MW00718083

Region and Place

A study of English rural settlement

To our wives

Jan Roberts and Sue Wrathmell

Region and Place

A study of English rural settlement

Brian K Roberts and Stuart Wrathmell

ENGLISH HERITAGE

2002

Published by English Heritage, The Engine House, Fire Fly Avenue, Swindon SN2 2EH

Copyright © English Heritage 2002

First Published 2002

ISBN 978-1-85074-775-8

Product code 50203

Reprinted 2012

British Library Cataloguing in Publication Data
A CIP catalogue record for this book is available from the British Library

All rights reserved
No part of this publication may be reproduced or transmitted in any form
or by any means, electronic or mechanical, including photocopying,
recording. or any information storage or retrieval system, without
permission in writing from the publisher

Design by English Heritage and Pauline Hull Design
Edited and brought to press by Karen Dorn and Andrew McLaren,
Publications, English Heritage
Indexed by Susan Vaughan
Designed by Pauline Hull Design

Printed and bound in Great Britain by 4edge Ltd, Hockley.

Contents

Figures

Tables

Acknowledgements

Without the support of English Heritage this project, which grew from our work on *An Atlas of Rural Settlement in England*, could not have been sustained. Special thanks are due to David Stocker and Graham Fairclough for their continuing encouragement. We are in considerable debt to Karen Dorn of English Heritage's publications department for her editorial skills and tact when dealing with our efforts and to Christopher Taylor for penetrating comments on the original text. From our employers, the West Yorkshire Archaeology Service, part of West Yorkshire Joint Services, and the Geography Department of Durham University, we have drawn both material and intellectual support.

We have quarried the work of other researchers without shame, and without them this volume could not have been brought to completion. Our most sincere thanks are due to all of them, scholars past and present. We are, of course, responsible for the misuse, misinterpretation and misquotations that must inevitably be present. Here we will mention only those who played an active part in the preparation of this work. Most of the maps are the responsibility of one of us (BKR), but the cartographic team in Durham, Arthur Corner and his successor David Hume, Chris Orton and Steven Allan made vital contributions, especially in solving computing problems. Chris also drew the maps for Chapter 4. Preparation of the case studies in Chapter 4 owed much to the work and advice of a number of people, especially Paul Everson, Stephen Rippon, Keith Stephenson, Christopher Taylor and Penny Ward. Chris Philo read the whole text and suggested a number of improvements to accuracy and consistency.

Finally, we acknowledge the forbearance and assistance of Jan Roberts and Sue Wrathmell who, through no fault of their own, have had to live with our running debate on rural settlement for almost a decade. Our only excuse is that we, too, have been the victims of our ideas.

Authors' preface

This book is the result of research that began in the early 1990s, research that originally had a rather limited and specific purpose. The initial objective, encouraged and funded by English Heritage, was to provide maps of England's dispersed and nucleated settlement patterns, to enable those patterns to inform the identification and selection of nationally important medieval settlement remains in the course of the Monuments Protection Programme. In some senses the final product of that work was *An Atlas of Rural Settlement in England* (Roberts and Wrathmell 2000a). It is a publication which attempts not only to provide contexts and frameworks for regional and local settlement studies; it also offers a series of models which illustrate our perception of the diversity of 'agrarian structures' in the regions we have defined. By 'agrarian structures' we mean not only the way in which habitation sites are distributed across the landscape, but also the way in which these sites interlock with – indeed, reflect – the decisions made by their occupants with regard to the exploitation of available agricultural resources: arable land, meadow, pasture, woodland and so on. Agrarian structures are the physical expression of those decisions.

The Atlas provided only limited opportunities to explore and elaborate such themes: hence this book. It provides few answers to those problems that have exercised rural settlement scholars and agricultural historians over the past fifty years. Indeed, we have to admit that it makes little attempt to do so. The reason is simple and personal. The process of creating the maps that appeared in the Atlas, and the many new ones that illustrate this publication, fundamentally changed our way of looking at rural settlement and agrarian structures, both spatially and chronologically.

The distribution maps have driven our evolving concepts. Thanks to the opportunities now available through computer mapping, we have been able to compare widely differing datasets with one another, and have explored the meaning of their correlations, negative as well as positive. This is in contrast to many of the national distribution maps supplied by archaeologists and historians; maps that frequently comprise little more than dots against a coastal outline, perhaps with a few major rivers, or at most with a relief map as background. Such 'backgrounds' are not neutral statements. They set intellectual parameters for those who read the maps; they structure the data. And if coastline and rivers do nothing more than enable the reader to locate, very roughly, a distribution in relation to the overall shape of England, then each symbol will say nothing more than: 'one was found here'. The arguments in our text are not simply illustrated by maps: they have been derived directly from the spatial correlations of a variety of mapped datasets – diachronic as well as synchronic. If readers wish to read new meanings into those maps, and to abandon those we propose in this volume, we shall still have succeeded in our primary aim. Our purpose is to offer a new direction for the course of research, not necessarily to anticipate its findings.

In practice, our argument builds around a presentation that is essentially retrogressive in character, beginning with nineteenth-century evidence and then reaching back in time to more remote periods. This procedure brings with it the danger of anachronism: as a rule, historical explanation is more reliably achieved by moving chronologically, so that in Gulley's words, 'causes precede result' (Gulley 1961, 306–9; Baker 1968, 243–4). Nevertheless, as he also pointed out, 'it is hardly possible to question the frequent necessity in research, of proceeding from a better documented period into the relative darkness of its predecessor'.

This volume is not, in the usual sense, a work of synthesis. We have not systematically searched the literature relating to local settlement and agrarian studies, in order to assemble them into a coherent national picture. Rather, we have approached from the opposite direction: assembling national data and then seeking to elaborate and explain the resultant patterns by reference to a limited number of local case-studies. Inevitably, our coverage of local studies is patchy, and fails to give sufficient weight to every region. In some measure this is deliberate: we have sought to give emphasis to some of the counties that have received little attention from researchers in the past thirty years. But at the same time, this book reflects the authors' own research experience. Just as the bibliography of a published work is frequently a reliable guide to the author's intellectual roots, so, too, the geographical emphases are an expression of his or her own research experience. As Christopher Taylor has pointed out, it is our own practical research experience that fundamentally shapes our approach to settlement studies, rather than the research of others (Taylor 1992, 9). We therefore acknowledge our northern and western bias, and ask researchers with a southern and eastern bias to redress it in future studies.

Further, we have deliberately ignored the constraints of conventional 'period' divisions, and have sought to make connections between datasets separated by centuries, even millennia. Our justification for doing so is that the maps reveal patterns and boundaries that seem to structure human activity over very long periods of time. This is not to claim that certain settlement forms or agrarian structures remained unchanged during these spans of time; but that each decision to alter or reform agrarian structures was informed not only by terrain but also by what had been laid out upon it: by what becomes, in our terminology, the antecedent pattern. One of the clearest examples is to be found in the West Midlands, in a regional study published elsewhere (Roberts and Wrathmell 2000b). There, we argue that the mid-nineteenth-century boundary between the nucleated settlements of the Feldon region and the dispersed settlements to the west, was already in existence in Roman and early Anglo-Saxon times. But at that earlier period it is not evident as a boundary between regions dominated by different settlement forms, but as a boundary between regions dominated by woodland or open land. The contrasts between woodland and open land informed the patterns of medieval settlement, and these in turn informed the patterns of nineteenth-century settlement. Different regions would respond to the same stimulus in different ways, because they started with different sets of attributes, cultural as well as 'natural'.

Chronological periods are simply a way of structuring data; in archaeology, they are a way of giving particular emphasis to what are perceived as major transitions in the character of material cultural assemblages. This is the context in which 'continuity' and 'discontinuity' become key issues of enquiry. Again in our West Midlands study, we have emphasised what is, in effect, an additional and underlying dimension to the succession of periods; one that also permeates this book. We have argued that the contrasting patterns of human activity to be found in the woodland areas and open land areas continued – modified but not eradicated – through the transitions in material culture from prehistoric, to Roman, to Anglo-Saxon, to medieval times (Roberts and Wrathmell 2000b, 91–5). Fundamentally, the lives of woodlanders guarding livestock or burning charcoal in Roman times might have more in common with their successors in Anglo-Saxon times, than with their contemporaries who laboured in the great tracts of intensively farmed arable land.

The significance of regions ...

Landscape is open to many forms of archaeological investigation. The history and physiography of every place or region are not exactly constants, but they do make insistent demands on every generation of historians and topographers; the archaeologist cannot switch them off. The sense of connectedness and progress which is the strength of landscape studies derives from the persistence of an agenda rooted in place ...

(Fleming 1998, 45)

Regional studies are at their most valuable when they are firmly located within wider debates, and when they examine the locally specific evidence within the context of the evidence from other contemporary societies. One cannot hope to understand what is unique about a region unless the broader context is first established.

(Hadley 2000, 26)

... and perceptions of regional identities

In 1240, Pope Gregory authorized the bishop of Coventry and Lichfield, in whose see Wybunbury then lay, to retain the church of Wybunbury for his own use because he had alleged 'that around Stafford and Chester there are woody tracts infested by sons of perdition who without the fear of God molest travellers' and that, as the bishop had to pass that way in the performance of his duties, he should therefore use it as a safe resting place.

(Sylvester 1956, 9)

As John Aubrey commented in the seventeenth century: 'In the dirty claey country they feed mainly on milke meates which cools their brains too much and hurts their inventions. These circumstances make them melancholy, contemplative and malicious... they are generally more apt to be fanatiques'; on the chalk, on the other hand 'tis all apon tillage, or shepherds and hard labour, their flesh is hard, their bodies strong; being weary after their hard labour they have not the leisure to read, and contemplate religion.'

(Lewis 1994, 171–2)

1
Rural settlement in space and time

Introduction

> It is so, that our soile being diuided into champaine grounde and woodland, the houses of the first lie uniformlie builded in euerie town togither, with streets and lanes; whereas in the woodland countries (except here and there in great market townes) they stand scattered abroad, eache one dwelling in the midst of his owne occupieng.
> *(Withington 1876, 20)*

These words by the Elizabethan scholar William Harrison cut straight to the heart of the subject matter of this book. Harrison was, as Homans noted, probably the first to comment upon the existence in England of two wholly different types of countryside (Homans 1960, 21). When he wrote, between 1577 and 1587, these contrasts were generally, but by no means consistently, being revealed by the mapping conventions used in Christopher Saxton's great atlas of 1579. Indeed William Cecil, Lord Burghley, may already have been in a better position to see them than Harrison, for he was in possession of the proof copies of Saxton's maps (Morgan 1979, 140). While the contrasts were most clearly seen at a county scale, in the division between wooded or mountainous areas and regions dominated by villages, they are also to be glimpsed in Saxton's important synoptic national map of *'Anglia'* (including both England and Wales: Ravenhill 1992). The freshness and vitality of this image and its impact upon perception and thinking cannot be understated (Morgan 1979). One of these major zones, termed 'champion', we now know comprised a broad band extending from the North Sea to the Channel. When Harrison was writing, it was still characterised by a type of husbandry whose most striking mark was its wide expanses of open, communally cultivated, subdivided fields. Outside this zone were 'woodland' countrysides which, though containing areas of subdivided fields, were more generally characterised by a prevalence of pre eighteenth-century enclosures associated with more hedgerow trees and surviving woodland blocks. Homans recapitulated Harrison's points with sharp precision: 'in the champion country were found compact villages; in the woodland was found some kind of dispersed settlement'. Rackham describes the same contrasts in more localised terms:

> England ... is divided by a remarkable contrast. On the one hand, as in Essex or Herefordshire, we have the England of hamlets, medieval farms in hollows of the hills, lonely moats and great barns in the clay lands, pollards and ancient trees, cavernous holloways and many footpaths, irregularly shaped groves with thick hedges with maple, dogwood and spindle – an intricate land of mystery and surprise. On the other hand, there is the Cambridgeshire type of landscape, the England of big villages, few, busy roads, thin hawthorn hedges, windswept brick farms, and ivied clumps of trees in the corners of fields: a predictable land of wide views, sweeping sameness and straight lines. *(Rackham 1986, 4–5)*

As Maitland noted (1897, 39), these are two different models which are held together by differing legal bonds and contrasting landownership arrangements. This division into two categories is, however, an over-simplified view of English landscapes. In our view England can be divided into three fundamental zones which we term the Northern and Western Province, the Central Province and the South-eastern Province. Each is defined by distinctive settlement characteristics and the thick black lines in Figure 1.4 represent the boundaries.

The Central Province is Harrison's 'champaigne ground', the 'champion' zone. The word 'champion' derives from the Latin *campus*, by way of the French *champagne* and the Anglicised *champaigne*. The equivalent English word *feldon* or *fieldon*, derived from *feld*, had the same root meaning of a 'tract of open country' (Smith 1956, 166–7). It appears in a grant by King

Edward the Confessor, of estates at Pershore and Deerhurst, made just before the Conquest of 1066: '*mid wuda. 7 mid feldan. mid laese. 7 mid haethe. mid maeden. 7 et mid e'i'tum.*' – 'with woodland and with open country, with pasture and with heath, with meadow and with eyots' (Harmer 1952, 366). The terms 'open fields' and 'common fields' appear frequently in the literature (Thirsk and Titow 1976, 10–56; Baker and Butlin 1973, 623), the former describing the appearance of the landscapes, the second describing their mode of operation. There is no doubt that field systems were often 'open', in that they lacked enclosing boundaries between the parcels, as well as 'common', being subject to communally agreed rules governing tillage and grazing arrangements. Indeed, they were normally 'subdivided' into a multitude of strip-shaped landownership parcels. Nevertheless, open fields need not be worked in common, common fields need not be subdivided, and open fields need not be organised into hundreds of strips. To this must be added two more levels of complication. First, the disposition of the strip holdings may be described as 'regular', following an ordered sequence throughout each furlong and each field or cropping unit; or they may be irregular, following no detectable sequence. Second, the sequence of crop rotation or shift may take place using two, three or more defined fields, each containing an approximately equal proportion of an individual's property; or it may be irregular, with furlongs grouped yearly on an *ad hoc* basis. In short, the diversity of field systems, seen in their physical layouts, husbandry practices and tenurial arrangements, are sufficiently complex as almost to defy rational classification. Campbell used an elegant form of principal component analysis to identify eight basic categories of 'open field system' in England. He did this to draw attention to the importance of regional variations, but the fact remains that we still know too little of the detailed distributions of the categories he recognised (Campbell 1981, 112–29). In broad terms, such field systems normally lacked permanent enclosure boundaries, although these could and did appear, both around and within the villages and hamlets. They could also occur along township and parish boundary lines and sometimes between the two or three great cropping units or 'fields'. However, the morphological characteristics of field systems, seen in the scatters of strips and unenclosed boundaries, are only one aspect of their substance. The relationships between the arable and the waste, the availability of fallow grazing over the arable, the arrangement of individual holdings, the regulation of cropping and the communal regulation of all these activities are all aspects of equal importance (Campbell 1981, 113–15; Kerridge 1992, 1, 116–17). As Kerridge emphasises, however, these are by no means always discussed in published studies.

Above all, whatever the details, communal field systems were pre-eminently the arable fields of each local community, the township or tithing, farmed by its inhabitants. For this reason, we have selected a northern term, *townfield*, for general use in this study. Avoiding the temptation to create any more closely defined categories, we have also employed a generalised contrast between *townfields* and *subdivided* fields. The latter, the results of division by inheritance or agreement, typically possessed no formal links with most of the local community, and hence were not truly townfields. Even the word *township*, by which we mean those ancient secular units of settlement and community, one or many of which could form a single parish, cannot be defined easily. At root, elements of communality are implied and were probably normally present, even if the inhabitants occupied dispersed dwellings rather than a nucleated village (Darling 1956, 282–8; Adams 1976, 62; Winchester 1990, 5–8, 19–34).

In contrast, the regions outside the Central Province have always tended to carry more trees and residual blocks of woodland. Such landscapes are termed *bocage* in France. The English term – now not commonly used – is *boscage* or *boskage*, often abbreviated to the adjective *bosky*: derived from the Latin *boscum* it implies land covered with growing trees or shrubs. Harrison uses the more general English term 'woodland' because the visible presence of trees in the coppices, in areas of brushwood and within the enclosing hedgerows and woodland blocks, provided a contrast with the characteristically open champion landscapes. Given the strong tendency in English historical writing to see townfield countrysides as a normative experience, from which all others are divergences, our efforts to classify and analyse these woodland landscapes in their own terms, in Chapter 6, are fraught with difficulties. Nevertheless, we believe this approach adds new perspectives to the study of landscape evolution, by re-emphasising the vast extent of former woodland and rough grazings, the raw material out of which assarts and other clearances were carved. Of course, this in no way excludes the possibility of temporary cultivation in areas that were later abandoned to nature. In tropical zones such tracts would effectively be termed 'savanna lands', where blocks and galleries of woodland coexist with large areas of unenclosed bush, more or less degraded, and tracts of bush and grass where recent cultivation had taken place. These are zones where through time a mixture of climatic fluctuations, fire, woodcutting and the grazing of domestic stock intermingle with varying degrees of cultivation, so that the consequent mosaic is the result of multiple interactions between nature and culture. The original form of vegetation is particularly difficult to reconstruct. This observation raises important terminological questions that will be addressed in Chapter 6.

In this study we explore and build upon the fundamental contrast between the two extremes of rural landscapes already discussed in *An Atlas of English Rural Settlement* (Roberts and Wrathmell 2000a). We argue that well before the ninth century, perhaps even by the Roman period, and conceivably much earlier, three fundamental landscape and settlement provinces had begun to emerge within England. While these possessed – indeed still do possess – distinguishable characteristics in terms of location, terrains, climatic conditions and edaphic potential, it is clear that they also reflect complex cultural and historical circumstances: they are all constructed landscapes and they cannot be explained or rationalised by simple physical, deterministic models. Precisely what models should be invoked must be argued in some detail, a step that will be preceded and supported by basic description and analysis.

It was Oliver Rackham who, in his formidable *History of the English Countryside*, saw that England comprised three fundamental cultural landscape regions, running north-north-east to south-south-west, approximately parallel to the escarpments of lowland England. Two of these, one lying to the south-east and the other to the north and west, he termed 'ancient landscapes'. These were separated from each other by the broad central swathe of 'planned landscapes', a tract which spreads north-east from Dorset, across the plains and scarps of the English midlands, the Trent Valley and the Vale of York, to the dissected coastal plateaux of Durham and Northumberland. This was the zone formerly dominated by the champion townfield landscapes. As far back as the turn of the nineteenth century, scholars such as E C R Gonner and Gilbert Slater had determined the essential geographical lineaments of this arrangement. In this matter, some criticism must be levelled at the sustained misuse of the work of one scholar, H L Gray, whose excellent formative study of English Field Systems (1915) contained a map that is often reproduced. This shows not 'field systems' as such, but the ways in which similar two or three-course rotational practices were followed within field systems that were, in reality, diverse in structure and character. Reproduced again and again, this map has, in the face of irrefutable evidence to the contrary (Slater 1907; Gonner 1912), been taken as a reliable indication of the zone typified by great arable fields, subdivided into two or three portions for the purposes of crop rotation. Extending this boundary too far to the west has obfuscated the underlying distribution eventually detected by Rackham. It has detracted from the fundamental characteristic of the Central Province, namely that in parish after parish, township after township, the communal townfields once occupied a substantial portion of the total land area, normally over 70% and perhaps as much as 80% or even 90% (Roberts 1976, 192; Hall 1995). It is this quality, linked with the dominance of nucleated settlements, which characterises the champion landscapes described by Harrison and underscores the contrast between these and the landscapes of what may be termed the 'outer' provinces to the north and west and south-east.

Methodological questions

This book is concerned with more than mere regional contrasts, important as these are. It is concerned with stability and change in regional structures throughout a period that extends over at least 1500 years. The underlying structure of this study is a retrogressive approach, working backwards through time: from evidence which represents over 90% of the potential total, to evidence which represents only a small proportion of what once existed (Taylor 1972, 109–13). Furthermore, a clear deficiency exists in what we present: our arguments have not been carried into Wales and Scotland. This is not because we believe that this could not or should not be done, but because our project was initiated by English Heritage. To have moved beyond the restricted English view would have placed even greater pressures upon our capacity to create maps, and would also have demanded the handling of more material and more diverse arguments.

The body of evidence we present is convergent, bringing together material from diverse sources which shows that the three provinces, originally identified by Rackham but redefined and refined by our present work, are cultural phenomena deeply embedded within the development of English local landscapes. Paradoxically, we neither assume nor argue that the landscapes we now see within each province need possess any great antiquity. There are dangers in the uncritical projection of the visible elements into earlier, more remote, centuries – in effect making assumptions about continuity and stability which may in fact be wholly unwarranted. In the course of 1500 years any landscape may pass through many transformations. Even if the three provinces can in some way be detected at both the beginning and the end of this immense span of time, we cannot, indeed do not, assume that the same landscapes were present 500, 1000, or, still less, 1500 years earlier. By way of illustration, the champion landscapes Harrison saw are no longer visible. What we see in the landscapes of this twenty-first century are patterns of enclosure – some imposed during the sixteenth and seventeenth centuries, but mainly in the eighteenth and nineteenth centuries – which differ subtly from the more ancient enclosures of the woodland landscapes. There can be no better illustration of the point we are making. We 'see' Harrison's landscapes in the mind's eye and in the details of what replaced the townfields: the latter are themselves no longer in any sense 'real' or present. Nevertheless, their transient existence accounts for the disposition and character of the enclosures that replaced them. In this we also glimpse the fundamental contrast between a 'retrospective' view,

looking backwards in time to explain the present scene, and a 'retrogressive' approach, using the evidence of past and present conditions to model the past (Baker 1972, 23–4).

The mapping and study of rural settlement

The language of settlement, as Harald Uhlig showed (1972, 55–91), poses particular problems. The absence of a commonly accepted terminology is an indication of core weaknesses within those disciplines concerned with the study of settlement as a cultural manifestation. A prescient small study published in 1952 by the geographer J H G Lebon successfully identified the essential characteristics of the three provinces. Lebon speaks of 'the great open fields, veritable giants' carpets of cultivated strips' running throughout the English Midlands, and contrasting with 'smaller, scattered patches of cultivation in those unenclosed parts of the country where open field husbandry did not prevail' (Lebon 1952, 14). These carefully chosen words suggest that he was well aware of the complexities present in those regions beyond the Central Province. Using mid-twentieth-century Ordnance Survey maps, Harry Thorpe compiled in 1962 a national map of rural settlement in the British Isles (Watson and Sissons 1964, fig 47). This study was much more detailed, but inevitably incorporated many obfuscating twentieth-century changes. He solved the methodological problem of how to show the characteristics of rural settlement on a national scale by adopting generalising procedures, but has left no account of precisely how this was done.

This brings us to the first structuring concept of our own project to map rural settlement: the terms nucleation and dispersion, broad but simple categories. A measure of legitimacy has been conferred upon them through long usage: they are, after all, descriptive contrasts employed since the sixteenth century. In practice, however, we emphasise that 'nucleation' and 'dispersion' represent opposite ends of a catena or gradation of types, and too little attention has been paid to intermediate forms, to what one of us has termed 'linked hamlet clusters' and 'linked farmstead clusters' (Roberts 1987, fig 7.1a, 7.7, 7.11). We should also recall concepts such as settlement 'chains' (RCHME 1970, xliv–vi),

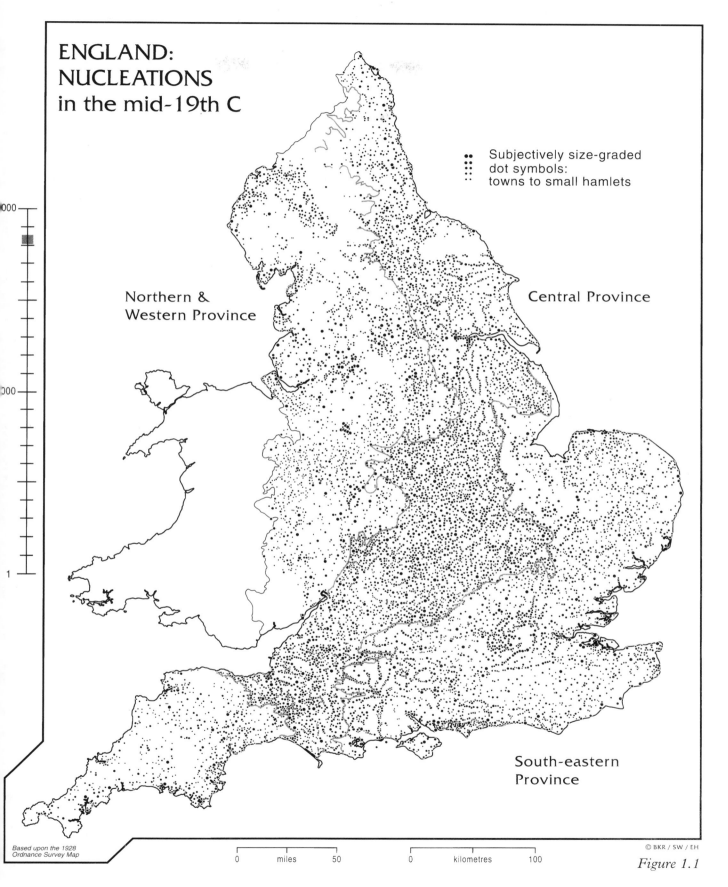

ENGLAND:
NUCLEATIONS
in the mid-19th C

Subjectively size-graded
dot symbols:
towns to small hamlets

Northern &
Western Province

Central Province

South-eastern
Province

Based upon the 1928
Ordnance Survey Map

0   miles   50

0   kilometres   100

© BKR / SW / EH

Figure 1.1

settlement 'girdles' (Jones 1953, 55, 60), and even the more commonly understood 'ribbon development' (Adams 1976, 68). The nucleated/dispersion contrast was employed by us in monument class descriptions prepared for English Heritage. It was intended to ensure that a review of scheduled and schedulable sites did not totally ignore those regions of England where nucleations have always formed a minor element in settlement history: regions characterised by the limited and often slight earthworks of dispersed settlements, as against the more prominent and extensive earthworks of deserted medieval villages. But if it were to achieve this, such regions had to be defined in maps. We have never assumed that the early nineteenth-century settlement pattern must substantially have the same characteristics as the medieval settlement pattern; indeed, the concept of a medieval settlement pattern is itself false, implying a stability which would fly in the face of half a century of research. The nineteenth-century distribution is seen instead as a master frame, within which can be unravelled long temporal threads of settlement change – both nationally and regionally – over the previous 1000 years and more. The approach we have adopted in this study is conditioned by three fundamental characteristics of the settlement forms and patterns we are discussing: the existence of three distinct national provinces; the existence within settlement patterns of a hierarchy of forms and associated functions; and the clear evidence for fundamental socio-economic transformations generating radical changes in both the form and function of settlements.

National provinces

The existence of three national provinces has already been sketched: they are seen in the four maps appearing as Figures 1.1, 1.2, 1.3 and 1.4. Their presence and limits have been determined by mapping the evidence for settlement found upon the Ordnance Survey Old Series One inch to one mile maps of the nineteenth century (Margary 1975–81). If evidence drawn from these maps is by no means perfect, neither is it merely a sample, for there is near 100% coverage of the whole country. This is an exceptional situation for historically or archaeologically based distribution maps. In practice, of course, the evidence varies in

quality; there are, for instance, clear-cut differences in the cartographic styles used by the Ordnance Survey draughtsmen. These have been well summarised by Richard Oliver:

> The general style is derived from late eighteenth-century county mapping ... Nevertheless by 1830 the style had become much more delicate, and delicacy would be characteristic of the one-inch style in the 1830s and early 1840s, though by the time that the Old Series was completed in 1874 a bold style was once more in favour. *(Hodson 1991, 5)*

There are further problems because the maps also vary in date. For England the year of publication for individual sheets ranges between 1805 and 1865, so that the cross section provided by the national map encompasses over a half century of economic development and landscape change. Nevertheless, the generalised distribution that can be constructed from this relatively homogenous source is extremely base-stable, and would be recoverable by anyone repeating the exercise. The spread of the sources used is emphasised in this and in other maps by the inclusion of a temporal as well as a linear scale.

It must be emphasised from the outset that when using this map several scales of analysis need to be undertaken. The three provinces represent only the highest level, but each province comprises a number of sub-provincial divisions, and these in turn have been divided into local regions, terms which have all been deliberately chosen to be neutral and avoid any great burden of meanings in other contexts. Thus, these are not 'natural', 'physical', 'environmental' or even 'cultural' regions: they are provinces identified using settlement characteristics. While we believe they possess wider implications, they are initially based upon observations drawn from the products of Victorian cartography. The construction of these maps has been more fully discussed in our Atlas, but basically the map of nucleations represents the placing of a simple dot symbol to represent cities and towns, market towns and large villages, average villages, small villages and even the larger hamlets (Fig 1.1). The fact that this was done by one person provides a consistency of approach that takes some account of variations in the sources. Repeating the exercise would generate the same map, but the texture of the distribution might vary a little.

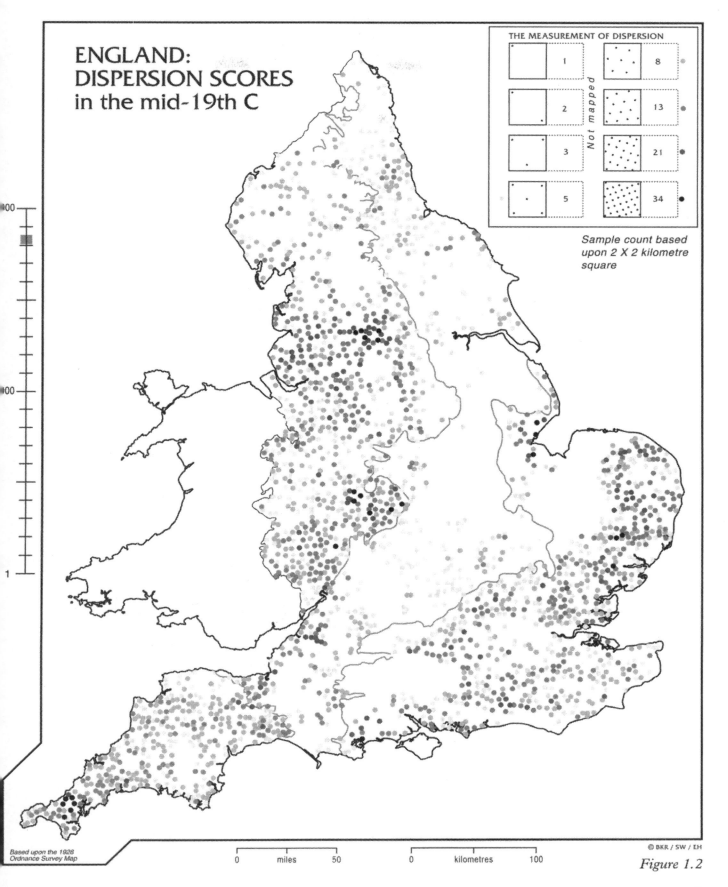

ENGLAND:
DISPERSION SCORES
in the mid-19th C

THE MEASUREMENT OF DISPERSION

Not mapped

Sample count based
upon 2 X 2 kilometre
square

Based upon the 1928
Ordnance Survey Map

0 miles 50

0 kilometres 100

© BKR / SW / EH

Figure 1.2

Dispersion was mapped by counting the dispersed entities within some 4,300 2 by 2km sample squares, and involved two elements. The first element is a 'dispersion score' comprising all units of dispersion – single farmsteads, houses, and so on. In addition there are more ambiguous groupings, where two or three farmsteads and associated cottages may cluster so tightly together as to be indistinguishable at the scale of the map. In the first count these were all reckoned as 'one' item. However, a second 'hamlet score' ('H3' etc) was also created, comprising all such ambiguous entities, ie farmsteads with any associated cottages, associations of two or three farmsteads, forges and ancillary dwellings and the like. Each 'dispersion score' was then related to the Fibonacci scale, namely 0, 1, 2, 3, 5, 8, 13, 21 and 34, for mapping purposes (Fig 1.2), and these numbers underlie the more generalised descriptive categories which appear in Figure 1.3. To give one example, a count of eight, nine or ten entities would score 8, while eleven, twelve or thirteen would score 13. This is a way of generalising great detail. It also allowed professional judgement to be exercised. For instance, scores in Swaledale were consistently reduced because it was appreciated that many of the isolated buildings were in fact barns, while in some industrial areas scores well in excess of 34 are recorded as that figure. Nevertheless, this maximum is an adequate indicator of the presence of great concentrations of activity. Hamlet scores, plus the larger hamlets that are shown on the map of nucleations, have been used to construct Figure 2.10.

These nineteenth-century settlement distributions are presented in some detail. We admit frankly that we cannot explore their full implications even within the compass of this study. Nevertheless, they have permitted us to identify the hierarchy of provinces, sub-provinces and local regions seen in Figure 1.4. We have no doubt that the precise characteristics and boundaries of each local region can be debated: we see these boundaries as mere tools, identifying tracts of 'settlement similarity' and would not take entrenched defensive positions concerning them. They are there to be both used and tested. Nevertheless, they represent real 'on ground' contrasts. The provinces are also tools, but we see these as less flexible. One specific case will illustrate both the problems and

the potential of the method. Sub-province CPNSL, 'the Pennine slope' (Fig 1.4), was defined and first placed in the Central Province on the basis of the numbers of nucleations it contained in the mid-nineteenth century. Further study has clearly shown that settlement intensification associated with the Industrial Revolution created most nucleations during comparatively recent centuries, and that the earlier provincial boundary lay along its eastern not its western limit, between the rising lands and the Trent valley. Similarly, there could be discussion over the inclusion of East Wessex (EWEXE: Fig 1.4) in the South-eastern rather than Central province. Nevertheless, endless debate over such details would miss the essential point: that the maps reveal at a national scale important settlement contrasts. Furthermore, they point unambiguously away from the deeply rooted research frameworks of the historic counties and away from modern units of local government. In this there is a fundamental challenge to all county-based records, accounts and enquiries.

The nineteenth-century settlement map, and the provincial boundaries derived from it, provide a context for a wide range of data which can be assembled as national distribution maps. The first example relates to those medieval nucleated settlements that were abandoned before the mid-nineteenth century: the relatively well-researched 'deserted medieval villages', or DMVs. Three successive versions exist of the national distribution of DMVs (Beresford and Hurst 1971, 66; Rowley and Wood 1982, fig 1; Atkin and Tompkins 1986, 4). That published in 1971 has been selected for inclusion here (Fig 1.5), as it contains fewer speculative identifications than the later versions. The chronological range of material represented in this distribution extends over many centuries. It encompasses villages depopulated in the Norman period or earlier, and those marking the retreat from marginal land in the later fourteenth and fifteenth centuries. It includes those resulting from conversions of arable fields to grazing lands in the Tudor period, and those depopulated during agrarian 'improvement' of the seventeenth and eighteenth centuries. The superimposition of the major provincial boundaries on this distribution reveals considerable general agreement with the map of nineteenth-century nucleations

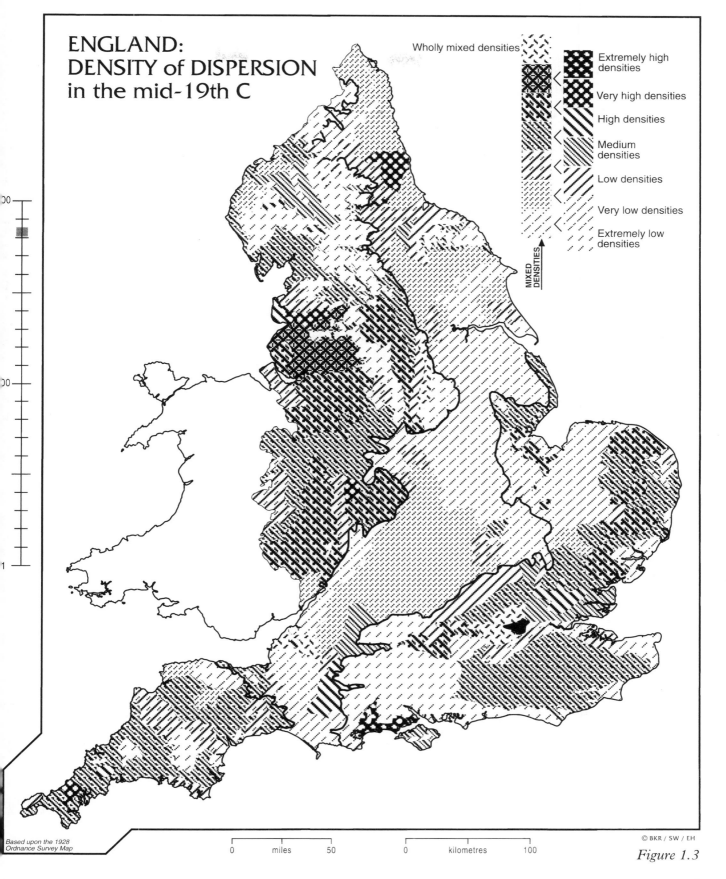

ENGLAND:
DENSITY of DISPERSION
in the mid-19th C

Wholly mixed densities

Extremely high densities

Very high densities

High densities

Medium densities

Low densities

Very low densities

Extremely low densities

MIXED DENSITIES

Based upon the 1928
Ordnance Survey Map

0   miles   50

0   kilometres   100

© BKR / SW / EH

Figure 1.3

9

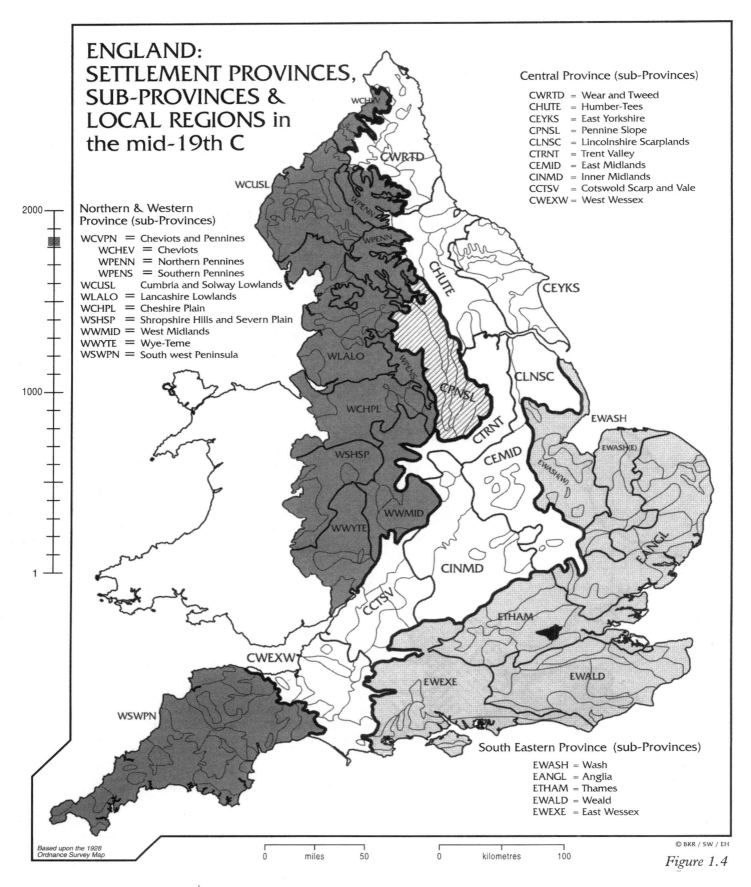

ENGLAND:
SETTLEMENT PROVINCES,
SUB-PROVINCES &
LOCAL REGIONS in
the mid-19th C

Central Province (sub-Provinces)

CWRTD = Wear and Tweed
CHUTE = Humber-Tees
CEYKS = East Yorkshire
CPNSL = Pennine Slope
CLNSC = Lincolnshire Scarplands
CTRNT = Trent Valley
CEMID = East Midlands
CINMD = Inner Midlands
CCTSV = Cotswold Scarp and Vale
CWEXW = West Wessex

Northern & Western
Province (sub-Provinces)

WCVPN = Cheviots and Pennines
WCHEV = Cheviots
WPENN = Northern Pennines
WPENS = Southern Pennines
WCUSL   Cumbria and Solway Lowlands
WLALO = Lancashire Lowlands
WCHPL = Cheshire Plain
WSHSP = Shropshire Hills and Severn Plain
WWMID = West Midlands
WWYTE = Wye-Teme
WSWPN = South west Peninsula

South Eastern Province (sub-Provinces)

EWASH = Wash
EANGL = Anglia
ETHAM = Thames
EWALD = Weald
EWEXE = East Wessex

Based upon the 1928
Ordnance Survey Map

0   miles   50

0   kilometres   100

© BKR / SW / EH

Figure 1.4

10

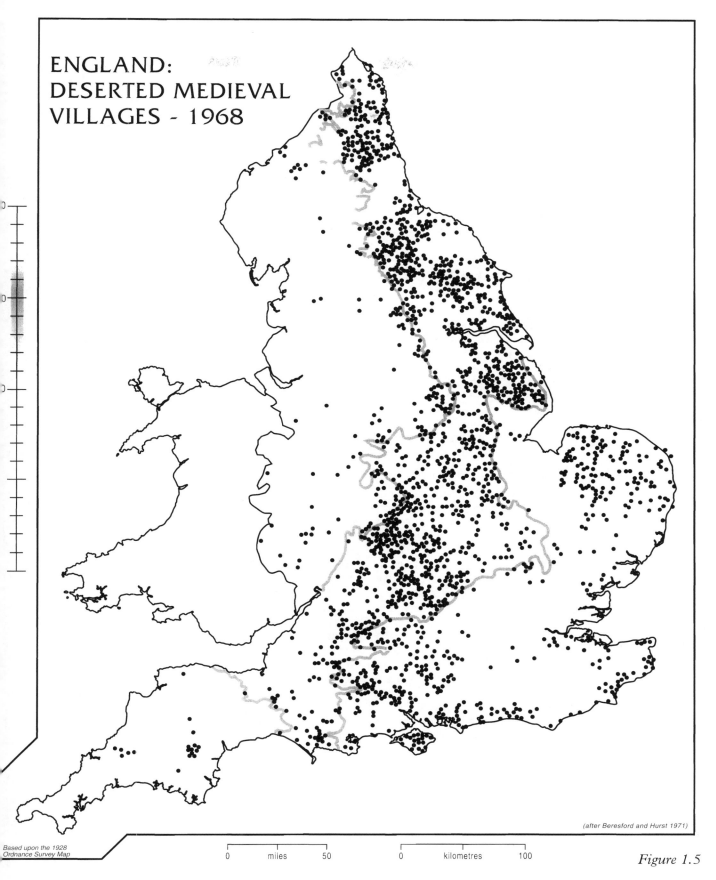

ENGLAND:
DESERTED MEDIEVAL
VILLAGES - 1968

(after Beresford and Hurst 1971)

Based upon the 1928
Ordnance Survey Map

0   miles   50   0   kilometres   100

Figure 1.5

(Figs 1.1 and 1.5). The areas of discord, however, raise important questions about the meaning of both maps. For instance, how far do the 'deserted villages' of northern East Anglia represent villages of the same kind as those of the Central Province? Our impression is that many of the East Anglian villages resulted from an infilling of spaces between dispersed farmsteads brought about by population increases. Thus documented 'deserted villages' may really be representatives of settlement types very different from the classic, tightly concentrated, composite villages of the midland type (Davison 1988; 1990; 1996).

Modelling settlement: a synoptic view

The complexity of the maps appearing as Figures 1.1 to 1.4 should not be underestimated. Based upon nineteenth-century data they compress into one plane that matrix of the time during which villages and hamlets were created: namely, all the 'periods' which have generated settlements that remained as living, functioning places into the middle decades of the nineteenth century. When comparing and contrasting what they show, the evidence they contain must be dissected with care. A synoptic view of some of the experiences affecting settlement is presented in Figure 1.6. It is introduced into the argument because it provides four broad views of the forces which generate settlement characteristics, and it allows us to glimpse the complex sequences of temporal spatial development. Beginning with the first column – 'Continuity' – the upper surface of the block represents the landscape of the present, with a scatter of settlements, while the vertical column reveals the presence of time. Of course, the word 'continuity' is not free of ambiguity, but in this context we imply continuity of settlement location: this need not imply a continuity of buildings, economy or social grouping. In itself this begs further questions, but no more than the practical problems associated with the thousands of nucleated settlements possessing both an Anglo-Saxon place-name and an Anglo-Saxon or Norman church, which also appear on our mid-nineteenth-century maps. Continuity, in some form, is present. Nevertheless, the model offers reminders that some settled

places disappear while others are created at later stages: this is indicated by the nature of the vertical lines recording settlement survivals. Of course, detailed excavations at sites such as Wharram Percy (Beresford and Hurst 1990) and Shapwick (Aston and Costen 1994) have revealed the vast complexity of the on-ground reality, but at this scale, approximately a 10 by 10km square, the generalisation serves well enough.

This is an ordered, wholly simplistic view of settlement. To this must be added a second column – 'cataclysm' – in which forms and patterns are affected by relatively rapid and far-reaching changes. It has long been recognised that the Harrying of the North, in 1069 to 1070, disrupted development and radically altered the temporal trajectories of many localities (Bishop 1962, 1–11; Sheppard 1976, 3–20). This is an exceptionally short-term change, but the effects of devastation, episodic in occurrence and uneven in its impact, were undoubtedly an ingredient of substantial importance in the evolution of settlement within many regions. The term 'cataclysmic' is usually applied to powerful short-term changes. Though the village depopulations of the fifteenth century were individually cataclysmic, they were often the end product of prolonged decline. Furthermore, the temporal range of these events extended, collectively, over at least a half century, often longer. Similarly, the enclosure of townfields by Act of Parliament brought cataclysmic change to parish after parish. Russell has documented this for Lincolnshire (see Bennett and Bennett 1993, 82–5). More generally, however, this particular portion of the wider enclosure movement extended between 1720 and the general Act of 1845 (Tate 1967, 88). Often the documentary record will not allow the close dating of each event, so that the shape of the graph resulting from plotting these events against a time axis cannot be determined accurately (Hodgson 1989, figs 6.1–6.4). It is likely that several temporally and spatially differentiated cycles are grouped together. For example, deserted villages appear in both Warwickshire and in Durham: in both cases they concentrate in the south-east of the county concerned. The former group, discussed by Beresford (1950) and then by Dyer (1982), is largely associated with final depopulation in the fifteenth century, but those of Durham were still shrinking in size in the period between 1676 and 1801, with

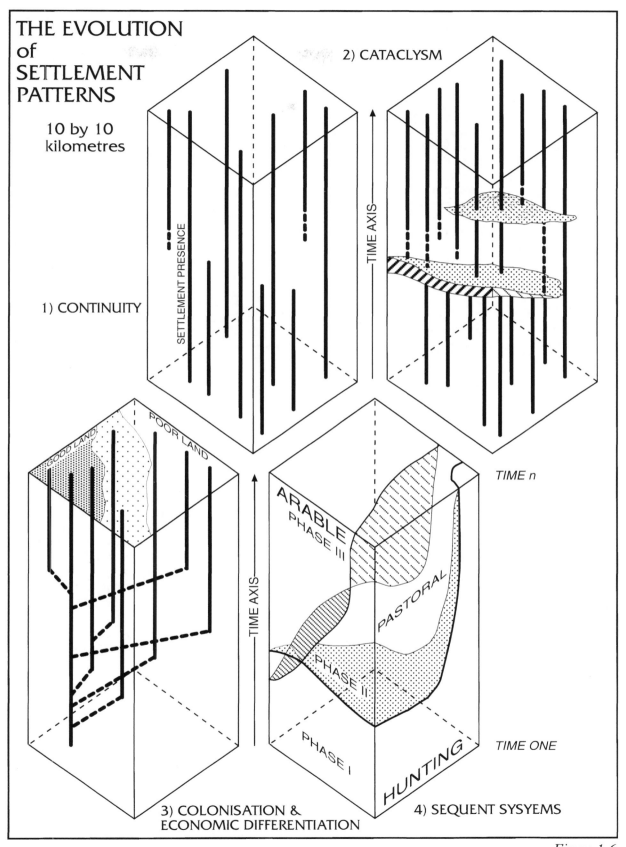

THE EVOLUTION of SETTLEMENT PATTERNS

10 by 10 kilometres

1) CONTINUITY

SETTLEMENT PRESENCE

2) CATACLYSM

TIME AXIS

TIME n

3) COLONISATION & ECONOMIC DIFFERENTIATION

GOOD LAND

POOR LAND

4) SEQUENT SYSYEMS

TIME AXIS

ARABLE

PHASE III

PASTORAL

PHASE II

PHASE I

HUNTING

TIME ONE

Figure 1.6

final depopulation after that date (Hodgson 1989, figs 5.1–5.3). In both areas earlier and later depopulations appear, but at the level of national mapping the inclusion of such refinements cannot yet be attempted. Nevertheless all levels – township, parish, estate, and, more rarely, sub-province – can experience rapid, far-reaching and dramatic changes of essentially cataclysmic character.

A third component is summarised by the word 'colonisation': changes which result from the expansion of settlement, or one type of settlement, into a new portion of territory. The model suggests that long-established settlements establish daughter settlements, and in time these, in turn, may establish grand-daughters. This usually takes place within the framework of varied land qualities, the darker shading representing good quality land, the lighter shading poor quality land. In his work on the 'multiple estate' Glanville Jones emphasised the role of local territorial lordship in framing such developments, and in particular the role of subinfeudation in estate fission and the stimulation of growth in peripheral settlement entities (Jones 1971, 252–64). Within this framework (Fig 1.7), not only does colonisation take place, but individual settlements may also change status: seasonally occupied sites become permanently occupied; single farmsteads become hamlets; hamlets grow, sometimes with radical restructuring, to become tenanted villages or even towns. His model, drawn initially from Welsh documentary sources, shows a scatter of hamlets based upon grain production around an estate centre in the lowland portion, but also drawing pastoral rents from the uplands where such grain as was grown was purely for local subsistence. The lord's officer, essentially a high status reeve, was located in a more important hamlet, and was responsible for rent collection, while church and court could either lie together in one hamlet or be located in adjacent hamlets. Jones' perception of the antiquity of the system is hinted at by including two Iron Age defensive sites.

Such an estate, he argued, could emerge, in historic times, as a territorial unit such as a hundred or hundredal manor. With the passage of time, and with economic development, population growth and the process of subinfeudation, the granting of portions – manors – to men of lower status, resulted in fragmentation. His drawing contained many subtleties, to

which we have added others. He included the explanation of directional place-names (eg Norton, Weston etc) and the presence of detached portions of manors, townships and parishes. He also included varied linguistic forms (British, Anglo-Saxon, Scandinavian and the like); status variations in names (as in -ton, -ham, -by, -thorpe, to which we have added -ley and -field) and even the presence of archaeological sites. His ideas have not been accepted without criticism, but were in strong measure supported by similar structures identified in Scotland by Geoffrey Barrow (Barrow 1973, 7–68). In a recent discussion, Rosamund Faith has integrated a view of Jones' work into what she terms 'extensive lordship' – namely 'the power to command goods and services from the population of an area' (Faith 1997, 10).

We would argue three things about the model. First, it creates a most useful, coherent framework within which to think about settlement development at the level of the local region. Secondly, it provides a possible link between, on the one hand, pre and protohistoric archaeological evidence and, on the other, the often confusing noise of the rich documentation of later centuries. Third, it presents a challenge to explore the historical roots of, and differences between rents and renders, tenures and the spatial framework of landholding, a challenge that has yet to be really taken up. Jones effectively raises fundamental questions about the gradual processes of internal colonisation and fragmentation within large territorial units that may have ancient origins. He touches deeper questions about the evolution of settlement patterns shaped by both continuity and in stability, by slow development and rapid change.

Settlement hierarchies and transformations

Within any pattern of settlement there is usually a hierarchy of forms: single-farmstead, hamlet, village and market town. All settlement patterns comprise varied quantities of each category, usually with far more small components than large ones. Two problems exist. The first is that even within a single country no single definition remains spatially or temporally constant (Roberts 1996a, 15–19). Thus, a settlement of 2500 or 3000 people which can be described as a market town in one location

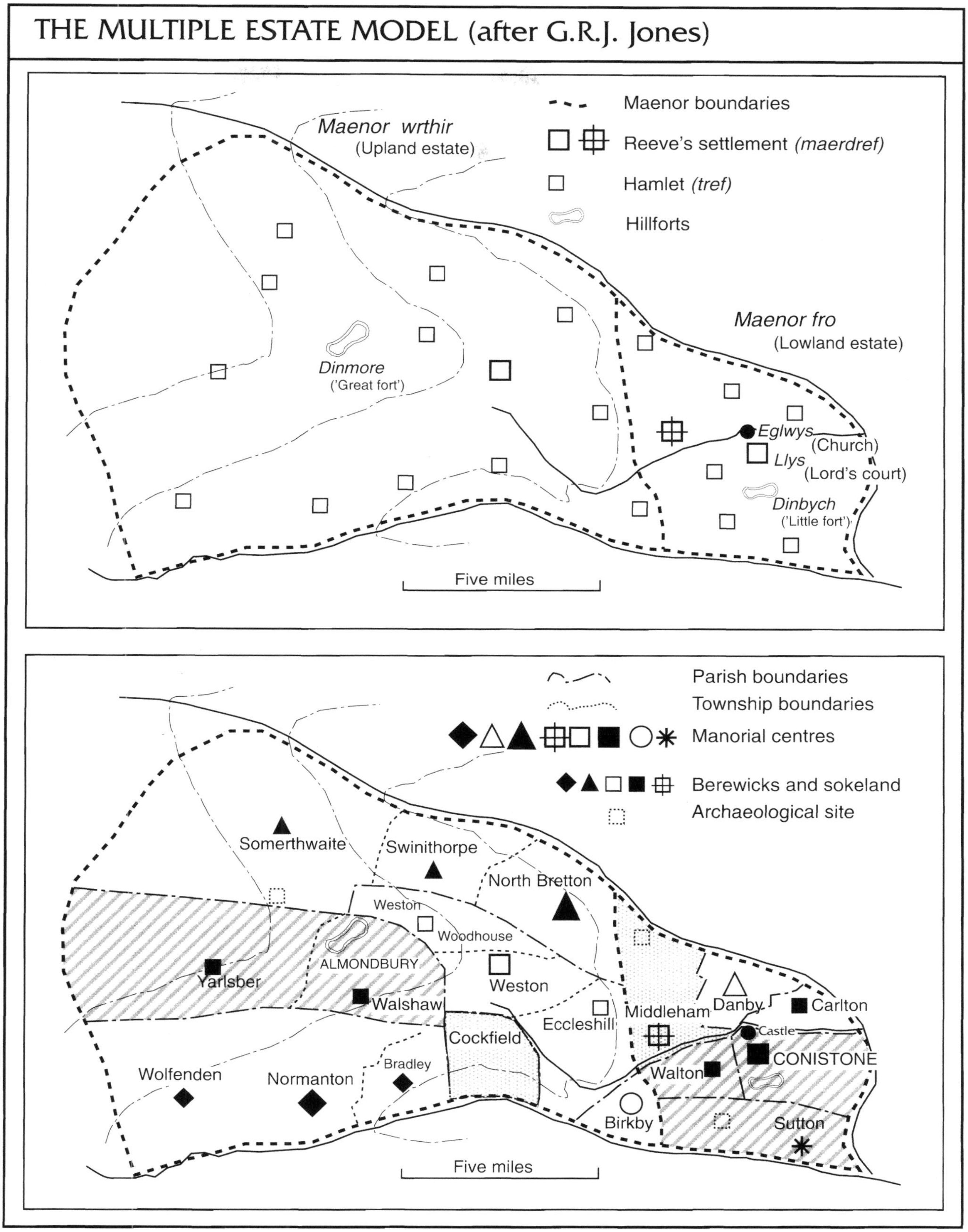

THE MULTIPLE ESTATE MODEL (after G.R.J. Jones)

Maenor wrthir
(Upland estate)

- - - Maenor boundaries
□ ⊞ Reeve's settlement *(maerdref)*
□ Hamlet *(tref)*
⬭ Hillforts

Maenor fro
(Lowland estate)

Dinmore
('Great fort')

⊞ ●*Eglwys*
(Church)
□ *Llys*
(Lord's court)

Dinbych
('Little fort')

Five miles

Parish boundaries
Township boundaries
◆ △ ▲ ⊞ □ ■ ○ ✳ Manorial centres

◆ ▲ □ ■ ⊞ Berewicks and sokeland
▫ Archaeological site

Somerthwaite
Swinithorpe
North Bretton
Weston
Woodhouse
ALMONDBURY
Yarlsber
Walshaw
Weston
Eccleshill
Middleham
Danby
Carlton
Castle
Walton
CONISTONE
Wolfenden
Normanton
Bradley
Cockfield
Birkby
Sutton

Five miles

Figure 1.7

or one century, may be viewed as a substantive town or a mere market village in other spatial or temporal contexts. Furthermore, individual places may undergo radical transformations, with a single farm becoming a hamlet, a village becoming a town etc. Nor need these transformations be uni-directional. For instance many deserted medieval village and hamlet sites, which may themselves have originated as very small settlements, are today occupied by no more than a single farmstead. Second, there is the problem of defining the particular mixture of settlement entities making up a given pattern. As noted earlier, 'nucleation' and 'dispersion' define two ends of a spectrum. At one end are patterns with most of the individual farmsteads or dwellings concentrated into clusters – a nucleated pattern – while at the other are patterns in which each farmstead or dwelling is set at a distance from its neighbours, a pattern dominated by dispersion. In reality, and more characteristically, each settlement pattern comprises a mixture of each type. No accurate measures can be made of these mixtures, and mathematical calculations offer no real solution (Houston 1963, 81–5). More importantly, few agreed terms exist to describe, and thus define, that portion of the settlement spectrum between a single farmstead and a large village. 'Hamlet' is commonly used, while, as noted earlier, one of us has defined 'linked farmstead clusters' and 'linked hamlet clusters' to designate the vast range of morphological possibilities between wholly nucleated and wholly dispersed forms. It is not our purpose to construct an elaborate terminology, but the absence of terms, and more profoundly the concepts linked to terms, means that models do not exist to describe subtle variations and temporal transformations which are important to understanding the realities of English settlement evolution. Classification and terminology must never become a Procrustean bed upon which to stretch reality, but both are essential to creating matrices within which data can be ordered and manipulated. Our solution here has been to use existing terms where possible, if necessary sharpening definitions, and generating appropriate new ones as occasion demands.

To return to the question of territoriality: the fundamental link between human societies and the land is to be found in landownership and landholding. The estates possessed by feudal landowners have been the subject of formal and detailed study by generations of historians. Some of their constituent parts may comprise elements of even older estates, but others represent components reassembled as the result of inheritance, the land market and royal or ecclesiastical favour. These are important to the study of settlement for three reasons. First, when owned by great magnates or ecclesiastical corporations they generate the administrative records from which the answers to questions can be sought, conclusions drawn and generalisations formulated. Second, they form the practical frameworks of management, within which decisions were taken and implemented, decisions that generated both change and stability. Third, because of their importance they constituted, no matter how diffuse their structure, nodes from which ideas were diffused or resistance elicited. Size and physical structure of estates varied greatly, from the substantially compact, for example those of the Duchy of Cornwall or the Bishop of Durham, to the notably fragmented, such as those of the Knights Templar or alien ecclesiastical corporations like the Abbey of Bec. All landed estates tended to contain mixtures of land of varied quality: good, intermediate and poor. In this respect they, and the functional entities of which they were constituted – township, parish, manor, hundred and honour – normally cut across both terrains and settlement regions. In all cases internal diversity offered varied economic opportunities.

In Figure 1.8 we map onto the distribution of Mowbray estates in c 1170 (taken from Greenway 1972, map 3), data concerning settlement characteristics derived from nineteenth-century maps: this is warranted as an initial generalisation despite the obvious dangers. We append to the map a model in which we suggest that at root there are distinct gradations of settlement characteristics, from areas with good quality land to areas of poor quality land. This is hardly surprising, but we add a further level of complexity by suggesting that this overall pattern was distorted by many intrusions of foreshortened sequences within subinfeudated estates. Where tenants holding from the Mowbrays developed hierarchies of settlement on their own more limited estates, these both echo and distort the general pattern, for example by intruding estate administrative centres into

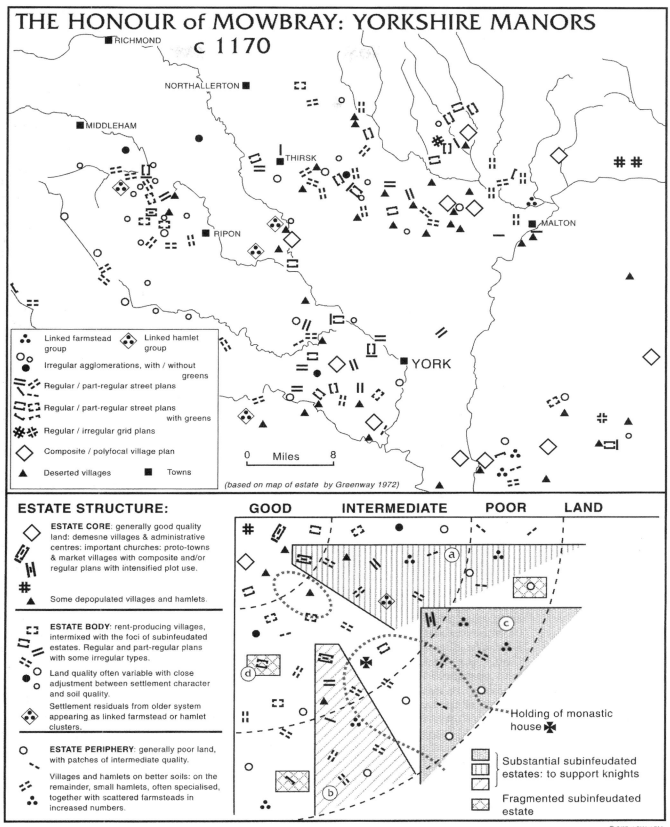

THE HONOUR of MOWBRAY: YORKSHIRE MANORS c 1170

RICHMOND

NORTHALLERTON

MIDDLEHAM

THIRSK

RIPON

MALTON

YORK

Linked farmstead group

Linked hamlet group

Irregular agglomerations, with / without greens

Regular / part-regular street plans

Regular / part-regular street plans with greens

Regular / irregular grid plans

Composite / polyfocal village plan

Deserted villages

Towns

0   Miles   8

(based on map of estate by Greenway 1972)

ESTATE STRUCTURE:

ESTATE CORE: generally good quality land: demesne villages & administrative centres: important churches: proto-towns & market villages with composite and/or regular plans with intensified plot use.

Some depopulated villages and hamlets.

ESTATE BODY: rent-producing villages, intermixed with the foci of subinfeudated estates. Regular and part-regular plans with some irregular types.

Land quality often variable with close adjustment between settlement character and soil quality.

Settlement residuals from older system appearing as linked farmstead or hamlet clusters.

ESTATE PERIPHERY: generally poor land, with patches of intermediate quality.

Villages and hamlets on better soils: on the remainder, small hamlets, often specialised, together with scattered farmsteads in increased numbers.

GOOD   INTERMEDIATE   POOR   LAND

(a)

(c)

(d)

(b)

Holding of monastic house ✠

Substantial subinfeudated estates: to support knights

Fragmented subinfeudated estate

© BKR / SW / EH

Figure 1.8

areas of intermediate or even poor quality land, simply because this represented the best land of the smaller estate. Further, the great monastic estates, also holding land from the Mowbrays, reflect different demands and policies.

Estates in land can endure for long periods: in Durham, the Raby estate, visible in the landscape because of the white-painted farmsteads created by tenancy agreements, was documented as an entity in the reign of Cnut (Hart 1975, 127). Of course, through time the internal arrangements will be restructured. If we follow Glanville Jones and picture an early rather simple socio-economic territoriality, with 'Dark Age' kings and lords sustaining a peripatetic exploitation of the land resources of large estates, then alienation to the church generated rather different patterns of exploitation, with centralised consumption invariably being focused at the locus of control, a great church or monastery. This innovation may either have been paralleled in the earlier needs of royal vills or could have been emulated by emergent royal palace centres. From these simpler structures, feudal estates and patterns of landholding and tenure evolved, leading to increased spatial and organisational definition, as well as greater fragmentation. The basic point is a simple one: for settlement development, estate structures were at least as important as the underlying land quality.

This conclusion leads directly to the final column in Figure 1.6 which models 'sequent systems'. In the model this is shown simplistically as a transition from an economy based upon hunting, via pastoral activity, to arable farming, although in reality this dimension of the model is infinitely complex. The qualities of land, and population pressures upon land, can never be wholly excluded from the argument but no crude determinism need be invoked. Good, intermediate and poorer quality land, measured on a locally relevant scale, is present in every local region, and these categories can be subsumed into wider sub-provincial, provincial and national scales. The three categories are not, of course, temporally constant, for good care and good husbandry can warm and improve even the poorer sorts of land, while over-cropping, over-grazing and soil deterioration may degrade land quality. Estates provide frameworks within which these developments occur; and while these devel-opments are not the theme of this book, they cannot be ignored when analysing settlement.

To conclude, we suggest that in order to grasp the true complexity of the evolution of settlement and farming systems, the four separate groups of columns in Figure 1.6 must be *combined* into a single model. Thus, in each and every 10 by 10km square at least this level of complexity is potentially present in a synoptic view, in which the visible elements of the landscape may be the end-product of several thousand years of development. Even in the localised view-point provided by a 10 by 10km square, it may in practice be near impossible to take account of so many levels of 'thick descrip-tion' (Geertz 1973, 6). The most detailed documentation will provide only limited glimpses of what happened. Nevertheless, we need to be aware of the potential complexity of what can happen in a matrix of time extending over 500 or 1000 years. If we carry these arguments, which have moved to the level of the individual estate, to the intricacy of the national settlement distribution, then the scale of the problem and the difficulty of generalising can be conceived.

The woodlands: 1086 and beyond

Figure 1.9 sets another distribution against our provincial boundaries: the record of woodland in Domesday Book, compiled more than seven centuries before the Ordnance Survey mapped settlement. It is based upon the labours of Sir Clifford Darby and his many co-workers, and assembles into a single distribution all the county studies they published. We have followed Darby's scheme for simplifying the complexity of the varied types of Domesday entry – leagues, acres, swine totals and swine renders – to three symbols (Darby 1977, fig 64), although, as he stresses, there can be no real equivalence between the different formulae adopted by the Domesday clerks. Underwood, brushwood and the like are included under the smallest symbol. There can be little doubt that the size of symbols adopted exaggerates the actual area of woodland involved. Further-more, the places at which Domesday records woodland were not necessarily the places where the woodland was actually located. The survey was concerned with

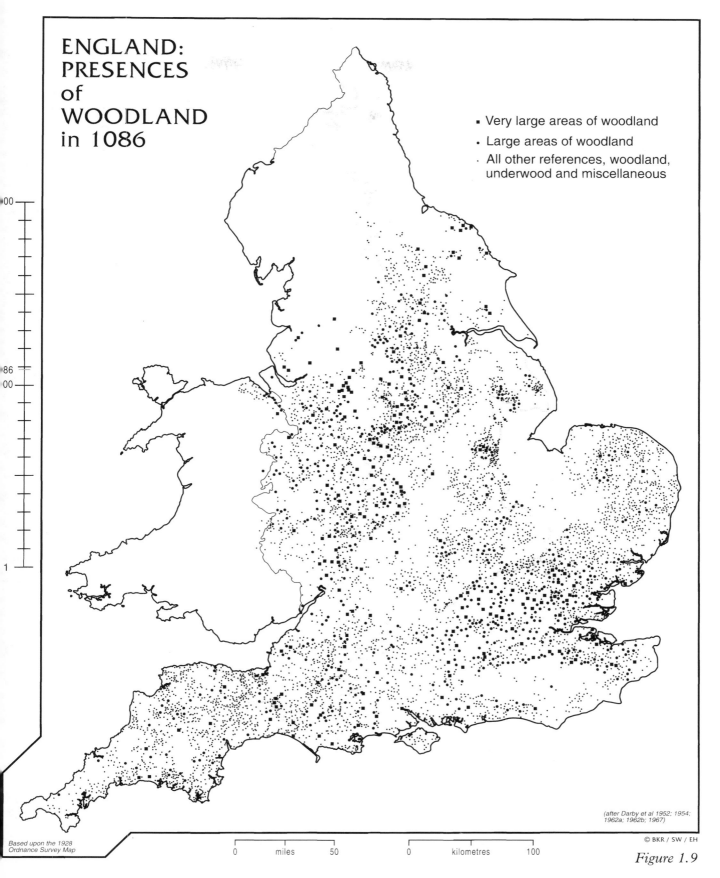

ENGLAND:
PRESENCES
of
WOODLAND
in 1086

■ Very large areas of woodland
· Large areas of woodland
· All other references, woodland,
  underwood and miscellaneous

*(after Darby et al 1952; 1954;
1962a; 1962b; 1967)*

© BKR / SW / EH

*Based upon the 1928
Ordnance Survey Map*

0   miles   50   0   kilometres   100

Figure 1.9

resources attributed to particular estates, and some of those resources – particularly woodland – might be in detached portions of the estate, some distance from the named estate centre. To give but one example, a very large single symbol stands out clearly in the south-western Midlands in a landscape largely free of recorded woodland. The woodland in question, some '3 leagues long and 2 leagues wide', is recorded (and therefore mapped in Fig 1.9) under King William's manor of Brailes, south Warwickshire. As Dugdale had noted as early as 1656, however, the woodland itself almost certainly lay at Tanworth, several miles to the north-west: part of the woodlands of the Forest of Arden. Moving this to its correct location – in a detached hamlet belonging to Brailes – would strengthen the impression in this part of the Midlands of a broad south-south-west to north-north-east cleared zone, facing a wooded frontier to the north-west, part of the Northern and Western provincial boundary (Gover *et al* 1936, xiii–xxxiv; Gelling 1978, 125–29; Hooke 1985a, 31–50; Roberts and Wrathmell 2000b). The same problem is particularly acute in the south-eastern counties, where portions of the woodland in the Weald were described under the names of the manorial centres of their parent estates set around its edges (Darby 1977, 191). Here, the places on the fringes of the Weald, where woodland was recorded, and where it has been mapped in Figure 1.9, are actually the places where there may have been little if any woodland.

Nevertheless, in spite of these qualifications, Figure 1.9 presents a useful, detailed and exciting picture. The variations in texture resulting from the assorted combinations of very large, large and small woodland symbols are surprisingly informative and raise many questions. In spite of its many deficiencies Domesday Book allows us to create a remarkable picture of later eleventh-century England. It is apparent that while some areas are devoid of recorded woodlands, in other areas, notably in the Chilterns and Essex, there were countrysides which still carried substantial woodland blocks, while in contrast Devon was characterised by large numbers of manors each with only a small amount of woodland attributed to it. Explaining these visible contrasts is difficult, for they may be as much a reflection of the way the data were recorded by the

commissioners, juries and clerks who assembled the evidence, as a reflection of real on-ground differences in the character of local woodlands. In this, it is likely that the character of local lordship was crucial. With large estates containing fewer subinfeudations there may have been a tendency to return larger 'blocks' of woodland, while areas where manorial fragmentation was more advanced, and many small manors had been created, could, when the data are mapped, result in the type of woodland distribution seen in Devon. Thus, tempting as it is to read directly from the map – and we will no doubt be guilty of this – Figure 1.9 should not be interpreted without careful analysis of Domesday Book. Finally, the account for Lancashire, surveyed in 1086, is demonstrably deficient in comparison with the rest of the country, while the northernmost four counties of Cumberland, Westmorland, Durham and Northumberland are wholly absent from the Domesday record.

In Figure 1.9 the provincial boundaries have been superimposed over the woodland distribution, an exercise that indicates two things. First, the nineteenth-century boundaries that demarcate the provinces dominated by dispersed settlement take, in large measure, the same course as the eleventh-century boundaries of those parts of the country dominated by woodland. Some of these may be seen to be entirely predictable. Others are undoubtedly physical yet possess a clear cultural importance, such as the northern scarp slope of the chalk escarpments running from northern Essex to the south-west. In contrast, the western boundary of the province winds across the Midlands and follows no clear-cut physical boundary until it reaches Sherwood, rising from the flat land of the Vale of Trent. Nevertheless, it is clear that to the south-west the course of the river Severn plays a part as a barrier.

Secondly, the division into woodland and open land provinces is by no means wholly clear-cut or absolute. In particular, the evidence shows that significant areas of woodland were present within the Central Province, notably in the south-west, in parts of the eastern Midlands and across portions of the Vale of York. We argue that these are real presences, and that tracts of wholly cleared land in this province intermingle with more wooded portions. Comparison of this map with the one showing settlement regions (Fig 1.4) suggests that there is a complex pattern of both accord and discord: this is a point we will return to below.

Pre-1086 woodlands

In a number of his publications Oliver Rackham has included a map of the Anglo-Saxon and Scandinavian place-names indicative of the presence of woodlands. This has been redrawn – and added to, in northern England – to appear as Figure 1.10. The interpretation of the precise meanings of these names is fraught with many questions; indeed, there are often indications that a given word may change meaning during its period of use. In our discussion of the name elements used by Rackham we follow Margaret Gelling's (1984) analyses of the four words:

1 *-leah* (-ley), as in the name Shirley, derives from an Old English word meaning – depending on context – 'forest, wood, glade, clearing', and later 'pasture, meadow' (Gelling 1984, 198). Broadly, the suffix is an indicator of the presence of woodland. While Gelling emphasises that subtleties must be considered through an examination of individual cases, her map of Derbyshire (Gelling 1984, fig 4) confirms that its distribution is supported and reinforced by other elements indicative of woodland, such as *-feld*, *-lundr* and *-wudu*. There is no clear way of dating this suffix, but Gelling cautiously suggests that it must have been used more after 730 than before that date (Gelling 1984, 198). The distribution of the names in *-leah* reflects closely the distribution of Domesday woodland areas. By 1086, when many are recorded for the first time, the names had become linked with settlements and presumably any cleared land associated with these: they had become in effect 'place-names'. It would in general be fair to argue that the presence of the element by 1086 is indicative of either a current or a former association with woodland.

2 *-hyrst* (-hurst) derives from an Old English word implying the presence of a 'wooded hill' (Gelling 1984, 197). Major settlements with the suffix *-hyrst* are of relatively late origin, and in Gelling's view grew up in areas not immediately

recognised by the Anglo-Saxons as appropriate to arable farming. Rackham's map shows that there is a heavy concentration in the Weald, but only a very thin scatter extending from the west Midlands to Lancashire. Within the Central Province a few examples appear in the southern portion of the east Midlands, which throughout our enquiries has gradually emerged as a complex mixture of landscapes with an exceptionally varied settlement history. They are wholly absent elsewhere.

3 *-thveit* (-thwaite) derives from an Old Norse word meaning 'clearing, meadow or paddock' (Gelling 1984, 210), and carries the implication of something being 'cut'. Its use may have extended into Middle English, and 'meadow and/or paddock' are possible later meanings. The Scandinavian conquests form a *terminus post quem* for its introduction, but the name form extends into post-Conquest usage. As a place-name it is concentrated within the Lake District and so does not complicate the general interpretation of the map.

4 *-feld* (-field) is a term that has been left until last because it is the most complex: it derives from an Old English word for 'open country', the opposite of *wudu*. For most of the pre-Conquest period it was used indifferently of land which might or might not be under the plough, with no specific connotation of arable. Nevertheless, it seems likely that it eventually came to mean 'arable land', particularly within the open-field farming systems in the second half of the tenth century, for example in the regional name 'Feldon' applied to the champion landscapes which appeared in south Warwickshire. Gelling suggests that the word had several phases of semantic development. First, there was an early phase of Anglo-Saxon encroachment on pasture land which gave rise to the numerous settlement names in *-feld*: this pasture must have included both open grass pasture and pasture mixed with varying amounts of woodland. Secondly, the end of the ninth and the beginning of the tenth centuries saw the next development, when the influx of Scandinavian farmers led to a great increase of arable land in the east and north of England.

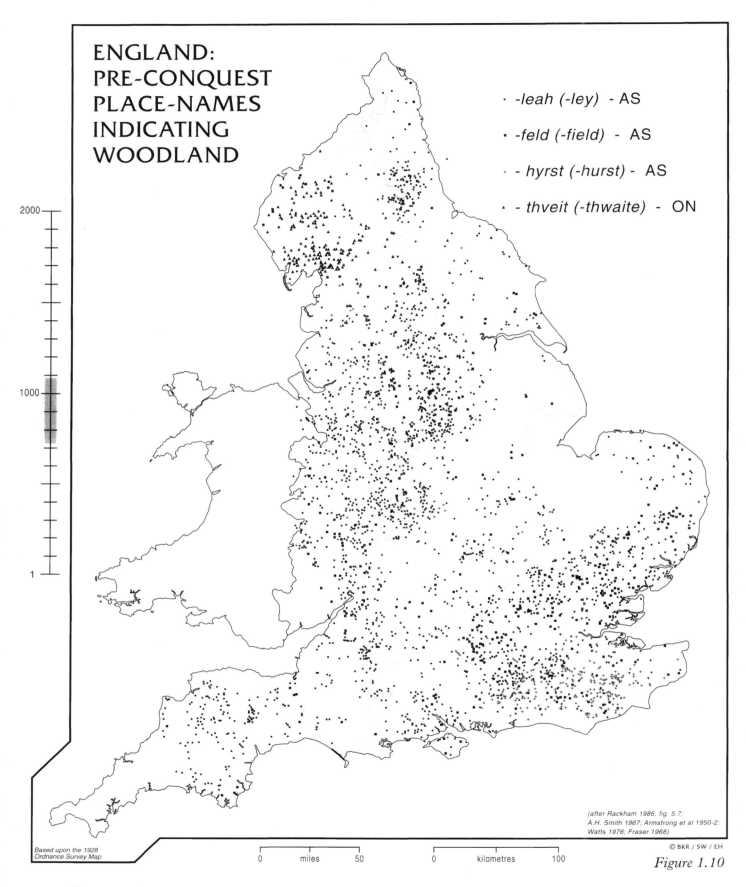

ENGLAND:
PRE-CONQUEST
PLACE-NAMES
INDICATING
WOODLAND

· -leah (-ley) - AS

· -feld (-field) - AS

+ - hyrst (-hurst) - AS

▲ - thveit (-thwaite) - ON

(after Rackham 1986, fig. 5.7;
A.H. Smith 1967; Armstrong et al 1950-2;
Watts 1976; Fraser 1968)

Based upon the 1928
Ordnance Survey Map

0   miles   50

0   kilometres   100

© BKR / SW / EH

Figure 1.10

Rough pasture was converted to arable, so that the plough was seen on the -feld. Thirdly, by the middle of the tenth century, in certain areas, a number of estates had little or no rough grazing or woodland inside their borders so that any open land was arable or meadow, and -feld meaning 'open land' may have become an appropriate term for the larger of these two divisions. Finally, as a term employed in naming villages -feld probably means 'open land previously used for pasture' and may be an indicator of areas converted to arable in the Anglo-Saxon period. To this we would add that any open land used for pasture might have once been arable at an earlier stage in its land use history.

These are intricate conclusions, and Gelling uses work by Cox to suggest that -feld 'was a prolific name-forming term in the early Anglo-Saxon period' – although ten examples before 730 hardly seem prolific when set against approximately 250 major settlement names containing this element. It may have remained in use in name formation until after 900 (Gelling 1984, 237–9). Rackham's map carries the argument a little further. If we exclude -thveit and -hyrst, which are respectively confined to the Lake District (where its meanings make sense) and the Weald, where a woodland context is unassailable, the distribution of the remaining two elements, -leah and -feld confirm the pre-1086 presence of the three provinces. To these may be added a further element appearing as -wold, -wald, and -weald, variants of the same word, seen most dramatically in the large tract of 'The Weald' of Kent, Sussex and Surrey and implying the presence of woodland or more probably of wood pastures. Fox has argued, with cogency, that such areas represent wood pastures, tracts of countryside characterised by grazing lands and isolated stands of wood, and were subjected to active colonisation during the ninth and tenth centuries (Fox 1989, 59–101). Because regions bearing such names are largely set within well-populated lowlands cleared and settled centuries earlier, their breaking for arable was associated with a great intensification of activity throughout all the champion regions.

The South-eastern Province carries many symbols indicative of pre-1086 woodland and in detail these conform closely to the distribution of Domesday woodlands, while the vast anomaly of the Weald on the map of the Domesday data is soundly and securely rectified. Were the element -denn (-dene) added to the map, meaning 'woodland pasture, especially for swine' (Gelling 1984, 234), then the concentration of symbols in the Weald would be even denser. In the Northern and Western Province there is again unambiguous confirmation of the provincial boundary between the Trent Valley and the rising land of Sherwood Forest and the ridges and escarpments beyond (the CPNSL sub-province). The west Midlands and Cheshire Plain are characterised by substantial numbers of these names, tending to form nodes separated by voids, presumably indicative of both the land cleared at an earlier stage as well as zones characterised by late surviving woodlands and commons. This scatter, thinning somewhat, continues into Lancashire – a zone not mappable in detail from the Domesday evidence – fading away in the Lake District where Anglo-Saxon place-names tend to be replaced by the Scandinavian -thveit. Overall, the distribution of these names confirms the presence of the three provinces. The Central Province contains a thin scatter throughout, excluding only north Durham and Northumberland, and small concentrations appear in the south-east Midlands, with greater numbers in the lowlands of the Vale of Berkeley and in the southern Cotswolds.

The distribution of these name-elements is an exciting example of convergent evidence. There is no way that the correspondence between, on the one hand, the distributions of woodlands in and before 1086, and on the other the distribution of nucleations in the middle decades of the nineteenth century, could be a product of unconscious manipulation of data. While there are many chronological uncertainties in this account, the massed place-name data suggest that the tripartite provincial structure has roots reaching back long before 1086. Furthermore, the three provinces, already characterised by different balances between cleared land and woodland in 1086, must surely have come into being long before the time when they can first be documented: the place-name mapping as currently constituted suggests an origin before the early eighth century. There is a further point: as the argument moves backwards in time the evidence does not suggest any great blurring of the provincial boundaries. We would not deny that there is confirmation for the presence of the wooded zones lying within the Central Province, including the regions with the element *-wold* (Fox 1989, 77–101). Some wooded tracts are still documented in 1086 particularly in the east Midlands. Nevertheless, the fundamental provincial contrasts appear to be deeply rooted.

The availability of timber

'Woodland' place-names provide us with one indirect dataset for the occurrence of woodland. Others could be constructed from, for instance, the records of industries that required large quantities of wood for their products, or charcoal for fuel. On a national scale, however, the most readily available data are those relating to vernacular timber buildings. Of these, perhaps the most important and influential existing distribution maps are for cruck construction (Fig 1.11), that for 'true crucks' being based on a plot of over 3000 samples (Alcock 1981, fig 2). One of us has argued elsewhere that the general distribution of crucks as evidenced in the present or recent stock of historic buildings reflects regions where cruck construction was used in medieval peasant houses; furthermore, that the regions to the east of the 'cruck-zone' were characterised by the alternative 'post-and-truss' method of construction (Wrathmell 1989a, 248–57). In the circumstances it is a matter of considerable interest that these zones show no correspondence with the three settlement provinces. It may be that the forms of settlement and land-use which generated the three provinces had no impact upon decisions as to how to support a house roof. On the other hand it may be that the cruck and post-and-truss patterning was established long before the emergence of the three provinces, or that other powerful practical or cultural forces have been at work.

The formation of external walling is, however, a different matter, and our starting point is none other than William Harrison, whose concept of champion and woodland regions began this chapter. He carries the distinction between these regions into his discussion of houses:

> It is not in vain, therefore, in speaking of building, to make a distinction between the plain and woody soils; for as in these, our

houses are commonly strong and well-timbered (so that in many places there are not above four, six or nine inches between stud and stud), so in the open champaign countries they are forced, for want of stuff, to use no studs at all, but only frankposts, raisins, beams, prickposts, groundsels, summers (or dormants), transomes, and such principals, with here and there a girding, wherunto they fasten their splints or raddles, and then cast it over with thick clay to keep out the wind. *(Withington 1876,113)*

The contrast is, therefore, not between houses constructed of timber and houses fabricated in other materials: the whole description relates to timber-framed structures of one sort or another. Rather, the contrast is between the houses in which generous quantities of timber studding were used in external walls, and houses in which a regional shortage of timber led to the use of wattle and daub to infill the timber frame. On this basis, we would expect the Central Province farmhouses of Harrison's day to have had the external appearance of clay-rendered buildings, while those of the wooded South-eastern and Northern and Western Provinces would display timbering.

Over thirty years ago, J T Smith published a study of timber-framed building in England in which he distinguished different regional traditions of external walls: an eastern tradition, characterised by the type of close vertical studding to which Harrison – a Londoner – is obviously referring; a western tradition of square panel framing, and a northern tradition which combines features of both with a distinctive use of the 'interrupted sill' (Smith 1965, 141–6, 153–6). Smith's study was based upon photographs of externally visible timber framing drawn from the National Monuments Record (Smith 1965, 135), and we should therefore expect to find a gap between the eastern and western traditions approximating to the Central Province. Figure 1.12 combines the information from a number of Smith's maps: those which plot ornamental panelled framing, herring bone framing, simple square panels and close studding (Smith 1965, figs 1–6). His plots of tie-bracing traditions have been ignored: bracing of one form or another would have been required even if the wall panels were wholly filled with wattle and daub.

There is no complete gap in Figure 1.12 to mark the Central Province; but there is a

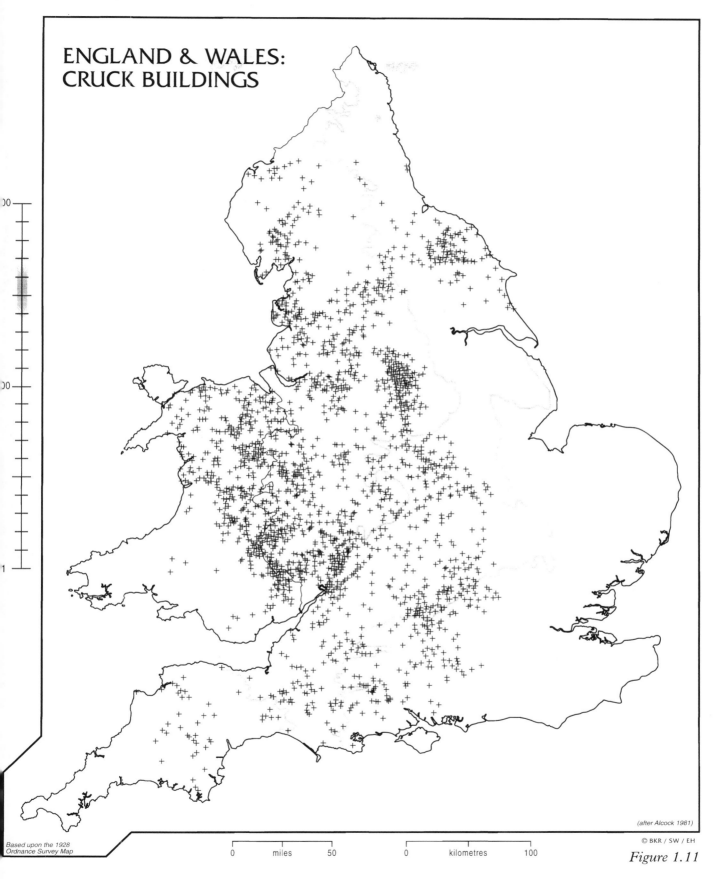

ENGLAND & WALES:
CRUCK BUILDINGS

Based upon the 1928
Ordnance Survey Map

(after Alcock 1981)

© BKR / SW / EH

0   miles   50   0   kilometres   100

Figure 1.11

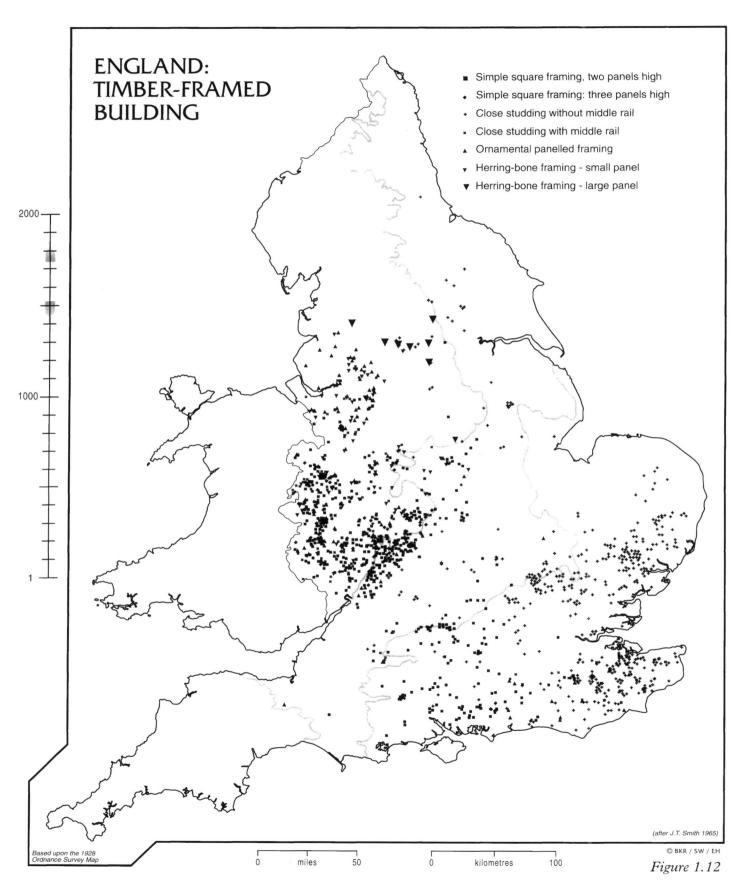

ENGLAND:
TIMBER-FRAMED
BUILDING

■ Simple square framing, two panels high
♦ Simple square framing: three panels high
✦ Close studding without middle rail
✕ Close studding with middle rail
▲ Ornamental panelled framing
▼ Herring-bone framing - small panel
▼ Herring-bone framing - large panel

2000

1000

1

*Based upon the 1928
Ordnance Survey Map*

0   miles   50   0   kilometres   100

(after J.T. Smith 1965)

© BKR / SW / EH

Figure 1.12

much thinner distribution of examples in this zone. We surmise that this scatter is related to several factors: the cartage of timber from woodland regions to adjacent champion areas; the inclusion in Smith's examples of high status buildings, such as manor houses, and the inclusion of town houses (eg Smith 1965, 137, 139). A glimpse of the movement of timbers is provided by Salzman (1952, 244–5) who notes, *inter alia*, the sale of 'bord' de Arderne' in Stratford-on-Avon in 1380, to be taken south for use at Woodstock. Taking these factors into account we would argue that Smith's distributions are broadly in line with Harrison's distinctions, and with our mapping of woodland and champion regions.

Two related issues should be considered at this point. The first is that the Central Province overlies the bands of Oolitic and Lias limestone which extend from Yorkshire to Dorset, and which were an important source of building materials for vernacular housing (Brunskill 1978, 187). The difference between the Central Province and those on either side is not, however, between a province with building stone and two others with timber; it is the difference between a province where building timber was scarce, and two others where timber was (in many but not all regions) plentiful. In short, the difference is not pre-determined by geology; it results from significant variations in the way agrarian resources were, and had been, exploited, and the impact of those variations upon the survival of woodland. As far as medieval peasant houses are concerned, the use of stone in the Central Province seems to have been confined to 'ground-walls', created by the collection of surface field stones rather than by quarrying stone. Only in post-medieval times were wattle and daub wall panels replaced by masonry walling, either leaving the cruck-framed trusses intact, or demolishing and rebuilding entirely. This kind of transformation is well recorded in the nineteenth century (Wrathmell 1989b, 8).

The second matter concerns the marked differences between Smith's eastern and western traditions of carpentry. In what circumstances did these differences arise? Our suggestion is that the emergence of a Central Province relatively bare of trees encouraged, to some extent, the independent development of local traditions on either side, in the South-eastern and Northern and Western Provinces. Of course, it is easy to overdraw the contrasts, and close examination of the distributions conflated into Figure 1.12 shows that the various styles of wall treatment do not have mutually exclusive distributions; rather different weightings. Nevertheless, it would be true to say that all distributions recorded in this book are a matter of weighting, proportion or variable density.

Finally, it seems, *prima facie*, almost inevitable that the provincial framework will also have had relevance to others aspects of building traditions – for example in the functional arrangements and plan-forms of farmhouses and outbuildings. For the present, however, our analysis depends on what others have reliably plotted at a national scale; we eagerly await more such distributions.

Rural settlement and woodlands – an overview

The data recorded in Figures 1.9 and 1.10 are brought together in Figure 1.13, showing the place-name evidence merely as small grey dots set behind the stronger symbols for the woodlands of 1086. The map is replete with massed data depicted at an exaggerated scale, and therefore it cannot be 'read' in detail. Furthermore, what appears must not be accepted uncritically. As noted above, the woodland data of 1086 cannot be mapped in an absolutely correct location, for even within a small township or manor the woodland was inevitably located some small distance from the locus of economic activity indicated by the place-name; in other cases this could be several kilometres. In theory at least, the two elements of the distribution, place-names and woodland, should occupy slightly different locations. None of the maps we are using is sufficiently accurate to allow any practical differentiation between the location of the name and the location of the woodland, but the distinction must be made. Furthermore, using the *English Place-Name Society* volumes for Cumberland and Westmorland (Armstrong *et al* 1950–52, maps; Smith 1967, maps), the work of Victor Watts for County Durham (Watts 1976, 212–25), and township names in the 1296 Northumberland Lay Subsidy (Fraser 1968), relevant Anglo-Saxon names for the four northern counties have been added to Rackham's distribution. This may in itself be in some need of

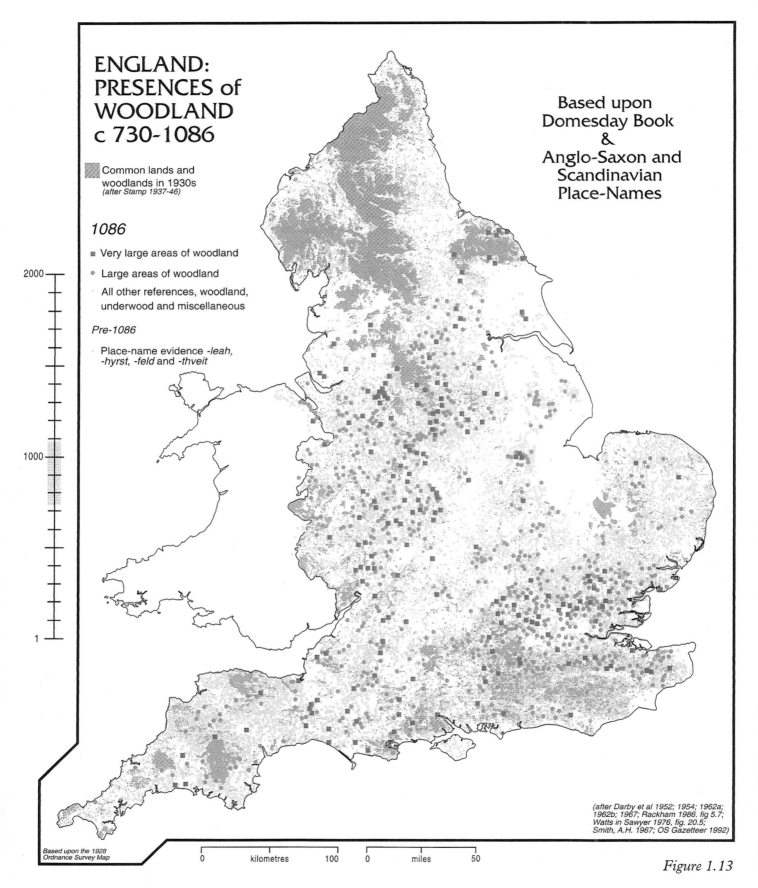

ENGLAND:
PRESENCES of
WOODLAND
c 730-1086

Common lands and
woodlands in 1930s
(after Stamp 1937-46)

1086

■ Very large areas of woodland

● Large areas of woodland

· All other references, woodland,
underwood and miscellaneous

Pre-1086

· Place-name evidence *-leah,
-hyrst, -feld* and *-thveit*

Based upon
Domesday Book
&
Anglo-Saxon and
Scandinavian
Place-Names

(after Darby et al 1952; 1954; 1962a;
1962b; 1967; Rackham 1986. fig 5.7;
Watts in Sawyer 1976, fig. 20.5;
Smith, A.H. 1967; OS Gazetteer 1992)

Based upon the 1928
Ordnance Survey Map

0   kilometres   100   0   miles   50

Figure 1.13

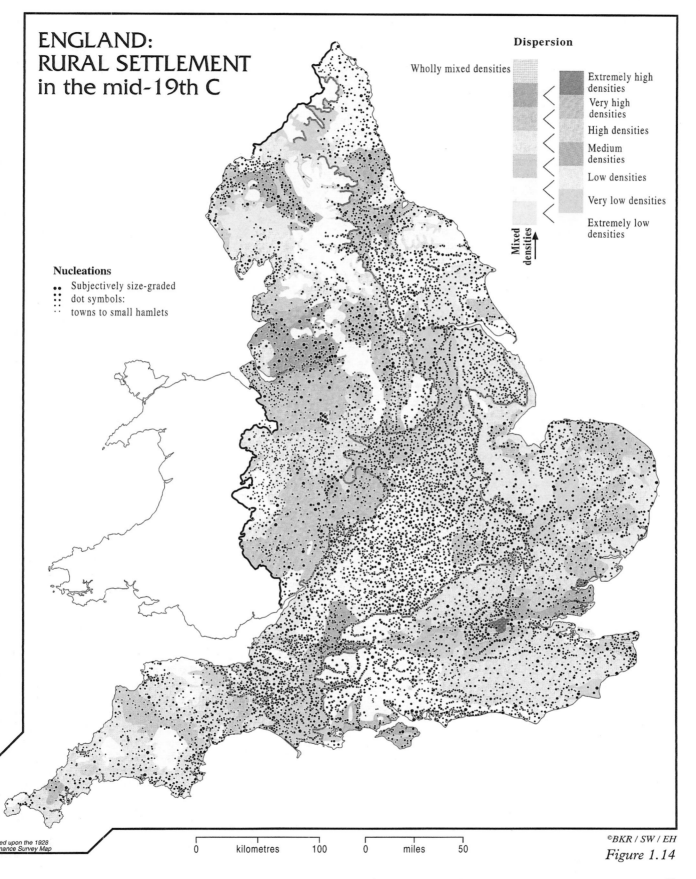

ENGLAND:
RURAL SETTLEMENT
in the mid-19th C

Nucleations

•• Subjectively size-graded
•• dot symbols:
•• towns to small hamlets

Dispersion

Wholly mixed densities

Extremely high densities
Very high densities
High densities
Medium densities
Low densities
Very low densities
Extremely low densities

Mixed densities

Based upon the 1928 Ordnance Survey Map

0 kilometres 100   0 miles 50

©BKR / SW / EH

Figure 1.14

revision, for we note discrepancies between Rackham's map and Margaret Gelling's mapping of some of the same names for the west Midlands (Gelling 1992, figs 3–7).

To enhance the image, we have also mapped all the common wastes and woodlands (excluding plantations) recorded during the 1930s and 1940s (Stamp 1937–44). This is by no means a perfect solution, but the addition serves as a reminder of the degree to which the better quality farmlands of the Northern and Western Province are fragmented and broken into separate cells by the presence of inhospitable upland masses.

There is unambiguous evidence of great swathes of land containing no symbols: we can only interpret this as land cleared during or before the Anglo-Saxon period, land which has persisted essentially as open for ten, twelve or even more centuries. The Domesday evidence of ploughs and ploughteams (Fig 3.5) suggests that a high proportion of it was arable, although we do not of course exclude intercalated tracts of common grazings. These merged into lands where the latter were more prevalent and where some woodland survived, often as underwood, but in one or two areas reaching high timber. In the remaining two provinces, as we move back through time, open land – perhaps grazing land – together with woodland formed a large colonisable reserve, which perhaps accounts for the presence of the name element -feld with its varied shades of meaning. By 1086 substantial tracts of cleared land can be postulated in the following areas:

1 East Gloucestershire, south Worcestershire and the Avon Valley and on the heavy clays and Marlstone escarpments of south-eastern Warwickshire and north Oxfordshire.

2 South-west and central Northamptonshire, most of Leicestershire (but excluding Charnwood Forest) and including south-east Nottinghamshire and north-west Kesteven.

3 Most of Lincolnshire and the East Riding of Yorkshire.

4 Excluding the special case of the Fenlands, most of Cambridgeshire, north-west Suffolk and the western third of Norfolk.

5 Hampshire, Wiltshire, Dorset and Somerset, often but not invariably linked with the chalk. (Somerset includes some of the most intricate terrains of the country.)

6 Substantial portions of southern Shropshire and southern Herefordshire.

Together these combine to create a broad south-south-west to north-north-east tract of cleared countrysides.

Further local studies will undoubtedly reveal more of the full significance of the fine detail of the woodland map, and correct some of our rather broad-brush descriptions. Nevertheless, even in its present unsophisticated state it represents an important statement, because it displays convincingly the national distribution of woodland both in and before the eleventh century. Even when we take into account its undoubted deficiencies and the many qualifications that must be attached to it, it is a remarkable picture for so remote a period and provides a firm foundation for further exploration. Figures 1.13 and 1.14 face each other. A comparison of these two composite maps, compiled from sources of widely differing character and separated by well over seven centuries, indicates the importance of reviewing as much archaeological and historical data as possible within this national and regional framework.

The distributions seen in these two maps result from interactions between many complex factors within the twin matrices of time and place. To begin to analyse and explain some of these linkages, we must isolate and dissect certain of these factors, and we will do this by examining a series of further distribution maps brought to the same scale. Chapter 2 will establish the broad character of England's physical geography, terrains, drainage systems, climatic conditions and edaphic factors. The rich evidence of nineteenth-century census materials will then be linked to settlement, leading to a broader assessment of the links between settlement types and demographic evidence. It will conclude with an analysis of other landscape and place-name evidence that has a bearing on the distribution of settlement.

Two fundamental caveats must be entered at this point. First, this study is retrogressive, moving from rich source material where the lineaments of arguments and hypotheses can be readily established, towards evidence which is more partial and thus less easy to interpret. Secondly, in this journey we will be using the work of other scholars – though we take full responsibility for the interpretations we place upon their materials. We appreciate that much published work used in this volume may now be in need of revision in the light of new discoveries, but the processes of collecting, re-evaluating and then remapping all the data would have been impossible within an acceptable time scale.

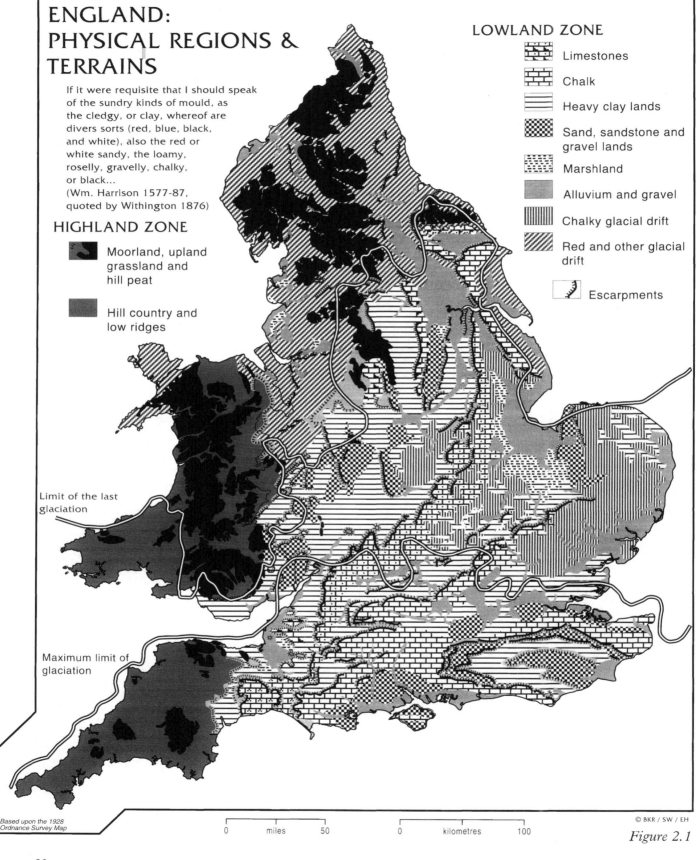

ENGLAND: PHYSICAL REGIONS & TERRAINS

If it were requisite that I should speak of the sundry kinds of mould, as the cledgy, or clay, whereof are divers sorts (red, blue, black, and white), also the red or white sandy, the loamy, roselly, gravelly, chalky, or black...
(Wm. Harrison 1577-87, quoted by Withington 1876)

HIGHLAND ZONE

Moorland, upland grassland and hill peat

Hill country and low ridges

LOWLAND ZONE

Limestones

Chalk

Heavy clay lands

Sand, sandstone and gravel lands

Marshland

Alluvium and gravel

Chalky glacial drift

Red and other glacial drift

Escarpments

Limit of the last glaciation

Maximum limit of glaciation

Based upon the 1928 Ordnance Survey Map

0 miles 50

0 kilometres 100

© BKR / SW / EH

Figure 2.1

2
Land and people

Introduction

Early last century Sir Halford Mackinder (1915, 63) pointed out that the terrains of England could be divided into two principal sections: 'the contrast between the south-east and the north-west of Britain, between the plains and low coasts towards the continent, and the cliff-edged uplands of the oceanic border ... depends upon a fundamental distinction in rock structure'. To the north and west lay a 'highland zone', dominated by uplands carved from rocks of Carboniferous age or older, while to the east and south a 'lowland zone' is characterised by young, softer rocks of post-Carboniferous age, sands, clays, friable sandstones, chalk and soft limestones. These contrasts are seen in Figure 2.1. The Midland clay plains form a distinctive tract between the uplands proper and the gently folded sedimentary rocks to the south and east where escarpments of chalk, limestone and sandstone alternate with long clay vales.

The contrasts between these broad regions are undoubtedly associated with differences in location, climate, soils, ecological conditions and ultimately farming potential. Sir Cyril Fox further developed Mackinder's ideas in his essay *The Personality of Britain* (1952) which brought the two zones to wider notice. While few scholars would now use crude physical determinism as a way of explaining all aspects of culture, there can be no question that local conditions undoubtedly affect *genres de vie* (Evans 1956, 217–39). There are, after all, real and important differences between the farming potential of Kent, the English Midlands and the Pennine uplands, differences that are apparent to any observant traveller. How can these contrasts be described and exemplified without over emphasising their importance? James Corner puts it well when talking about the landscapes of contour ploughing in America: 'these striking landscapes of curves, rolls and turns are literally measured expressions of

the farmer's elaborate negotiations with topography, soils and weather. A dimensional vocabulary accompanies such measures, including phrases such as slope tolerance, pitch, strike, plow depth, plow line, overplow, cross-sow, and datum' (Corner and MacLean 1997, 131). To these we would add for earlier landscapes of England, 'furlong, wong and daywork, nook and gore, land, selion, dole and hade, water-furrow and dyke', the language of the land and those close to it (Adams 1976). In these technical vocabularies, one modern, one traditional, there is no crude determinism, for while the land often dictates, it may also be coaxed and nudged, helped and nurtured. We believe that our settlement 'local regions' are the product of an endless process of such 'negotiations' between human societies and the land. Rooted in land qualities, local regions derive many of their characteristics from human endeavour. Of course, even the soil itself is rarely delivered complete from the hand of nature: many of the most fundamental attributes it now possesses are the end product of centuries of stone picking, cultivation, manuring, cropping and careful management. Anyone who doubts this should observe the use of flint as a building stone in chalk countrysides: much of this material must have been picked from the land. Aspects of these crucial and elaborate negotiations are explored in the next two chapters through discussion of three themes: land, people and agrarian systems.

The physical context: the terrains

Mackinder provides an important clue about where to begin framing an understanding of the terrain of England (1915, 110): the upland masses are so placed that the rivers are longer on the eastern slope than on the western (Fig 2.2). The great divide of the English drainage system runs along the high range of hills extending from

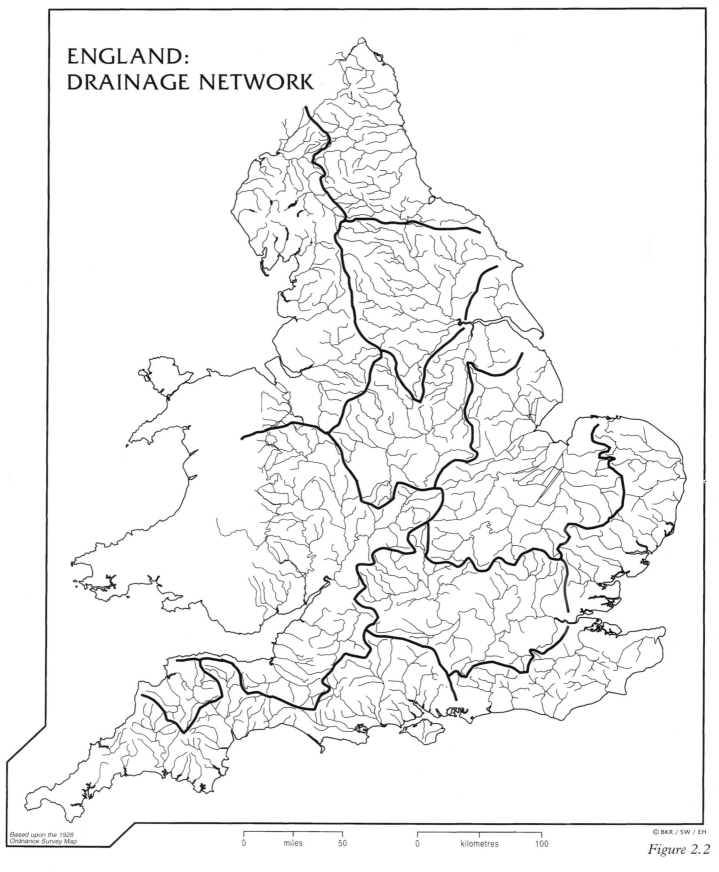

ENGLAND:
DRAINAGE NETWORK

Based upon the 1928
Ordnance Survey Map

0   miles   50

0   kilometres   100

© BKR / SW / EH

Figure 2.2

the Cheviots along the Pennines – nearer to their western than to their eastern edge. It then curves southwards from the Pennines across the Cheshire Plain to the Welsh mountains, and then between the basins of the Dee and the upper Severn, in such a way that all of the main Pennine rivers come down eastwards to reach the sea in the Humber estuary. In fact, some 25% of the drainage of England is expelled through this great waterway. As Mackinder pointed out, there are three considerable rivers, namely the Yorkshire Ouse, the Trent, and the Avon-Severn, whose combined courses form a vast curve, extending across England from north-east to south-west. The lowlands they create curve round the southern limit of the northern upland and are also roughly parallel to the escarpment of Jurassic limestone, which begins in the hilly plateau of the Cotswolds and sweeps north-east into Yorkshire. To the east and south of this escarpment drainage is in three directions: to the Wash, to the North Sea and to the English Channel, depending upon the placement of two further south-east to north-west watersheds. The skeleton of the lowlands is structured around the upstanding large escarpments of the Jurassic and the Chalk. The latter forms the complex nodes in Salisbury Plain and the Marlborough Downs, with three downland ridges extending to the north-east, east and south framing the drainage systems of the Witham-Welland-Nene-Great Ouse, the Thames and the smaller river systems flowing to the south coast.

The result of all this is a set of basins. In the south these are separated by substantial hill ridges, low hills or low plateaux, but the divides between the Avon and the Trent, the Trent and the Weaver and the Trent-Avon and Wash systems are merely higher portions of what is essentially a continuous Midland plain. East Anglia and parts of eastern Yorkshire both have some of the qualities of disconnected 'islands' of land. It is no accident that these contrasts are echoed, although never closely followed, in the ancient contrast between the counties of the south and east and the Midland shires. Furthermore, London, York and Gloucester, while not occupying sites at the absolute head of navigation, all lie at or near the head of navigation for sea-going ships (Bristol being a replacement for Gloucester, allowing shipping to avoid the treacherous reaches of the lower Severn). Nevertheless, the Trent, the Severn and the Yorkshire Ouse all formed highways for small boat traffic, and the importance of inland ports such as Boroughbridge, Tadcaster, Doncaster, Nottingham and Bridgnorth should not be underrated, even before water levels were maintained by weirs, necessitating portages around any unnavigable obstacles.

Comparison between Figure 2.1 and Figure 2.2 serves to emphasise the broad links between the river systems and terrain, and reiterates the role of the larger drainage systems in creating the great tracts of terrace and alluvial lands. These give rise to tracts of warm, well-drained cultivable soils as well as flood-prone bottom lands such as are seen in the lower Severn and Avon and, most dramatically, in the Fens. In fact, the terraces are normally reworked glacial drift – that complex, varied, rather poorly mapped and frustrating substance which plasters much of northern and eastern England. Drift is derived from both distant and local sources, lifted, moved, deposited and often then reworked and redeposited by moving ice and meltwaters, eventually deposited in thick belts across much of midland and eastern England (Fig 2.1). The importance of drift is fundamentally simple: dig, build or plough and it is these 'superficial' deposits which are most commonly encountered; entrench, excavate and quarry, and country rock is normally reached – sandstone and marl, clay, chalk, limestone and the hard rocks of pre-Carboniferous date. In contrast, the alluvial deposits, found not only on the lower terraces and flood plains of the larger rivers but also in small amounts along the tributaries, streams and smallest brooks, represent the downwashings from slopes whose soils were rendered less stable by woodland clearance. Beneath lie the older, earlier gravels. In this, the role of cultural influences in generating seeming 'natural' elements in our long-settled landscapes should never be underestimated (RCHME 1960; Shotton 1978, 27–32; Catt 1978, 12–20; Bell and Boardman 1992: Fulford and Nichols 1992).

This account of some of England's physical characteristics has been included because human occupation of the land has responded to the variations described, as can be seen in a comparison of Figures 1.13 and 1.14 with Figure 2.1. For early human societies the differences between lowlands, some with glacial deposits and others without glacial deposits, were probably at least as important as the more obvious contrasts between land above and below the 300m contour. It is a great leap to move from our perception to theirs. There must have been great contrasts between landscapes with well-developed drainage systems and those, more recently glaciated, where there was an immature drainage network associated with soil conditions ranging from lake clays to pervious sands, over quite short distances. In turn, these presented qualitative differences from the more homogeneous landscapes of valley and plateau chalk, limestone scarp and dipslope, the larger areas of well-drained sands, or even the rolling hill slopes of many of the uplands. The post-glacial development of the varied drainage basins was important in laying the foundations of what were to become farming landscapes. Furthermore, in this account the lithological qualities of country rocks and drift have been emphasised, rather than their precise geological ages, the structures of which they are a part, or the terminology applied to them. Lithology is closely associated with chemical constituents, and with the amount of stones, coarse sand, fine sand, silt, fine silt or clay that are by-products of *in situ* weathering. Above all, lithology affects the proportion of calcium carbonate naturally present: lime, which controls soil acidity and the potential for agricultural production. Human hands have modified many components of landscape, but their basic mineralogical constituents have always been the gift of nature.

When Figures 2.1 and 2.2 are compared with Figure 1.14 the coincidence of certain of the settlement boundaries with physical divides is clear. Terrain contrasts, and all that they imply in terms of land resources, have undoubtedly 'affected' the location of the cultural boundaries, as can be seen in the five areas selected for detailed discussion. First, an important contrast in settlement occurs along the northern edge of the Chalk escarpment, as far east as the point where its degraded edge disappears beneath the boulder clay plains of East Anglia, somewhat east of Saffron Walden. The escarpment is itself a complex feature: varied beds of chalk have a cumulative thickness of the order of 250m and overlie the Upper Greensand, the Gault Clay. There are occasional outcrops of Lower Greensand and finally Kimmeridge Clay of Jurassic age, into which is cut the Vale of

the White Horse. This succession brings several distinctive qualities to the landscapes of the chalk scarp: a physical diversity, seen in stepped slopes, with varied often loamy soils, where country rock mixes with chalk and other downwash materials. It is a varied landscape with attractive agricultural potential; there is an assured water supply, provided by springflow from the base of the absorbent chalk. Finally, viewed from above, there is a banded cross-scarp succession of downland wold on the chalk itself, further diversified by deep valleys and superficial deposits. There are varied landscapes and soil potential along both scarp and scarpfoot, where downwash generates lime-rich soil diversity – a preferred settlement zone according to Dominic Powlesland's terminology. Eventually these give way to mixed arable and meadow land on the clays below the scarp, where drainage is more impeded. This is a recurrent landscape pattern culturally linked with parishes and townships organised as a series of strips cutting across the grain of the land at right angles (Havinden 1966, 17–30).

Secondly, the western edge of the Fenlands presents a marked contrast between the flat lands of the peat fen and the softly rising driftlands and low plateaux of the eastern Midlands. Similar slight but important rises characterise the northern limits of the fenlands. It is no accident that our provincial boundary, mapped from the perceived density of nucleations, follows the wetland/dryland break around the rim of the fenland basin. This depression was scoured out by ice and subsequently infilled with a mixture of peat fen, alluvial and marine deposits. In broad terms the area is divided by a low ridge of silt that parallels the coast of the Wash. On the landward side is peat fen, and on the seaward side are salt marshes. Well-settled in Roman times (Phillips 1970) the area then suffered a marine transgression, followed by subsequent reclamation of the coastal marshes between the silt ridge and the sea, using a succession of sea dykes (Hallam 1965). Fen, clay fen islands, silt ridge and marshlands together logically form one distinctive sub-province (Fig 1.5). Once again, townships and parishes often take the form of strips, crossing the grain of the land from driftlands to fen or from silt ridge to fen and salt marsh, giving access to contrasting resources. Preferred settlement zones appear as a denser than normal concentration of villages on the rising land at the basin's rim and on the silt ridge and larger fen islands (Fig 1.1). In fact, on a national scale, we can say that such bands of very regular strip parishes and townships are substantially limited to such zones, where well-marked environmental contrasts offer varied local economic potential.

Thirdly, the Pennine edge of northern England constitutes a less distinct boundary. The lower ridges of rising foothills form a transition zone between the riverine plains, sometimes flat, sometimes undulating, and the sloping, scarp-divided, dissected plateaux of the eastern side of Pennines. The approximate line of the 300m contour has been adopted as the provincial boundary, for it is often followed by the head dyke – the line between improved and unimproved land. Nevertheless, in general the deeply incised main dales have been seen as forming part of the Northern and Western Province. In practice, of course, no boundary 'line' can ever be satisfactory, and indeed on the ground the transition between two landscape types is normally found to be a zone. This can often be substantial, possessing the width of a few kilometres. Like the preferred settlement zones along scarps, it is often associated with on-ground contrasts in economic potential so that the territories of parish, township and manor cut across it at right angles.

Fourthly, the south-eastern edge of Sherwood Forest is associated with the presence of Keuper Sandstones and Bunter Series, both of which possess soils which tend to be sandy and 'blow' under intensive cultivation. In fact, between the Trent Valley and the Pennines lies a complex set of north to south escarpments, broken and eroded away by the drainage systems of the Aire, the Yorkshire Ouse, the Don, the Tarne, the Idle, Meden, Maun and Rainworth Water. As noted before, the initial provincial boundary was drawn to the west of this zone, west of the 'Pennine slope' sub-province (CPNSP: Fig 1.4). Subsequent, more detailed investigations have suggested that an earlier provincial boundary once lay further east, sweeping around the western edge of the Trent Valley, leaving Sherwood and the associated local regions along the Pennine edge in the Northern and Western Province.

Finally, a comparison of Figures 1.13 and 2.1 shows that a great tract of anciently cleared land runs from the chalk northwards, embracing the clays of the upper Thames, the limestones of the Cotswolds, and sweeping north-east, across the rolling clay lowlands of the Midlands into the Trent valley. A similar but smaller tract lies to the south and east of the Fenlands in the east Midlands and East Anglia. The rich diversity of soils within these areas cannot be sufficiently emphasised, and while we appreciate that a more detailed level of resolution would reveal many subtleties in the relationships of settlement and land, the evidence of our mapped data suggests that these great tracts were essentially without significant woodland.

The physical context: climate, vegetation and soils

The preceding section shows that in England immense variety is found within quite short distances, most easily seen in the changes in the height, texture and colours of landscapes, and culturally encapsulated in vernacular building styles, field patterns and land use. Few observant drivers can fail to notice that the same short distances are often associated with quite marked changes in weather patterns. Longer-term familiarity with, and movement through, any tract reveals that what is really happening is the generation of quite marked local climatic differences. Historically, climatic conditions – generalised weather – have never been constant, and climate, vegetation and cultural activity interrelate in particularly diverse and subtle ways (Lamb 1966; Parry 1978; Lamb 1982). For much of England the normal growing season falls in the seven to eight months with mean temperatures above 6° C. Only in the extreme south-west does this rise to nine to twelve months, but in the higher parts of the Pennines the growing season may be as low as five to six months (Fig 2.3). Mean annual rainfall has normally been highest in the uplands and lowest in East Anglia, with variability also being least in the west and highest in the east. As recent decades have shown, this 'normal' pattern can shift sharply by the year, and may have varied greatly in the past when periods of drier than average conditions have greatly exceeded wetter than average conditions. Some rainfall data are incorporated into Figure 2.3, and the cross section reveals how the Pennines are in a rain shadow occasioned by the Welsh mountains and the Lake District.

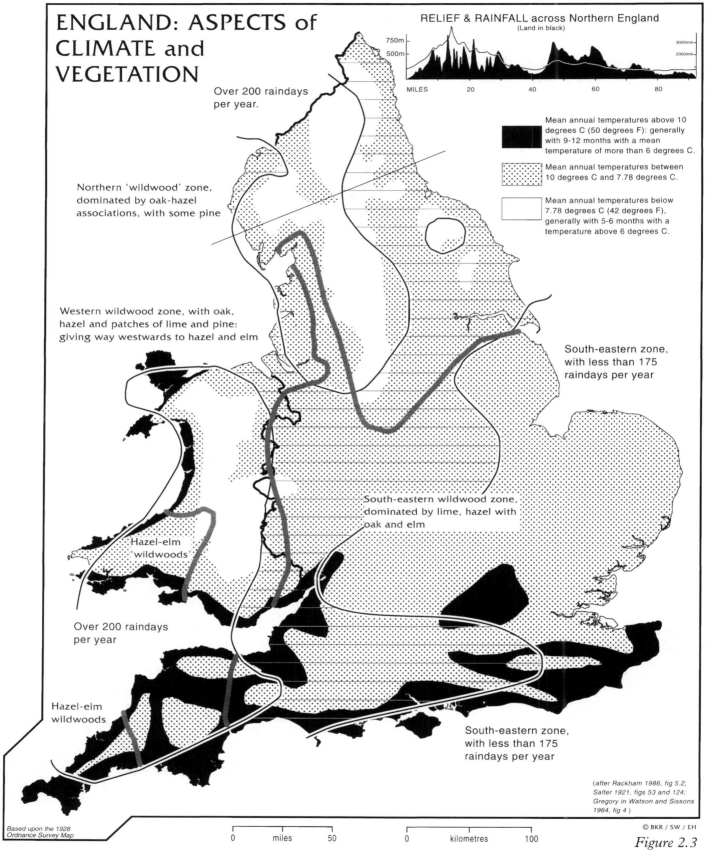

ENGLAND: ASPECTS of CLIMATE and VEGETATION

RELIEF & RAINFALL across Northern England
(Land in black)

750m
500m
3000mm
2000mm

MILES   20   40   60   80

Over 200 raindays per year.

Mean annual temperatures above 10 degrees C (50 degrees F): generally with 9-12 months with a mean temperature of more than 6 degrees C.

Mean annual temperatures between 10 degrees C and 7.78 degrees C.

Mean annual temperatures below 7.78 degrees C (42 degrees F), generally with 5-6 months with a temperature above 6 degrees C.

Northern 'wildwood' zone, dominated by oak-hazel associations, with some pine

Western wildwood zone, with oak, hazel and patches of lime and pine: giving way westwards to hazel and elm

South-eastern zone, with less than 175 raindays per year

Hazel-elm wildwoods

South-eastern wildwood zone, dominated by lime, hazel with oak and elm

Over 200 raindays per year

Hazel-elm wildwoods

South-eastern zone, with less than 175 raindays per year

(after Rackham 1986, fig 5.2; Salter 1921, figs 53 and 124; Gregory in Watson and Sissons 1964, fig 4)

Based upon the 1928 Ordnance Survey Map

0   miles   50

0   kilometres   100

© BKR / SW / EH

Figure 2.3

Every locality shows small variations between windward and leeward slopes, or valleys parallel to or athwart the prevailing winds, variations that national data are simply too generalised to reveal. So it is that slight secular variations in climate can have profound impacts upon human life. An overall slight warming extends the area of over nine months growing season, pushing the national average conditions upwards towards eight months. Thinking in terms of practical farming, this shortens the period when beasts needed to be stall fed, and moves growing seasons of five to six months higher up mountain slopes. What all this could mean in practice is indicated in a pollen diagram from Weardale in the Pennines, from which it appears that wheat was being cultivated at a height of some 400m above sea level in the later thirteenth century (Roberts *et al* 1973, 207–21). Extensive traces of former cultivation at high levels around most upland areas affirm the existence of climatic variations as well as economic and social pressures (Parry 1978).

By about 5000 BC post-glacial warming had brought woodland cover to large parts of the country. Much of this was undoubtedly oak woodland, but there were admixtures of other trees. Elm and lime appeared on the more base rich soils, with alder in the damper valleys. Birch appeared on the poorer soils, particularly in the north and west, with Scots pine in the northern Pennines. For England, Rackham (Fig 2.3) identified five wildwood provinces, and presents a picture rather different from the 'mixed oak forest' most of us see in the mind's eye. He has suggested that pollen diagrams underestimate the importance of lime and ash, because they shed less pollen than oak or birch. Similarly hazel, which can form a canopy tree rather than a mere shrub, also produces less pollen when overshaded by taller neighbours. Rackham placed most of lowland England in the Lime Province, arguing that the two commonest trees were lime and hazel, with oak and elm as the next most abundant. Pools and fens were fringed with alder, while pine woodlands appeared in the eastern Fenlands, birch woodland in the Somerset levels and ash woods in south Norfolk. Further north and west lies the Oak-Hazel Province, containing mosaics of these trees, perhaps with oaks appearing on the less fertile soils, with local patches dominated by elms and pine. Finally, in

Cornwall appears a type more dominant in south-west Wales and Ireland, the Hazel-Elm Province (Rackham 1986, 68–73). These provinces in no way conform to those we have identified, but we note that there is a relatively strong correlation between the distribution of the sessile oak (*Quercus petrea* or *Quercus sessiliflora*) as mapped by Perring and Walters (1962, 186) and our two outer provinces. Tansley (1939, 303–4) suggests a correlation with soils in which high acidity is a common factor. In contrast the common or pedunculate oak (*Quercus robur L*: Perring and Walters 1962, 186) is universal.

As Rackham emphasises, the conversion of millions of acres of wildwood into farmland was unquestionably the greatest achievement of any of our ancestors (Rackham 1986, 72). Beginning in the Mesolithic period, openings were established in this forest by hunting, gathering and fishing communities; these were followed by land taking clearances of farmers in the early Neolithic, but by the Iron Age, felling, agriculture and intense grazing ensured that pollen diagrams begin to reveal some landscapes already as open as those of today. From the Anglo-Saxon period until about 1300, somewhat warmer, less stormy conditions, with warm summers and cold winters prevailed, conditions favouring grain harvests and the extension of grain cultivation into higher latitudes and upland environments. After about 1300, conditions changed, and cooler, wetter, more unsettled conditions made harvests more uncertain (Lamb 1984, 423–73). These circumstances were associated with a retreat of settlement from the uplands, sometimes perhaps the direct result of deteriorating climatic conditions, but more probably the result of complex economic and social changes. In detail these changes had varied repercussions upon different terrains. Clearing the woodlands and draining the land led to the erosion of surface soil and the accumulation of silt, while recession led to the establishment of grasses and bushes on former arable and pasture, slowing movements on hillslopes and reducing the supply of sediment lower down the basins. Neither alluvial flood plain, nor saltmarsh, nor limestone pavement, nor upland or lowland peat bog can be excepted from this tally: all have felt the impact of culture. The succession of seasons and the longer swings in climate have been, and still are, beyond human control. Above all else however, it has been an increase in the numbers of people and changes in their distribution which have been linked, in complex relationships, with the most fundamental developments in settlement, clearance and landscapes.

What did clearance for agriculture mean for people's way of life? One view is provided by the poet George Mackay Brown:

To drudge in furrows till you drop
Is to be born.
(George Mackay Brown, 'Stations of the Cross; First Fall', *Collected Poems 1954–92)*

It is worth reflecting on this, especially in a society that has come to romanticise the life of the pre-industrial peasantry. Each acre of tillage represents an accumulation of almost unimaginable labour. Suppose a single quarter-acre, open-field strip or 'selion' of arable measures 5.5 yards by 220 yards (one furlong) in length; suppose also that this demands the cutting of 22 ploughed 'bouts', or slices, reckoning that each plough slice is some nine inches wide (Passmore 1930, 52): then the ploughman must walk some 22 furlongs or 2.75 miles, to cultivate *each single quarter-acre strip, and 11 miles for each acre* (a figure confirmed by McConnell 1922, 60). If a standard holding of 30 acres is being tilled under a two-course rotation (half fallow; half under crop), then the ploughing requirement is 15 acres for the crop and twice for the fallow of 15 acres, 45 acres in all. This means that 45 x 11 miles per acre are walked, a total of some 495 miles for the holding. These figures of distance, and the ploughland:cropland ratio achieved, offer a surprising revelation of the advantage of the three-course rotation. For if the 30 acres were ploughed as 10 acres for each of the two crop fields and 10 acres x 2 for the fallow field, then some 55 fewer miles need be walked. Of course, over a year such distances are relatively small, but these figures are merely for ploughing, and do no include harrowing and harvesting requirements. We must imagine the struggle with the stilts, or handles, to keep the plough in work, the battle with stones and mud, and the prodding of the recalcitrant oxen with their neck sores caused by the ill-fitting yokes: the realities of 'contact with the soil' become starkly clear. Furthermore, all these figures assume that the land has already been broken for the plough.

Population trends and regional distributions

Population levels have been a crucial control factor affecting the relationships between human beings and the land which supported them – the spring that drives the clock – seen most clearly in the changes wrought since the advent of the Industrial Revolution. Nevertheless, it would be quite wrong to assume that prehistoric levels were universally or even markedly lower than those present in later feudal centuries. In both periods there were substantial local variations in population, itself a powerful factor generating further regional differentiation. While the gross prehistoric total was probably lower than that, say, of 1300, there may have been local regions that actually possessed higher prehistoric populations than were present at the latter date. The evidence up to 1983 was summarised by Fowler (Fig 2.4) who, with appropriate qualification, concluded that the achievements of the later Iron Age population were 'appropriate for a population in the region of a million living, in some areas, at a density approaching the norm of medieval rural England' (Fowler 1983, 32–8). It is no criticism of his courageous assessment to add wryly 'if only we knew the latter figure', but the point is taken. The Butser Hill experiment with 'prehistoric' agriculture has produced surprisingly high seed:yield ratios, even in the absence of manure, using spelt and emmer, ranging between 1:7 to 1:59 but averaging 1:40. These are far higher than medieval yield ratios tabulated by van Bath (Reynolds 1981, 108–9; van Bath 1963b), indeed comparable with late nineteenth-century data (Mercer 1981, 232). Roger Mercer concludes that 'farming practice in British prehistory had the potential to support massive populations' but rightly points out that a bad year could bring appalling hardship heralding widespread disease and death (Mercer 1981, 236).

At this stage we must attempt to provide some fixed points at which estimates of gross population levels can be established (Fig 2.4), before assessing what these may mean in terms of settlement and landscape. In 1851 there were some 16.76 million people in England, to which must be added 1.165 million in Wales. This, the first modern census, represents the only accurate estimate of historic population: that of 1801, showing 8.3 million in England and

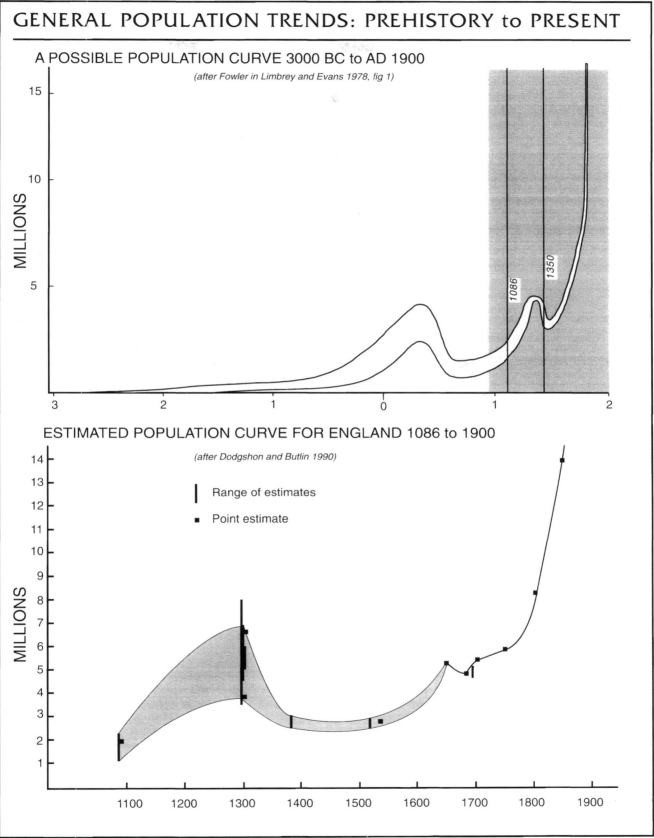

GENERAL POPULATION TRENDS: PREHISTORY to PRESENT

A POSSIBLE POPULATION CURVE 3000 BC to AD 1900

(after Fowler in Limbrey and Evans 1978, fig 1)

ESTIMATED POPULATION CURVE FOR ENGLAND 1086 to 1900

(after Dodgshon and Butlin 1990)

Figure 2.4

41

0.588 million in Wales, while broadly reliable, is based upon mere tally sheets and is almost certainly not fully accurate. For England, the overall percentage increase between 1750 and 1801 was of the order of 33% but that between 1801 and 1851, as industry burgeoned, was some 102%, a wholly different order of magnitude (Lawton and Pooley 1992, 33, table 3.3). These reasonably accurate data put all earlier figures in perspective. The earliest reliable national estimate, the work of the Lichfield statistician Gregory King in the later seventeenth century, suggests a total of 5.2 million souls for England and Wales in 1695, although Glass's corrected figure is 4.8 million (Glass and Eversley 1965, 203–4). Glass's investigations reveal something of King's methods; more particularly they show a link between the formal place-name listings by Adams and Spelman, the maps of Christopher Saxton and King's first attempts to estimate the national total (Glass and Eversley 1965, 176–8, 185–7). Francis Bacon foreshadowed the methods of historical demography when he claimed in *of the Greatenesse of Kingdomes*' that 'the population [of a state] may appear by Musters, and the number of Cities and Townes by Cartes and Mappes' (Morgan 1979, 147). The medieval clerks of the Exchequer created national lists of place-names (Glasscock 1975), together with some indication of each locality's status; indeed Domesday Book, listing some 13,000 places in England (with a few in Wales) falls into this category. In many senses Saxton's important maps of 1579 are indexical, effectively converting settlement listings into maps. Gregory King reasoned – and four copies of his list make this reasoning wholly clear – that if it were possible to group elements of the gross settlement lists into categories, and then to estimate the average population of the average settlement in each of the categories, a process of simple multiplication would generate the required total. King spent much energy wrestling with likely household size in his varied categories – town, village, hamlet and the like – a crucial figure in the multiplication process. Hearth Tax data, giving the number of taxed houses in each settlement, allowed him to refine the method. There is, of course, more to population than gross totals. Rates of growth between 1801 and 1851 averaged 0.66% per annum, and between 1851 and 1901, under the influ-

ence of a quickening industrial economy and imperial expansion, averaged 2.04% per annum. Lawton calculates that for England and Wales in 1701–31 the annual rate of increase was 0.28%; in 1731–81, 0.73%; in 1781–1801, 1.10%, and in 1801–31, 1.72%. These rates of growth are founded upon voluminous and reasonably accurate data, both national and local.

In summary, it appears that for the last two decades of the seventeenth century the population of England and Wales was of the order of five million people. It is worth recalling the country to which this relates: post-Restoration, post-fire and post-plague London, a time of quickening activity on coalfields, with Defoe describing trade in vivid terms. In woodland areas, in coal-fields, in ports and in parts of the country-side, mining, iron production, cloth industries, brewing and leatherworking, indeed all aspects of manufacturing and trade were expanding in response to rising population and extending colonial interests. The two totals, of somewhat under 5 million for 1680–1700 and somewhat over 8.3 millions after industrial 'take-off' in 1801, must be kept firmly in mind when evaluating all earlier estimates, for these figures represent our only really secure foundations. This is why they have been discussed at some length.

The problem with English demographic history has always been to fill the gap between these post-medieval estimates and that based upon Domesday Book. The basic figures for 1086 can be quickly stated. Some 13,278 places were listed, and by adding all of the recorded population together and counting all, even the slaves, as heads of households, and then multiplying by five (for the number of people in a household) a grand total of some 1.59 million is achieved. This is a figure that Darby, after much careful qualification, considers 'may be not far from the truth' (Darby 1977, 87–91). Sawyer formulated an important argument when he suggested that 'the rural resources of England were almost as fully exploited in the seventh century as they were in the eleventh and that although some settlements were established or moved in the late Anglo-Saxon period, the settlement pattern is, in general, much older than most scholars have been prepared to recognise' (Sawyer 1976, 2). He showed that for Kent, while in 1086 some 347 localities are listed by name, another 159 places are known to have existed from earlier documentation, places important enough to possess baptismal churches. Domesday Book, as is widely admitted, conceals or omits much evidence. The ratio of places listed in Domesday Book to the documented total in Kent is at least 347:506 or 1:1.46. Multiplying 1.5 million by 1.46 produces nearly 2.2 million, a crude adjustment, for the individuals who actually lived in 'unmentioned' settlements may have been returned under tenancies in the entry for the main manor. Nevertheless, Postan has suggested that the number of households present in 1086, the base figure from which all calculations begin, may be 50% higher than the number of tenants actually listed (Postan 1972, 28). Working these figures, approximately 300,000 recorded householders multiplied by 50% give 450,000, and multiplying this by a number per household as low as 3.5 gives 1.5 million, and by a figure as high as 5.0 gives 2.25 million. We take the latter as a base figure, and use it in the discussions that follow.

Bruce Campbell (1990, 93) suggests that rates of population growth in England after 1086 could range between 0.5 and 1.3% per annum. A rate of 0.5% applied to a base population of 2.25 million in 1086 would give some 6.54 million by 1300, before the drastic declines of the fourteenth century. Were the rate to have been 1% per annum, then the 2.25 million of 1086 would have given 11.5 million by 1250 and 12.75 million by 1300, both improbably high figures. Once again, we can only stress that any generalisation must conceal both temporal and spatial variations in the rate of growth. The estimate of 6.54 million in 1300 approximates to Postan's view that at that date there were 'nearer 7 millions than [Russell's] 3.7 million'. Hallam, beginning with a base of 2 million in 1086, and founding his opinion upon an examination of dozens of manorial surveys falling between 1086 and 1300, suggests a figure for 1300 of between 4.5 and 7 million (Hallam 1988, 512), with a conservative estimate of 5.25 million. These figures must be compared with the 4.8 million estimate for the 1690s. While uncertainties are involved, there are clear grounds for suggesting that in England the population in the latter part of the thirteenth century exceeded that present in the closing decades of the seventeenth century; indeed, it may have been substantially in excess of the latter total. In the two and a quarter

centuries between 1086 and 1300, growth may have varied between as much as 1.3% per annum and as little as 0.1%. Indeed, in the period between 1066 and the decades of the civil war, between 1135 and 1154, some estates may even have shown an overall decline in population, without affecting the overall 1086–1300 general trend.

Earlier population estimates pose even greater problems. Sheppard Frere, working with towns, forts and vici, estimated that by the end of the second century the population of Roman Britain may have amounted to 'almost three million' (Frere 1987, 301–2). Millett's detailed calculations offer a rather higher figure, at about 3.7 million (Millett 1990, 181–5). Even without this, however, it is remarkable how easy it is to achieve a figure far in excess of the base estimate for 1086.

This discussion has led us to conclude two things. First, that Francis Bacon and Gregory King were right that the number of settlements, set against some information on the likely number of inhabitants within each, is a foundation-stone of pre-censal estimates of population. This has implications for future work on settlement listings. Second, pre-seventeenth-century population estimates, when compared with our first reliable estimate for the later seventeenth century, are often significantly high. The countryside was populous, and a populous countryside will be subjected to great pressures from usage.

Regional detail

These estimates are important but frustrating. They are important because they ask questions about the relationships between population and settlement development. They are frustrating because they do not allow the all-important regional components making up the gross totals to be assessed. To do this we have again adopted a retrogressive approach, beginning with the nineteenth-century sources, and feeling our way backward through time. Four fundamental points are revealed in Lawton's analysis of regional population trends in Great Britain between 1701 and 1901 (Dodgshon and Butlin 1990, 292–3) and in his mapping of the data for 1801 (Lawton 1964, 228; Lawton 1986, 11; Lawton and Pooley 1992, 118). First, densities of 64–128 per square mile

(100–199 persons per 1000 acres) prevail through most of the Central Province. Exceptions are parts of the east Midlands, the Cotswold scarps and vales and the west Wessex sub-province (CINMD, CCTSV and CWEXW: Fig 1.4), where they reach 128–256 per square mile (200–399 per 1000 acres) and above. These regions all possessed local industries. Of course, wherever coalfields intrude into the province higher concentrations appear. Secondly, the textile areas of Lancashire and Yorkshire in the Northern and Western Province carry even higher densities, normally 256–449 per square mile (400–700 persons per 1000 acres), and in some areas reaching levels in excess of 513 per square mile (800 persons per 1000 acres). Thirdly, there is a clear tendency for the woodland areas of the two outer provinces to carry densities falling between 128–256 per square mile (200 and 399 per 1000 acres), although there are important exceptions. In the northern portion of East Anglia (parts of EWASH(E) and EANGL) in the plain of Hereford (WWYTE) and the chalklands (EWEXE: all Fig 1.4), densities of 64–128 per square mile (100–199 per 1000 acres) prevail. Finally, in the higher parts of the Pennines, moorland countrysides with only scattered farmsteads and few nucleations, there are densities of 63 persons per square mile (0–99 persons per 1000 acres). These very generalised statements are drawn from maps in which the administrative cells, the units of record for population data, sit uncomfortably over contrasting terrains and settlement realities.

By the mid-nineteenth century, further population increases had undoubtedly blurred the elements of the 1801 distribution, but Figures 2.5 to 2.8, based upon the work of John Dewdney, show the parish by parish distribution for England in 1851. The level of detail is too great to be considered at length here, but these maps are part of the vital bridge between the poorly documented worlds of the more distant past and the rich data of recent statistical sources. Four maps each show a different quartile of the distribution and enhance our understanding of the map of rural settlement in the mid-nineteenth century. The picture catches the Industrial Revolution just at the point when a 'drive to maturity' is in progress (Rostow 1971, 9–10). The top quartile (Fig 2.5) emphasises the raised population levels in Lancashire and

western Yorkshire, the results of a burgeoning of comparatively long-established cotton and woollen industries. London, the capital of an expanding empire, had already reached 2.3 million, although there were already problems of definition and the conurbation was probably something under 2.7 million, approximately 15% of the total for England and Wales (Best 1979, 25; Best and Rogers 1973, 57-9). The London area and the mining districts of Cornwall, parts of the west Midlands, Derbyshire, and Durham all lie in this top quartile, as do the smaller industrial and coalfield areas of Gloucestershire and Somerset, parts of the Yorkshire, Derbyshire and Nottinghamshire coalfield and the east Cumberland coalfield. The extent to which rural areas were already involved in these general increases can be judged from the widespread distribution of parishes falling within this band.

To simplify the problems of generalising about an exceedingly complex distribution at a national scale, without becoming drawn into specific local detail, we have identified three characteristic 'types' of pattern in Figures 2.5 to 2.8:

Type A consists of high density blocks, zones where many adjacent parishes contain high levels of population, most clearly seen in the upper quartile elements (Fig 2.5). All are areas of eighteenth and nineteenth-century industrial and urban expansion, the direct products of the Industrial Revolution, and must mask out all traces of earlier population distributions deriving from antecedent levels of economic development. Portions of Lancashire, Cheshire, Durham and Cornwall fall into this category, while the concentration around London is pre-eminent.

Type B is formed by low density blocks, zones where population is absent or very low, appearing amid the lowest quartile of the distribution (Fig 2.8), and representing unsettled, negative areas, mostly the inhospitable uplands. The northern Pennines, Cheviots, the Lake District, North York Moors, Exmoor, Dartmoor and portions of Cornwall all fall into this category. The low densities on the chalk country tend to involve discontinuous chains of smaller blocks of parishes which appear in this quartile, along with significant portions of Herefordshire, the East Riding of Yorkshire, Lincolnshire and the Brecklands. There are clear grounds for arguing that all

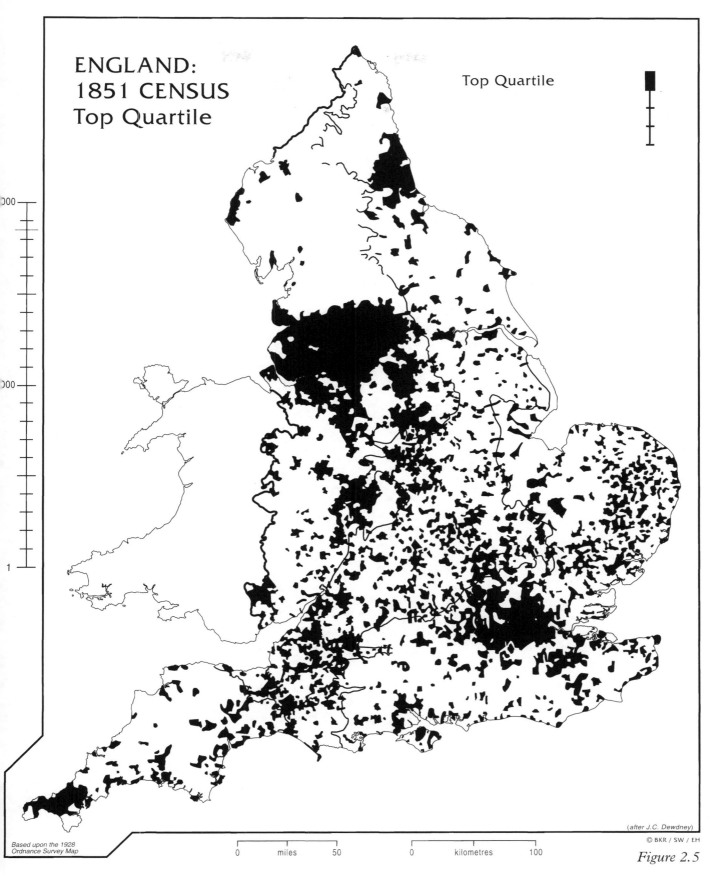

ENGLAND:
1851 CENSUS
Top Quartile

Top Quartile

Based upon the 1928
Ordnance Survey Map

(after J.C. Dewdney)

© BKR / SW / EH

0   miles   50   0   kilometres   100

Figure 2.5

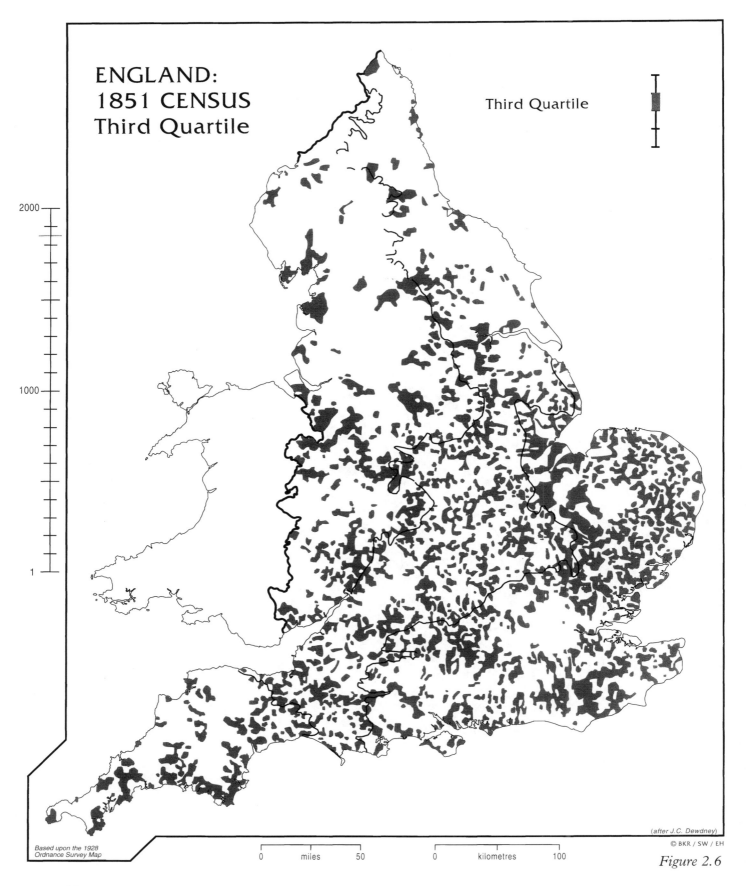

ENGLAND:
1851 CENSUS
Third Quartile

Third Quartile

(after J.C. Dewdney)

Based upon the 1928
Ordnance Survey Map

0   miles   50

0   kilometres   100

© BKR / SW / EH

Figure 2.6

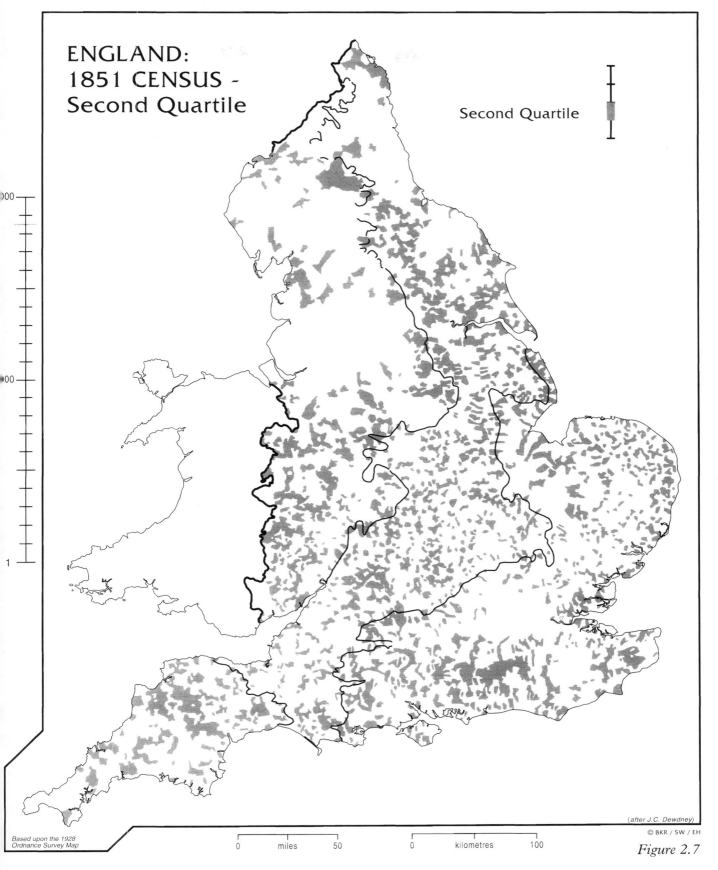

ENGLAND:
1851 CENSUS -
Second Quartile

Second Quartile

(after J.C. Dewdney)

© BKR / SW / EH

Based upon the 1928
Ordnance Survey Map

0 miles 50

0 kilometres 100

Figure 2.7

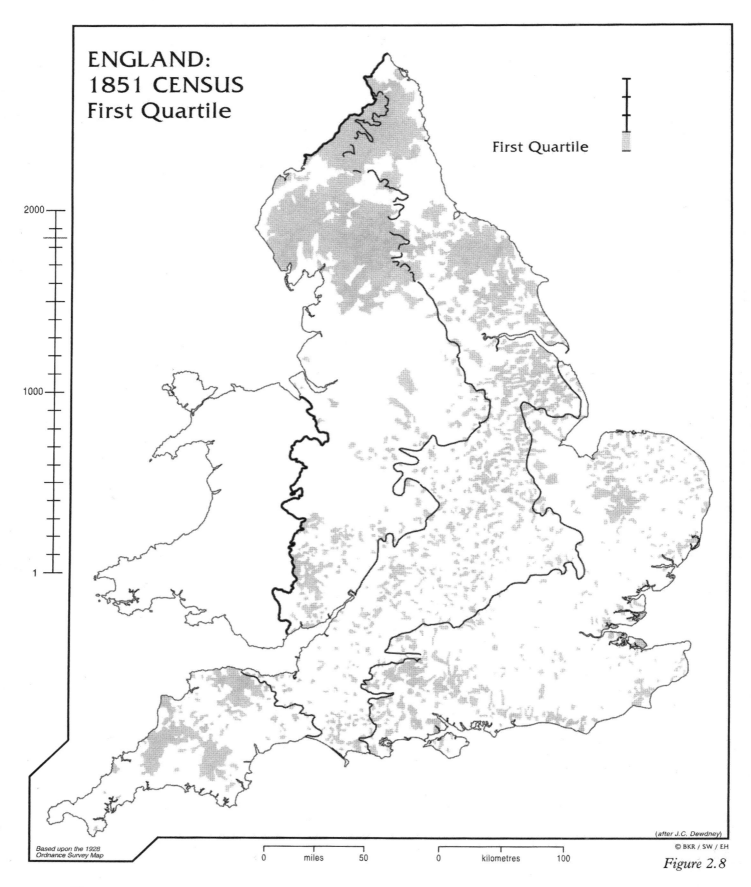

ENGLAND:
1851 CENSUS
First Quartile

First Quartile

(after J.C. Dewdney)

© BKR / SW / EH

Based upon the 1928
Ordnance Survey Map

0   miles   50   0   kilometres   100

Figure 2.8

had long been negative areas, carrying populations significantly lower than those normal for adjacent well-settled zones. The characteristics are such that while they could be, indeed were, exploited for cultivation, their soils were subject to relatively rapid declines in natural fertility, through pan formation, leaching or both, a process only reversible through intensive inputs of labour for draining and manuring.

Type C marks variable density zones, where parishes with high densities jostle with others with intermediate and very low densities – the term 'patchy' is best applied to these. They occur in all maps, but are most clear in those of the two middle quartiles (Figs 2.6 and 2.7). Of course, more extensive blocks do sometimes appear, but there are substantial areas possessing great local parish to parish variety. This patchiness reflects, on the one hand, the natural variations in soil quality, but more importantly, on the other, the impact of landownership within essentially fertile and intensively occupied terrains, and the varied ways in which estate components were managed.

This way of describing the characteristics of extremely detailed population distributions was originally worked out by Rosalyn Leighton in experimental work on demographic distributions. She compared the distribution of households recorded in the Compton Census of 1676 with that of the inhabited houses recorded in the first census of 1801, ie before the main impact of the Industrial Revolution (Leighton 1995). She noted a tendency, whatever the actual population levels involved, for the distribution of the three types of pattern to remain relatively constant throughout the period between 1676 and 1851. Furthermore, she explained Type C – the 'complex patchwork' – in terms of the network of 'closed' and 'open' parishes. The former lay under strong seigniorial influence and control. The 'open parishes' were often split among several controlling interests, or wholly lacked any direct seigniorial control, so that they more easily accreted both population and diverse economic and social components, most notably craft, mercantile and industrial elements. The differences are such as to affect the trajectories through time of each individual parish to a substantial degree, sustaining and enhancing the variations. Mills defined and discussed these differences for the eighteenth and nineteenth centuries but it

is clear that similar contrasts, between settlements under strong lordship and settlements subjected to less intense seigniorial control, have been present since medieval centuries (Mills 1980). Even in the village-dominated Central Province there were already, by the later thirteenth century, considerable local variations in manorial structure, expressed in terms of both size and crucial variations in the balance between demesne, villein and free land (Kosminksy 1956, 90–1, 100); there was already also a fundamental contrast between ecclesiastical and lay manors (Kosminksy 1956, 110–111; Roberts 1982, 125–46). These contrasts were deeply rooted. They are a reflection of long-established land occupation, and while the act of granting land to a particular owner or corporation may provide a direction for its subsequent temporal trajectory, other contrasts, including some elements of the manorial structure and settlement characteristics, undoubtedly take their origin from ancient settlement circumstances.

It is these contrasts, seen upon nineteenth-century demographic maps, that reach the heart of our enquiry, that of seeking meaning in rural landscapes and the societies they have supported (Geertz 1973, 5). If these claims, drawn from mapped data of the 1851 census, appear inconceivable given the long periods of time which are being considered, then Figure 2.9 makes the crucial point that even within a 'late' distribution more ancient elements can persist. This draws together in one map the lowest quartile of the 1851 distribution, and the 1968 map of deserted villages (as black dots: Beresford and Hurst 1971, 66). The correlation is remarkably close, and shows that the abandonment of nucleated settlements between, largely, the mid fourteenth and early eighteenth centuries, still left its mark on the population densities of 1851.

To return to the main theme of characterising population distributions, Types A-C are undoubtedly useful as a simple, descriptive model. Of course, the 'blocks' in themselves have no absolute meaning, being a quirk of statistics; but they do represent areas within which there are only relatively small variations between each parish and its neighbour, whereas in the 'patchwork' areas the variations between parishes are relatively large. This is a fundamental distinction, affecting the character of local regions. In fact, our discussion has led

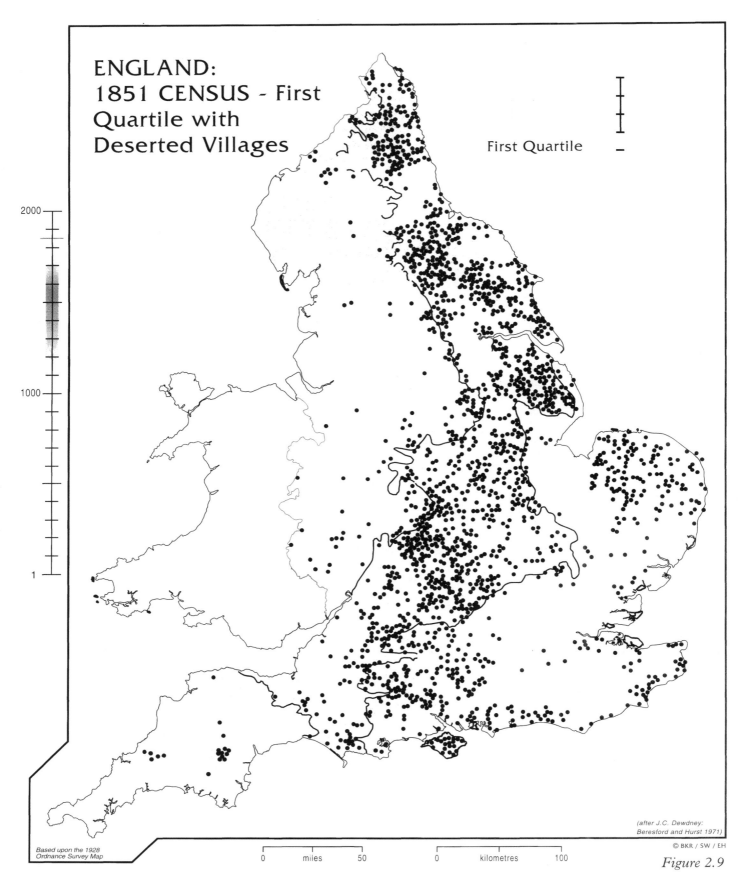

ENGLAND:
1851 CENSUS - First
Quartile with
Deserted Villages

First Quartile

2000

1000

1

*Based upon the 1928
Ordnance Survey Map*

0   miles   50

0   kilometres   100

*(after J.C. Dewdney:
Beresford and Hurst 1971)*

© BKR / SW / EH

Figure 2.9

towards a simple conclusion: there is no general relationship between type of settlement and population density. Both nucleation and dispersion are associated with varied levels of population density. More specifically, extremely low densities of population undoubtedly correlate with low densities of dispersion, while high levels of population correlate with those areas where dispersion has the potential to become so dense as to create a single sprawling form, what the Germans term *Schwarmsiedlung* – 'swarm settlement' (Grenzbach 1984). Of course, the absolute levels achieved by 1801 and 1851 in areas where there was contemporary coal extraction or woollen cloth production are not likely to have been present in the medieval period. Nevertheless, a degree of local enhancement of dispersion densities by industry operating within the framework of the dual economy was probably already present in medieval times. The identification of this distinctive patching of population in late sources frames an understanding of demographic estimates and settlement.

Turning to the regional population densities recorded in Domesday Book, Darby's figures show that if the recorded population per square mile is plotted (Darby 1977, fig 34) three fundamental zones appear. Throughout eastern England figures in excess of 10 are normal, with parts of eastern Norfolk and central Suffolk reaching 15 and even 20 and more. Throughout the remainder of the South-eastern and Central Provinces (excluding only the Weald, parts of the Chilterns, the Brecklands and the fens and levels) figures range between 5 and 10, while the Northern and Western Province returns figures below 2.5. If we multiply each of these by the low figure of four, to estimate family size, then 40, 60 and 80 per square mile are suggested for eastern England, with between 20 and 40 being normal throughout the lowlands elsewhere, and below 10 in the north and west. Moreover, if we then reckon, as calculated above, that a base population of 2.25 million in 1086 had increased to 6.5 million by 1300 with an overall average growth rate of 0.5% per annum, then at the same rate of growth, 10 per square mile would have increased to 29, 20 to 52, 40 to 116, 60 to 174 and 80 to 232 per square mile. These are not vastly inflated estimates, and real figures may have been higher. The result is that for many rural areas, the numbers suggested

by these estimates overlap the middle ranges of the concentrations present in 1801. Bruce Campbell is right in his conclusion that, before the demographic crisis of the mid-fourteenth century, the medieval countryside was 'literally teeming with people' (Campbell 1990, 73).

The medieval regional pattern

To turn to the medieval regional pattern, we can form a view about the increases in tenant populations between 1086 and 1300 documented by Hallam, even if we take account of the fact that sub-tenancies may well be concealed by the Domesday record. Table 2.1 is abstracted from Hallam's (1988) summary of population changes between 1086 and the decades between 1300 and 1350 on the basis of recorded tenancies.

While these figures (Hallam 1988, 537–93) represent an important sample of manors scattered across the country, the marked variations in the sample size should be noted. So, too, should the organisation of this material, on a county basis: it means that it is difficult to apply Hallam's valuable analysis directly to our provincial structures. The recasting of data along provincial lines might provide a more meaningful picture of regional variability. For both 1086 and 1300–50 the regional distribution of population is generalised in the percentages for each period. The increase in northern England was to be expected, but eastern England sustains a significant lead. This is manifest in the high levels seen in the Poll Tax returns of 1377 (Baker 1973, fig 42). With the exception of southwest England (here meaning Devon and Cornwall), the east Midlands, an area substantively dominated by champion lands, have the lowest rate of increase between 1086 and the first half of the fourteenth century. Hallam's analysis of the trends in the east Midlands suggests that 1086–1244 saw rapid increase, 1244–80 considerable decline, increasing again between 1280–1312. David Hall argues that in Northamptonshire the tenurial structure tended to become fossilised because of the pressure of population, with yardland levels achieved before, at or soon after 1086, persisting right through the Middle Ages (Hall 1995, 80–2). In contrast, in other regions growth was associated with both the expansion of assessed

Table 2.1 Accumulated recorded tenancies 1086–1300/1350

county groups	total 1086	% of total	total 1300–1350	% of total	% increase between 1086 and 1300–50
Eastern England (Lincs, Norfolk, Cambs, 45 manors)	1238	19.6%	5367	25.5%	433%
South-eastern England (Middx, Surrey, Sussex, 26 manors)	523	8.3%	1998	9.5%	382%
East Midlands (Notts, Rutl, Leics, Northants, Bucks, 39 manors)	901	14.3%	2302	10.9%	255%
Southern England (Wilts, Hants, Dorset, Somerset, Berks, 63 manors)	1202	19.0%	3673	17.5%	305%
West Midlands (Staffs, Worcs, Gloucs, Oxon, 54 manors)	956	15.0%	3038	14.5%	318%
South-western England (Cornwall, Devon, 23 manors)	880	13.9%	1675	8.0%	190%
Northern England (Yorks, 58 manors)	422	6.6%	2430	11.6%	576%
The Marches (Hereford, Salop, Cheshire, 45 manors)	198	3.1%	529	2.5%	267%
		100% (99.8%)		100%	

land in townfields and the creation of enclosures in severalty.

In the final section of this chapter we turn to three maps which show further aspects of settlement and population, beginning with a map of hamlets, a by-product of the main map.

The distribution of hamlets

Figure 2.10 integrates two sets of information: first, the distribution of the smallest nucleations on Figure 1.1 (category E); and secondly, the distribution of 'H' scores derived from the map of dispersion (Fig 1.2). These are used to create a national distribution of the smallest clustered settlements, here termed 'hamlets'. It is not wholly consistent, integrating into a single map the smallest elements of a 'pure', total distribution, while other evidence comes from the hamlet scores derived from a set of samples. Nevertheless, it represents a first attempt to create a national map of hamlets, and certain significant points emerge from an analysis. First, the 'E' hamlets are widely scattered, with concentrations appearing as follows:

1 In the west Midlands, particularly in Shropshire, but extending eastwards

into Staffordshire and to a degree north and south along the Welsh Border;

2 Through the South-eastern Province, except for the lands immediately to the east of the Wash (EWASH: Fig 1.4), and the lower lands of the Thames Basin;

3 In Cornwall and Devon, but extending into the southern portions of the Central Province;

4 In the Pennine foothills, a small concentration extending eastwards into Lincolnshire.

Second, the high 'H' – or hamlet – scores are much more closely limited to regions peripheral to the Central Province: throughout East Anglia (EANGL and the northern parts of ETHAM: Fig 1.4); in Cornwall, parts of Devon and Somerset, and through the remainder of the Northern and Western Province. In the borderland tract embracing Cheshire, Shropshire and Herefordshire, the 'E' hamlets and high 'H' scores complement each other. Given the volume of mapping from which these data have been abstracted it is unlikely that this distribution is merely a fiction of the mapping technique.

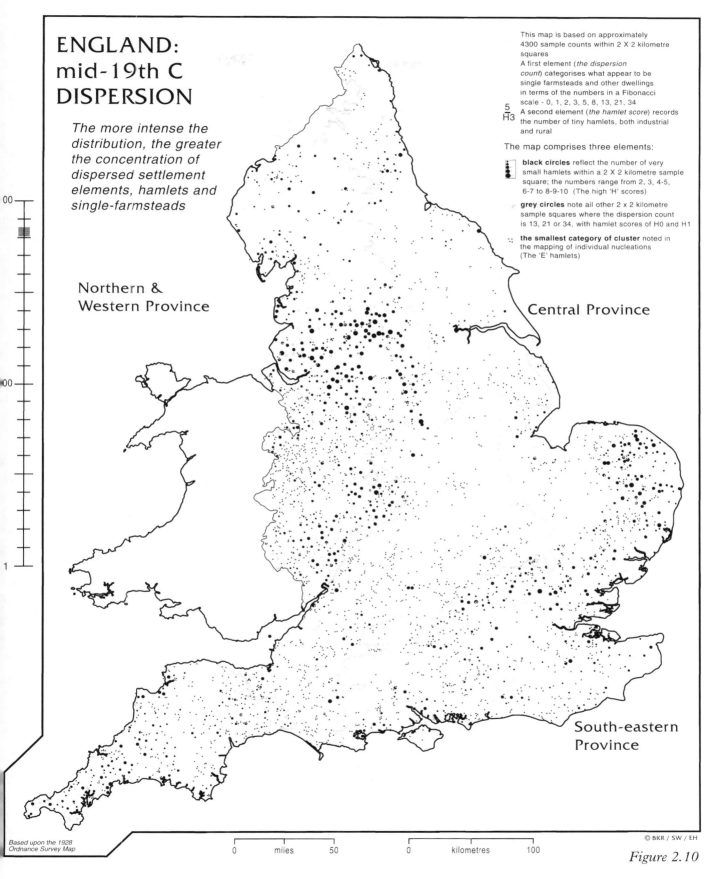

ENGLAND: mid-19th C DISPERSION

The more intense the distribution, the greater the concentration of dispersed settlement elements, hamlets and single-farmsteads

Northern & Western Province

Central Province

South-eastern Province

This map is based on approximately 4300 sample counts within 2 X 2 kilometre squares

A first element (*the dispersion count*) categorises what appear to be single farmsteads and other dwellings in terms of the numbers in a Fibonacci scale - 0, 1, 2, 3, 5, 8, 13, 21, 34

5
H3
A second element (*the hamlet score*) records the number of tiny hamlets, both industrial and rural

The map comprises three elements:

black circles reflect the number of very small hamlets within a 2 X 2 kilometre sample square; the numbers range from 2, 3, 4-5, 6-7 to 8-9-10 (The high 'H' scores)

grey circles note all other 2 x 2 kilometre sample squares where the dispersion count is 13, 21 or 34, with hamlet scores of H0 and H1

the smallest category of cluster noted in the mapping of individual nucleations (The 'E' hamlets)

Based upon the 1928 Ordnance Survey Map

0   miles   50

0   kilometres   100

© BKR / SW / EH

Figure 2.10

What then does this mid-nineteenth-century distribution tell us about settlement? Two general points appear that draw the argument back to the basic distributions seen in Figures 1.1 and 1.2. This evidence confirms the extent to which the three provinces represent deep structural elements within England's settlement geography. Hamlets represent an element of local settlement diversity which is by no means universal; indeed, it is subject to sharp spatial variations over relatively short distances. It is clear that even if we attempt to filter out the hamlets which are the result of industrial accretions – and this, we should recall, may be as true of East Anglia as Lancashire and Yorkshire – there are areas of the country where hamlet clusters are significant components of the total pattern. What this means is not immediately clear at the present stage of analysis, though more detailed, regional studies may indicate a correlation with the policies for agrarian management adopted by major landowners such as the Crown and ecclesiastical institutions. To give an example: a comparison of Figures 2.10 and 2.11 suggests that in parts of East Anglia and to a lesser extent in the south-west Midlands, small hamlet distributions and place-names with the affix 'Green' show mutually exclusive distributions. To explain this is not easy; it is a distribution which may or may not possess 'meaning'. Furthermore, it is too easy to emphasise the concentrations within the outer provinces, and miss the fact that there are portions of the Central Province within which hamlets are present in sufficient numbers to generate notable concentrations. The density in Durham is to be linked with the coalfield, but the more concentrated scatter further south implies the existence of different settlement landscapes.

Place-names with the affix 'Green'

A second distribution records those settlements including the element 'Green'. The map, Figure 2.11, was created by Robert Shirley, and results from an assiduous search of the *Ordnance Survey Gazetteer of Great Britain* relating to the Landranger map series (1992). The distribution, closely reflecting the three provinces, was not foreseen. There is no doubt that documentary work would add far more 'greens',

for many have not survived to reach the Ordnance Survey maps. For instance W Faden's map of Norfolk in 1797 shows many more (Barringer 1996). Nevertheless, Shirley's map represents a simple, coherent level of documentation. The sample is a large one, and further work is unlikely to destroy the fundamental coherence of the pattern revealed by the distribution.

Two points must be made. These 'greens' are not 'green villages', and in most cases, no matter how they may now be regarded, they are not true village greens. 'Green villages' comprise planned layouts, geometrically devised, with farmsteads and tofts arranged around a formalised central open space subjected to certain communal rules of management. In contrast the affixed 'greens' mapped here, even where they are parish or township centres, appear normally to have developed from an area of open common waste around which farmsteads and cottages accreted. It is the attachment of a separate element 'green' to the place-name which in general provides the clue. This distinction needs emphasis, for it is fundamental to the problem. In County Durham only one true 'green village' – Byers Green – specifically incorporates the word 'green', and this developed in the decades after 1183 on the site of what was then an assart. Settlements including the name element 'green' tend to be first documented in the thirteenth and fourteenth centuries. Of course, 'green' also appears as a first element, as in Greenham, Greenstead, Grindley and Grendon; but as a second element, -grene is considered to be Middle English, and to develop in a post-Norman Conquest context (Smith 1956, 209). Furthermore, when 'green' appears as a second element, such settlements tend not to appear in Domesday Book, or the 'green' affix has subsequently been appended to what is clearly an older name element, notably to a settlement which is distinct and separate from the original focus.

A few cases indicate that the date of the accretion of the affix may bear no relationship to the antiquity of the place-name. *Plumtuna* in Essex, documented in 1086, became Plunker's Green; while Kineton in Solihull and Mappleborough in Studley, both in Warwickshire and both mentioned in Domesday Book, appear to have had the element 'green' added at a later date (Mawer and Stenton 1936, 70, 226). Like Byers Green, these are exceptional.

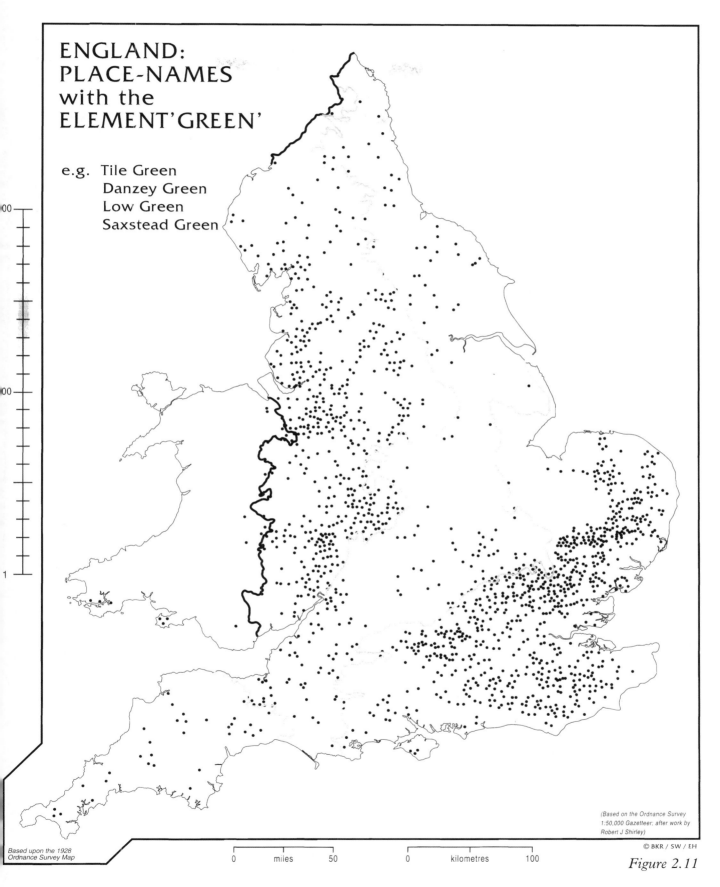

ENGLAND:
PLACE-NAMES
with the
ELEMENT 'GREEN'

e.g. Tile Green
     Danzey Green
     Low Green
     Saxstead Green

(Based on the Ordnance Survey
1:50,000 Gazetteer; after work by
Robert J Shirley)

Based upon the 1928
Ordnance Survey Map

0   miles   50

0   kilometres   100

© BKR / SW / EH

Figure 2.11

Furthermore, even if the settlements to which the affix 'green' was eventually applied were indeed present in 1086 – and this is not impossible – they were in general not places of sufficient status to achieve specific mention in Domesday Book, and it is normally assumed that they are post-1086 developments. Certainly, in the Forest of Arden many such 'greens' were associated with specific family names, and seem to represent congregations of farmsteads, smallholdings and cottages clustering in a rather irregular manner around an informal area of open space, common waste or even a roadside strip (Roberts 1965, 461–9). To describe these as 'squatting' settlements would not necessarily always be true; but, on the other hand, subsequent encroachments added to the numbers of dwellings around many 'greens'. The open area may vary in size from a few acres to a very large tract, with dwellings sprawling around what is identifiable as an area of common land. In East Anglia, Peter Wade-Martins (1980) has demonstrated medieval origins on the basis of pottery scatters recovered from the sites of former homesteads along the margins of such greens.

We postulate three phases in the development of 'green' names, the first of which includes two elements. The first element is settlements in which the term 'green' is added to an older name, perhaps because the original focus lost status relative to other places. The second element is settlements subsidiary to more important places, where the name 'green' has been added to an older settlement name to identify a subsidiary focus. In practice it is often difficult to differentiate, because a 'green' settlement bearing a township or parish name may be a larger nucleation than the higher status church/hamlet focus. The second phase may itself include two categories: those settlements which bear an ancient family name, putatively post-Conquest in origin, and those which bear a name indicative of a craft or other activity, perhaps even more recent. In the great parish of Tanworth, in the Forest of Arden, over half the family 'greens' were present before 1400 (Roberts 1965, 465–6), and were perhaps already in existence, undocumented, before about 1300. As a third, and final phase, we must recognise that once the nomenclature was established it was natural that the term would be applied to any developing cluster of small farmsteads and cottages beside an area of common waste. These could form either an irregular cluster, or a straggle along broad roadside verges or the edges of commons.

'Green' is not the only name associated with such settlement structures. With them are also associated the name-elements 'street' and 'end'. Though we have not yet attempted a full plot of 'end' names comparable to that for 'greens', an examination of the mid-nineteenth-century one-inch maps makes it clear that these, too, are linked to landscapes with late surviving woodlands and extensive tracts of common grazings. Though the bulk of 'green' names occur in the two outer provinces, there are also scatters of 'green', 'end' and 'street' in the Central Province: none of the data mapped in this volume is confined to one or another of our three provinces; in all cases, the arguments are based on weighting. Nevertheless, it is instructive to examine in more detail one of the slight but noticeable concentrations of 'green' names in the Central Province: that in northern Bedfordshire and north-east Buckinghamshire. An examination of Figures 1.13 and 1.14 shows that this part of Bedfordshire and Buckinghamshire is a zone where there is evidence for patches of late-surviving woodland. It is also a zone where the settlement map shows areas of dispersed settlement breaking up the homogeneity of the landscapes dominated by villages. The concentration of 'green' names is, therefore, consistent with two other independent datasets in marking a part of the Central Province that was never wholly assimilated into the dominant pattern of agrarian structures.

Finally, the name elements 'green', 'street' and 'end', identifying hamlets and even, after substantive growth, what appear to be 'villages', carry the discussion to those settlement forms that lie on the threshold between true nucleation and true dispersion: linked farmstead clusters and linked hamlet clusters. We have yet to map and analyse the numbers involved, and the varied relationships they have to the (presumably) older foci indicated by pre-Conquest place-name forms and documentation in Domesday Book. Nevertheless, as our later arguments will show, this is by no means a peripheral theme, for it has a direct bearing upon the ways in which the village-dominated landscapes evolved from more ancient structures and forms.

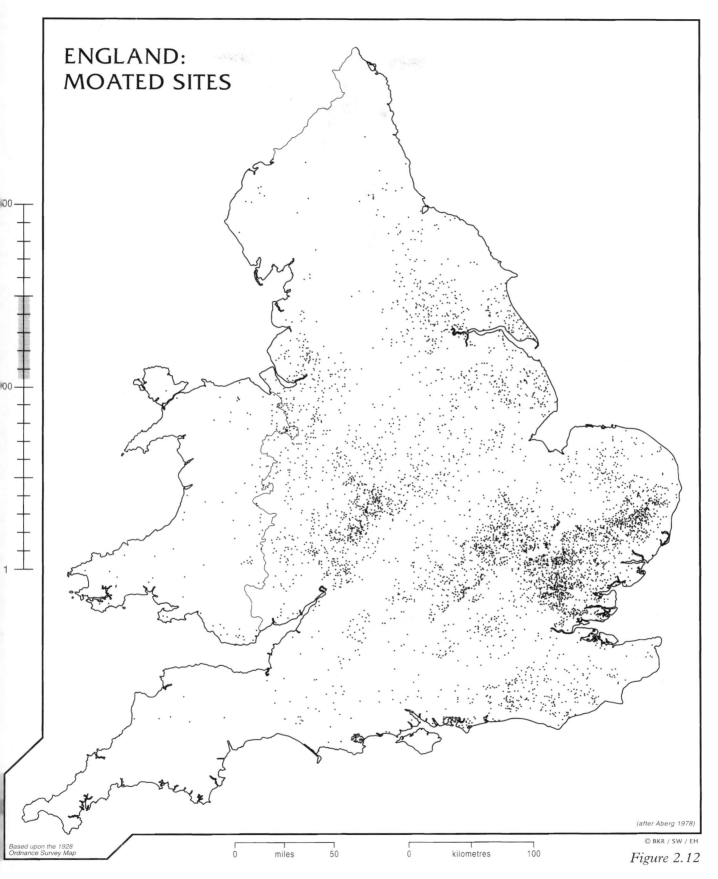

ENGLAND:
MOATED SITES

(after Aberg 1978)

Based upon the 1928
Ordnance Survey Map

© BKR / SW / EH

| 0 | miles | 50 |
| 0 | kilometres | 100 |

Figure 2.12

Moated sites

Moated sites have been widely recognised as a social phenomenon. They were created by aristocrats, by members of the knightly class and also by franklins, men of relatively humble status who accumulated sufficient wealth to acquire land. These semi-fortified dwellings signalled status, and protected movable property from fire and casual brigandage by a substantial water-filled ditch crossed by a bridge. By no means confined to the claylands, examples are known where the subsoil was sandy. At Weoley Castle in the West Midlands this necessitated several feet of puddling clay. Excavation has tended to date their construction to the twelfth and thirteenth centuries, and they appear to be essentially a distinctive offshoot of the ringwork and motte and bailey traditions translated down the twin scales of relative importance and social status. Furthermore, the stimulus of the practical need for a ditch around a farmyard to provide drainage in low-lying countrysides is also likely. They form a distinctive and numerous medieval settlement feature, and in limestone and stone country are replaced (in higher status homesteads) by an enclosing wall. Their distribution reveals that they had close links with woodland landscapes, particularly areas which were experiencing active colonisation in the period between 1100 and 1300. In the Forest of Arden they can be linked with 'small manors', estates accumulated piecemeal by a social class below that of the knight but above that of the ordinary peasant, ie freeholders or franklins (Roberts 1965, 469–76; Aberg 1978). Aberg's distribution map (Fig 2.12) shows that the heaviest concentration appears in Essex and Suffolk (EANGL: Fig 1.4). Notable concentrations also appear in the local region based on the Forest of Arden, south of Birmingham, but neither of these represents a closely circumscribed concentration, and thinner scatters appear in the Weald, along the Welsh borderlands and northwards into Cheshire and Lancashire. Moats also appear throughout the Central Province, in the Midlands, in Lincolnshire and into the Vale of York (le Patourel 1973). The most notable and significant concentration, however, appears in the southern portion of the south-eastern Midlands, in south-west Cambridgeshire, Hertfordshire, Huntingdonshire, Bedfordshire and Buckinghamshire, the same zone as that which, as we have noted in the

discussion of 'greens', contains a distinctive mixture of characteristics, some associated with the Central Province, others more closely linked with the South-eastern Province.

Explaining this distribution is by no means easy, not least because, like all the others we are discussing, it compresses a temporal phenomenon into the flat plane of a map, compacting time and obscuring any regional variations in the rates of moat construction. Nevertheless, it is quite clear that the distribution map of moated sites bears a relationship to the three settlement provinces. The differences between them, however, pose questions. Unfortunately, while the records of the Moated Sites Research Group differentiate between moats in villages and moats associated with isolated dwellings and farmsteads, this difference has not yet been mapped nationally. We suspect that the moats of the Central Province largely represent the dwellings of manorial lords, set in or near villages; we cannot yet demonstrate this. In contrast, it is likely that the highest concentrations of moated sites in the other provinces are associated with the presence of freeholders, although some were clearly granges, park lodges and the like (Aberg 1978). The limited range of excavated evidence suggests that they were constructed over rather long periods of time. Their use extends over an even longer period; indeed, many are still occupied. They emerged to become characteristic features of some woodland landscapes because these landscapes were contexts within which small freehold 'manors' could and did appear. It is no criticism of the many excavators to suggest that they have usually concentrated on discovering and dating the history of the moated site itself; equally important is any evidence for pre-moat occupation. It is too easy to see the moated site as the result of intrepid colonists pushing forward the frontiers of land improvement into landscapes of woodland assarts. As their overall distribution shows, moated sites are a social phenomenon, reflecting the needs, accumulated wealth, fears and social aspirations of diverse individuals.

Rural settlement does not exist in a vacuum: it has the practical function of housing and serving the inhabitants who are deriving a living from the land. It is to farming systems and landscapes that we now turn.

3
Farming systems and landscape characteristics

Landscapes and regions, countrysides and cultures

Differences in settlement are linked to variations in farming regimes. Figure 3.1 which shows farming systems in the period between 1500 and 1640, is redrawn from an original by Joan Thirsk (1967, fig 1). Her classification scheme builds around three farming types. There were the grass-growing uplands, where the principal asset was stock, and where farms were based upon limited areas of improved land – be this in open strips or enclosed fields. These systems utilised the vast areas of open pastures on the fells, with their poor, thin soils and inhospitable climatic conditions. In the lowlands, the character and condition of the land varied greatly, but was generally more favourable than the uplands for mixed farming, integrating corn production with grass and stock. A fundamental distinction must be recognised between those areas where corn, sheep and stock were variously combined in the great vales and on downlands and wolds, and the areas of wood pasture, where the production of some grain was combined with stock rearing, fattening, pig and horse breeding and dairying in tracts of woodland and common grazing. Thirsk has explored the ways in which these farming regions tended to be associated with distinctive field systems, social and manorial structures, inheritance practices, settlement and landscape characteristics and even industrial activities. She concluded that the recurrent features observed suggested that 'some institutions in the life of local communities are intimately linked with, and dependent upon, one another'. On the other hand, detailed studies emphasise 'at the same time many aspects of life in which each community was unique' (Thirsk 1967, 15).

Thirsk views her map as very tentative, stressing that it is the boundaries of the regions which are the most uncertain and noting that they 'will certainly require amendment in the light of more detailed local investigation' (Thirsk 1967, 4). Figure 3.1 attempts to bring out, through shading, her tripartite division, and superimposes the boundaries of the three provinces. There is no doubt that each of the three provinces contains examples of each of the three fundamental farming types: what differs is the overall balance of these between each province. Further, we should emphasise that Thirsk's map was not used while framing our map of settlement: the two maps are independent creations, so that the accord and discord between them pose legitimate questions.

Set opposite Thirsk's map is a redrawn copy of a map published in 1907 by Gilbert Slater titled 'The Enclosure of Common Fields by Act of Parliament' (Fig 3.2). This work was based upon a parish by parish compilation, although the individual amounts of such land in each parish varied greatly – as we now know from Tate and Turner's work (Slater 1907, 73, 196, 197; Turner 1978). Shading the whole parish exaggerates the area of townfield lands, to a much greater degree in some areas than in others, but the map remains the most precise view we have of their distribution in the late eighteenth and nineteenth centuries. Tate's analysis of 1967 suggests that the pre-1801 enclosures involved about 2.5 million acres of 'common field' (ie townfield land), as against 0.83 million acres of waste. After 1801 the proportion was 1.8 million acres of common field as against 1.25 million acres of waste (Tate 1967, 88). The shading of Figure 3.2 has been structured so that the removal of the lightest element reveals the pattern of common fields in 1801, when many of the classic systems of the Central Province remained intact.

For areas outside the Central Province the picture of townfields is enormously complicated by the existence of 'enclosure by agreement'. Around many villages and small towns there is only limited evidence for the Parliamentary enclosure of town-

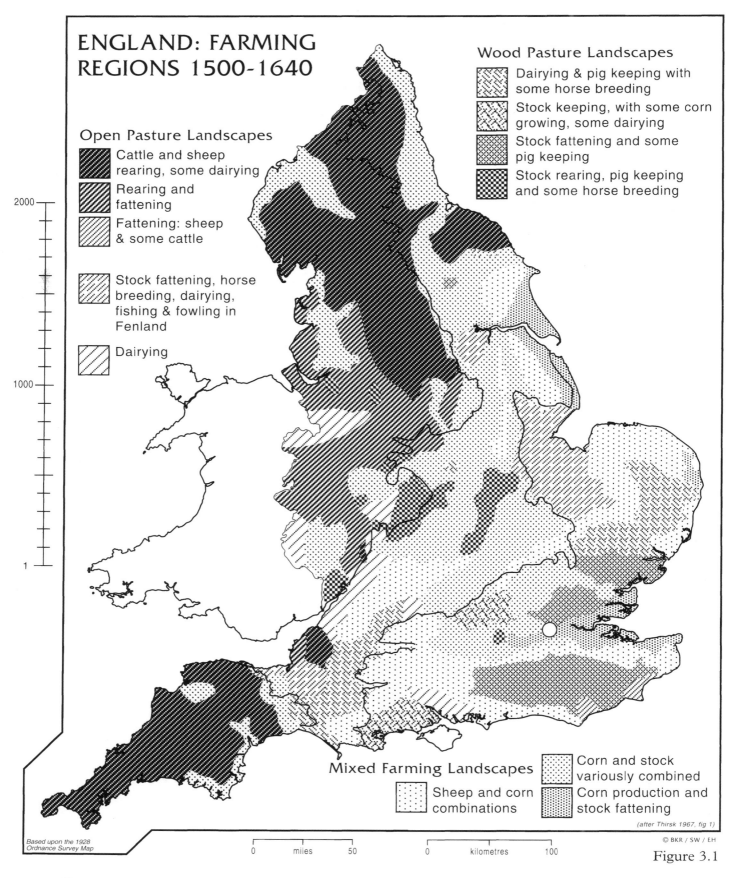

ENGLAND: FARMING
REGIONS 1500-1640

Open Pasture Landscapes

Cattle and sheep
rearing, some dairying

Rearing and
fattening

Fattening: sheep
& some cattle

Stock fattening, horse
breeding, dairying,
fishing & fowling in
Fenland

Dairying

Wood Pasture Landscapes

Dairying & pig keeping with
some horse breeding

Stock keeping, with some corn
growing, some dairying

Stock fattening and some
pig keeping

Stock rearing, pig keeping
and some horse breeding

Mixed Farming Landscapes

Sheep and corn
combinations

Corn and stock
variously combined

Corn production and
stock fattening

(after Thirsk 1967, fig 1)

*Based upon the 1928
Ordnance Survey Map*

0   miles   50

0   kilometres   100

© BKR / SW / EH

Figure 3.1

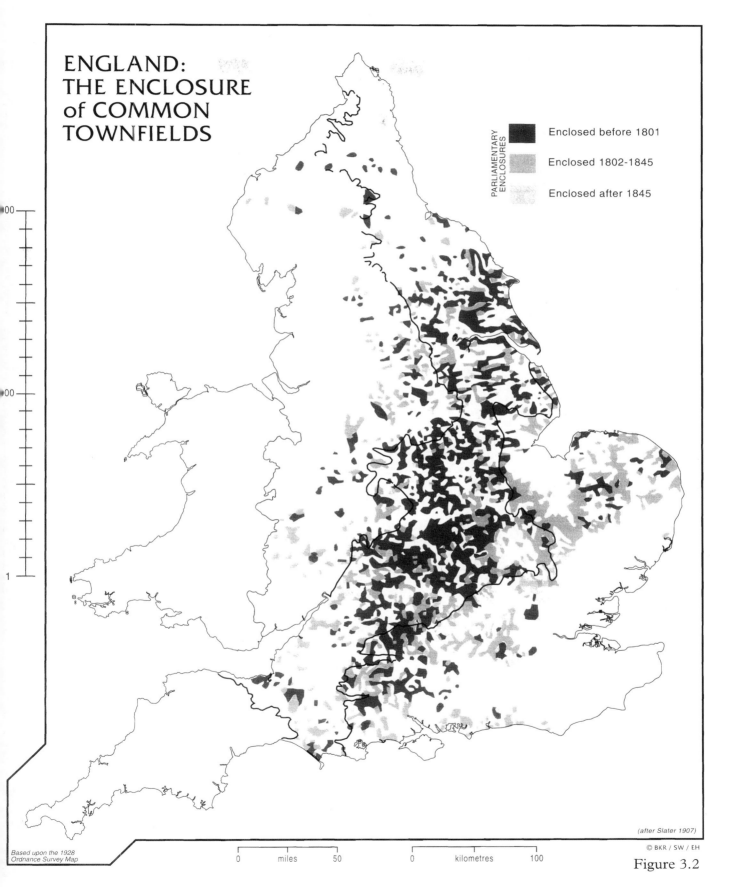

ENGLAND:
THE ENCLOSURE
of COMMON
TOWNFIELDS

PARLIAMENTARY
ENCLOSURES

Enclosed before 1801

Enclosed 1802-1845

Enclosed after 1845

(after Slater 1907)

Based upon the 1928
Ordnance Survey Map

0   miles   50

0   kilometres   100

© BKR / SW / EH

Figure 3.2

fields; yet at the same time, field boundaries displaying reversed-S aratral curves are a frequent occurrence. These are visible on eighteenth and nineteenth-century maps and as surviving field boundaries, and establish a picture of former landscapes in which significant areas of common arable and meadow supported nucleated settlements. In effect this is the classic 'midland' model carried into the two outer provinces. In a discussion of 'piecemeal and partial enclosures', Yelling drew together examples from Worcestershire, Gloucestershire, Somerset and Essex, and made a number of points relevant to an understanding of this widespread process (Yelling 1977). In the first place, piecemeal enclosure varied in pace, from slow to rapid. Secondly, it is often poorly documented: indeed, there is often documented emphasis upon only a few holdings, eg the glebe. Thirdly, piecemeal enclosures must be studied in the context of the 'more permanent features of the rural scene: the settlement and farming regions'. Fourthly, communal townfields may have a better chance of survival around nucleations: the larger the nucleation, the greater the chance of survival, because of the sustained power of communal organisation and the fragmentation of holdings. Finally, the interconnections between common field survival, settlement form and environment need detailed analysis. Within the Central Province extensive enclosure by agreement is also known to have taken place in the North-east and parts of the Midlands (Hodgson 1989; Gay 1902–3), but it is only at the most intricate level of local detail that piecemeal enclosures can be dissected and mapped. The result is that wide scale generalisation is difficult, a matter to which we will return in Chapter 6.

Comparison between Figures 1.14 and 3.1 shows that by the late sixteenth and early seventeenth centuries the Central Province, dominated by nucleated settlement, was sustained by mixed farming based upon corn and stock variously combined. Only in the extreme south-west of the province do more varied types of system appear: sheep and corn combinations in the Cotswolds and on the downlands of Dorset; stock fattening, horse breeding, pig keeping and dairying amid the extremely diverse terrains of Somerset and north-west Wiltshire. Of course, even in the Midlands there is a measure of diversity, with a tract of wood pasture farming types along parts of the Jurassic limestone escarp-

ment extending across Northamptonshire. Further north, the North York Moors form a distinctive island of upland England intruded into the Central Province, but the Durham and Northumbrian coastal plain and associated escarpments carry mixed farming landscapes as far north as the Scottish border. Nevertheless, Figure 3.2 emphasises that much of this same tract was characterised by open, communally organised townfields that were largely subjected to enclosure in the period between 1720 and 1850. The map omits the townfields of the south-western portions of the Central Province and the north-east coast, which were enclosed in a different manner and at an earlier time (Gonner 1912, maps C and D).

In contrast, the South-eastern Province contains a great mixture of farming types, the majority based upon wood pastures, grazing sheep and other stock amid open commons and woodlands. Substantial areas of the Chalk country and the lighter lands of north-eastern East Anglia were given over to sheep and corn farming, with varied combinations adapted to local circumstances and taking place within farms that were structured around varied combinations of open arable and enclosed lands. As Slater's map emphasises, only in some areas – on the Chalk, in the Thames valley and in parts of the Chilterns and northern East Anglia – was Parliamentary enclosure an important ingredient of the landscape. Pre-seventeenth-century enclosure was the more usual, and these areas correlate reasonably closely – but never absolutely – with Thirsk's wood pasture landscapes. Coastal marshlands and the Fenlands form distinctive farming regions. In contrast, the systems of the Northern and Western Province are grounded in the presence of great tracts of hill pasture, notably in the north and west. In the Eden valley, the Lancashire lowlands, south Staffordshire and the Herefordshire Plain versions of the mixed farming types characteristic of the Central Province appear. The province was characterised by stock production supported by generally less extensive – but individually no less large – areas of subsistence arable, often organised in the form of open, strip fields. However, throughout both of these outer provinces a large proportion of the townfield farms included at least some enclosed land, while many were worked wholly as enclosed lands held in severalty.

We have not reproduced Thirsk's map for 1640–1750 because the farming regions of that period were highly complex (Thirsk 1984–5, fig 1). Nor, for the same reason, have we introduced the complex map of farming regions created by Stamp during the 1940s (Stamp 1962, fig 171). In the previous chapter, the discussion of the distribution of population in 1851 explored some of the impacts of industrialisation on the intensification of both nucleation and dispersion, a process developing since the seventeenth century but reaching a crescendo during the nineteenth. Nevertheless, at root, the settlement base is largely rural in origin, even where this has been substantively overlain by industrial components. The diversity seen in the local regions delineated in Figures 1.14 and 3.1 is a product of interactions between land, people and very long periods of time. Processes of creation, decay, adaptation, renewal, sometimes with dramatic transformations occurring over long or short periods of time, generate what the historian Maitland termed 'that complex palimpsest' (1897, 38), bearing comparison with a parchment overwritten not once but many times. An inherited cultural landscape is, in M R G Conzen's words, the 'geographical record of its own evolution' (1949, 76).

Figure 3.3, is a summary of landscape types in England. Heavily dependent upon work by Joan Thirsk and Alan Everitt, it provides a simplified regional pattern, drawing upon an understanding of farming regions but also touching elements of the physical structure, and creating a schedule of eight categories (Everitt 1985, 1–59). Thirsk summarises matters as follows:

> Grain growing regions were the downland and wold areas; the emphatically pastoral were the forest and moorland areas. At both these extremes of the spectrum some changes in land use were in progress [in the sixteenth and seventeenth centuries], though they were muted simply because these arable and pastoral regions had the natural attributes, and hence the best economic reasons, for continuing to grow grain and grass respectively. *(Thirsk 1987, 38–9)*

New crops, land drainage, agricultural price variations and the advantages of location were bringing changes to all other regions. This simplification provides a general framework and, as Thirsk puts it, the eight categories 'should serve as an introduction to the more elaborate, the more local, or sometimes more idiosyncratic, regions that

are, or may be, devised in specialist studies' (Thirsk 1987, 37). We concur with this view, although we have used her map as a framework for our own, rather than merely copying it. In effect these generalised landscape types, with names which readily convey the appearance and character of the dominant landscapes within them, form a most valuable framework for any discussion of the evolution of landscapes and regions.

Landscape practicalities: forms and patterns

Settlement, field and farm relationships offer a bewildering range of possibilities. Van Bath (1963a, 54–8) created a useful generalisation when he noted that four basic types of settlement field relationship could be historically identified. First, square or block fields, generally with length to breadth proportions of 1:1 to 1:2, are associated with either hamlets or scattered dwellings. Secondly, strip fields, generally of the proportions 1:10 to 1:20, are associated either with scattered dwellings or with chains of farmsteads. The latter, as population increase occurs and subdivision of holdings takes place, have a tendency to develop into street villages. To this we may add that these types may be either largely 'open', substantively lacking formal enclosure boundaries, fences, hedges, wall, banks and ditches and the like, or 'enclosed' with each parcel defined by a carefully constructed bounding feature. This classification is useful and has the real advantage that it lacks the burden carried by such terms as 'open fields'. Nevertheless, it is inevitably flat, lacking both the functional and developmental dimensions of the real systems, which involve much more than the immediately visible structures and in which varied methods of cultivation are applied and varied crops produced.

Basically there are three possible methods of cultivation that might be applied in these structures. First, temporary or shifting cultivation may occur, breaking land, sowing a crop, harvesting, repeating the cycle for a few years, and then deserting the plot, so that it can become revegetated by wild growth: at first grasses and heathers; eventually shrubs and trees. This is a method of exploiting the natural productivity of the soil, which will eventually suffer exhaustion, so that yields decline to such a degree that the farmer deems the input of labour to be no longer worthwhile.

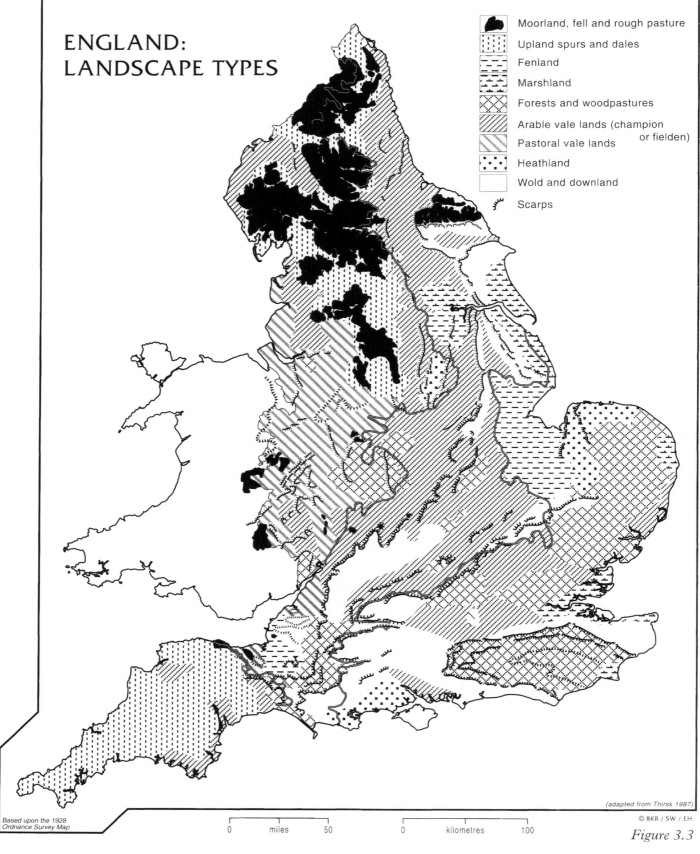

ENGLAND: LANDSCAPE TYPES

Moorland, fell and rough pasture
Upland spurs and dales
Fenland
Marshland
Forests and woodpastures
Arable vale lands (champion or fielden)
Pastoral vale lands
Heathland
Wold and downland
Scarps

(adapted from Thirsk 1987)

Based upon the 1928
Ordnance Survey Map

0 miles 50

0 kilometres 100

© BKR / SW / EH

Figure 3.3

Secondly, some form of manure, human and animal ordure, plant material, turf, seaweed or nutrient-rich mineral materials (such as shell sand) are applied to the plot to sustain fertility and yields in the face of continued cultivation. Thirdly, a cropping cycle is adopted so that the plot is 'rested' for a period of time: a crop and fallow system, in which the cropping may be for one or two years, followed by a period of either bare fallow – when the land is ploughed to rid the soil of weed growth and prepared for the next seed bed – or grass fallow, when native plants are allowed to grow, to be used for grazing purposes. The cycle 'crop-fallow-crop-fallow' represents the well known two-course rotation or shift, while the cycle 'crop-crop-fallow-crop-crop-fallow' is the three-course rotation. Both of the cropping systems normally interlock at some level with the physical layout of the arable fields.

Of course, there are many possible variations of each, but all of these ways of maintaining soil fertility have been part of agricultural practices for millennia. It was possible to incorporate all three within an almost infinite range of combinations to create many and varied farming systems within the structured frameworks of plot and field layout. It is this great range of possibilities that provides diversity to the study of field systems. Here we will do no more than note that this short account omits the integration of pasturing arrangements, cultivation procedures and practices, the management of meadows, woodlands and commons, and, not least, the disposition of holdings and the tenurial arrangements associated with them. This plethora of factors gives a dynamism and complexity to the real world, which is often successfully concealed by 'text book' cases, models to which generalisations necessarily refer. Further, as Yelling pointed out, field systems may integrate both open lands – divided into many strip parcels, each open to its neighbour – with enclosed plots, held by individual farmers. This blurs the boundary between communally organised systems and systems in severalty (Yelling 1977). In spite of two extremely important foundation studies (Gray 1915; Baker and Butlin 1973), we await a national study of field systems; indeed this hiatus has posed persistent problems for our present study. We have constantly been forced to sidestep these problems, to use surrogates, and above all to recognise that our primary objective must be a broad view of settlement not the development of field systems. Nevertheless, we believe that our pattern of provinces and local regions forms a viable framework within which to conduct future studies of the regional differences in field systems.

The model appearing as Figure 3.4 is a compromise, adopted for present purposes. Based upon a drawing originally devised by Uhlig, which it adapts considerably, it shows as nine vignettes numerous types of linkage between nucleated and dispersed settlement and field systems (Uhlig 1961, 285–312; 1971, 93–125; 1972). It is one way of classifying the possible diversity of settlement, field and farming systems. We will proceed by examining each vignette in turn, starting with case C.

Case C is a 'classic' nucleated arrangement with a village whose arable and meadow are divided into dozens of strip plots, each of which was open to its neighbour. In this case, three fields are depicted: one, W, for winter grain (wheat), one, S, for spring grain (barley) and the other, F, at rest as fallow. The surrounding woodlands and common pastures are suggested by shading, as is the holding of a single farmer. This is a model of a settlement system of which many variations were once widespread throughout the Central Province. Cases A and B represent simpler, and in practice, smaller versions of a strip plot system. They are the kind of 'core' arable structures which were widespread in the two outer provinces, and which will become familiar in Chapter 4, with the case studies of actual townships. Case B, with farmsteads girdling the core arable – whether curvilinear or rectangular – is particularly relevant, while in case A, two options are shown for the relationship of arable to core settlement: one with farmsteads in a cluster; the other with them placed in rows. In both cases open and enclosed elements, strips and blocks, are both present, begging many questions about their relative chronologies and subsequent development; this will be considered in later chapters.

In case C, soil fertility is maintained by a cycle of crop-crop-fallow, but in cases A and B, because of the smaller area of arable, fertility can be maintained by adding manure to the strip field kernel, making it a form of 'infield'. Temporary tillage of portions of the common pasture, as 'outfields', allows natural fertility to be tapped. In the enclosed lands, some plots could be manured or

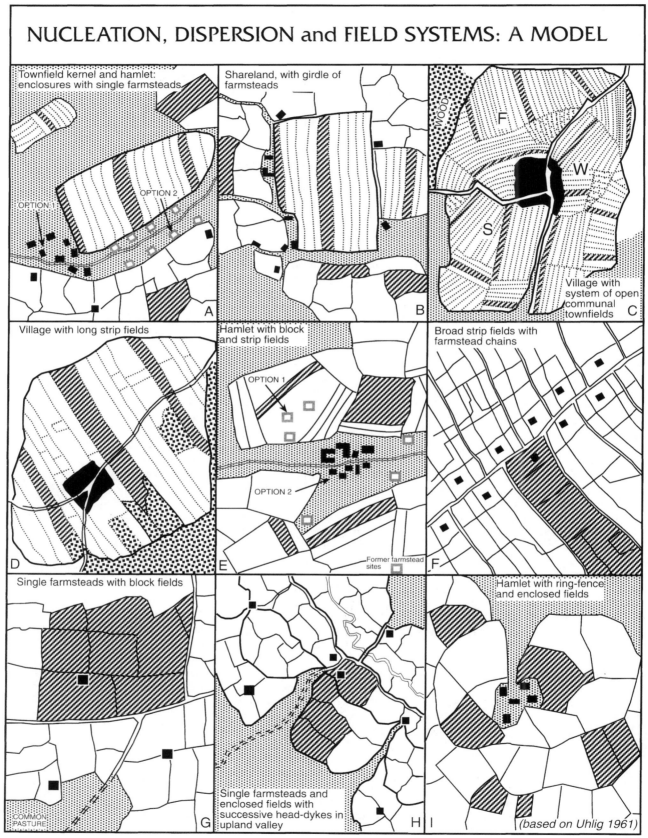

NUCLEATION, DISPERSION and FIELD SYSTEMS: A MODEL

A Townfield kernel and hamlet: enclosures with single farmsteads

B Shareland, with girdle of farmsteads

C Village with system of open communal townfields

D Village with long strip fields

E Hamlet with block and strip fields

F Broad strip fields with farmstead chains

G Single farmsteads with block fields

H Single farmsteads and enclosed fields with successive head-dykes in upland valley

I Hamlet with ring-fence and enclosed fields

(based on Uhlig 1961)

Figure 3.4

sustained by a rotation incorporating fallow, while others are merely for pasture. Of course, the wider geographical contexts of these 'cases' are important. Variants of case C are found across the great fertile plains of much of northern Europe, while cases A and B are met with throughout the environmentally more difficult peripheral European margins, in a great arc from Finisterre to Finland. Nevertheless, it is also possible that in cases A and B we can glimpse something of the antecedents of the more highly structured systems modelled in C.

Cases D and F are, much more than the others, derived from Continental sources, the latter comprising a rather 'broad' strip, the width of a single farm, representing the classic German '*Waldhufen*' or '*Marschhufen*' (Mayhew 1973, 66–77). They are included for two reasons. On one hand they are a powerful reminder of the role of planning in the creation of settlement and field systems. On the other hand, they are apparently absent from England, although the 'strip' parishes of certain parts of eastern and southern England present some formal similarities. By these arrangements terrain is divided among communities, parishes, townships and manors, rather than individual farmers (Havinden 1966; Taylor 1970, 56–9; Owen 1981, 2.3). Although differing in scale, these arrangements clearly possess the same underlying motivation: namely the approximately equitable sharing of varied resources. There is no doubt that enclosed versions of case F also appear; indeed, there are parallels with the prehistoric 'reaves', and with the prehistoric or later 'co-axial' systems noted by various scholars (Fleming 1988; Warner 1996, 44–53). Case D, drawn almost without alteration from Uhlig's version depicting a '*Gelängeflur*', shows a village territory divided into a series of long, broad strips. The scale is often somewhat smaller than in case F, where the strips extend beyond the compass of the page, and may even reach several kilometres. It is, however, significantly larger than in case C, where individual strips tend to be approximately 200m (220 yards or one furlong) in length, with two or three falling within a width of about 15m (16.5 yards or one rod, pole or perch). This example has been included because there are indications, from the Midlands and from east Yorkshire, that similar long strips, 300m, 400m, 600m or even longer may underlie the strips of systems such as that modelled in case C.

In Derbyshire, east Yorkshire and Cumberland and Westmorland, cases have actually survived, and can be seen on late maps and on the ground. At the very least, D is a reminder that there are in reality many more types of communally organised field system than are characterised by the model seen in case C. Some of these, not closely documented here, will be discussed in detail in later chapters.

Case E, deliberately placed at the centre of the model, comprises a mixture of blocks and strips, which may be open or enclosed, and may be associated with either dispersed (option 1) or clustered (option 2) farmsteads. Its relative simplicity is misleading, for it possesses the potential to develop into many other types. Following expansion, the result of population increase, it could be transformed into case C or case G, or it could have case D or F superimposed upon it after a radical replanning of the landscape and a redistribution of its resources. Or it could simply, and quietly, survive, with little alteration.

Case G is a simple situation, with a ring-fenced farm surrounding a single farmstead. These blocky plots may, of course, be open, although they are more characteristically enclosed. Such types are found throughout many of the vale landscapes in England and result from late enclosure of former townfields. H is a special case, in an upland valley location. Successive head dykes, the boundaries between the enclosed land and the open common grazings, give rise to distinctive patterns of funnel-shaped driftways for moving stock, and often to chains or girdles of farmsteads along each side of the valley. Such patterns are typical of the upland dales of northern England, the Welsh Borders and the uplands of the South-west; but they also appear throughout the forest and wood pasture zones of the South-eastern Province. Finally, case I may also have various contexts. The hamlet could be derived either from an upland shieling, a site formerly occupied only on a temporary basis, or from an ancient area of improved land in a lowland environment. While the sample holding is shown with block fields, strips are possible, such cases appearing in the uplands of the South-west and the North-west.

The models of Figure 3.4 provide a working framework, in which a series of essentially simple images allows us access to the complex field morphologies, farming arrangements and temporal development of field systems. Two fundamental points of criticism could legitimately be levelled against them. First, we have undoubtedly treated scale in a rather cavalier manner, so that cases C, D, F and H cover far larger tracts of land than the remainder. This we admit; but correct scale representation within the compass of this small diagram was not feasible. Secondly, we have said too little about the role of *transformations*, with one system being developed, either gradually or suddenly, into another. Either is equally possible. These simple models are icons for an infinitely complex reality that takes us far beyond the mere classification and manipulation of forms. They present questions and challenges concerning their socio-economic contexts, their place in development or stasis, and their temporal and spatial relationships. Amid what often appears as a mass of bewildering and often contradictory evidence, they provide reference points intermediate between documentation and the physical evidence.

One further aspect of the models should be noted: an additional element of classification which has instructive implications for the genesis of the whole set. Case E is a category that is essentially *unspecialised*. It could appear and function well in diverse habitats and climates, whereas, with the possible exceptions of cases G and I, all of the others represent a strong degree of *specialisation*; they mark adaptations to particular physical, social or economic circumstances. For instance, some of these types appear in areas largely dominated by poor soils, where highly productive arable plots were laboriously maintained by human effort (cases A and B). Others appear in areas of communal colonisation and/or communally sustained grain production (cases C, D and F). Fragmented, piecemeal colonisation in difficult upland environments (case H) and group expansion of former grazing grounds (cases A, B and I) generate other types. Cases I, G and particularly E, however, are unspecialised, essentially irregular arrangements, and lie at the root of all systems.

Finally, to summarise our argument so far, Figure 1.14 implies that there are different settlement types appearing, in varying proportions, within each of the provinces. This analysis of the links between settlement and farming systems suggests that each province will contain varied mixtures of the varied types defined in Figure 3.4. In general, it is clear that while each province contains mixtures of terrain types (Figs 2.1 and 3.3), there are broad brush contrasts between the provinces: between the extensive cultivated, open lands in the Central Province; the wooded lands together with some open grazings and cultivated areas in the South-eastern Province, and the open grazing lands, with some wood pastures and woodlands and with smaller areas of cultivation, in the Northern and Western Province. This creates a spatial setting for Harrison's contrasts with which we began Chapter 1. Further, each of the provinces will consist of distinctive assemblages of varied proportions of the farming structures defined in Figure 3.4. Subsequent chapters will attempt to define these, qualitatively if not quantitatively. We reiterate strongly at this stage that the settlement map (Fig 1.13), the woodland map (Fig 1.12) and the farming systems map (Fig 3.1) show the convergence of separate evidence, not merely the copying or unconscious replication of patterns revealed by Thirsk, Darby or Stamp. The characteristics of sub-provincial landscapes have been modelled in our *Atlas* (Roberts and Wrathmell 2000a), and while we recognise that these represent frameworks for further regional discussions, our intention here is to concentrate on an appraisal of the national picture. We continue with further evidence from Domesday Book.

Ploughteams and provinces in 1086

Figure 3.5 is another replotting of the county studies from Darby's *Domesday Geography*. There must always be questions about the extent this map conceals the presence of the smallest of settlements such as the unnamed berewicks and other dependencies. As we noted in the discussions of population in Chapter 2, Sawyer has drawn attention to the substantial number of settlements in the Weald which simply do not appear in Domesday Book yet are documented in earlier sources (Sawyer 1976, fig 1.1). Furthermore, Darby found that it is impossible to generate settlement by settlement ploughteam plots for the northern counties, so that in these areas the record of teams has been replaced by a small dot showing the presence of each recorded settlement. The break line is shown by an emphasised boundary. While this map

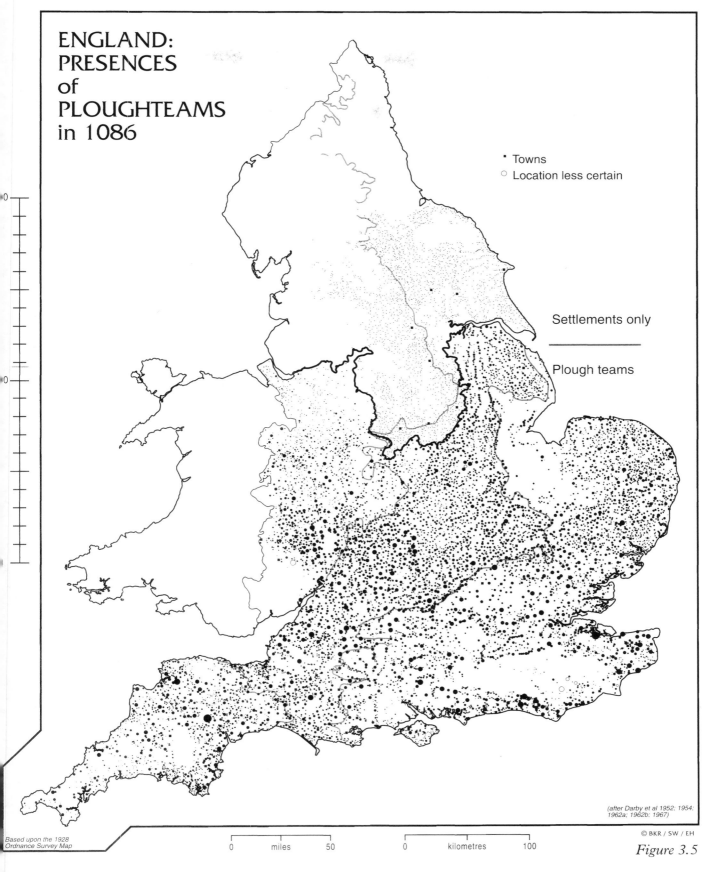

ENGLAND:
PRESENCES
of
PLOUGHTEAMS
in 1086

• Towns
○ Location less certain

Settlements only

Plough teams

(after Darby et al 1952; 1954; 1962a; 1962b; 1967)

© BKR / SW / EH

Based upon the 1928 Ordnance Survey Map

0 miles 50

0 kilometres 100

Figure 3.5

generally confirms the existence of stretches of both boundaries of the Central Province, the record of cultivated lands in the two outer provinces means than in comparison with the map of woodland the picture is more blurred. This provides a more accurate image of on-ground conditions by emphasising that cultivation was a necessary prerequisite of permanent settlement throughout all the provinces. It is also a stark reminder that the provincial boundaries, which appear on so many of our maps, were strongly permeable. There were continual interactions across provincial boundaries, such as those described in the study, by Tina Jolas and Françoise Zonabend (1977, 126–51), of the social and economic interactions between two communities near Chatillon sur Seine. The presence there of an open plain surrounded by a mass of communal forest immediately pointed to a contrast between 'the periphery and the centre, the wild and the cultivated, the communal and the private'. The distinction extended to those 'who had land and cows' and those who had 'a goat, a pig and a few chickens', ie the tillers of the fields and the woodspeople (Jolas and Zonabend 1977, 129).

Seen in terms of ploughteams, there were in 1086 strong general similarities between the distributions seen in the inner Midlands and East Anglia (Fig 3.5). This emphasises that, in terms of the capacity of farmers to till substantive areas, the differences between the two regions were less marked than the distribution of woodland might seem to imply. Distinct patterns of tillage are to be seen along the chalkland valleys and in the Thames Basin, while recorded settlement is notably absent from the Weald, where cultivation is seen to be concentrated on the claylands and loams of the surrounding valleys. Of course, like woodland, the ploughteams were recorded under the manorial centres rather than at their actual locations, so that elements of circular argument are always present. On a broader scale, the South-eastern and Central Provinces maintained pre-eminence in terms of population and prosperity between 1086 and the sixteenth century. Distribution maps created from thirteenth and fourteenth-century taxation rolls, the Poll Tax of 1377 and sixteenth-century taxation rolls, all confirm this point (Darby 1973, figs 11, 21, 22, 35, 42 and 43; Glasscock 1975, map 1). In 1086 the South-east was economically dominant. By 1334 there was a distribution in which nodes of very high and higher than average prosperity were scattered between the South-eastern and Central Provinces (Darby 1973, fig 35). The concentration of large amounts of economic activity and population further west and north (Darby 1973, figs 3.6–3.10), is largely a product of post-medieval technical developments, not least the harnessing of steam power. Further, it is interesting that in spite of the presence of woodland throughout the South-eastern Province, lands in the area were not generally drawn into royal forest (Fig 3.6), except in parts of the Thames Valley and east Wessex (EWEXE: Fig 1.4). Figure 3.6 serves to emphasise the degree to which royal forest was a legal rather than an ecological concept, for while areas so designated are often associated with areas of Domesday woodland, particularly in the Central Province, the most heavily wooded areas were not necessarily involved. Royal forests, simply because of their legal status, served to give some protection to standing timber, and thereby created a contrast with what was happening in the surrounding countryside (Glasscock 1973, 164–7; Tubbs 1968).

Careful study of Figure 3.5 reveals slight peculiarities in the pattern, which serve as a warning of buried problems. First, a cluster of settlements with larger ploughteam totals appears in the northern portion of the east Midlands, but checking shows these to be in Rutland, where distinctive tenurial characteristics led to the summation of numerous settlements under a few centres (Phythian-Adams 1977, 63–84). No doubt other slight variations in the texture of the map, local and regional, must have been generated both by real on-ground variations and by differences in the way that information was collected and collated by the royal officials and juries. It will be noted that the greater density of settlements with larger numbers of teams tends to appear in the southern portion of the west Midlands, in contrast to the scatter of smaller concentrations in the east Midlands. Hill's work tells of a concentration of royal manors in this area (1981, fig 179; but see also Fig 5.9 below), but we cannot be certain if we are seeing actual differences in the distribution of teams or differences in their recording. Besides variations in the record, the more subtle differences in the texture of the distribution undoubtedly reflect variations in local terrain conditions. These points serve to emphasise the very real problems involved in 'reading' this distribution. The fact that

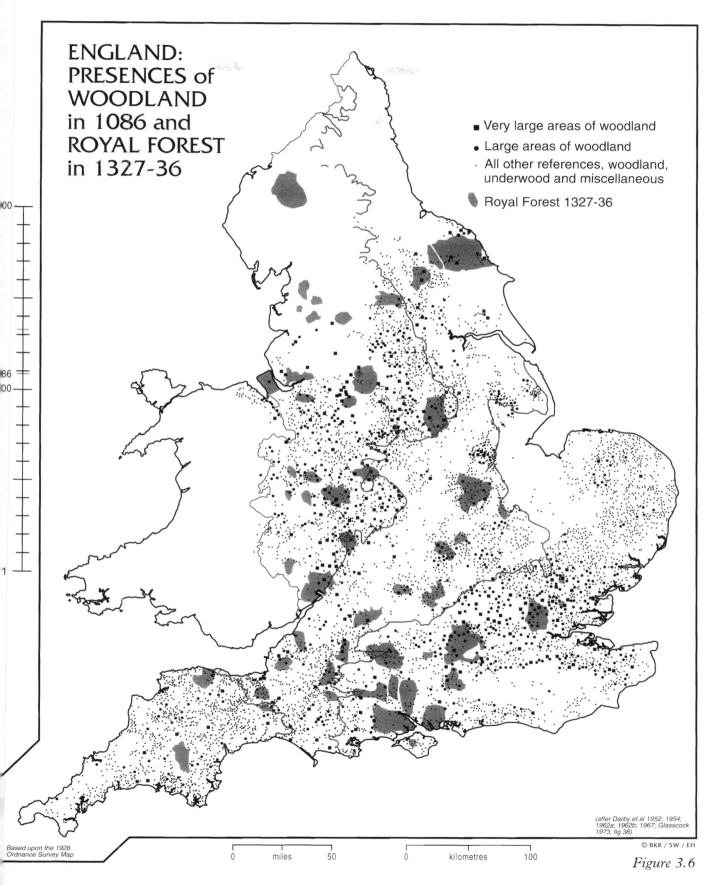

ENGLAND:
PRESENCES of
WOODLAND
in 1086 and
ROYAL FOREST
in 1327-36

■ Very large areas of woodland

● Large areas of woodland

· All other references, woodland,
underwood and miscellaneous

Royal Forest 1327-36

*(after Darby et al 1952; 1954;
1962a; 1962b; 1967; Glasscock
1973, fig 38)*

Based upon the 1928
Ordnance Survey Map

0   miles   50   0   kilometres   100

© BKR / SW / EH

Figure 3.6

such nuances can be detected leads us to believe that further study may reveal elements in this mapping that cannot at the moment be distinguished, or indeed even imagined.

Presences and absences in varied concentrations create a patchy distribution throughout the remainder of the south-east, there being clear links between agriculturally attractive and less attractive terrains. The distributions of ploughteams and woodlands are broadly complementary. Many other points could be made: the thin skein of recorded teams on the siltlands of the Fens; the slightly increased densities along the preferred settlement zone where the driftlands meet the fenlands; the cartwheel pattern of cultivation along the water-favoured valleys of the dry chalklands, paralleling the presence of nucleations seen in Figure 1.14, and the surprisingly dense scatters of small settlements throughout Devon and Cornwall, sweeping around the upstanding moorland masses. These all have an interest and are worthy of further analysis. Of more immediate interest is an extension of ploughlands westwards, from the team rich lands of the lower Warwickshire Avon and lower Severn valleys, spreading into the valleys of the middle Wye, the Lugg and the Arrow, with a small gap being clearly visible around what was later termed Malvern Chase (Fig 3.5). This draws the plain of Hereford, in our classification set within the Northern and Western Province, into the zone dominated in 1086 by arable cultivation.

In conclusion, it is important to emphasise that while it is possible to identify, in 1086, a tract that may correspond to the Central Province as defined in nineteenth-century sources, Domesday Book itself affords no evidence at all about the presence of nucleated or dispersed settlement. The place-names it records apply to the territories of vills or townships, not to the fixed locations of nucleations, a warning against the unwarranted assumption that the settlement forms of later centuries were already present in 1086. This point we will return to in later chapters.

Antecedent landscapes: Early Anglo-Saxon and Romano-British roots

The distribution of woodland recorded by Domesday Book and mapped in Figure 1.9 is a one moment snapshot of this resource (and one which is, as we have seen, distorted in places). Nevertheless, the woodland recorded then was clearly long-established. This is indicated by the way in which Anglo-Saxon 'woodland' place-names – some going back perhaps to the mid-eighth century – intensify and marginally extend the distribution (Fig 1.10): the kind of relationship one would expect in an environment of continuing, long-term clearance, especially in what became the Central Province. None of this should be contentious, given the current consensus on the expansion of arable farming in Middle and Later Saxon periods.

Perhaps more contentious will be our application of this same broad patterning of woodland to the fifth to seventh centuries. Our hypothesis is that the broad patterning of woodland recorded in Late Anglo-Saxon England provides – with appropriate extensions – the woodland context for early Anglo-Saxon activity. There are, of course, alternative hypotheses: that there was much less woodland in the fifth to seventh centuries than later; or that the woodland of the fifth to seventh centuries had some entirely contrary patterning to what was there a few centuries later. Either alternative seems, on current evidence, incredible.

To explore the relationship of our preferred hypothesis to Early Anglo-Saxon data, we turn first to the distributions of imported grave goods published by J W Huggett (1988). The distribution maps that accompany Huggett's analyses take the form of black dots set against a background of white space demarcated by a coastal outline. The important point here is that the viewer's perception of a distribution – and what may or may not be important in relation to that distribution – is shaped by what other data the author has included. In the case of imported grave goods such as the amber beads (Huggett 1988, fig 1, redrawn here as Figure 3.7), the coastline has an obvious significance since the objects have arrived by sea. Furthermore, on the basis of variations in the composition of assemblages, two distinct exchange systems between England and the Continent have been proposed (Huggett 1988, 78). Those of us who have stared long and hard at the Late Anglo-Saxon woodland map, however, have focused not on the coastline but on the blank areas between Kent and the main south-west to north-east spread of find-spots. For these blanks are regions where substantial woodland areas are recorded in later centuries. Early Anglo-Saxon material

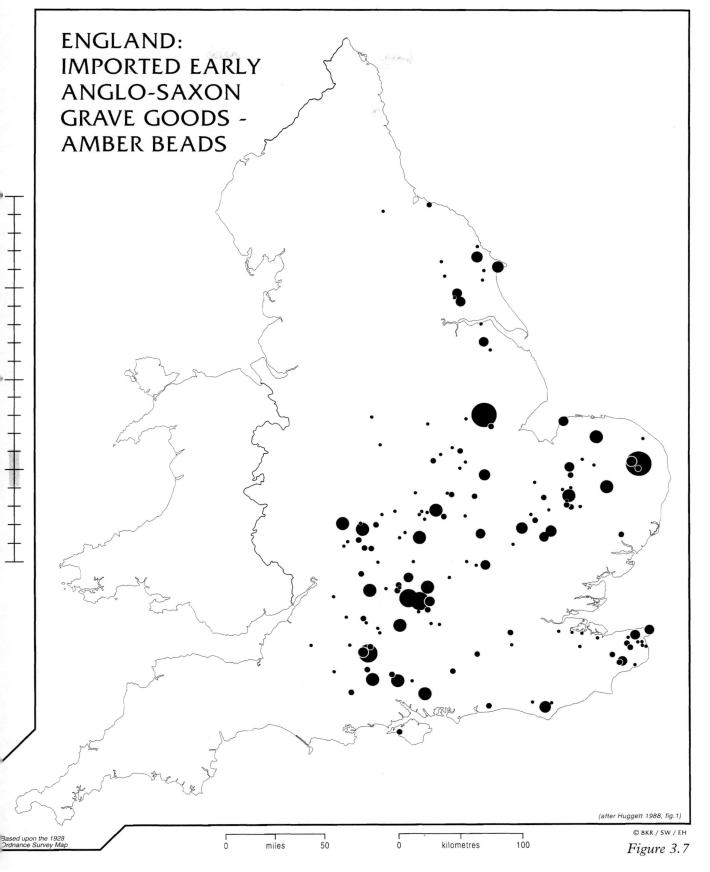

ENGLAND:
IMPORTED EARLY
ANGLO-SAXON
GRAVE GOODS -
AMBER BEADS

(after Huggett 1988, fig.1)

© BKR / SW / EH

Based upon the 1928
Ordnance Survey Map

0   miles   50

0   kilometres   100

Figure 3.7

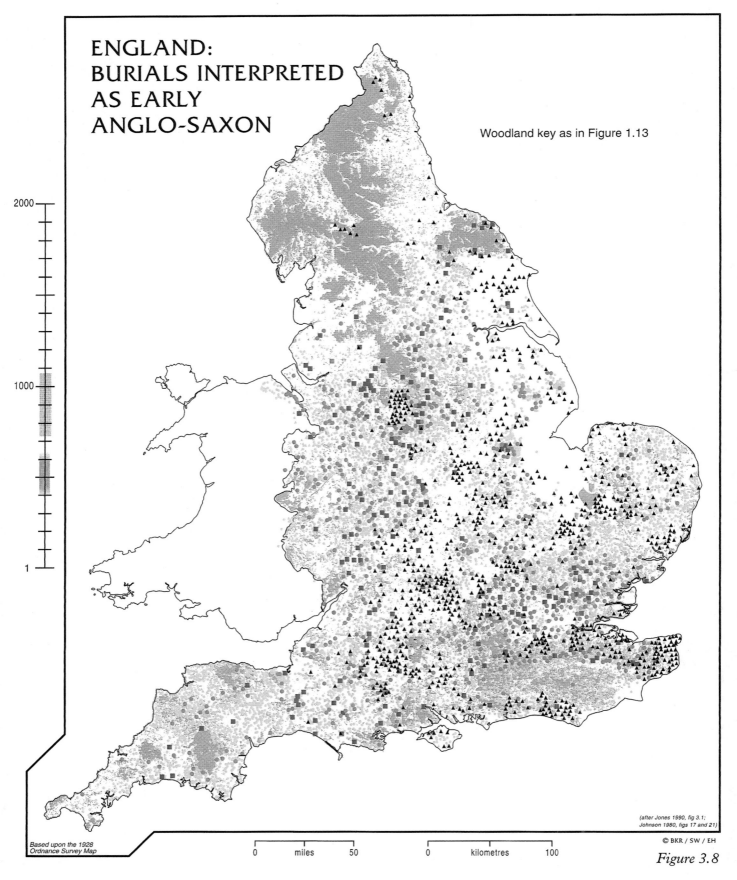

ENGLAND:
BURIALS INTERPRETED
AS EARLY
ANGLO-SAXON

Woodland key as in Figure 1.13

2000

1000

1

Based upon the 1928
Ordnance Survey Map

0   miles   50   0   kilometres   100

(after Jones 1990, fig 3.1;
Johnson 1980, figs 17 and 21)

© BKR / SW / EH

Figure 3.8

culture has traditionally been described as having a southern and eastern distribution in England. This is obviously true in the sense that its distribution is not northern and western. Nevertheless, there are significant regional variations within the south and east, variations that warrant more detailed study of the kind published for East Anglia by Christopher Scull (1992, 10–14).

Figure 3.8 shows the overall distribution of Early Anglo-Saxon cemeteries. Once again the main concentrations coincide broadly with those areas that in Late Anglo-Saxon times were characterised by a greater proportion of open land to woodland: in the zone that later developed as the Central Province, as well as around various estuaries along the East Anglian and South-east coastline. That said, there are indications that the Central Province cemeteries tend to cluster around the fringes of woodland nodes, rather than lying squarely within the cleared areas. This may indicate that in England, as in some parts of the Continent, cemeteries were sited on the edge of woodlands rather than in their communities' main cultivation grounds.

The absence of cemeteries from what we believe were the main tracts of contemporary woodland does not, of course, mean that those woodlands were outside the control of the communities that created those cemeteries. In an earlier survey of the west Midlands woodland boundary zone (Roberts and Wrathmell 2000b), we noted previous studies that had mapped the trackways extending from the open zones to tracts of woodland, giving communities of cultivators access to distinct seasonal grazing lands (Ford 1976, 280–82, fig 26.4; Hooke 1985b, 138–41, fig 10.10; 1998, 161, fig 55). Such patterns of exploitation may well have been inherited from earlier generations in the Iron Age, as Peter Warner has suggested in relation to the 'co-axial' trackways of Suffolk (Warner 1996, 47–9). What we envisage here is a patterning in the distribution of material culture that reflects not patterns of 'occupation' or 'control', but patterns of behaviour informed by access to diverse resources. Figure 3.9 shows, as well as fifth-century Anglo-Saxon burials, the main concentrations of -ingas place-names: across the woodlands of Suffolk and Essex, in clusters in Norfolk and along the fringes of the Weald (Gelling 1978, 106–29; Dodgson 1966, 1–29). Such names perhaps record the attribution of woodland to kinship groupings after the 'primary settlement' phase.

In the regional survey of the west Midlands mentioned above, we elaborated a series of conclusions by Margaret Gelling, W J Ford and others: that the boundary between woodland and open land evident in Late Anglo-Saxon times was already in place in the Roman period; that the south-west to north-east line of the Avon and Trent valleys was a major zone of cultivation – serviced by the Fosse Way – continuing from Roman into Anglo-Saxon times; that the percentage of this zone's population identified by Early Anglo-Saxon grave goods was small, and that long-established but archaeologically invisible agricultural communities continued to form the bulk of the population (Roberts and Wrathmell 2000b, 91–2). It would be unwise to argue the same case for all regions – either with regard to the size of the 'Anglo-Saxon' population or in relation to continuity of cultivation. Indeed, a recognition that some regions may have experienced a continuation of their agrarian structures, while others experienced complete dislocation, could go some way towards resolving the contradictions in the archaeological evidence.

The final maps in this series (Figs 3.10–3.11) show Roman distributions against the Late Anglo-Saxon woodland background. The first of them (Fig 3.10) indicates the location of 'Romanised' buildings, or structural material (roof tile, hypocaust flue tiles, brick, stone foundations etc) derived from such buildings. It is based on the gazetteer published by Eleanor Scott (1993), with additional information on Norfolk (courtesy of David Gurney). This can be compared with Figure 3.11, which is based on the map of Roman villas published a quarter of a century earlier by Rivet (1969, 209–16). It is notable that numerous discoveries made in the intervening years have intensified the distribution, but have not significantly extended it. It seems, therefore, that for once we have a reasonably reliable archaeological distribution of occurrence, rather than one shaped by the pattern of exploration.

The very patchy distribution of Romanised buildings can be compared with the statement by Ken and Petra Dark, that the 'villa landscape' of Roman Britain 'was centred on south-east England and was dominated by a pattern of romanized farmsteads and country houses' (Dark and Dark 1997, 11). As with Early Anglo-Saxon distributions, this statement is true only in the most generalised sense: significant tracts

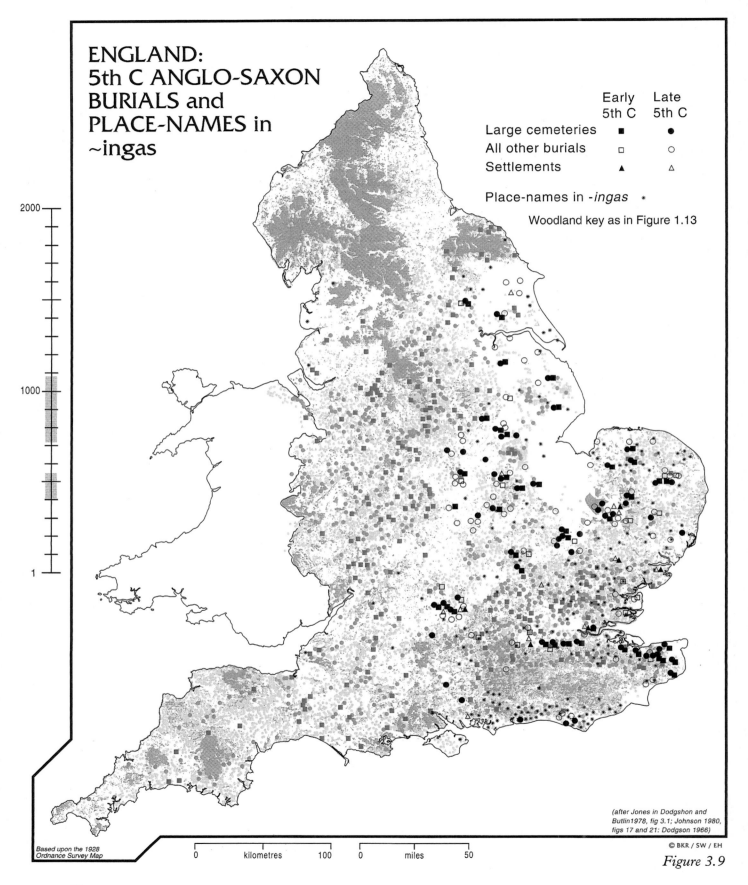

ENGLAND:
5th C ANGLO-SAXON
BURIALS and
PLACE-NAMES in
~ingas

Early 5th C   Late 5th C

Large cemeteries   ■   ●
All other burials   □   ○
Settlements   ▲   △

Place-names in -ingas   ✳

Woodland key as in Figure 1.13

(after Jones in Dodgshon and
Butlin 1978, fig 3.1; Johnson 1980,
figs 17 and 21: Dodgson 1966)

© BKR / SW / EH

Based upon the 1928
Ordnance Survey Map

0   kilometres   100   0   miles   50

Figure 3.9

of south-east England were not dominated by Romanised buildings, for whatever reason. Martin Millett has emphasised that 'villas' formed only a small proportion of the rural settlements of Roman Britain; that they related to the 'public towns' rather than to the agricultural productivity of the various regions, that they were built for the display of wealth, not for its production through agriculture. Villas are an index of the Romanisation of the native elites whose tribal territories became the *civitates* of Roman Britain (Millett 1990, 91–2, 117–20, 195). Millett's maps display one specific background to various archaeological distributions: the supposed boundaries of the *civitates*. He saw these territories, and the tribal groupings of the Late pre-Roman Iron Age on which they were based, as the key to explaining variability in the extent, chronology and character of Romanisation (Millett 1990, 66–7).

There is no reason to deny the primacy of social explanation for the patterns of Romanisation in Britain, and the absence of distribution maps of non-Romanised farming settlements makes it difficult to take matters further. Nevertheless, a few possibilities for interpreting Figure 3.11 can be outlined. Some of the gaps in the distribution of villas no doubt represent farming regions where, for social and political reasons, Romanised building traditions did not take hold; but others, such as the Weald, the New Forest and the stretch of territory north of London, may have been significantly wooded in Roman times and therefore subject to different patterns of activity from those in the open lands. Certainly the area north of London was well wooded in the mid-first century BC, judging by Caesar's account of his campaign against Cassivellaunus (Caesar, *Gallic War V*, 19). The relationship between the Romans and the tribes occupying these areas, and the disposition of *civitas* boundaries, may not be a complete explanation for some of the gaps in villa distribution where woodland was extensive seven centuries later. They may be areas of woodland that remained largely intact from the Late pre-Roman Iron Age down to the eleventh century. In marked contrast, concentrations of Romanised buildings are to be found in the Chilterns, to the west and south-west of Verulamium, where Early Anglo-Saxon burials are few in number, and where again there was extensive woodland seven centuries later. Such cases may signify a major discontinuity in settlement, where formerly cleared lands were subject to woodland regeneration in the post-Roman period. Elsewhere, as in the valley of the Warwickshire Avon, we have already suggested an alternative regional experience: continuity in the cultivation of land that had been largely cleared of woodland by the Roman period and remained open thereafter.

At present we offer no more than a few possibilities from the range of possible explanations, and any of these might be refuted in detailed studies. It will, in particular, be interesting to compare our data with the growing number of dated pollen sequences. The geographical biases in the provenance of samples, and the problem of inferring general patterns from particular cases should not be underestimated. Nevertheless, there seems to be some support for the idea that the Northern and Western Province (the Darks' native landscape) 'was relatively well wooded, and seems not to have been exploited to the full extent of its agricultural potential' in the Roman period (Dark and Dark 1997, 32). Be that as it may, the point we seek to emphasise is that, in Early Anglo-Saxon, in Roman and in pre-Roman times Britain was not a blank space defined by a coast, but an island containing varying environmental contexts that informed patterns of human activity and, thereby, patterns of deposition of material cultural remains. Large and long-standing areas of woodland will have been used for seasonal grazing for millennia; areas of cleared land will have continued under cultivation for millennia. We may not be able, as yet, to define them; but we do not doubt they existed. And over the centuries, human responses to changing socio-economic conditions will have affected these different areas in different ways.

The pattern of the provinces

The preceding part of this chapter explored, in plan, the way in which the Central Province of nucleations and townfields seems to have been generated from open land/woodland patterns in Roman and earlier times. The purpose of this part, following the methodology of archaeological excavation (which also, of course, proceeds retrogressively), is to cut, figuratively, a section through the three provinces, to explore the various ways in which they

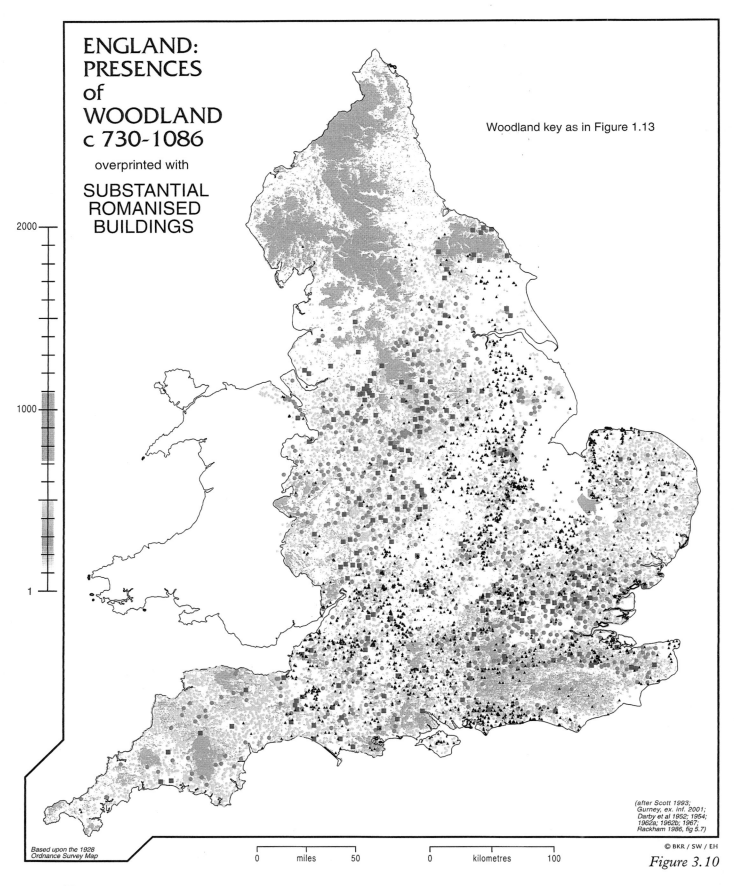

ENGLAND: PRESENCES of WOODLAND c 730-1086

overprinted with

SUBSTANTIAL ROMANISED BUILDINGS

Woodland key as in Figure 1.13

2000

1000

1

(after Scott 1993; Gurney, ex. inf. 2001; Darby et al 1952; 1954; 1962a; 1962b; 1967; Rackham 1986, fig 5.7)

Based upon the 1928 Ordnance Survey Map

0   miles   50   0   kilometres   100

© BKR / SW / EH

Figure 3.10

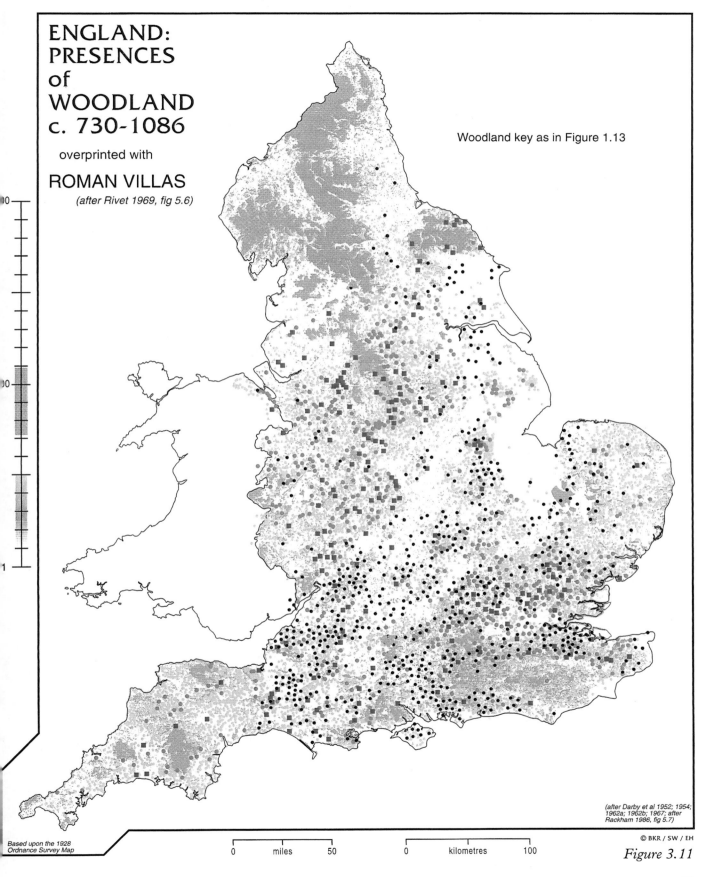

ENGLAND:
PRESENCES
of
WOODLAND
c. 730-1086

overprinted with

ROMAN VILLAS

(after Rivet 1969, fig 5.6)

Woodland key as in Figure 1.13

(after Darby et al 1952; 1954; 1962a; 1962b; 1967; after Rackham 1986, fig 5.7)

© BKR / SW / EH

Based upon the 1928 Ordnance Survey Map

| 0 | miles | 50 |

| 0 | kilometres | 100 |

Figure 3.11

may be related in stratigraphic terms. We are not yet in a position actually to determine such relationships: this is the start, not the end of the enquiry. Nevertheless, we can propose some models which might frame the course of that enquiry.

Model (a) in Figure 3.12 represents Oliver Rackham's (1986) distinction between 'planned countrysides' and 'ancient countrysides', the former being the rectilinear patterns of fields which resulted from the post-medieval enclosure of townfields. The townfield zone, ie the Central Province, is seen in model (a) to overlie part of a uniform base of 'ancient' countrysides.

Model (b) owes much more to the Highland Zone/Lowland Zone contrasts. In this, the boundary between the Central Province and the Northern and Western Province is a more fundamental divide than that between the Central Province and the South-eastern Province. It implies a more 'developed' central and south-eastern zone, contrasting with a less well-developed northern and western zone, though with some diffusion westwards. At root we have here Sir Cyril Fox's idea that new cultures, brought by immigrants, were *imposed* on the lowlands and *absorbed* in the highlands (Fox 1952, 88, proposition xi). While this deterministic view cannot now be accepted without substantial qualification, the presence of south-east to north-west contrasts in the physical character of the land and its biological potential cannot be ignored when settlement and cultural contrasts are being studied. One effect of these contrasts might be seen, for instance, in Robin Glasscock's map showing the extent of moveable wealth in 1334 (Glasscock 1975, map 1).

In model (c) there is still an initial uniformity, but then each of the three provinces follows a separate trajectory. We might envisage type Ai, the Central Province, resulting from the removal of woodland over a part of type A. In type C, however, there is a deliberate preservation of woodland in a different socio-economic environment which allows the support of high density populations without the results of Ai. Type B represents a much lower population density, and more limited areas of cultivation, in a zone characterised by degenerated soils. Model (d) shows roughly similar trajectories, though with each zone undergoing more complex changes.

Finally, in model (e) a complex diagram builds upon the idea that a series of regions with differing characteristics have generated the three settlement provinces. Their relationships in the middle decades of the nineteenth century are represented in the model by the line Time 1. The transition from B to A, in the Central Province, can be envisaged as the entire enclosure movement, whose several phases – the Tudor enclosures, enclosures by agreement, and the full impact of the Parliamentary enclosures – utterly transformed the landscapes of the province. This is a transformation we can document and in measure explain. Certainly the literature is large. It will be reconsidered in Chapter 5. The largely homogeneous shading of landscape types C and D – our two outer provinces – is misleading, but for the purposes of clarity the phases of change they passed through have been treated very simply.

Further subtleties have been introduced. Even in the upper portion of the diagram the zigzag lines between A/B and C and D carry the implication that the provincial boundaries need not have been wholly static when viewed at the scale of the sub-province or the local region (Fig 1.4). On the ground they represent a band of transition rather than a hard line. Linked with this idea, the zigzags in the lower portion of the diagram serve to suggest two things. First, local regional diversity may well have been substantial at earlier stages in landscape evolution: to any natural physical diversity must be added the presence of wholly cleared and uncleared lands as well as those at intermediate stages of development. The varied patterns crossed by the line at Time 2 suggest this local variety. Secondly, we are suggesting that the three provinces seen in Figures 1.13 and 1.14 evolved through the gradual assimilation of local regions towards a provincial 'norm'. This is suggested in model (e) (Fig 3.12) by the arrow leading upwards through the complex pattern towards the relative simplicity of type B. This can be postulated most clearly for the Central Province, which became a planned landscape of nucleated villages supported by extensive townfields. This hypothesis, which has important implications for our picturing of landscape change, will be assessed in Chapter 5.

We cannot, as yet, say which of these models, or which aspects of these models, isolated or combined, will eventually provide viable research frameworks for investigating rural settlement diversity on the ground. Some indications can, however, be gleaned from the case studies to be outlined in Chapter 4.

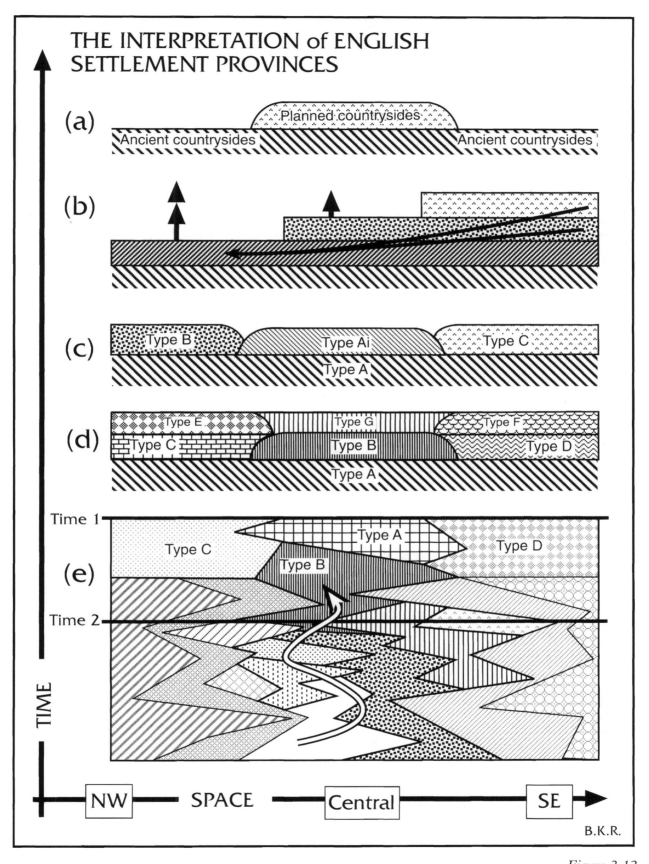

Figure 3.12

Conclusions and directions

Four conclusions emerge so far from our analysis of Figures 1.13 and 1.14 and the materials with which we have compared them. First, the provincial boundaries are broadly stable for long periods and, subject to some qualification, there are grounds for arguing that they were present in 1086 and indeed must predate the Domesday Inquest by several centuries. It is clear that the main provincial boundaries show some adjustment during this time, and we should remind ourselves that no less than 800 years have passed. Thus, some elements of the nineteenth-century boundaries are evidently very ancient. Others result from both the coarse changes brought by industrialisation and the more subtle ones wrought by more localised developments such as the expansion and replanning of field systems and depopulation and enclosure. Secondly, although physical factors were undoubtedly involved in determining the location of some elements of these key boundaries, to invoke physical determinism to explain them is wholly unsatisfactory: powerful cultural factors must also have been at work. Thirdly, there is no doubt that at the later stages of landscape development industrialisation has had a major effect, making villages into sprawling towns, hamlets into villages, and single dwellings into hamlets. Figure 1.14 bears testimony to all of these developments. Fourthly, in this account we have barely taken our arguments beyond the rather general level of the provinces, although close comparisons between the varied maps show that the distributions reveal important elements of continuity and change at the level of both the sub-provinces and local regions.

In Chapter Four, we present a series of detailed short studies within the broader context of the patterns revealed by the national maps of settlement and early woodland. These linkages are important, because they show the ways in which we believe this study provides a setting and context for local-scale investigations. This step opens the way for two more lengthy analyses of the provinces. First, there is an indisputable connection in the Central Province between the presence of nucleated settlement forms and the extensive open, common, subdivided field systems. These must be further explored, for the genesis of the townfields and the origins of the nucleations they supported are likely to be closely interrelated. If the origin of this Central Provincial settlement system can be resolved, and if the extent to which it represented a planned, imposed arrangement can be established, we will then be in a position to approach the more difficult questions of what landscapes preceded the development of the townfields. These landscapes, destroyed by the imposition of extensive townfields, may or may not have shared features with those of the Northern and Western and South-eastern Provinces. This will involve an exploration of some of the features of the model seen in Figure 3.11 (e). It will also be closely associated with an attempt to describe, characterise and analyse the landscapes of the two outer provinces, notably the balance between the areas of townfields and the varied types of enclosed landscapes. Above all, a chronology of development of each type must be established. Finally, while the provinces are 'real' entities, visible both on the ground and on maps, we must again emphasise the ways in which they were tied together through tenurial and other socio-economic linkages.

4
The characteristics of place: cases and studies

Introduction

Any attempt to construct national distributions can start from one of two places. It is possible, once criteria and classifications have been established, to begin assembling detailed data in one particular locality, county or region, and then to work across the whole of the country in a systematic fashion. The advantage of this kind of 'progressive' approach is that, as it is based on detail, the resulting distributions and synthetic statements have a high degree of reliability. The disadvantages are, however, considerable: it requires either many years' research or the application of considerable resources to achieve a worthwhile conclusion. Furthermore, much depends upon getting right the classifications and categories of information at the beginning of the project, and maintaining their relevance and coherence for its duration. The other way of constructing national distributions – the one chosen here – is to use more generalised data which are already available, or which can be readily assembled, to create a framework for subsequent detailed research: a 'top-down' approach. The first of these procedures is more likely to mark the conclusion of a particular phase of research, whereas the alternative marks the beginning of a programme of investigation. The principal challenge for the 'top-down' approach is to establish its relevance to detailed studies of particular communities and localities. Such is the purpose of this chapter: to demonstrate that what has been observed in detailed, local research can be used to elaborate the national patterns; and equally, to show that the national framework can be used to invest studies of particular localities and communities with new meaning.

This chapter, therefore, offers the reader a dramatic shift in scale. It comprises a series of township-scale case studies (Fig. 4.1), and using either the original or new interpretations, it seeks to link these studies together within the context of the national framework. We stress that the cases assembled here are *not* the result of rigorous, systematic research or selection procedures. Nor do they represent an attempt to characterise regional variation in any aspects other than those of direct concern here. They are pieces of work, in some instances by the writers but mainly by others, that have been to hand, and that seem to offer something of relevance to the generalising hypotheses proposed elsewhere in this book. The review of individual case studies begins with the Central Province, the province that has traditionally supplied the models for medieval settlement and townfield structure. The few examples we include here are used to highlight the considerable variety of agrarian structures in what appears, at a national scale, to be a relatively uniform zone. They are also used to explore some anomalous regions, also identified at a national scale, where nucleation either never occurred, or came only in post-medieval times. The final study for the Central Province explores the evidence for the survival of the settlement structures that preceded townfield layout and nucleation.

Case studies from the South-eastern, and Northern and Western Provinces will be seen, by contrast, to emphasise the commonality of underlying structures despite the enormous variations in terrain, tenure and other conditions. This is quite deliberate, and builds upon a hypothesis, published in an earlier article (Wrathmell 1994, 182–6), that the kinds of agrarian structures observed in East Anglia could also be detected in the Pennine foothills, on the other side of the Central Province. The implications of this hypothesis for settlement history will be reviewed at the end of this chapter; for the moment, the point that needs reiterating is that these case-studies either provide new interpretations of existing data, or emphasise particular aspects of other researchers' findings, in order to explore this hypothesis.

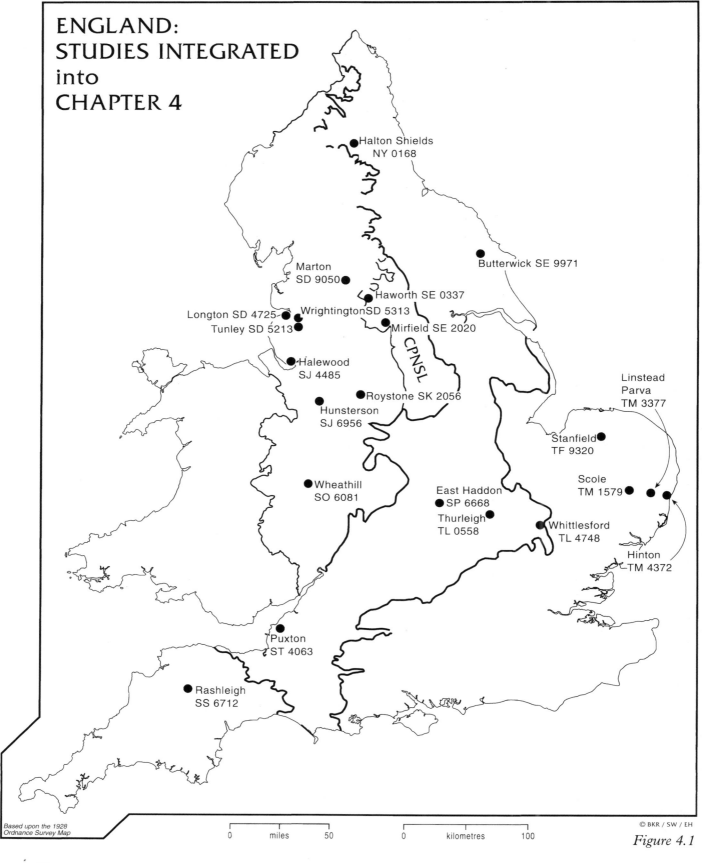

ENGLAND:
STUDIES INTEGRATED
into
CHAPTER 4

● Halton Shields
  NY 0168

● Butterwick SE 9971

Marton
SD 9050 ●

● Haworth SE 0337

Longton SD 4725 ● Wrightington SD 5313 ●
Tunley SD 5213 ●

● Mirfield SE 2020

CPNSL

● Halewood
  SJ 4485

● Royston SK 2056

Hunsterson
SJ 6956

Linstead
Parva
TM 3377

Stanfield ●
TF 9320

Scole
TM 1579 ● ●

● Wheathill
  SO 6081

East Haddon
● SP 6668

Thurleigh
TL 0558

● Whittlesford
  TL 4748

Hinton
TM 4372

Puxton
ST 4063 ●

● Rashleigh
  SS 6712

Based upon the 1928
Ordnance Survey Map

0   miles   50   0   kilometres   100

© BKR / SW / EH

Figure 4.1

Variations in the Central Province

Townfield structures: scale and chronology

The first case study is intended to typify the classic 'Midland' open-field township with single, nucleated settlement. It has been drawn from Northamptonshire, where the work of David Hall and others has done much to characterise the regular, ordered structure of such vills:

The single holding, yardland or virgate, can be related to the ground evidence. Normally one such holding will consist of a single ridge in every furlong throughout the system… Most field systems had a regular order of tenants holding strips… the same neighbours always being adjacent. The number of lands in a furlong is frequently a multiple of the yardland rating for the vill. *(Hall 1989, 195)*

Such a high degree of regulation implies that the townfields were laid out, or wholly reorganised, at a single time. Furthermore, the documentary evidence indicates that

Figure 4.2

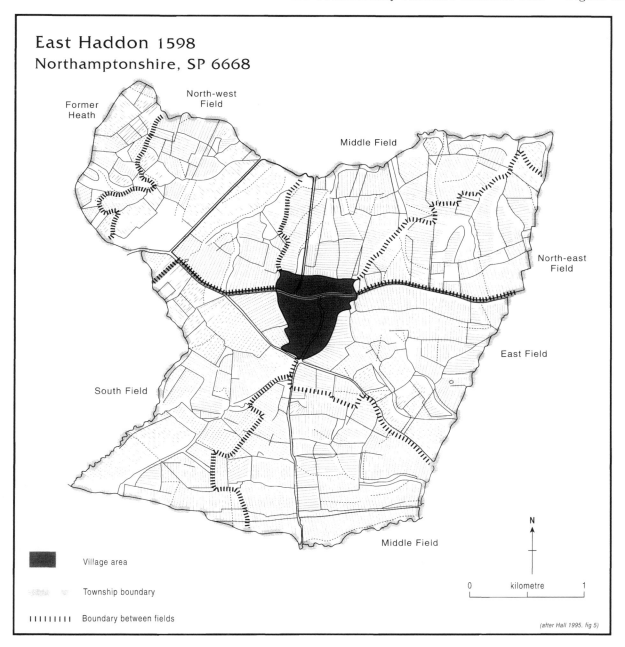

East Haddon 1598
Northamptonshire, SP 6668

Former Heath

North-west Field

Middle Field

North-east Field

East Field

South Field

Middle Field

N

Village area

Township boundary

Boundary between fields

0   kilometre   1

(after Hall 1995, fig 5)

this regularity was sustained for centuries. Such inflexibility in the agrarian structure should probably be linked with a second characteristic of the great majority of Northamptonshire vills: the way in which almost the whole of the township area was covered by the townfields, with little or no woodland or permanent pasture.

East Haddon, shown in Figure 4.2, is one such township, though its field structure was rather more complex than might at first appear. There was a double field system, the two parts divided by the east-west village street. Hall argues that this arrangement may pre-date the Norman conquest (Hall 1995, 277). One part, the North Fields, was itself divided into three fields, and there is evidence that the tenants' strips were in a regular order. They amounted to 38 yardlands. The South Fields were also in three parts, and once again there is evidence of regularity in their laying out: 'the fields had been laid out in roods that represented a yardland when added up through all the tenurial cycles' (Hall 1995, 282). The system contained 21.5 yardlands.

Northumberland, at the northern end of the Central Province, provides markedly contrasting structures with those of the east Midlands: townships where nucleation occurred centuries later than it did south of the Humber; townships in which the arable townfields encompassed a much smaller proportion of the community's agrarian resources; townships in which extensive, permanent common grazing lands persisted throughout the Middle Ages. The case study chosen here is Halton Shields, a township in the medieval lordship of Halton (Wrath-mell 1975, 70, 194, 393–5). Figure 4.3 shows Halton Shields as it appeared in J Forster's survey of 1677 (Northumberland Record Office ZBL 269/1). The settlement is shown as a single block of seven tofts, some with symbols marking associated messuages, others without. Further structures lay to the south, in enclosed ground called Greenside Field. The tofts occupied the line of Hadrian's Wall. To the north of the village were its three townfields: East, Middle and West. South of Greenside Field was the extensive area of rough grazing called Shildon Common, which served as inter-common for the surrounding communities.

Halton Shields, on the evidence of its name, began as a seasonally occupied settlement, to facilitate exploitation of grazing on Shildon Common during the summer months. The place does not appear as a separate vill in the taxation records or inquisitions of the thirteenth and early fourteenth centuries; its earliest listing as a vill appears to be in 1524 (*Northumberland County History*, VI, 101). Given the political, social and economic instability of the Border region during the fourteenth and fifteenth centuries, it seems likely that the creation of Halton Shields township, with its village and three-field system, was an event of the early sixteenth century. If so, it can be seen as one of the last manifestations of the nucleation-townfield revolution that had begun some six centuries earlier in the east Midlands.

The survival of dispersed settlement: cases from Bedfordshire and Buckinghamshire

The late Anglo-Saxon and Domesday woodland map (Fig. 1.13) shows that extensive patches of woodland survived at that time within the Central Province. Figure 1.14 indicates that some of them had a sufficiently prolonged impact on settlement forms to remain detectable (vicariously, as areas of dispersed settlement) on the nineteenth-century settlement map. There is a group of small patches of relatively high dispersion in north Bedfordshire and north-east Buckinghamshire (Fig. 1.2). These could, of course, be the result of post-medieval developments, rather than a sign of long-lasting woodland environments. Fortunately, the area has seen a number of important investigations by Tony Brown and Chris Taylor, and these, we believe, resolve the issue.

Thurleigh is one of a group of townships in north Bedfordshire where there is 'a classic mixture of dispersed and nucleated settlement. On the whole, the villages are generally small, and are surrounded by numerous small hamlets and single farmsteads' (Brown and Taylor 1989, 61). The 'village' of Thurleigh lies at the centre of the township; its principal elements, Bury Farm and Church End, may signify its origin as a hall-church focus. There are numerous hamlets and scattered farms elsewhere in the township: the hamlets of Scald End, Park End and Cross End; and the ancient farmsteads of Blackburn Hall, Whitwick Green Farm and College Farm in Backnoe End. Of these, Scald End was a string of farmsteads, some now represented only by earthworks and pottery scatters, which seems to have been established after the eleventh century, partly at least on former arable land. As late as the beginning of the nineteenth century there were still extensive areas of open field, shown on Figure 4.4, though most of the outer parts of the township comprised anciently enclosed fields.

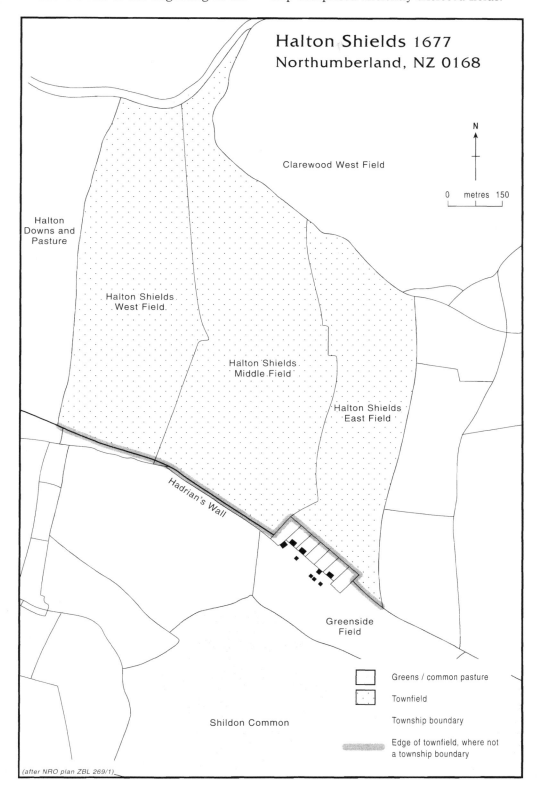

Halton Shields 1677
Northumberland, NZ 0168

N

0 metres 150

Clarewood West Field

Halton Downs and Pasture

Halton Shields West Field

Halton Shields Middle Field

Halton Shields East Field

Hadrian's Wall

Greenside Field

Shildon Common

Greens / common pasture

Townfield

Township boundary

Edge of townfield, where not a township boundary

(after NRO plan ZBL 269/1)

Figure 4.3

87

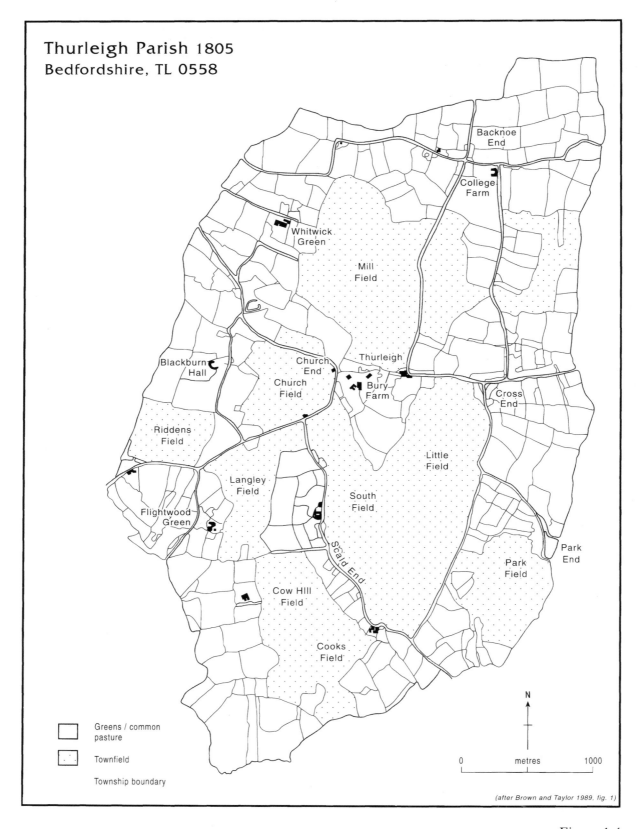

Thurleigh Parish 1805
Bedfordshire, TL 0558

Backnoe End

College Farm

Whitwick Green

Mill Field

Blackburn Hall

Church End

Thurleigh

Church Field

Bury Farm

Cross End

Riddens Field

Little Field

Langley Field

South Field

Flightwood Green

Park End

Park Field

Scald End

Cow Hill Field

Cooks Field

N

Greens / common pasture

Townfield

Township boundary

0   metres   1000

(after Brown and Taylor 1989, fig. 1)

Figure 4.4

Combining medieval records of manors and virgates with the post-medieval cartographic evidence, Brown and Taylor have argued that at Domesday the only significant area of virgated open-field land may have been that of the principal manor, centred on Bury Farm. Elsewhere in the township, small scattered settlements such as Cross End and Whitwick Green could already have been in existence on the periphery of the woodland. During the next two centuries the open-field lands were expanded at the expense of the formerly extensive wood-pasture, and the small settlements acquired lands in these fields – though clustered near the settlement rather than scattered uniformly around the open fields. The distinctive Scald End settlement was probably established during this period of expansion (Brown and Taylor 1989, 67–9). The pre-expansion pattern of settlement postulated by Brown and Taylor seems, therefore, to include a hall-church settlement in the centre of open-field arable, with peripheral dispersed settlements associated with greens such as Flightwood (Brown and Taylor 1989, fig. 3). In short, it is much the same pattern as will be described in case studies from both the Northern and Western Province, and South-eastern Province. The expansion of population and townfield land in the mid to late twelfth century did not result, as elsewhere in the Central Province, in the nucleation of settlement. Brown and Taylor suggest two reasons for this: the existence of very substantial areas of old enclosure, and the organisation of the open fields in small 'fields' grouped into scattered 'seasons':

> A type of farming is indicated in which a topographically less concentrated approach was possible in cropping systems and regular fallowing. Given this, then a nucleated settlement pattern was simply unnecessary. (Brown and Taylor 1989, 68)

What Brown and Taylor have offered here is the definition of an alternative model to the classic nucleated, townfield model, rather than an explanation as to why the one was chosen at Thurleigh rather than the other. That explanation should perhaps be sought in the differing antecedent patterns of land use and agrarian structure: in the extent to which, in pre-nucleation times, townships had already come to be dominated by arable farming; in the extent to which wood-pasture resources had been preserved. Inevitably, such antecedent patterns in turn require other layers of explanation, relating to even earlier cultural patterns as well as soils and terrain.

As will be evident in the case studies from the South-eastern Province, dispersed settlement townships which escaped the village revolution owed much of their spatial patterning to long-established networks of trackways. At Chellington, in the same region as Thurleigh, there were four distinct settlement areas in the Middle Ages. Brown and Taylor, in their study of this township, emphasise the importance of the road and track system for understanding the pattern of medieval settlement; they also suggest that some of these tracks may be prehistoric, once again emphasising the role of antecedent structures:

> The general picture is one of gradual change within the framework fixed by an ancient trackway system. There seem to have been two broad periods during which really fundamental change took place – the (probably) late Iron Age and earlier Roman periods ... [and] the late medieval/earlier post-medieval period ... But the evidence we have does not suggest that any of these changes was particularly abrupt. (Brown and Taylor 1999, 109)

A final example from these pockets of dispersion is a very instructive one, in that it highlights the conceptual problems which have resulted from too great an emphasis on the remains of medieval nucleated settlements. Hardmead, in north-east Buckinghamshire, makes a rather unexpected appearance in the definitive publication on deserted medieval villages (Beresford and Hurst 1971, fig.7A–C). A plan of 1638 indicates many more houses than existed there in 1960. They were clustered at two 'ends' of the township, east and west, more than half a mile apart, with a manorial site and church half-way between them. The assumption that these represented a 'now-deserted village in semi-decay' (Beresford and Hurst 1971, 49) seems, three decades on, unwarranted, in view of Brown and Taylor's work in the area, and given what we know of the character of dispersed settlement in general. The seventeenth-century pattern is much more likely to be in substance a reflection of what was there in the Middle Ages.

Late nucleation on the Pennine Slopes

Another part of the Central Province deserving special consideration is the sub-province labelled CPNSL (Figs 1.4, 4.1). It had a dense enough distribution of nucleations to be originally included by us in the nineteenth-century Central Province, but it seems to have been part of the well-wooded Northern and Western Province in the eleventh century (Fig. 1.13). Our working hypothesis has been that the change in affiliation resulted from the conversion of dispersed to nucleated settlement during the period of industrialisation, and associated massive population growth, in the eighteenth and nineteenth centuries. It is always encouraging to find that the broad

generalisations which have emerged from our work are in accord with detailed regional studies, especially where the one has not been influenced by the thinking behind the other. The initial publications of the CPNSL hypothesis (Roberts and Wrathmell 1998, 101–2) coincided with a detailed study of settlement in Nidderdale (Muir 1998), at the north end of CPNSL. The conclusions reached by Richard Muir about settlement in the 'Middle Valley zone' of Nidderdale are worth quoting:

> The pattern of settlement was a dispersed one, including hamlets, which were often loosely organised around small greens or had their cottages and farmsteads strung out along a length of track...the pattern of nucleated settlement seen today is the product of a

Figure 4.5

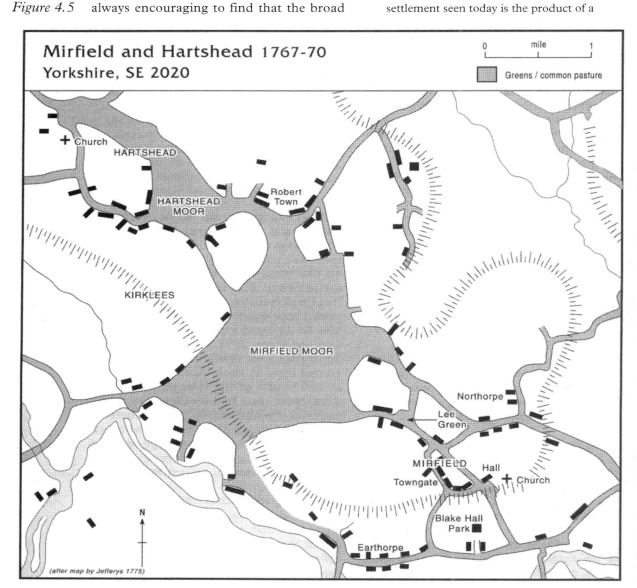

Mirfield and Hartshead 1767-70
Yorkshire, SE 2020

0   mile   1

Greens / common pasture

HARTSHEAD

Church

HARTSHEAD MOOR

Robert Town

KIRKLEES

MIRFIELD MOOR

Northorpe

Lee Green

MIRFIELD   Hall

Towngate   Church

Blake Hall Park

Earthorpe

N

(after map by Jefferys 1775)

process of 'late nucleation'...[linked to] industrialisation and related processes.
(Muir 1998, 75)

The case-studies presented here are from a little further south in CPNSL, from the Calder and Aire valleys where the impetus for nucleation came from the rise of textile manufacture. Villages were created, through population growth, by infilling between existing settlement foci, and by ribbon development along the margins of enclosed land and common pastures. The patterns of change are strikingly similar to those which had affected parts of Norfolk six centuries earlier, during the rapid expansion of an agricultural population (e.g. Wade-Martins 1980, 22–3, 27).

The pre-nucleation patterns of settlement can be seen in the first case-study, which combines the West Riding townships of Mirfield and Hartshead, and the hamlet of Robert Town in Liversedge. These can be seen on Figure 4.5, a redrawing of Jefferys' 1775 map, based on a survey of 1767–70. At that period, Hartshead settlement consisted of a church with a couple of houses near the north end of Hartshead Moor, and a scatter of farmsteads along both sides of a lane to the south. It is evident, however, that the enclosed block of land to the north of the farmsteads had been taken in from the Moor after 1700, as it is not shown on a map of c.1700 (Scargill and Lee 1986, 8). The same is true of a further block to the south-west of Robert Town, though the smaller enclosure immediately south of Robert Town was there by 1700. Thus the settlement at Hartshead seems to have been a 'moor side' development, and the one at Robert Town had been established where the moorland funnelled down into a trackway. Both settlements are medieval: Robert Town was recorded as Liversedge Robert, one of three hamlets in a dispersed township, in the fourteenth century (Faull and Moorhouse 1981, 436); Hartshead was a Domesday vill. Hartshead church is partly mid-twelfth century and was first recorded, as a chapel, in 1147 (Faull and Moorhouse 1981, 389).

To the south-east, beyond the expanse of Mirfield Moor, were two small post-medieval intakes. Beyond them the enclosed lands of Mirfield were formed by two large oval areas on each side of smaller enclosures, defined by trackways, at Towngate and Blake Hall Park. Settlement was peripheral to these ovals: a scatter of farmsteads along

Towngate; a small hamlet on the northern edge of the eastern oval, called Northorpe, and a scatter of buildings along the southern edge of the western oval, originally called 'Earthorpe'. At a hall-church focus between the ovals, the medieval manor house, demolished to make way for a new church in 1871, itself replaced an adjacent Norman motte. The ruined medieval church is thirteenth-century and later, but there is also a late Anglo-Saxon gravestone (Pevsner 1967, 368). Northorpe is first recorded in the thirteenth century, and Towngate and Earthorp in the sixteenth century (Smith 1961a, 199–201). Both main ovals seem, on the first edition of the Ordnance Survey 6 inch map, to have enclosed parcels of former townfield strips; one of them may have been le Westefeld recorded in the early fourteenth century (Smith 1961a, 202).

The general pattern of medieval settlement in the West Riding part of CPNSL is of hall-church foci and common-edge settlement on the periphery of cultivated or other enclosed ground. It is a pattern that will be instantly recognisable to those familiar with dispersed settlement in East Anglia. There are, of course, exceptions, such as the township of Clifton, adjacent to Hartshead, that in the Middle Ages had a linear, nucleated village with extensive townfields (Crump 1925, 105–35). Most of the nineteenth-century nucleations visible in this region on the nation map are, however, the result of an intensification of housing in post-medieval times.

The process of nucleation can be examined in detail at Haworth, about 15 miles north-west of Mirfield. Those who make the pilgrimage to the home of the Bronte sisters will see dense housing on each side of Main Street, the principal village street; but this is very much a nineteenth-century development. Figure 4.6 shows that the earlier settlement foci were at each end of Main Street, which was then simply a lane. At the north end was a hamlet called Town End, set around a triangular green formed by an intersection of lanes. An eighteenth-century map shows the remnants of townfields on either side of the lane running westwards from this green. At the south end lay Hall Green, another triangular green formed by intersecting trackways. This was surrounded by enclosed fields in the nineteenth century and bore no sign of former subdivided strips. The evolution of Haworth is evident in the dating of its stock of historic buildings. The only medieval structure

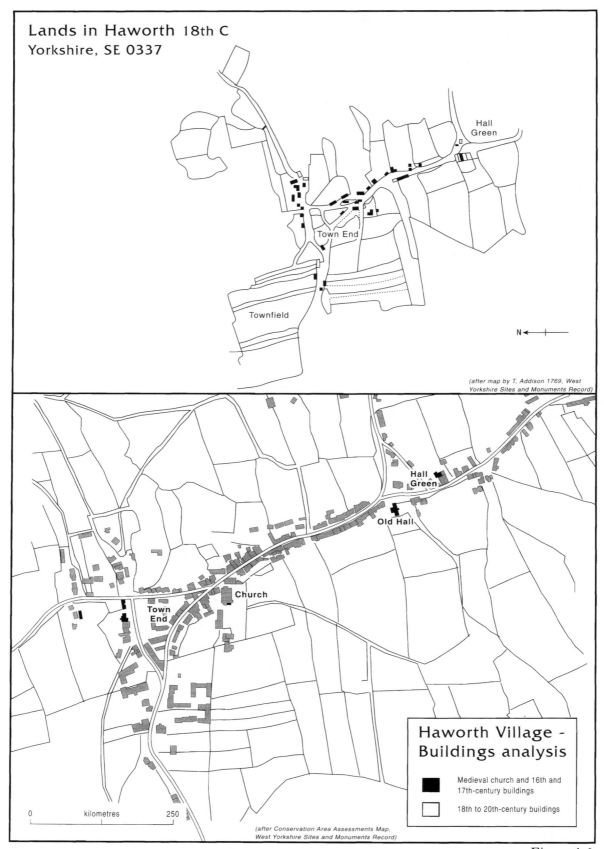

Figure 4.6

is part of the parish church, which lies close to the southern end of Town End green. On the north side of this green are three sixteenth and seventeenth-century buildings. The other surviving structures that predate the eighteenth century are the sixteenth-century Old Hall and part of a seventeenth-century farmhouse, both at Hall Green. The conversion of Haworth into a large village, through the expansion of housing around and on these greens, and along the sides of what became Main Street, linking these foci, can be related to the development of the textile industry in the later eighteenth and nineteenth centuries.

The townfield revolution

Though long drawn out, the change from dispersed to nucleated settlement and the introduction of highly regulated and stable townfield systems were cumulatively a revolution of immense significance for the lives and livelihoods of those who experienced them. The transformation is signified in the east Midlands by the recovery of Early and Middle Saxon pottery from habitation sites which later disappeared beneath medieval furlongs. In some cases, the memory of the earlier settlement was preserved by the habitative name of a furlong (Hall 1995, 130). Since the Second World War the flattening of townfield ridges, and the expansion of cultivation over land formerly maintained as permanent pasture have revealed once more, through the medium of cropmarks, the habitation sites and associated fields and trackways predating the townfield revolution. It has to be said, however, that there have been few attempts to undertake comparative analysis of the agrarian structures pre-dating and post-dating that revolution: some scholars have studied the 'ancient landscapes'; others have concentrated on the ridges, furlong boundaries and strip orientations of the medieval townfields. This is unfortunate, because such comparisons represent an ideal opportunity for detailed investigation of continuity and discontinuity in agrarian structures.

As an example of the potential of such comparative analysis we can review the township of Butterwick, on the Yorkshire Wolds. Its village settlement and townfield structure were recorded on a map of 1563 when, apart from the village enclosures themselves, the whole of the township area was given over to open fields (Fig. 4.7; Harvey 1982, 30–31). The length of the

parcels of land varied considerably: those in Kirkdales furlong, North Field, were nearly 2km long, whereas several furlongs around the village were small. In the sixteenth century Butterwick was assessed at 101 oxgangs, and Domesday Book, five centuries earlier, had assessed the township at 96 bovates. This suggests that the open fields had not been expanded to any significant degree in the intervening centuries (Harvey 1982, 38). Indeed, it could be argued that the agrarian structure visible in the sixteenth century was already largely in place by 1086. The regular distribution of tenants' lands in the furlongs and across the open fields as a whole (Harvey 1982, 34–6) indicates a comprehensive redesign of the agrarian system carried out perhaps on a single occasion. Figure 4.7 shows this agrarian structure superimposed on the cropmarks of earlier settlements, field boundaries and trackways as recorded by RCHM(E) (Stoertz 1997, fig. 44). The large-scale published map of cropmark information covers only the northern half of the township. Nevertheless, it provides extensive evidence of the structures that preceded the township. They include forms that are evident in other parts of the Wolds, for example in the Wharram parishes (Hayfield 1987, figs 44 and 104): small clusters of rectilinear enclosures, often subdivided, such as numbers 8 and 10 on Figure 4.7; and extended linear systems of rectangular enclosures, 'ladder settlements', like number 6 on Figure 4.7. These structures and the associated trackways seem to have had no influence on the layout of the townfields; nor, for that matter, on the location of the township boundaries themselves. Such clustered enclosures and 'ladder settlements' have been dated elsewhere to the later prehistoric and Roman periods (Hayfield 1987, 92–4, 183). They represent, therefore, prima facie evidence of a complete discontinuity in the post-Roman, pre-Norman period.

There is, however, a further element in the pattern of cropmarks: a cluster of small, curvilinear settlement enclosures a short distance to the south-west of the medieval (and modern) settlement. This cluster, and several others with similar formal characteristics, have been tentatively ascribed to the Anglo-Saxon period (Stoertz 1997, 20, 59). It is conceivable, therefore, that this complex belongs to the period before the creation of the open fields, as might indeed be assumed from the circumstance that it

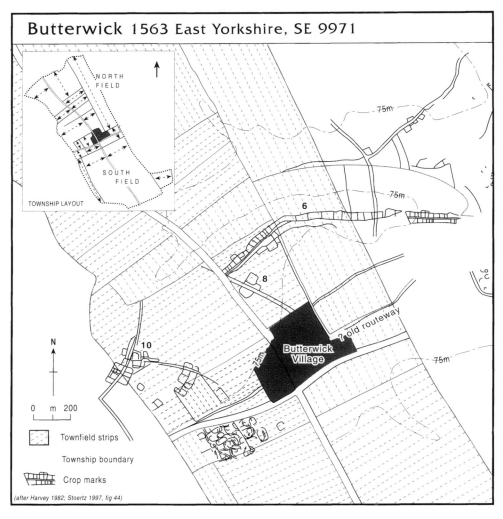

Butterwick 1563 East Yorkshire, SE 9971

NORTH FIELD

SOUTH FIELD

TOWNSHIP LAYOUT

6

8

10

Butterwick Village

? old routeway

75m

0   m   200

Townfield strips

Township boundary

Crop marks

(after Harvey 1982; Stoertz 1997, fig 44)

Figure 4.7

lies beneath one of the furlongs. Yet appearances may be deceptive. The furlong in which it is located was small, and could have been added to the pattern of townfields some time after the major reorganisation. A cropmark east-west trackway just north of the enclosure complex might have once linked up to a minor routeway running east from the church, along a furlong boundary, later replaced by a route (the modern road line) diverted south of the present settlement. Whether any of these speculations provides a sustainable view of Butterwick's nucleation and townfield development is not a matter of concern here. The point of the discussion is to demonstrate that comparative analysis of medieval and earlier agrarian structures holds considerable potential for exploring such issues. It is a point which can be underlined by Susan Oosthuizen's study of Caxton, in west Cambridgeshire, where some of the furlong boundaries immediately

around the village seem to owe their alignment to a pre-Roman field system (Oosthuizen 1997, 147–8). In fact, as will become evident in the discussion of Whittlesford, west Cambridgeshire is one part of the Central Province where pre-nucleation agrarian structures seem to have survived the townfield revolution exceptionally well.

Comparisons between the outer provinces

Structures of the Northern and Western Province

In the Northern and Western Province, the characteristics of the Central Province are inverted. Nucleated settlements and extensive townfields, although they are to be found in almost all regions, become a minor strand in the pattern. The dominant rural theme is townships with dispersed patterns of farmsteads and hamlets and small town-field cores, surrounded by enclosed fields and by wood-pastures or open heaths and moors.

Lancashire is one such county. Angus Winchester has provided a valuable overview of the area's rural settlement and agrarian structures, emphasising the tripartite division between the cleared arable lands in the western, coastal lowlands, the wooded areas further east and the open moorlands on the hills (Winchester 1993). One of the lowland areas, the Fylde, bears a name meaning 'a plain', which is closely related to *feld*, or open country (Winchester 1993, 11). It is characterised by large nucleated settlements with regular, planned layouts that Winchester compares with those in Yorkshire and Durham. He suggests they resulted from 'a wholesale transformation in the aftermath of the [Norman] Conquest' (Winchester 1993, 13). Longton, on the Ribble estuary, is one of these large villages. On the first edition of the OS 6 inch map, it can be seen to lie within an extensive area of long, sinuous fields whose pattern clearly preserves the outlines of consolidated townfield strips, the result of piecemeal enclosure in the seventeenth century (Fig. 4.8; see Winchester 1993, fig. 2). Indeed, there is a hint of planning in advance of determining the township divisions, in that some of the long curving boundaries seem to extend northwards into the adjacent township of Hutton. A series of fourteenth-century deeds provides detail on parcels and furlongs in Longton's townfields. One of these deeds, dated 1318, records a selion with a tongland (i.e. tongueland) in *le Tunstedes*, a furlong known from post-medieval sources to have been located some distance to the south of the village (Winchester 1993, 13–14), as shown on Figure 4.8. It almost certainly marks the site of a pre-nucleation farmstead (see Field 1993, 215), the tongueland, or tapering strip, perhaps originating as a driftway which gave access to the steading.

The woodland and moorland regions of the county provide a contrasting picture, with far more restricted areas of cultivation supporting dispersed settlements. Mary Atkin (1985) has published studies of dispersed settlements and associated oval enclosures in Leyland Hundred. The ovals frequently occurred in pairs, one arable and one pastoral, bounded in some instances by substantial hedged banks. The farmsteads associated with the arable ovals were usually

located on their periphery, and some of the land may have been held and used in common (Atkin 1985, 173). The case study presented here (Fig. 4.9), Tunley in Wrightington, is an oval that Atkin interpreted as being divided into two parts: arable to the north, pastoral to the south. Their eastern boundary is marked by massive hedgebanks. 'Aratral curves, and butt ends of strips showing in the field boundaries, ran both east-west and north-south, suggesting an interlocking pattern of arable strips of rather short length' (Atkin 1985, 175). On the other hand, two phases of growth may be represented, as is suggested by the layout of some farms.

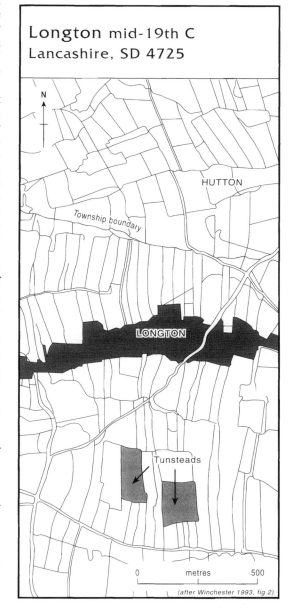

Longton mid-19th C
Lancashire, SD 4725

N

HUTTON

Township boundary

LONGTON

Tunsteads

0   metres   500

(after Winchester 1993, fig 2)

Figure 4.8

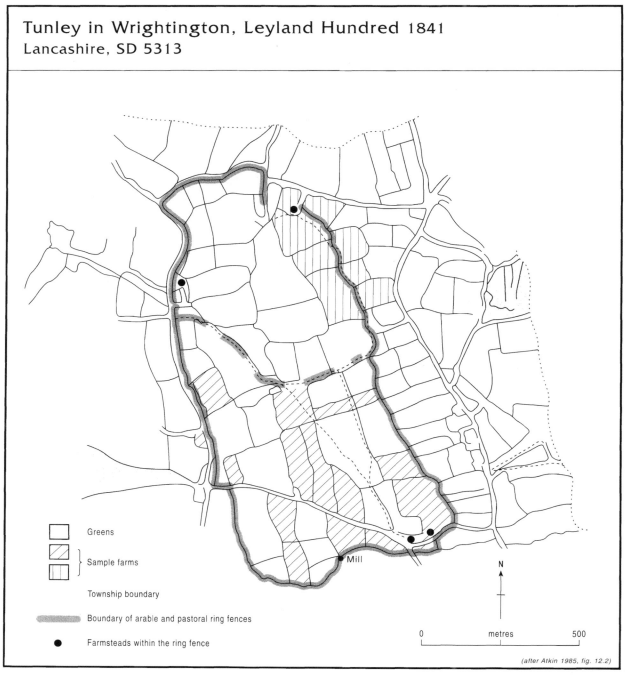

Tunley in Wrightington, Leyland Hundred 1841
Lancashire, SD 5313

Greens

Sample farms

Township boundary

Boundary of arable and pastoral ring fences

Farmsteads within the ring fence

Mill

N

0   metres   500

(after Atkin 1985, fig. 12.2)

Figure 4.9   Further south in the same county, the pattern of coastal and estuarine nucleations with inland dispersion continues. The township of Hale, on the north bank of the Mersey, contained a nucleated settlement with townfields. Immediately to its north, however, the neighbouring forest township of Halewood was dispersed. In the seventeenth and eighteenth centuries, Halewood encompassed two distinct areas: Halewood North End, alias Halewood Green, at the north-west end of the township, and Hale Bank End at the south-east end (Fig. 4.10). This division was evidently long-standing, as the two parts were in different manors and different ecclesiastical jurisdictions (Hollinshead 1981, 16). Indeed, it is reflected in a collection of thirteenth and fourteenth-century charters (Wrathmell 1992, 1–4). By the later thirteenth century the township contained a number of sub-manorial freehold estates, and some of the freeholders had houses as well as lands in the township. This is suggested by their surnames, including 'of the Bank' (or *le Bonker*) and 'of Halewood', as well as by direct and unambiguous references, such as one to land in Halewood on either side of Roger Carpenter's house. Some of the houses were probably isolated, set within their own fields: this is indicated by the archaeological record of four, possibly five isolated moats whose locations are shown on Figure 4.10. There were, however, at least two places within the wood where messuages were grouped more closely together, and where fields were in multiple ownership, subdivided into small parcels. One of these was in Hale Bank, where in 1347 William *le Bonker* leased to John of Ireland 3 acres in *Bonkerfield*. The other place is named in the medieval deeds as *Crosbyhouses*. It is a name that has not apparently survived into recent centuries, but is presumed to be the area later known

as Halewood North End. In the late thirteenth or early fourteenth century William of Halewood granted to Ralph, son of Elen, three acres in Halewood in the field called *Crosbihowsys*, between the land of Henry son of Adam and the land of Richard son of Simon.

By the eighteenth century the pattern of settlement had probably intensified, as the last vestiges of woodland were cleared. There were then about 90 houses and cottages in the township, mainly in isolated positions but still with concentrations around Halewood Green and Hale Bank End (Hollinshead 1981, 16). The manor courts still distinguished between the two ends for administrative purposes, each having a separate rota list for appointing constables and supervisors of highways (Hollinshead 1981, 30–1). When the final fragments of common land were enclosed in 1803 (Lancashire Record Office DDX 1171), what remained was largely in the

Figure 4.10

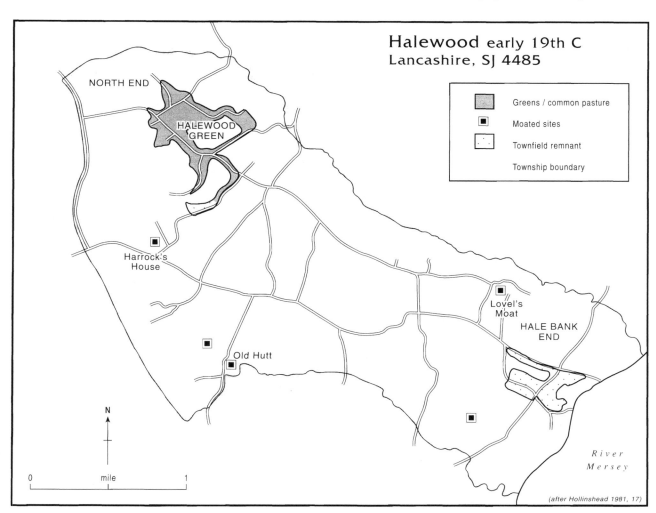

Halewood early 19th C
Lancashire, SJ 4485

Greens / common pasture

Moated sites

Townfield remnant

Township boundary

NORTH END

HALEWOOD GREEN

Harrock's House

Lovel's Moat

HALE BANK END

Old Hutt

N

0 mile 1

River Mersey

(after Hollinshead 1981, 17)

form of irregular green lanes, which were converted to standard width roads. Figure 4.10 does not show most of these strips of commons, but indicates the two most extensive areas. One was at Hale Bank End, where the shape of some of the field boundaries suggests former townfields. The other was at Halewood Green, and involved the enclosure of that green. To the south, three small parallel strips remained to be enclosed, and these might conceivably have been fragments of North End's townfields.

Moving southwards again, the rural settlement forms and field patterns of Cheshire were the subject of several publications by Dorothy Sylvester in the 1940s and 1950s. Leaving aside her speculations on the role of ethnicity in determining the various agrarian arrangements, her general conclusions could serve as a model for much of this province. There were few large villages, and these were often, though not *Figure 4.11* invariably, associated with the ecclesiastical

centres of multi-township parishes; several have *bury* names, including Astbury, Bunbury, Prestbury and Wybunbury (Sylvester 1949, 10–12, 24). She defined a type-series of townships on the basis of settlement form and agrarian structure, including nucleated hamlets with townfield, dispersed or semi-dispersed with townfield and dispersed with no townfield (Sylvester 1949, 24). There is, therefore, no clear correlation between particular forms of settlement and the existence of *some form* of open or subdivided field land. Over 250 Cheshire townships provide evidence of 'open arable lands' (Sylvester 1956, 2, 31): 'the custom of division into strips and of intermixed holdings was widely practised, not only in the arable fields but in meadows and on the peat mosses' (Sylvester 1956, 4). On the other hand, these townfields were mainly small core areas of arable, covering only a very restricted portion of the township. Beyond them were irregular patterns

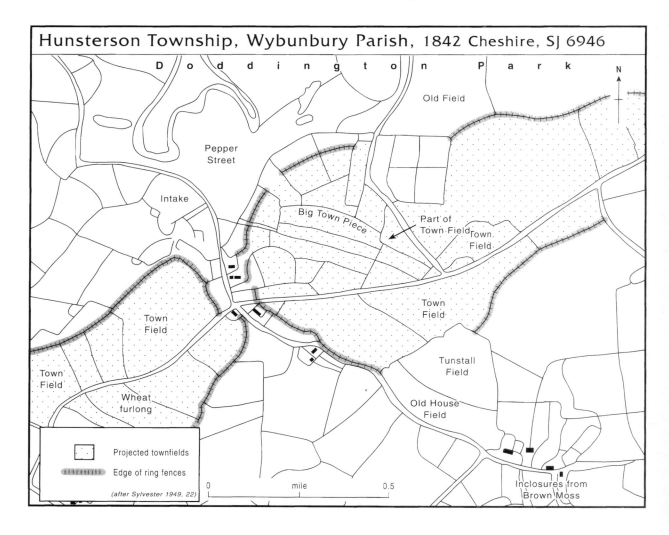

Figure 4.11

of enclosed fields, some bearing the name *ridding*, a term specifically linked to the clearing of woodland. Contemporary evidence for thirteenth and early fourteenth-century assarting is widespread, and this seems to have been a time of great fluidity in agrarian structures:

> the extension of population and new ploughlands had evidently been too rapid for adjustment to keep pace. It seems that ploughing strips were to be found in all kinds of places: fields, furlongs, crofts and riddings as well, perhaps, as bundles of two or three acres in sundry places. *(Sylvester 1956, 26)*

As at Halewood, and in common with many other parts of this province, there is no evidence as to how these townfields were managed. Our knowledge of even their extent within the township is largely post-mortem, based upon post-enclosure field shapes and the occurrence of residual *Town Field* names in Tithe surveys. The reason is that enclosure came early, relative to the main period of enclosure in the heartland of the Central Province. This is not necessarily true of the larger nucleations:

> In the villages and market towns, the custom of community ploughing seems to have been sufficiently deeply entrenched to have survived, albeit often in a decreasing area and in a smaller number of fields, until the 18th and 19th centuries. *(Sylvester 1956, 32)*

In other townships, however, especially those with dispersed settlement and small townfield cores, conversion to severalty seems to have begun as early as the fourteenth century (Sylvester 1956, 15–17, 24). The process can be associated with the county's emerging tradition of pastoral farming, especially dairy farming.

To turn to a specific case, the parish of Wybunbury, in the extreme south-east of Cheshire, encompassed 18 townships. Wybunbury township contained one of three large nucleated settlements in the parish. It had a 'Town Field, a possible outfield, open peat moss held in strips... old farms of square adjacent fields, and small, irregular hamlets on a now-enclosed heath' (Sylvester 1949, 19). Hunsterson, one of the subsidiary townships in the parish, was classified by Sylvester as 'semi-dispersed and dispersed'. Her copy of the 1842 Tithe Map (Sylvester 1949, 22) has been redrawn here as Figure 4.11. It shows

a scatter of houses around the cross-roads, and around them, evidence of former town-fields in the shapes of the fields and in the occurrence of *Town Field and Town Piece* names. There were other scattered farms, and a hamlet in the south-east part of the township was presumably established when the moss was enclosed. One possible interpretation of these patterns is that Hunsterson's arable was formerly in two townfield areas contained within elongated ovals. Their putative extents are shown on Figure 4.11. The scatter of farmsteads north and south of the crossroads could then be seen as common-side settlement peripheral to the ovals. It is impossible to say whether they were founded in medieval or later times. Two other field names, however, probably signify the former presence of one or more medieval farmsteads on the southern periphery of the larger oval. They are Old House Field and Tunstall Field, *tunstall* meaning 'farmstead, (the site of) a farm and its buildings' (Field 1993, 215).

Oval enclosures such as those identified in Lancashire and Cheshire were presumably in use in the Middle Ages, but their origins – or at least the origin of this form of agrarian structure – could be much earlier. At Roystone in the Derbyshire Peak District, the Romano-British settlement and field complex investigated by Hodges (1991) and Wildgoose (1991) is remarkably similar to those recorded by Atkin in Lancashire. A detailed typological analysis of field walls in the area of Roystone led to the identification of the pair of conjoined, oval enclosures shown on Figure 4.12. Atkin has already compared this with a very similar pair of medieval enclosures at Goosnargh in Lancashire, covering about twice the area of Roystone (Atkin 1985, fig. 12.4). Even the suggested agrarian regimes expressed in these structures are comparable. The Lancashire ovals are thought to have had different functions: one for arable, one pastoral (Atkin 1985, 173–5). At Roystone the western oval, which contained on its margin the settlement site, was thought to have been used for stock; the eastern oval, 'by contrast, appears to have been parcelled up into fields. Some of these fields resembled strips...' (Wildgoose 1991, 227). Furthermore, the ovals were partly defined by circumferential trackways as well as by walls, just as the Lancashire ovals were often defined by lanes as well as hedge banks (see Atkin 1985, 173). The longevity of agrarian structures is a matter that will be considered again in relation to the South-eastern Province and in the concluding section of this chapter.

The Shropshire case study, the township of Wheathill (Fig. 4.13), is based upon the published work of the RCHM(E) (Everson and Wilson-North 1993). It has been selected because it represents another region, like Cumbria and Kent, where deserted medieval villages have, in the past, been pursued too assiduously: none of the proposed deserted medieval village sites in the parish – Wheathill itself, Egerton, Bradley's Farm or Cold Green Farm – is ever likely to have supported a village settlement. The nineteenth-century settlement pattern, of individual farmsteads and small hamlets, 'though not static is probably of some antiquity' (Everson and Wilson-North 1993, 65–6). The settlements recorded in medieval times were Wheathill, Egerton and Bromdon. Egerton was recorded as a separate vill in 1316, though under the lord

Figure 4.12

of Wheathill, and in 1324 Roger of Bromdon gave lands and tenements in Egerton to John of Bromdon. The 1327 Lay Subsidy entry for Wheathill lists its lord, Walter Hacket, John of Bromdon and Johanna of Egerton, together with two other payers who might have lived in any of these settlements. Alternatively, one of the unattributed taxpayers may represent *Leverdegrene*, a place recorded in the twelfth century which is possibly to be identified with the nineteenth-century farmstead called The Green, at 'a common-edge location at the eastern funnel-shaped end of Cold Green Common' (Everson and Wilson-North 1993, 65–6, 69–70).

Wheathill itself contains Wheathill Court and a church recorded in the twelfth century as a dependent chapel of Stottesdon minster (Croom 1988, 74): it should perhaps be categorised as a hall-church focus. Egerton is an abandoned settlement, but may formerly have contained two or

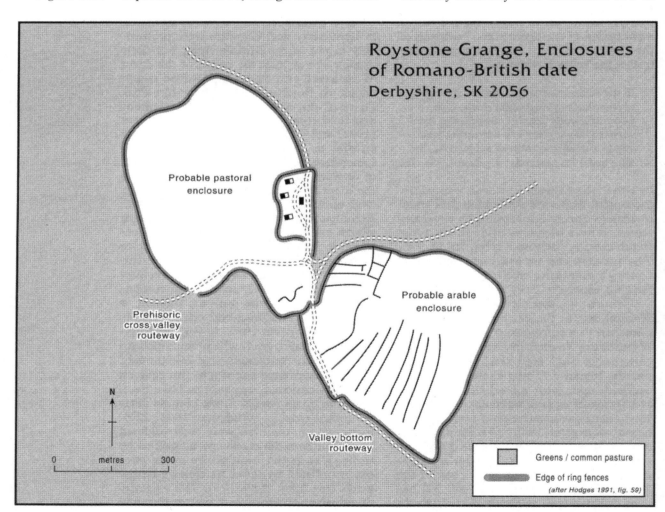

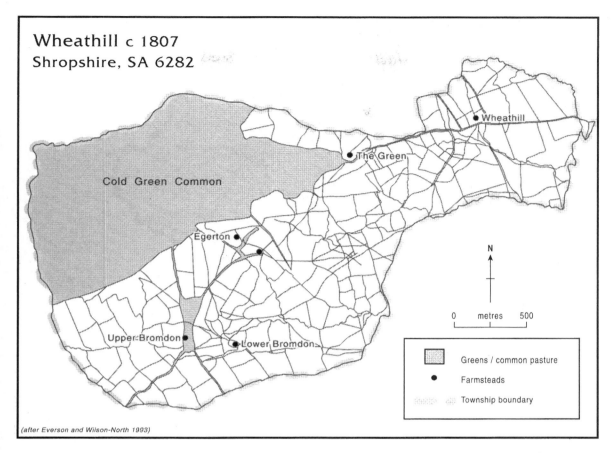

Wheathill c 1807
Shropshire, SA 6282

Cold Green Common

Wheathill

The Green

Egerton

Upper Bromdon

Lower Bromdon

N

0   metres   500

Greens / common pasture

Farmsteads

Township boundary

(after Everson and Wilson-North 1993)

three farmsteads. It, too, could have had a common-edge location in the Middle Ages, given that the extent of Cold Green Common on Figure 4.13 is, minus encroachments, what survived in 1807 (Everson and Wilson-North 1993, 66–9). Bromdon, to the south of Egerton, was two farms in the late nineteenth century: Everson and Wilson-North suggest Lower Bromdon as the medieval site. The field boundaries and tracks shown on the 1883 OS 6 inch map hint at a former green running northwards from Upper Bromdon farmstead. Everson and Wilson-North conclude that:

> the medieval pattern was one of isolated farmsteads or small hamlets scattered across the landscape ... The numerical correspondence of five holdings [in Domesday Book] with the five persons taxed in the early 14th century is striking and suggests that the later settlement pattern was already established by the 11th century.
> *(Everson and Wilson-North 1993, 70)*

It is a conclusion which serves as a strikingly appropriate introduction to a case-study from the south-western portion of the province: Rashleigh in Devon.

Rashleigh, in the parish of Wembworthy, was included by W G Hoskins in a study of Domesday manors in the Highland Zone. His aim was to determine how units larger than the single farmstead, but without a known village settlement, might have been constituted on the ground in 1086 (Hoskins 1963, 21). He concluded that, in Devon, 'the pattern of settlement in 1086 was virtually what it is today. There have been no significant changes' (Hoskins 1963, 45). The name Rashleigh means 'at the ash wood or clearing' (Gover, Mawer and Stenton 1932, 372), indicating that in later Anglo-Saxon times this was a wooded countryside experiencing clearance. The Domesday survey records a manor with five villeins, three slaves, five bordars and two swineherds, and Hoskins sought to identify these with the various farmsteads and hamlets depicted on a map of the manor of 1769 (Devon County Record Office 211M/P5). This same map has been used, along with the first edition Six Inch Ordnance Survey map, to create Figure 4.14. The manorial holding, where Hoskins

Figure 4.13

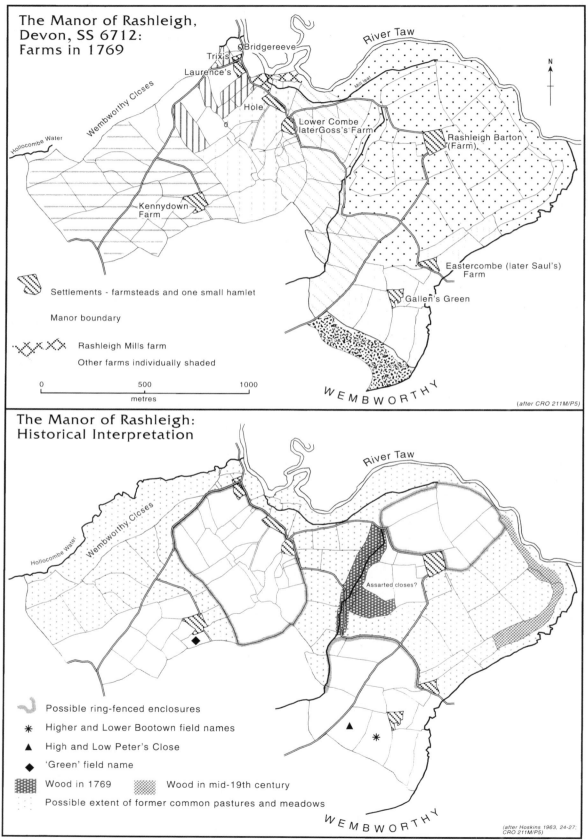

The Manor of Rashleigh,
Devon, SS 6712:
Farms in 1769

River Taw

Bridgereeve
Trixs
Laurence's
Wembworthy Closes
Hollocombe Water
Mill leat
Hole
Lower Combe
(laterGoss's Farm
Rashleigh Barton
(Farm)
Kennydown
Farm
Eastercombe (later Saul's)
Farm
Gallen's Green

N

Settlements - farmsteads and one small hamlet

Manor boundary

Rashleigh Mills farm

Other farms individually shaded

0   500   1000
metres

WEMBWORTHY

(after CRO 211M/P5)

The Manor of Rashleigh:
Historical Interpretation

River Taw

Wembworthy Closes
Hollocombe Water
Assarted closes?

Possible ring-fenced enclosures

* Higher and Lower Bootown field names

▲ High and Low Peter's Close

◆ 'Green' field name

Wood in 1769   Wood in mid-19th century

Possible extent of former common pastures and meadows

WEMBWORTHY

(after Hoskins 1963, 24-27;
CRO 211M/P5)

Figure 4.14

suggested the slaves should be located, was represented in 1769 by Rashleigh Barton, then comprising a mansion house and chapel. Its farmhold, at over 220 acres, amounted to about a third of the total area of the estate, just as, at Domesday, it had been rated at one virgate out of three (Hoskins 1963, 25–6).

Hoskins also identified the other farms, all much smaller, with the five villeins holding two virgates in 1086. These were Saul's Farm, known as Eastercombe in the Middle Ages, Goss's Farm, formerly Lower Combe, Kennydown, Hole and Bridge Farms. By 1769 Bridge Farm had been divided into two equal parts: Lawrence's Farm and Trix's Farm. A group of three cottages at Gallen's Green, each with a share of the small green there, were suggested as 'the lineal descendant of the small colony of five bordar households in 1086 (Hoskins 1963, 25–7). In 1769 two fields immediately adjacent to Gallen's Green bore the name 'Bootown', We suggest a link with the Middle English word *boie*, meaning 'boy' or 'servant' (Smith 1956, 40). A 'settlement of servants' would accord with Hoskins' suggestion.

Whilst accepting Hoskins's general conclusions, it is possible, from analysis of the 1769 map, to suggest further developmental stages in Rashleigh's agrarian structure. Clearly, as Hoskins noted, the proportions of the township in demesne and in tenant holdings were broadly the same in 1086 and 1769. This does not, however, mean that these units covered the same amount of land at those two dates. Beginning with the Barton: in 1769 it contained woodland on the north-east and north-west fringes of the estate, on the slopes of valleys. Another stretch of woodland, Westerwood, occupied a valley, perhaps 'Westercombe', on the west side of the farm. No doubt these, presumably more extensive and perhaps accompanied by further woodland at the southern edge of the estate, provided the eleventh-century swineherds with a living. The settlement at Eastercombe, a farmstead and cottage in 1769, may have been located on the margin of the Barton ring fence, once that had reached its maximum extent. It is, however, conceivable that the Barton ring-fenced land was originally a much smaller oval of arable on the north side of the settlement, as indicated on Figure 4.14.

The tenanted farms, the areas of which are shown on Figure 4.14, may also, at an early stage, have been confined to a smaller oval ring-fenced area defined by trackways and primary field boundaries. In 1769 this oval contained the whole or parts of Trix's and Lawrence's Farms, Hole Farm and Lower Combe Farm. The steadings of the first two of these were sited at Bridgereeve, a hamlet at the north end of the oval which also contained a couple of cottages. Hole and Lower Combe were located to the south-east, but again on the margin of the oval. The oval itself contained the intermixed lands of Trix's and Lawrence's, and the field boundaries hint at an even greater mix of lands in earlier times. Added to this, some of the fields had names including the word 'quillet', signifying small parcels or strips within an enclosed field (Slater 1907, 42).

In this reading, the tenant farmsteads may, at an earlier stage, have had all their arable lands intermixed in the oval, with their farmsteads on the margins to allow easy access to different resources. To the north-east of the oval were the shared meadow lands along the river Taw; elsewhere, there would have been tracts of open and woodland pasture, and to the east the Barton ring-fence farm. Gallen's Green may well have supported the group of medieval smallholdings described by Hoskins. Though in 1769 the cottages and green were wholly surrounded by the fields of Saul's Farm, two of these fields south-west of the green were called High and Low Peter's Closes; and one of the Gallen's Green cottages was called John Peter's cottage. It may be that the cottage holdings had earlier been rather larger than they were in 1769, incorporating some of the surrounding small fields. Kennydown Farm may have originated from a similar arrangement, as the fields immediately south of the steading bore the name 'green'. At this stage we can go no further with interpretation, but this reading would imply far more dynamism in Rashleigh's agrarian structures than Hoskins supposed. It should be noted that we have attached no chronology to any of the suggested changes.

Rashleigh is our final case study from the Northern and Western Province, and it is worth noting, in conclusion, that many of its features, described and inferred, bear comparison with structures much further north. In particular, the disposition of tenant lands and steadings in relation to the 'tenant oval' is strikingly similar to that already described at Tunley in Lancashire. Similarly, other aspects, such as ring-fenced

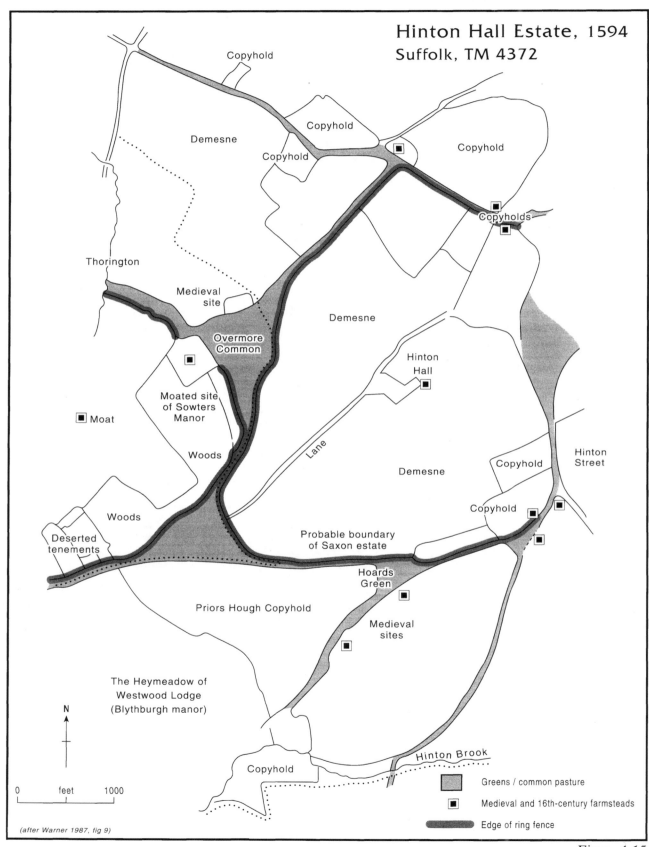

Figure 4.15

demesne farmsteads and marginal tenant holdings associated with greens, are ones that will appear again in the case studies from the South-eastern Province.

Structures of the South-eastern Province

The review of settlement in the South-eastern Province concentrates on East Anglia, where various scholars have carried out and published impressive research over several decades. The agrarian structures they have identified bear close resemblance to many of those that have been described in the Northern and Western Province. One of the Norfolk structures, the oval at Stanfield (Wade-Martins 1980, 49–52), has been reserved for discussion in a comparative study with Whittlesford, later in this chapter. In Suffolk, Peter Warner has recognised 'hall-farm' cores as primary settlements, along with secondary and more transient settlements along the fringes of greens and commons between the primary blocks (Warner 1987, 29). Hinton (Fig. 4.15) is one of his examples of primary settlement. The core is a hall standing alone in the centre of the estate (perhaps itself comprising a core area and an extension to the north-west) reached by a long trackway that passes through the middle of the demesne. The demesne was enclosed by a long, curving ring-fence boundary that Warner believes may be Anglo-Saxon or earlier. It 'fits into a pattern of similar curving boundaries and triangular greens and commons on the clay land side of the estate', and predates the establishment of tenements on the edge of those greens and commons (Warner 1987, 31). A group of tenements at Hinton Street, bordering the commons on the edge of the estate, may have originated in the six freeholds that Domesday records as being attached to Hinton. Other tenements, singly and in clusters, were scattered elsewhere on the periphery of the estate, along the fringes of triangular commons, at the interstices of Hinton and neighbouring estates.

This kind of structure is very similar to that already described at Mirfield, West Yorkshire, in the CPNSL sub-province, which was originally part of the Northern and Western Province: the hall-church core and secondary settlements along the lanes and common edges. Even more striking, perhaps, is the similarity of structures that Warner has defined as 'secondary parishes'. These appear to have had only small 'core' areas, and to have been focused much more on the secondary green-side settlements. Linstead Parva is one of them (Fig. 4.16). In many cases they are 'demonstrably late creations. Some are sub-divisions of more ancient mother-church territories ... they appear as a rationalisation of a parish

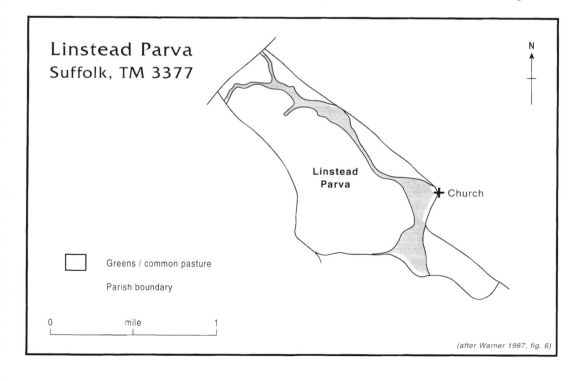

Linstead Parva
Suffolk, TM 3377

Linstead Parva

✝ Church

□ Greens / common pasture

Parish boundary

0   mile   1

(after Warner 1987, fig. 6)

Figure 4.16

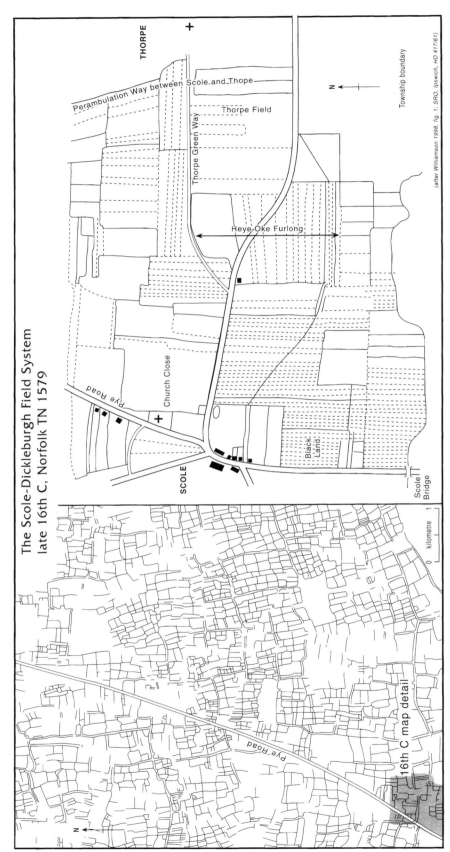

Figure 4.17

pattern which had been overtaken by settlement development on green-side sites' (Warner 1987, 17). Linstead Parva is mirrored by Hartshead, near Mirfield (Fig. 4.5), which seems also to have served green-side development. The church at Hartshead was established in the twelfth century as the centre of a chapelry carved out of the extensive *parochia* of Dewsbury's Anglo-Saxon minster. Once again the parallels are clear.

The case studies selected thus far have been intended to show the remarkable degree of similarity between agrarian structures in the two outer provinces. There are, however, significant tracts of the South-eastern Province where the layout of fields and lanes owes much to a larger, rectilinear scheme of land division – so-called 'co-axial' field systems. The evidence has been summarised by Tom Williamson:

> The essential pattern of boundaries and roads displayed a measure of regularity, suggesting organisation at a scale larger than that of the medieval manor, vill or parish. Moreover, in some places such structured frameworks were apparently slighted by Roman roads, suggesting – following the normal rules of horizontal stratigraphy – that they must pre-date them.
> *(Williamson 1998, 19)*

These 'structured frameworks' have been explored in southern Essex (Rippon 1991), in north Suffolk (Warner 1996, 44–53) and in south Norfolk (Williamson 1998). There has been much debate about their dating, with Rippon opting for an Anglo-Saxon origin for his Essex patterns (Rippon 1991, 53, 57), rather than the alternative late Iron Age or early Roman date suggested for those frameworks which appear to ignore the alignments of Roman roads.

In many ways the evolution of ideas about these rectilinear systems, in terms of both dating and composition, has been shaped by scale changes in the various regional studies. Rippon analysed the broad patterns in southern Essex, rather than focusing in on their more regular parts, and he modelled the processes of expansion, regression and recolonisation which might have led to the evident shifts in axial alignment over the various blocks (Rippon 1991, 41). Similarly, in south Norfolk and north Suffolk, Warner mapped the broad pattern of long-distance lanes and droveways that frame and link the impressive rectilinear

systems of Scole-Dickleburgh and South Elmham-Ilketshall (Warner 1996, figs. 3.4, 3.6). He compared these long-distance lanes with the transhumance droveways that crossed the North Downs of Kent and gave access to the wood-pastures of the Weald (Everitt 1986, 36). He also noted the difference between the very long trackways on the flat clay interfluves on either side of the Waveney Valley, and the shorter lanes which run at right-angles to the more diverse river systems further south (Warner 1996, 48–9). Though the rectilinear systems were oblivious to small-scale variations in terrain (Williamson 1998, 23), they have, nevertheless, a clear *broad* correlation with terrain, because the lanes which frame them were designed to give access to the varied agrarian resources which were themselves structured by terrain and soils. As Williamson has acknowledged, whilst at least some of these lanes are evidently pre-Roman, many of the field boundaries which form the infill between them could be medieval or even post-medieval (Williamson 1998, 26).

The way in which these rectilinear patterns informed the agrarian structures of medieval communities is explored in the next case study, the vill of Scole on the Norfolk-Suffolk boundary. Williamson (1998, fig. 1) has mapped the rectilinear pattern of fields and lanes known as the 'Scole-Dickleburgh field system', which appears to ignore and therefore predate the alignment of the Roman road now called Pye Road (Fig. 4.17). A plan of the later sixteenth century shows open-field furlongs and parcels intermixed with closes, between Pye Road and the adjacent vill of Thorpe Parva (Suffolk Record Office, Ipswich, HD 417/61). Whatever the inaccuracies of the alignments shown on the plan, it seems clear that the course of Pye Road north of the junction at Scole had remarkably little impact on the orientation of adjacent boundaries, for example those of the closes around the church. In the face of this evidence, it is hard to escape the conclusion that not only the wider network of lanes but also the more detailed land division recorded on the plan was in place before construction of the Roman road. Some of the rectilinear enclosure boundaries may, therefore, have survived from prehistoric times, in much the same way as has been claimed for some furlong boundaries at Caxton in Cambridgeshire (Oosthuizen 1997). Others may, however, have a less direct relationship to the pre-medieval land divisions: they may represent the piecemeal amalgamation and enclosure of adjacent open-field strips whose alignment was itself determined by the alignment of prehistoric boundaries.

Of the other roads shown on the plan, the two running eastwards from Scole follow furlong boundaries in some stretches, but in others cut through the open-field parcels diagonally. Only the enclosure in the fork between the highway (*via regia*) and Thorpe Green Way seems to have been influenced by them in its alignment. Similarly, what appears to be an earlier, abandoned line of the *via regia*, to the south of the road as marked, seems also to have followed furlong alignments in some places but to have cut across open-field parcels in others. The township boundary, described as the perambulation way between Scole and Thorpe, has similar characteristics, zigzagging around some of the closes but also cutting through some of the open-field strips. Were the roads and township boundary later than the open-field strips, as well as being later than the rectilinear boundary patterns? This is, after all, what a simple reading of the stratigraphic evidence would indicate. Whatever the circumstances leading to the preservation of such early rectilinear frameworks, their impact upon medieval agrarian structures was superficial rather than fundamental. The frameworks housed dispersed settlement, some of it clustered around greens. Some of the greens appear to have obliterated blocks of rectilinear enclosures; others were irregular in shape and caused local contortions in the grid. This can be seen in the South Elmham-Ilketshall system which, as Rackham remarked, had 'inserted into it ... the usual medieval furniture of greens, parish boundaries, scattered farmsteads, churches, and at least 23 moats' (Rackham 1986, 158). It contained, in short, settlement elements similar to those in the parts of Suffolk where curvilinear rather than rectilinear patterns dominated. The curvilinear patterns may themselves, of course, be pre-medieval in some cases (Warner 1996, 46–7, 52).

The South-eastern Province case studies presented so far are all from East Anglia: the aim here has been to sample variation and uniformity in agrarian structures across the provinces, not to attempt a synthetic study embracing all regions. Nevertheless, an obvious line of further enquiry will now be to determine whether the patterns observed in East Anglia were also widespread in other parts of the South-eastern Province. There are, indeed, indications of comparable patterns. Warner's comparison of droveway lanes in Suffolk with those in Kent has already been noted. Alan Everitt's map of the droveways crossing the Kent downland shows long, roughly parallel, sinuous tracks between half a mile and a mile apart – a spacing roughly in accordance with the Scole-Dickleburgh trackways. Furthermore he, too, has postulated a pre-medieval date for their creation (Everitt 1986, 36–9). The form of Kentish medieval settlement was isolated farms and hamlets, with numerous isolated parish churches. Though there were once many places with subdivided fields, these were not communally organised like those in the Midlands. There is also evidence of late green-side settlement (Everitt 1986, 39–42). Similar droveways to those in Kent can be seen in Sussex, for example in the Burgess Hill area, providing access to the clay weald commons (Warne 1985, figs 1 and 2). They became a focus for marginal settlement including, at St John's Common, a chapel that may be late medieval (Warne 1985, 132–3). Further west, in the area around Basingstoke, Hampshire, yet more common-edge settlement has been identified, some of it represented by sixteenth-century hall houses. The vill of Lockerley is said to comprise 'several large greens around which there are farms and cottages. These elements link together to inclose a large sub-circular area within which there is evidence for open field strips' (Edwards 1995, 12). The applicability of this description to many of the case studies in both outer provinces hardly needs further emphasis.

Comparisons between provincial border zones

If the Central Province of predominantly nucleated settlement with regular open fields has superseded irregular, dispersed farming structures, then we might expect that, at an appropriate scale of analysis, the earlier pattern will reveal itself as a continuous archaeological record beneath the more recent layer of deserted medieval villages and associated townfield ridges and furlongs. With records such as those for Butterwick, discussed above, we can hope to analyse the replacement of one agrarian structure by another, but we shall not observe interaction between the two. For that we must turn instead to the fringes of the Central Province, to the locations where nucleations intrude upon dispersed patterns but do not entirely obliterate them. One such area is south-west Cambridgeshire, on the eastern margin of the Central Province. Here, there is evidence for the intrusion of nucleations into a surviving framework of dispersed settlement. The other area is the Craven region of Yorkshire, which provides similar evidence.

The Case of Whittlesford

In 1989, Christopher Taylor published an account of the evolution of his thinking on the origins and development of Whittlesford, his home village in west Cambridgeshire. He demonstrated, with an enviable measure of intellectual self-awareness, how his understanding of what Whittlesford represented had been shaped, and re-shaped on a number of occasions, by his experiences of investigating other rural settlements. Whittlesford became 'not so much the study of the development of a village, but more the development of the mind' (Taylor 1989, 209). He also issued a challenge: 'to develop new and stable concepts to replace the traditional and obviously outmoded ones' (Taylor 1989, 227). The two major research problems at Whittlesford appear to be the chronology of occupation in various parts of the settlement area, and the relationship between population estimates and the extent (and density) of settlement at various points during the Middle Ages (Taylor 1989, 213–14, 219).

Until recent expansion, Whittlesford comprised the units of settlement shown in Figure 4.18 . There was a discrete hall-church focus near the River Cam and, to the south-west, nucleated settlement along High Street and West End. A further scatter of farms extended along North Road and at Middle Moor, at the north-west end of North Road. Field evidence, in the form of earthworks and pottery scatters, has indicated thirteenth and fourteenth-century occupation for most of the length of North Road, along the Middle Moor road and at the west end of West End, as well as in the gap between the church and High Street. In our reading, a key aspect of Whittlesford's layout is that the projected pattern of medieval habitation seems to be determined by a series of linked trackways, roughly

defining an oval area. The oval marks an area of gravel which was completely surrounded by ill-drained marshlands: it may be the 'island' (*eg*) which has been detected in the name *Rye Croft* (C C Taylor, pers. comm.; see also Gelling 1984, 36–7). Rye Croft was a relatively small area of open field, enclosed in the early nineteenth century along with the larger Bridge Field (south of the village), Stone Hill Field (west of Bridge Field), and Bar Field (north of Stone Hill Field). Also enclosed at that time were the common grazings of Middle Moor and Mitch Moor (copy of 1812 enclosure map in Cambridgeshire County Record Office, courtesy of C C Taylor). The course of High Street south-westwards, beyond its junction with the road through West End, seems on the enclosure map to be taken up by the curving line of a series of field boundaries. On present evidence it is at least conceivable that this once marked the southern boundary of another area of common grazing, the northern edge being the line of the present road through West End. There is some evidence for successive reductions in the size of 'The Green' at West End (Taylor 1989, 222).

Ignoring for the moment the nucleation on High Street-West End, the general pattern of fields, commons and farmsteads is very similar to agrarian structures recorded in the South-eastern Province. To exemplify the similarities we have chosen Stanfield in Norfolk (Fig. 4.19), one of the settlements in Launditch Hundred published by Peter Wade-Martins (1980). There is a hall-church focus, on the edge of what was clearly an oval of subdivided fields which seem to have continued south of the oval. The oval was partly defined by trackways, partly by common grazing land (Wade-Martins 1980, 50). Medieval pottery was recovered from various fields, though not in any great quantity. Nevertheless, Wade-Martins regarded it as sufficient to postulate areas of former occupation along the lane leading westwards from the church, and along the margins of the commons where that lane or driftway had formerly funnelled outwards into the large area of common (Wade-Martins 1980, 51–2). This pattern, repeated in other Norfolk parishes, can also be detected at Whittlesford *if one ignores the nucleation*: the two townships are comparable both in structural form and in scale. Was the settlement along Whittlesford High Street, exhibiting features consistent with 'planning' (Taylor 1989, 225), planted into an agrarian structure similar to Stanfield's? The alignment of the village crofts along High Street would be consistent with parcels of former open-field strips, taken out of a core open field extending from Rye Croft into Bridge Field. The

incorporation of Stone Hill Field and Bar Field into the open-field system might have occurred when the High Street village was planted on the arable, and when the West End Green came to be occupied by increasing numbers of dwellings. Taylor

Figure 4.18

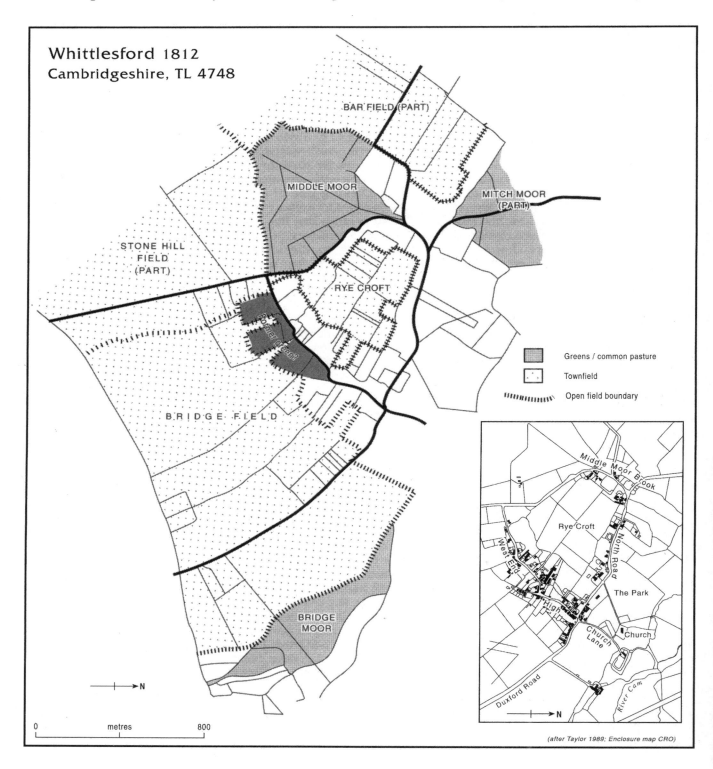

noted the massive, three or fourfold increase in the population of Whittlesford between Domesday and 1279 (Taylor 1989, 213). This could be explicable as a short-term event rather than as gradual growth, if the village had been intruded into the township in the twelfth or thirteenth century. Making no allowance for differences in soils, terrain or tenure it is interesting to observe that the 1334 lay subsidy assessment for Whittlesford was three times the size of that for Stanfield (Glasscock 1975, 27, 207). This is, surely, to some degree a measure of the impact of nucleation.

Is there, finally, any indication that the development proposed here for Whittlesford was experienced in other Cambridgeshire communities? There is at least one possibly comparable example at Haslingfield, north-west of Whittlesford. The RCHM(E) inventory for Haslingfield notes that the main village area, articulated by the High Street, occupies 'an oval area of about 100 acres, the perimeter of which is outlined by lanes' (RCHME 1968, 136). The same entry offers the suggestion that the oval had formerly been a green, but the accompanying plan shows a number of field divisions within the oval reminiscent of parcels of former open-field. This is, therefore, another *prima facie* case of a nucleation being intruded into an arable oval. The medieval parish church of All Saints, though it stands at the south-west end of the village, also adjoins the lane which marks the perimeter of the oval on the south and west sides. It may, therefore, have originally related to perimeter settlement rather than to a village within the oval. It has been suggested that the large ovals in the adjacent parishes of Haslingfield, Barrington and Harlton are related to the control of this area by a specific Anglo-Saxon population group, the *Haeslingas* (Oosthuizen 1998, 103). The argument here is that such ovals are far more widespread than such a conclusion would imply, and reflect the agrarian arrangements of

Figure 4.19

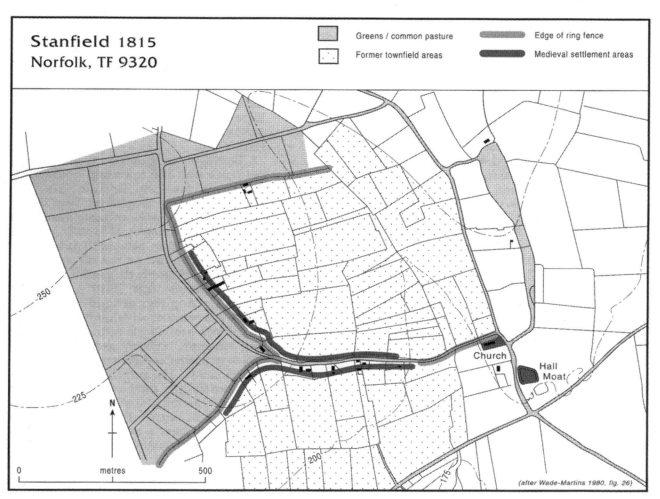

Stanfield 1815
Norfolk, TF 9320

Greens / common pasture

Former townfield areas

Edge of ring fence

Medieval settlement areas

0   metres   500

N

(after Wade-Martins 1980, fig. 26)

people in western as well as eastern England.

The case of Marton

Craven is a region, nominally in the Northern and Western Province, where nucleated settlements have spilled over the Central Provincial boundary, through the Aire Gap into Ribblesdale. Some of the vills in Upper Airedale acquired nucleated settlements, and others did not. In the ecclesiastical parish of Marton-in-Craven, about 8 km west of Skipton, we can infer a partial nucleation of what had earlier been wholly dispersed settlement (Fig. 4.20). In the mid-nineteenth century Marton was composed of three townships whose sizes and settlements varied considerably: West Marton, which had a village settlement, amounted to 1885 statute acres; East Marton, covering 729 acres, contained dispersed settlement, and Ingthorpe Grange was a single farm of 189 acres (OS First Edition, Six Inch Map; surveyed 1848–50). The medieval records for the parish provide, we argue, a reasonably convincing picture of how this mix of settlement came about; and crucial to the argument is the evidence for Marton's fiscal assessment in terms of carucates, or ploughlands, at the time of Domesday Book and later.

We have not identified any document that gives us the individual carucages for East and West Marton, but the two together were assessed at 9 carucates in a series of records from 1166 to the mid-sixteenth century (Clay 1947, 233; *Feudal Aids*, VI, 8; Yorkshire Archaeological Society DD1 21/29/3). Ingthorpe's assessment, at 2 carucates, seems similarly to have remained static during that period (Brown 1906, 101; Clay 1947, 241; Kershaw 1970, 14–15). The picture changes, however, when we work back to the relevant Domesday entries. *Martun* was recorded there as three manors which had been in the hands of Archil, Orm and Ernebrand, and was assessed at 6 carucates; *Vcnetorp* was in two manors, which had been in the hands of Uctred and Archil, and was assessed at 2 carucates (Faull and Stinson 1986, 30W26, 27). The inference is that between 1086 and 1166 the fiscal assessment of Ingthorpe remained static, whilst that for Marton increased by 50%. Can this substantial increase be linked to the apparent recording of only one *Martun* in Domesday Book, and

the occurrence of two Martons in later documents? To attempt to explore this question further, we can usefully draw in a few other strands of evidence.

The most impressive archaeological remains in the parish are those of the manorial homestead of the Marton family, which survives as a group of prominent rectilinear earthworks in East Marton, close to the medieval parish church. There are further earthworks, possibly representing fishponds, nearby, but nothing to indicate a deserted village settlement: this was clearly a hall-church focus of dispersed settlement. The church itself is first recorded in 1152–3 when the existing chapel gained parochial status (Farrer 1916, no.1471). The place-name *Martun* refers to a pool (Smith 1961b, 39), no doubt the large pool which lies (now dry) a short distance to the east of the hall and church. It is conceivable that the Domesday entry *Martun* subsumes what were already two separate vills of East and West Marton. For the purposes of our current hypothesis, however, we have taken the information at its face value: that there was one township of Marton at Domesday (along with Ingthorpe). Given this, the focus of Marton vill was undoubtedly the hall-church complex at East Marton, whereas the vill and village of West Marton are best interpreted as a later offshoot. This hypothesis is supported by a reference in 1284-5 to *Morton cum West Morton* (*Feudal Aids*, VI, 8).

There is, in general terms, strong evidence that the township boundaries shown on the First Edition, Six Inch Ordnance Survey maps of the West Riding are surviving medieval township boundaries (Faull and Moorhouse 1981, 17), and the township boundary between East and West Marton, as shown on the relevant map, indicates quite clearly the partitioning of an earlier, larger unit (Fig. 4.19). The boundary dog-legs around rectangular fields in a manner which indicates that it was drawn around, or through, an earlier field structure, probably open-field furlongs which were later consolidated into enclosed, several fields. The pattern of field boundaries generally in these townships indicates open-field farming over much of West and some of East Marton. Furthermore, in West Marton village, a two-row village on a north-south axis now partly obscured by the east-west Turnpike road, the crofts appear to follow the same alignment as the boundaries marking consolidated open-field strips behind them. It seems, in short, that the village may have been formed along a boundary between adjacent, pre-existing furlongs.

To sum up, the hypothesis we propose for the mixed settlement in Marton parish is as follows. At Domesday there was one large vill of Marton with a smaller, probably offshoot township of Ingthorpe. Marton had dispersed settlement, with a hall-church focus, and Ingthorpe was presum-ably either a single, small hamlet (it later became a monastic grange) or a series of dispersed farms. Marton already had open-fields of some kind. By 1166 Marton had been split into two townships, the new part having a village settlement created in former open-field land. The creation of the new unit should presumably be related to an intensification in arable cultivation: its impact can be seen in the 50% increase in the Martons' carucage. A feature of the

Figure 4.20

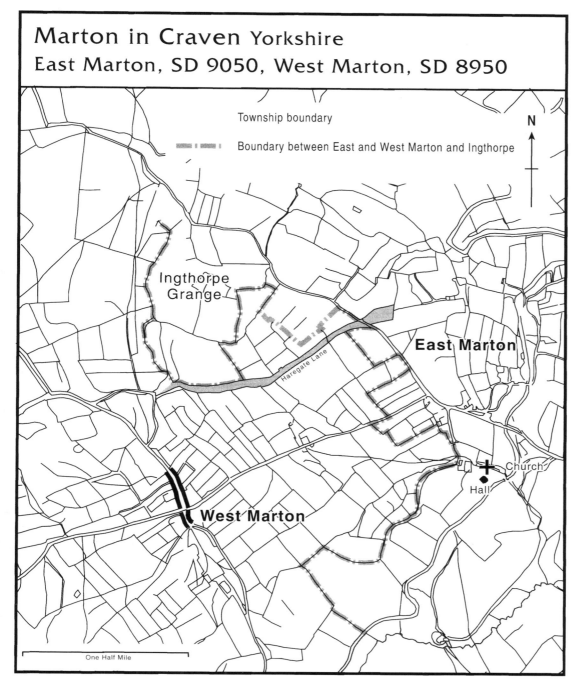

Marton in Craven Yorkshire
East Marton, SD 9050, West Marton, SD 8950

Township boundary

Boundary between East and West Marton and Ingthorpe

N

Ingthorpe Grange

East Marton

Haregate Lane

Church

Hall

West Marton

One Half Mile

creation of villages, or parts of villages, *de novo* is that it is often marked by the imposition of uniform bovate holdings. Though evidence of the full tenurial composition of East and West Marton has not been assembled, there does seem to have been a significant frequency of two bovate holdings in West Marton, even as late as the sixteenth century (Yorkshire Archaeological Society, DD121/29/3). There remains the question of when the split (and the creation of a village) took place. The first certain reference to two Martons is in the document establishing Marton chapel as a parish church: it refers to *'jus parochiale de utraque Marton...'* (Farrer 1916, no.1471). This document has been dated to 1152–3 (Gurney and Clay 1971, 19). Therefore, nucleation is likely to have taken place between 1086 and 1153.

The implication of this line of argument is that there may be a close relationship between changes in the assessment of carucage, and changes to the level of arable exploitation in a vill. Furthermore, whilst some changes may be the result of reorganising field systems, others may signify township splitting and the planting of nucleations. This is not the place to explore such issues further, except to note that much information on the organisation and reorganisation of settlements and fields may lie buried in Domesday Book, again under the guise of changes in assessments of ploughs and ploughlands. Reductions may in some cases signify township splitting rather than difficult times; significant increases may mark village plantation and extension.

The dating of agrarian structures in the outer provinces

These case studies have provided descriptions of select agrarian structures, but have offered little information on their origins and chronological development. As noted above, the oval enclosures at Roystone, Derbyshire, seem to indicate that such structures were being created and/or used in the Romano-British period, and it may be that some of the other examples described here go back at least this far, as Warner has suggested for Suffolk. There is, however, no reason to suppose that all predate the Middle Ages: the oval form is most readily interpreted as a 'primary' agrarian structure, unconstrained by any pre-existing boundaries in a particular locality.

One region in which an early medieval origin can be reliably inferred is the North Somerset Levels. Environmental evidence suggests that reclamation in the Roman period was followed by inundation in post-Roman times, to be succeeded by a new reclamation in the early medieval period (Rippon 1998, 78). Stephen Rippon's extensive research has led him to define a series of reclamation episodes in medieval and later times on the basis of field morphology. The earliest, in the higher, coastal areas, is typified by irregularly shaped fields that often incorporate the meandering lines of watercourses:

> Other characteristics include sinuous droveways with an abundance of roadside waste and funnel-shaped commons ... Settlement was abundant, usually dispersed, and occasionally associated with small, oval-shaped enclosures defined in the pattern of field boundaries. *(Rippon 1997, 149)*

He identifies these ovals, which he calls 'infields', as 'the earliest reclamations/settlement sites in a newly recolonised marsh' (Rippon 1997, 172).

One such oval, named Church Field, is at Puxton, a manor that Rippon has investigated in considerable detail (Fig. 4.21). On what may have been its northern fringe stands a medieval church, built (or perhaps rebuilt) in the late thirteenth or early fourteenth century (Rippon 1998, 75). Immediately south-east of the church is a raised platform which Rippon has shown to be an early occupation site. Ceramic evidence indicates it was used from the tenth century until abandonment in the thirteenth century. Since, however, post-Roman Somerset was aceramic until the tenth century, a significantly earlier start date cannot be ruled out. The rest of Church Field contained small fields and paddocks (Rippon 1998, 69). There is some evidence, from aerial photographs, that the earthworks bounding the 'oval' had originally continued much further west and north (Fig. 4.21), perhaps defining a much larger original 'infield', extending almost to Mays Lane. Beyond Mays Lane was a further group of settlement earthworks, including building platforms, along the road running northwards from the church. The more southerly platform bordered a triangular area of roadside common enclosed in 1816. Excavation has indicated that settlement in this part of Puxton came later than in the oval, beginning in the twelfth or thirteenth

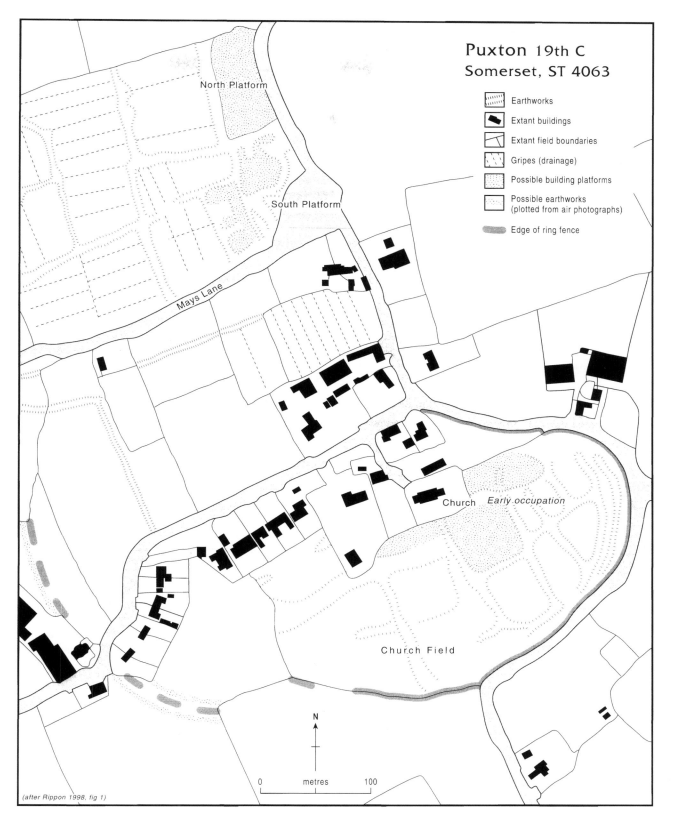

Puxton 19th C
Somerset, ST 4063

Earthworks

Extant buildings

Extant field boundaries

Gripes (drainage)

Possible building platforms

Possible earthworks
(plotted from air photographs)

Edge of ring fence

North Platform

South Platform

Mays Lane

Church *Early occupation*

Church Field

N

0   metres   100

(after Rippon 1998, fig 1)

Figure 4.21

century and continuing into late and post-medieval times (Rippon 1998, 73–8).

Rippon's study of reclamation and settlement on the Levels has produced structures which can be interpreted in a manner not dissimilar to some of those recorded in the South-eastern Province and in the Northern and Western Province. The earliest element at Puxton was an oval containing the primary settlement focus, with secondary settlement spreading along one of the droveways leading away from the oval, through the enclosed fields, towards the common pastures.

Conclusions

As indicated at the start of the chapter, this review of individual townships makes no pretence to be a comprehensive synthesis. Those readers whose interests lie south of a line from Cambridgeshire to Shropshire will feel particularly neglected, but there are large blanks, too, in the North. Nevertheless, the bulk of the cases forms a broad transect extending from Lancashire to Suffolk, and allows regional variation in the three provinces to be sampled in such a way as to provide data relevant to general hypotheses on rural settlement diversity. We have claimed to detect a basic uniformity in the agrarian structures of the South-eastern Province and the Northern and Western Province. Where such structures were uninfluenced by earlier boundaries the enclosure of ground for arable produced broadly oval shapes. The hall-church settlement is frequently found to be associated with such manifestations, sometimes within the oval but more often at its margin. Other farmsteads, especially those created subsequently during periods of rising population and increasing numbers of farming units, spread along the periphery of the oval, by the side of circumferential trackways. Habitation sites were fluid, they came and went; more durable was the framework of land boundaries and trackways.

The rationale of such structural characteristics is the convenience of placing farmsteads on the boundary between contrasting agrarian resources – typically, on the edge of the arable to allow easy access not only to the arable but also to the surrounding pastures: hence the 'girdling' of arable ovals with farmsteads. Such arrangements seem to have been widespread and long-lived. They were, of course, the structures which

Glanville Jones cited to typify certain kinds of Welsh rural settlement (Jones 1985, 157), and they were again invoked by Richard Hingley when modelling Roman period settlement in eastern England (Hingley 1989, 98–100). The ovals at Roystone demonstrate that such forms could predate the Middle Ages, though the example from Puxton shows that they might equally originate in Anglo-Saxon times.

There is evidence from a number of the ring-fenced ovals in both outer provinces that the cultivated ground within them was held by the tenants in intermixed strips. It is impossible to determine the extent to which these resembled the townfields of the Central Province in their structure and use, as they were largely eradicated at a much earlier date than the latter, and are therefore far less well documented. But it is likely that the strips attached to a particular holding were bunched together in the vicinity of its homestead rather than spread uniformly across the oval. The generation of intermixed strips was probably the result of the workings of partible inheritance. Again, such characteristics are not limited to medieval England: the Welsh 'girdle' settlements had lands in strips or 'quillets' (Jones 1985, 163–4, fig. 11.2), and strips are indicated by field evidence at Romano-British Roystone.

Rectilinear land divisions, typified by the co-axial systems of East Anglia, offer an alternative structural model. Like the ovals their origins are, at least in some cases, pre-Roman, though debate continues as to exactly how much of the framework which we see was articulated at that period. If the key element is, indeed, the roughly parallel trackways giving access from the main settlement areas in the valleys to remote wood-pasture grazings, then we might profitably look for more examples around the Weald and in the west Midlands, where other parallel trackways and transhumance routes have been identified. The sharpness of the contrast in framework morphology should not, however, lead us to over-emphasise the differences between rectilinear and curvilinear structures in counties like Suffolk where both are present. The networks of trackways skirting arable lands and linking greens, the presence of track-side and green-side settlement, the evidence of intermixed arable strips in the fields, are common to both.

Some parts of the South-eastern and Northern and Western Provinces saw the development of villages with extensive townfields, notably in the coastal districts and main river valleys, where sloping well-drained lands of no great altitude were concentrated. Such development was, however, more characteristic of the Central Province. Its villages and townfields appear to constitute not so much a contrasting system as one in which certain aspects of the basic agrarian structure have been developed at the expense of others: an assymetry or imbalance has been fostered. There are, of course, parts of the village/townfield zone where extensive common pastures were available, for instance around the Dunsmore plateau in Warwickshire. Nevertheless, the heartlands of the province saw the expansion of townfields over major portions of each township area. In such circumstances the location of homesteads on the boundary between differing resources was not an option. At places like East Haddon and Butterwick, the clustering of farmsteads at the junctions of the townfields was the most convenient alternative. The flexibility of arrangements evident in the outer provinces could not be sustained in such conditions. A high degree of regulation and stability was required: hence the necessity of impartible inheritance; hence the survival of yardland holdings for as much as eight centuries; hence the need for Acts of Parliament to break these structures.

The exploration of the pre-townfield agrarian structures at Butterwick is only one example of the kind of diachronic analysis which should be undertaken far more widely. It has the potential to contribute substantively to general hypotheses on long-term variation and stability in these structures. Were the 'ovals' of the North-west, for example, preceded by different forms of field and settlement patterning in later prehistory? Do the recti-linear field patterns of East Anglia overlie even earlier curvilinear patterns? One of the key questions about the Central Province is whether it developed in a landscape that was already different from those to either side: whether the overturning of mixed farming regimes had already occurred in parts of the Midlands before the end of Roman Britain; whether extensive cultivation continued unabated here in the early Anglo-Saxon period; whether nucleation and townfield development were simply a means of reducing systemic pressures, or of increasing efficiency.

The aim of this chapter has been to demonstrate the value of placing case studies of individual townships within the framework of regional variation that has been explored in earlier chapters. Without such a context it is difficult to assess the significance of similarities and differences. One example of such difficulties is the long debate over whether nucleation and the development of regular townfields occurred in pre or post-Conquest times. Debate might have been abbreviated if it had been recognised that the answer could be 'either, depending upon which part of the Central Province the examples came from'. Equally, the debate on 'continuity' from Roman to Anglo-Saxon times might have taken a different course. It has been said that 'the evidence for continuity from the field patterns of the prehistoric and Roman periods to the initial organisation of medieval common fields is both contradictory and inconclusive' (Oosthuizen 1997, 145). Contradictions may simply reflect different experiences in the various provinces and their regions. Single case studies, or groups of cases confined to a particular locality, may provide valid generalisations for their region, generalisations that may, at the same time, be entirely inapplicable to other parts of the country.

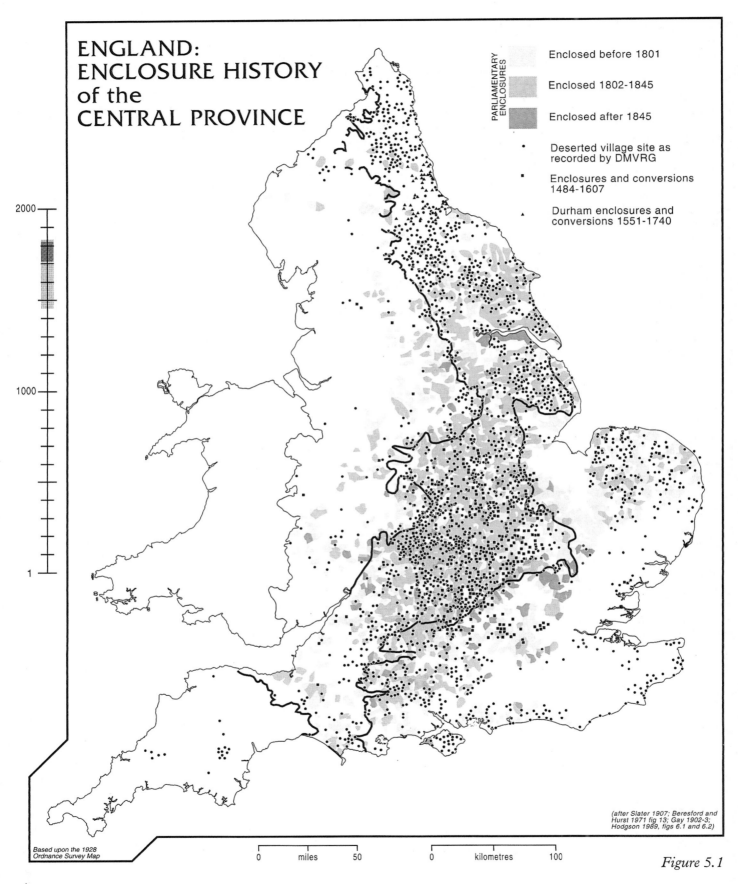

ENGLAND:
ENCLOSURE HISTORY
of the
CENTRAL PROVINCE

PARLIAMENTARY ENCLOSURES

Enclosed before 1801

Enclosed 1802-1845

Enclosed after 1845

• Deserted village site as recorded by DMVRG

■ Enclosures and conversions 1484-1607

▲ Durham enclosures and conversions 1551-1740

2000

1000

1

(after Slater 1907; Beresford and Hurst 1971 fig 13; Gay 1902-3; Hodgson 1989, figs 6.1 and 6.2)

Based upon the 1928 Ordnance Survey Map

0   miles   50

0   kilometres   100

Figure 5.1

5
The Central Province:
a reappraisal

Introduction

The Central Province has been defined on the basis of differences in the form and density of mid-nineteenth-century settlements, but there can be no doubt that these relate in large measure to variations in the patterns of landholding and landuse. By the 1850s the course of industrial growth had modified patterns of agrarian-based settlement in a significant number of regions in diverse ways: intensifying dispersion in some areas and generating nucleated settlements in others. Nevertheless, we argue that the settlement patterns observable in the mid-nineteenth century are substantively a reflection of agrarian structures whose antecedents can be traced back to the Middle Ages, and whose roots are likely to be even earlier.

Open-field enclosure

Enough evidence has been accumulated in local and regional studies (for example Vinogradoff 1908, 264–84; Harvey 1965, 17–31; Spufford 1974, 58–64; Hall 1995) to indicate that the province's medieval nucleated settlements were normally associated with extensive 'open field' systems. These open fields predominated among the resources available to the community in their territory or township: hence we have used the term 'townfield' systems in our discussions. In some parts of the country such townfields achieved a high degree of regularity, with strips allotted to individual farmers in a set order – and the same order – within each furlong, an order that was reflected in the sequence of the farmers' tofts within the village. The beginning and end of the sequence were determined by reference to the conventional direction of the progress of the sun. In Scandinavia this system was termed *solskifte* – 'sun-division' (Homans 1960, 94–100; Göransson 1961, 80–104).

The subdivision of fields into small strip parcels held by individual farmers is a phenomenon detectable through medieval England. What distinguishes the townfields associated with the Central Province from the subdivided fields characteristic of the two outer provinces is the degree of regularity present, their extent in relation to the township area, and their servicing by a single community housed in a single location. The trends towards settlement expansion and field subdivision, in themselves widespread features, have here been harnessed to serve public and private policy. Planning has led to uniformity and regularity: social structures, including mechanisms for transferring holdings from one generation to another, have been developed to maintain indefinitely such regularity and uniformity (Homans 1960, 109–59; Raftis 1964, 33–62; Howell 1983, 237–70).

There is no dataset available to map the occurrence of townfield systems during their lifetime, but there is post mortem information: records of their enclosure and replacement by new ring-fenced farms, not least by Act of Parliament. Figure 5.1, a composite map, draws into a single distribution the evidence available for the enclosure of the communally organised townfields. Three principal sources have been drawn together, namely Gilbert Slater's map, published in 1907, Gay's map of enclosures and conversions in the period 1484–1607 (Gay 1902–3) and Beresford and Hurst's 1968 map of deserted villages (Beresford and Hurst 1971). These have been supplemented by some other sources, particularly for the north of England (Hodgson 1989, figs 6.1–6.4). The dominance of the Central Province is clear and supports the hypothesis set out above. There are, however, some interesting divergences from the provincial settlement model, divergences which provide a route towards a better understanding of the genesis of both townfields and nucleations.

In the South-eastern Province significant numbers of townfield enclosures are recorded for three sub-provinces and their local regions: the Eastern Wash (EWASHE), the Thames Valley (ETHAM) and East

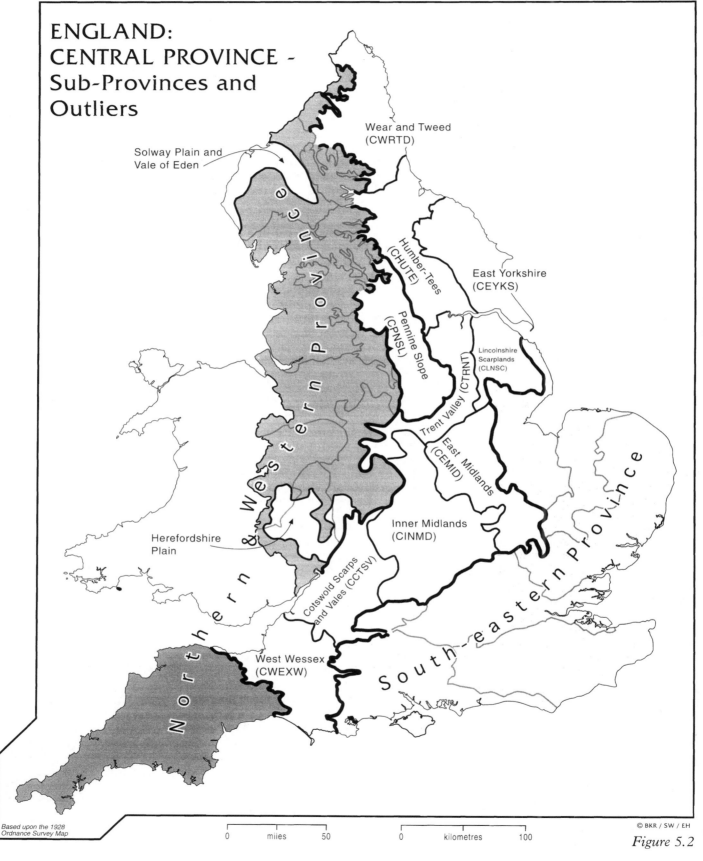

ENGLAND:
CENTRAL PROVINCE -
Sub-Provinces and
Outliers

Wear and Tweed
(CWRTD)

Solway Plain and
Vale of Eden

Humber-Tees
(CHUTE)

East Yorkshire
(CEYKS)

Pennine Slope
(CPNSL)

Lincolnshire
Scarplands
(CLNSC)

Trent Valley (CTRNT)

East Midlands
(CEMID)

Northern & Western Province

Herefordshire
Plain

Inner Midlands
(CINMD)

South-eastern Province

Cotswold Scarps
and Vales (CCTSV)

West Wessex
(CWEXW)

Northern

Based upon the 1928
Ordnance Survey Map

0   miles   50

0   kilometres   100

© BKR / SW / EH

Figure 5.2

Wessex (EWEXE: all Fig 1.4). All of these are discussed to varying degrees of detail in Chapter 6, but one point is worth making in relation to Figure 5.1. Slater's mapping of Parliamentary enclosure, simply by blocking in a parish area (Slater 1907, 196–7), is too crude to pick up important scale variations. Turner's recasting of Tate's lists shows that, in Norfolk for example, the amounts of land enclosed are consistently smaller than those of classic open field areas in the Central Province (Turner 1978, 178–84; see also Homans 1960, 19–21). Further divergent regions can be detected in the Northern and Western Province, though not so much on the basis of enclosure records as on other data. These are dealt with in the present chapter. The first is the Eden Valley in Cumbria, an area of nucleations and townfields which effectively forms a north-western outlier of the Central Province (Fig 5.2). The second is the Herefordshire Plain which, at an early period, seems to have formed a similar emergent outlier, on the evidence of its exceptionally high density of plough teams in the Domesday record (Fig 3.5).

Figure 5.1 also shows considerable variation within the Central Province itself. Both the south-western and more obviously the northern parts have few recorded Parliamentary enclosures, though they have reasonably high densities of nucleations and (again in the north) numbers of deserted medieval village sites. For the north at least there is a ready explanation: in the counties of Durham and Northumberland most townfield enclosure was carried out not through Act of Parliament, but by agreement in the Halmote court or by private agreement among freeholders (Hodgson 1989, 213–50, fig 6.14; Wrathmell 1975, 275–81). Figure 5.3 summarises the sequence of enclosure for the period 1600–1899 in the southern part of the historic county of Northumberland, roughly that part south of the Wansbeck, and for County Durham in the period 1550–1850. In Northumberland it distinguishes between those enclosures which related to townfields and those concerned with common pastures. It shows that Parliamentary enclosure played only a minor role in the later stages of the process and was mainly concerned with waste: the bulk of the townfields had been abolished earlier and by private agreement. Similarly in Durham the vast majority of the enclosures before 1700 took place by a process of 'surrender and admittance' within the Halmote court of the bishops, and was primarily concerned with townfields. A second wave, occurring between 1750 and 1850, was essentially concerned with the enclosure of common pastures in the western part of the county. Furthermore, it should be noted that in Northumberland other townfield enclosures took place without the need of any form of agreement, where the township was in the hands of a single landowner. The abolition of tenant right on the Scottish Borders left customary tenants in a weak position: they were effectively tenants at will (Wrathmell 1975, 179–80).

It is pertinent to ask why there should be such a difference in enclosure experience between the northern counties of the Central Province and those further south, and what other variations might relate to it. One clear distinction can be made in terms of the proportion of the township area contained within the townfields. In the north, townfields normally encompassed only a small proportion of the whole township area (eg Butlin 1964, 101, 106). This gave greater opportunity for making changes to the agrarian structure through, for example, the periodic ploughing up of the waste. Further south in the Central Province, the proportion of the township occupied by townfields was far greater. In Northamptonshire, for example, the 'most striking feature of the county was its open-field land, stretching almost unbroken over the uplands and along the Nene Valley. Within this region nearly all the ground was cultivated, having very little woodland, heath or pasture' (Hall 1995, ix). Those regions in which townfields encompassed almost all the township resources were the ones which had least flexibility, the ones which required a Parliamentary Act to effect enclosure. They are also, as is argued later, the regions that saw the earliest development of townfields, core zones of the Central Province, to which other more peripheral regions gradually accreted. It was, we suggest, these later accretions that were in general the earliest to be enclosed. This argument forms the substance of this chapter.

Figure 5.1 compresses into a single plane a vast amount of data spanning many centuries. It encompasses records of enclosure from the later fifteenth to late nineteenth centuries. If we perceive the various episodes of enclosure as elements of a single

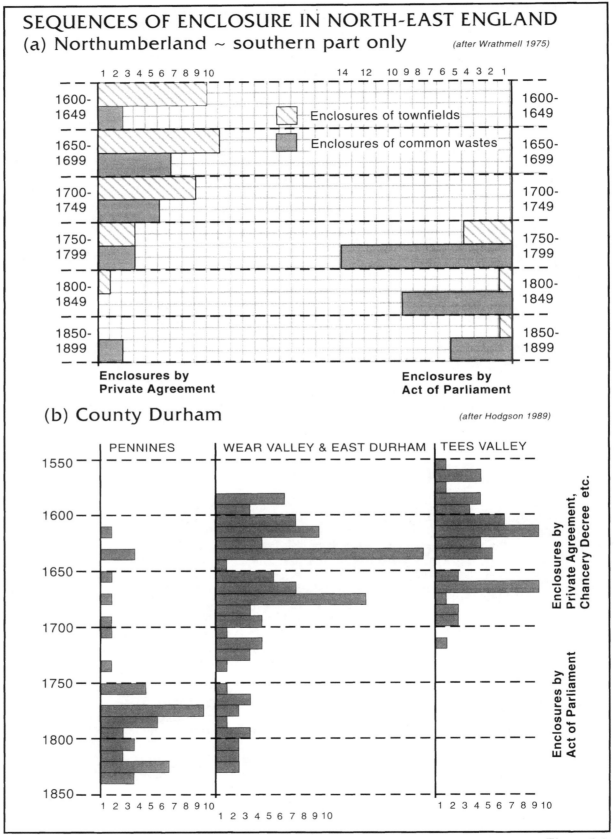

SEQUENCES OF ENCLOSURE IN NORTH-EAST ENGLAND
(a) Northumberland ~ southern part only *(after Wrathmell 1975)*

Enclosures of townfields
Enclosures of common wastes

Enclosures by Private Agreement

Enclosures by Act of Parliament

(b) County Durham *(after Hodgson 1989)*

PENNINES | WEAR VALLEY & EAST DURHAM | TEES VALLEY

Enclosures by Private Agreement, Chancery Decree etc.

Enclosures by Act of Parliament

Figure 5.3

movement, we see a movement that continued for more than four centuries in one part or another of this province. This is a significant timespan; one that we argue is of the same magnitude as that which had witnessed the creation of the Central Province in the first place. We accept Harold Fox's conclusion that the townfield system was fully developed, in terms of both its organisation and its extent, by the twelfth century – or in the North, perhaps by the thirteenth century. As early as the tenth century, perhaps earlier, complicated systems with intermixed acre strips had developed in some Midland townships, and it is possible that at some of these places two or three-field systems had been put into operation at that early date (Fox 1981, 88).

Figure 5.2 is an abstraction from Figure 1.4 and shows sub-provinces identified on the basis of settlement characteristics. These were created pragmatically, to establish intermediate units between provinces and the local regions. We have shown that the provinces appear in distributions based upon different sources derived from varied periods, and the temporal persistence of their boundaries implies that they represent deeply embedded spatial structures. We are, however, aware of the fact that it would be perfectly feasible to identify somewhat different divisions on the basis of maps of other evidence. Figure 5.1 is a case in point, providing data that would allow the Central Province to be divided into rather different sub-provinces from those identified on the basis of nineteenth-century settlement characteristics. Regions, relatively homogeneous areas identified on the basis of defined criteria, are basically tools. While their manifestation as visible landscapes affects our perceptions, the many elements of regional character do not conform to a single, simple boundary, for life is more complex than the map.

Field systems and fiscal tenures

Figure 5.4 includes a range of symbols showing two and three-field systems documented up to 1334 (Glasscock 1973, fig 23). The two-course rotation is the older, providing a crop-fallow-crop-fallow cycle in one of the fields, and a fallow-crop-fallow-crop cycle in the other. Towards 1200, however, there is evidence for village territories organised into three fields (Glasscock

1973, 83), a more intensive rotation, producing the best results only on the richer soils. This distribution shows a clear concentration within the central and south-western portions of the Central Province, but with a cluster in the East Wessex sub-province (Fig 1.4). It is interesting to note that Göransson's map of systems with evidence of *solskifte* (Fig 5.5), again drawn from twelfth and thirteenth-century data, broadly complements this distribution, being concentrated in that part of the province between the Wash and the Tees. This may have structural and historical significance in the evolution of the townfields.

In Figures 5.5–5.7 we have mapped various kinds of data relating to tenure and the diverse terminology of tenurial assessment. They also incorporate data relating directly to Scandinavian settlement. It will be immediately apparent that most of these distributions have not been informed by the provincial structures we have defined from variations in settlement pattern. Nevertheless, *within* the Central Province they may have themselves informed regional differences in agrarian structure – for example, in the density of *solskifte* vills within the Danelaw. Figure 5.5 includes, in addition to Göransson's data (1961, fig 9), Jolliffe's map of fiscal tenements (1935–6, 171). The extent of Danish settlement is shown more precisely in Figure 5.6. This marks settlements with the name element *-by* together with those names with a mixture of English and Scandinavian elements – the Grimston hybrids (Smith 1956, fig 10; Hill 1981, fig 68). A final map of this series, Figure 5.7, draws together a more subjective body of evidence suggesting the types of manor present in the post-Conquest period. It is accepted that the roots of these variations lie in pre-Conquest centuries (Aston 1958; Kosminsky 1956, 68–151; Rees 1963, fig 5; Loyn 1962, 53; Hill 1981, fig 174; Hart 1992, map 1,1) and a rather broad and indistinct east to west division of the Central Province, at or near the Danelaw boundary, is detectable in Figures 5.4, 5.5 and 5.6. It probably represents an important structural divide, present in the earlier stages of the evolution of settlement and field systems, yet not visible in any of the characteristics mapped from the post-medieval evidence. Nevertheless, it is possible that evidence for the sustained presence of a divide might emerge from the mapping of elements such as field names or the morphology of furlongs for which

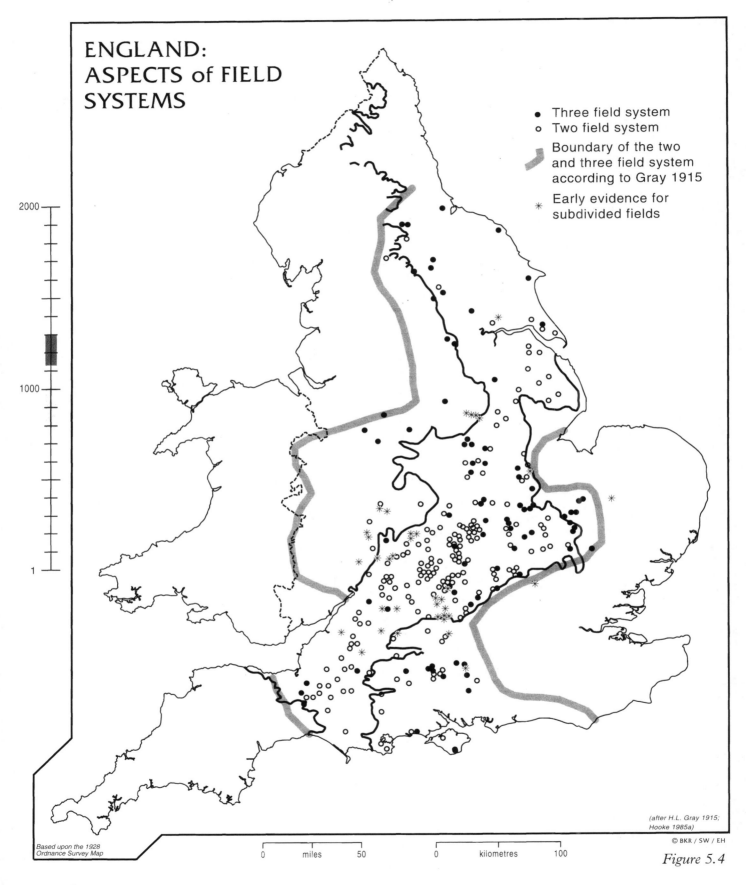

ENGLAND: ASPECTS of FIELD SYSTEMS

- Three field system
- Two field system
- Boundary of the two and three field system according to Gray 1915
- Early evidence for subdivided fields

2000
1000
1

(after H.L. Gray 1915; Hooke 1985a)

© BKR / SW / EH

Based upon the 1928 Ordnance Survey Map

0   miles   50

0   kilometres   100

Figure 5.4

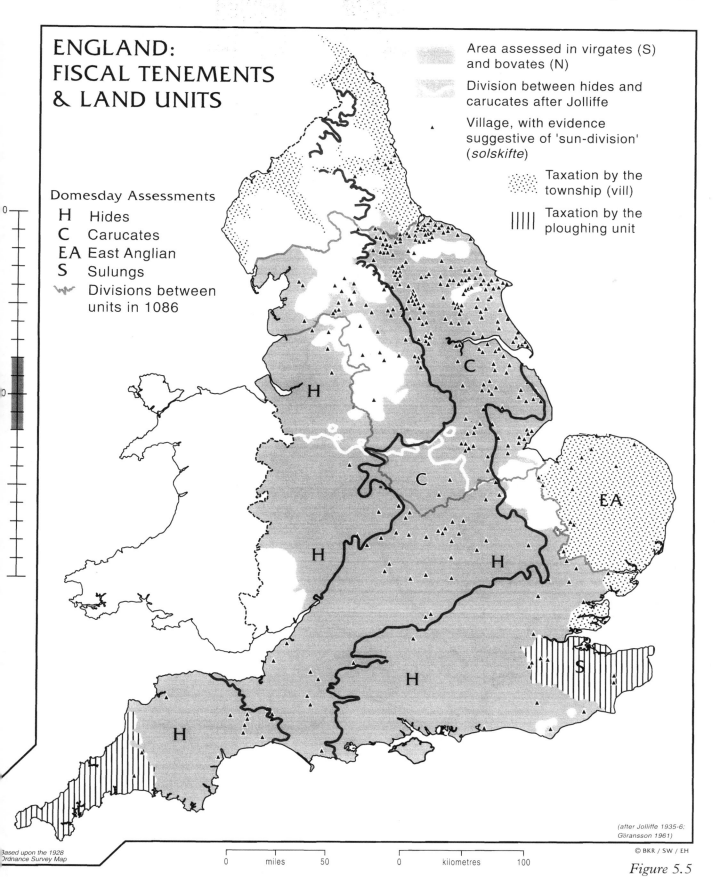

ENGLAND:
FISCAL TENEMENTS
& LAND UNITS

Area assessed in virgates (S)
and bovates (N)

Division between hides and
carucates after Jolliffe

▲ Village, with evidence
suggestive of 'sun-division'
(*solskifte*)

Taxation by the
township (vill)

Taxation by the
ploughing unit

Domesday Assessments

H   Hides
C   Carucates
EA East Anglian
S   Sulungs
    Divisions between
units in 1086

(after Jolliffe 1935-6;
Göransson 1961)

Based upon the 1928
Ordnance Survey Map

0   miles   50

0   kilometres   100

© BKR / SW / EH

Figure 5.5

125

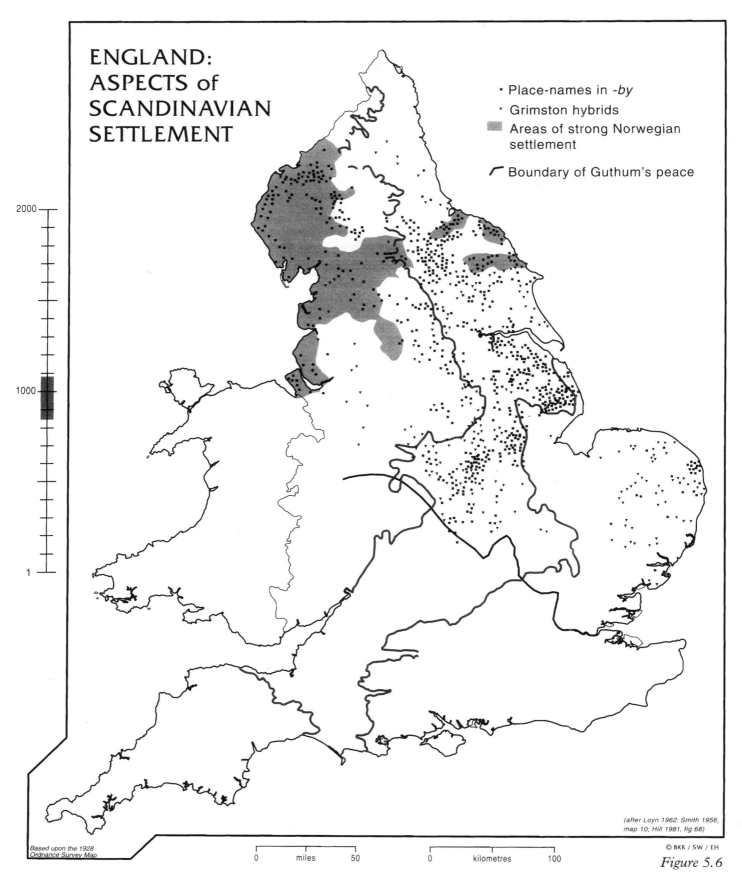

ENGLAND:
ASPECTS of
SCANDINAVIAN
SETTLEMENT

· Place-names in -by
▾ Grimston hybrids
Areas of strong Norwegian settlement
Boundary of Guthum's peace

(after Loyn 1962: Smith 1956, map 10; Hill 1981, fig 68)

© BKR / SW / EH

Figure 5.6

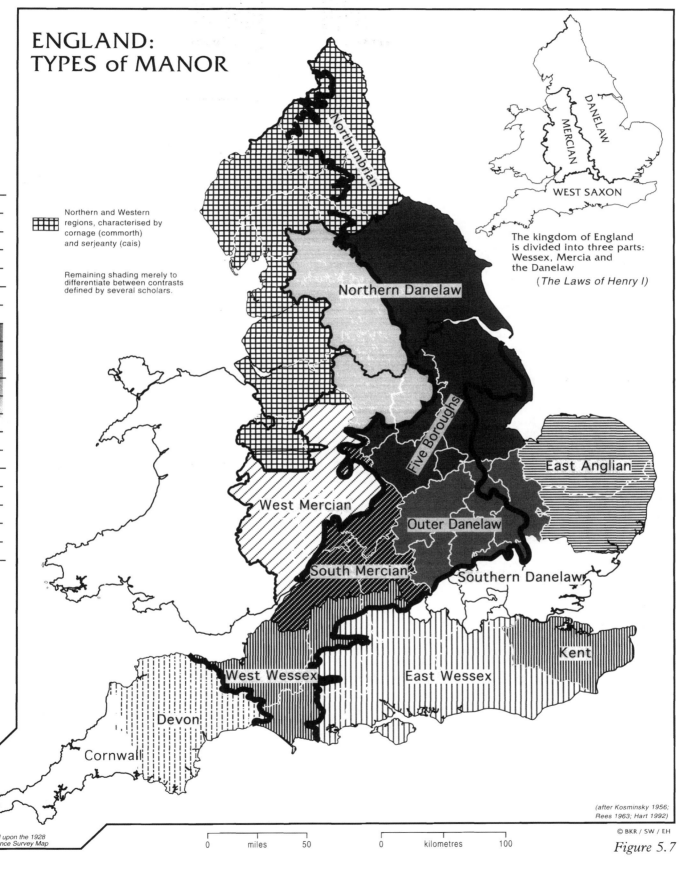

ENGLAND:
TYPES of MANOR

Northern and Western regions, characterised by cornage (commorth) and serjeanty (cais)

Remaining shading merely to differentiate between contrasts defined by several scholars.

Northumbrian

Northern Danelaw

Five Boroughs

West Mercian

East Anglian

Outer Danelaw

South Mercian

Southern Danelaw

Kent

West Wessex

East Wessex

Devon

Cornwall

DANELAW

MERCIAN

WEST SAXON

The kingdom of England is divided into three parts: Wessex, Mercia and the Danelaw

(*The Laws of Henry I*)

(after Kosminsky 1956; Rees 1963; Hart 1992)

Based upon the 1928 Ordnance Survey Map

0 miles 50

0 kilometres 100

© BKR / SW / EH

Figure 5.7

127

regional scale data are not currently available. While we will continue to use the sub-provincial divisions seen in Figure 5.2 as a framework for discussion, we reiterate that other divisions are possible, and we will have occasion to refer to them.

Figure 5.4 also includes a star symbol that shows all the locations where there is documentary evidence dating from before the Norman Conquest for townfields or proto-townfields, indicators of divided holdings (Gray 1915, 57–8; Sawyer 1968, nos 972, 1363, 1448; Finberg 1972a; Finberg 1972b, 488–9, 491–2; Hart 1975; Hooke 1985a, 194–5; Hooke 1998). The distribution can reflect only those estates mentioned in charters. More particularly, it relates closely to those documents which have detailed bounds (Hill 1981, 22–5), for it is in these that appears the terminology perhaps indicative of communal, subdivided townfields. Even within the areas possessing charters with bounds, the concentration of references is most marked in a area embracing parts of Berkshire, Oxfordshire, Worcestershire, Gloucestershire and northern Somerset, in spite of numerous boundary clauses documented elsewhere (Hill 1981, fig 31 and 35). Areas that had long been densely settled would tend to produce situations of local conflict, where the strips of one community abutted those of another. This in turn would tend to bring such detail into the documentary record. The material is mainly of tenth-century provenance, but some is of eighth and early ninth-century date. The quantity is limited but two points can be teased out. First, approximately two-thirds of the symbols lie within the limits of the Central Province. This can hardly be pure chance, given the occurrence of charters with bounds elsewhere. Secondly, of the remaining third, while scattered references appear in the Breckland, in south Yorkshire and on the edges of the chalk in the East Wessex sub-province, the majority – thanks to the survival of much Worcester material – appear in the Northern and Western Province, amid essentially woodland landscapes flanking the Severn valley. They suggest that the processes generating early townfield systems were by no means confined to the Central Province, where they eventually came to predominate.

The sequence of the discussion we have adopted requires some comment, for it necessarily intermixes temporal and spatial arguments. First of all we examine the outliers of the Eden Valley and Hereford-shire plain, and then the two ends of the province's main tract, in the north-east and the south-west. This is followed by an assessment of the pre-Conquest origins in the Midlands, followed by a discussion of the Danelaw.

The outliers of the Central Province

The Eden valley

Separated from the lowlands to the east by high and bleak moorland passes, the Eden valley had been absorbed into the English state by 1100, yet long remained a march-land with distinctive economy and social customs (Kapelle 1979; Higham and Jones 1985; Higham 1986; Winchester 1987; Roberts 1989, 59–75). The Norman take over of 1092 saw the appearance of town-field systems based upon very long strips, each forming a field kernel attached to a planned nucleated village, concentrating a former scattered population (Roberts 1993; 1996b). The dimensions of these strips should be appreciated. A 'normal' townfield parcel tended to be 200m (220 yards or one furlong) in length, but these cores contain strips that are 250m, 400m, 600m in length, or even longer. To these initial units more furlongs were gradually added, eventually resulting in the appearance of more conventional townfield systems (Elliott 1973, 41–92). This was by no means universal. At Cumwhitton, expansion around the core resulted in a wedge-shaped pattern of what were essentially consolidated farms, arranged radially around a small strip-field core (Roberts 1987, fig 3.12). Two-course rotations are likely to have been followed, for the area was not penetrated by the three-course rotation (Elliott 1973, 57–8), but in the early stages the long strips must have formed the arable field. This kernel is likely to have been in continuous cultivation and sustained by manuring, but producing only one crop a year (Elliott 1973, 55–6). The crucial transition to a formal two-course shift must, as new furlongs accreted, have been conditioned by the availability of sufficient manure from the stock wintered in byres. There are hints of the temporary cultivation of some areas of common waste as 'outfields' (Elliott 1973, 63–7; Winchester 1987, 74–7), adding to the arable area.

Detailed fieldwork suggests that the imposed townfield agriculture replaced an earlier pattern of more scattered hamlets, each surrounded by small enclosed fields whose system of usage cannot now be determined (Roberts 1993). We are left with the impression of a communal system in a less than completely developed state.

The emergence of townfield systems dominating the land surface of each township was inhibited by a number of factors. In the first place there was the late date of the take over by the English state. Secondly, there was the availability of large areas of common waste, which allowed the keeping of substantial numbers of animals. Thirdly, the qualities of local terrains and soils were variable. Fourthly, there was a prevalence, initially at least, of relatively low population levels. Finally, there was possibly also a form of tenant right which demanded a willingness to take part in border defence (Kerridge 1969, 43-5, 58–60; Thirsk 1967, 16–28), associated with the persistence of border conflict until the accession of James I. These systems illustrate well why we use the term 'townfields' rather than 'open fields' or 'common fields'. All of the 'inby' land – at first the cultivated arable core – was no doubt securely fenced, while the 'open' boundaries between individual large strips varied from substantial earthen lynchets to dumps of field clearance stones and boulders, and banks made of these. Such broad boundaries may account for the 'unploughed strips' described by Elliott amid the arable field areas, grazed by tethered stock (Elliott 1973, 59). More significantly, grazing lands were present in such abundance that pasturing townfield fallow – although never wholly absent – was unnecessary, and indeed was made difficult by the needs of high intensity cultivation within the limited areas manured as arable.

The characteristics of the Eden valley give a useful glimpse of the arrangements which may have preceded the more formalised, more complex systems elsewhere. A development towards a more formalised system would involve a distinct sequence of physical changes. First, there would be the gradual clearance of field stones and the destruction of incipient boundaries by the removal of material for buildings and road construction (particularly in areas lacking surface field stone). Next would come the addition of more furlongs and the adjustment of ploughing directions to the details of local topography.

Finally, there would be the imposition – in areas of greater arable potential – of formalised two and three-course rotations, normally coupled with formal distribution and sometimes the redistribution of holdings. All represent steps towards the appearance of what Fox termed the 'Midland system' (Fox 1981, 64–8). The Eden valley systems, seen in early seventeenth-century maps of the Howard of Naworth archives, show all stages of these developments.

Herefordshire Plain

By 1086 the Herefordshire Plain already carried high densities of recorded plough teams (Fig 3.5). The area encompasses the county's plains and ridges. To the east, these are separated from the champion lands of the Central Province by the Malvern ridge and associated low plateaux, which still carry areas of open common waste, and by the river Severn. Gray included it within his zone of regular two and three field rotations (Fig 5.4). Sylvester's work shows that post-medieval three field and multiple field systems extended into the middle Wye and Lugg valleys, although multiple systems tend to predominate. Kingsland, in the upper Lugg valley, had by 1709 an extraordinarily complex pattern of open arable townfields and older enclosures. Faced with the presence of townfields amid areas dominated by dispersed and semi-dispersed settlement, Sylvester postulated the existence of a 'pre-existing Celtic pattern' (Sylvester 1969, figs 3, 21, 23, 375); she suggested that the 'Mercians' and the 'Anglo-Normans' introduced the 'Midland type' field systems, with nucleated settlements, into the region. In fact the system at Kingsland is more likely to be Norman in origin, for as Merlen (1987, 20–21) points out the Norman church lies outside the motte and bailey castle, and the settlement represents a post-Conquest plantation of English peasants to support the garrison. The key problem, in both this and many other portions of the outer provinces, is to get any clear view of the balance between documented townfields, piecemeal enclosures of former townfield land, enclosures taken from waste peripheral to townfields, and any more ancient enclosures, perhaps antedating the townfields.

Kingsland can be usefully set alongside three other cases. Sheppard (pers comm 1979) examined a 1720 map of Marden lying north of Hereford in the more favoured, wider valley of the lower Lugg. The manor comprised three substantive villages, Sutton St Michael and Sutton St Nicholas with Marden, plus a dozen smaller hamlets and ten large, isolated homesteads. All but the last possessed some townfield lands. Those of Sutton, while nominally in three great fields, concealed a situation in which the strip holdings of all three settlements were intermingled within various portions of the fields. The remainder of the manor comprised a chaotic, unstructured mass of townfield and meadow blocks and enclosed land. Using this material as a foundation Sheppard reconstructed the manor in about 1300. At that stage there were possibly seven settlement clusters associated with three open arable townfields, accounting for over two-thirds of the surface area, indeed more if the meadows are included. In addition, there were also some very small areas of common waste and some woodland. Thus, between 1300 and 1720, piecemeal enclosure created the fragmented pattern found at the latter date. Sheppard attempted a reconstruction in the later eleventh century, basing her arguments on the evidence of furlong structures and place-names. She identified a series of arable fields associated with a scatter of some nine 'settlements' – essentially hamlets, some with demesne, some with bond tenants and others with freeholders. At that date a significant proportion of the estate was waste, and she could not of course in any way determine which of the arable areas were already subdivided townfields. Assarting of the waste between 1086 and 1300 added new furlongs to the arable. She argued that some of the small furlongs north of Sutton village developed within frames established by 'Celtic' fields.

A contrasting situation was documented by Lord Rennell of Rodd, who in his study *Valley on the March* (1958) created a remarkable picture of the valley of the Hindwell Brook, a tributary of the upper Lugg. Cut by Offa's Dyke, yet with the Welsh border pushed further to the west, the manors are all described as 'waste' in 1086; indeed Domesday Book specifically records 'on these waste lands have grown woods in which ... Osbern goes hunting and he has from them what he can catch. Nothing else.' He pointed out that we cannot assume that no habitation or cultivation was sustained (Rennell of Rodd 1958, 51); the term 'waste' merely implies that the estate was not an organised enterprise

which could pay full dues and taxes in money or kind. Given that devastation probably occurred in 1052, it was perhaps a reduction of grazing intensity – the result of the removal and killing of stock – that allowed the regeneration of woodland in the 34 years between the two dates. As we have stressed before, the peasants who survived would have needed to till land in order to live. Against this background he identified a series of groups of what he termed 'old manor arable fields': these were generally of the size 200 by 684m (220 by 748 yards), with 201 by 603m (220 by 660 yards) being equal to about 30 acres (12ha). He postulated a very rough correlation between these and Domesday hidages, a single hide manor having approximately two 9 by 31m fields (in fact 10 by 34 chains, 'say 70 acres': Rennell of Rodd 1958, 113–17). He was, however, careful to stress that the figures possessed no exactness, merely that a two-hide manor had more arable acreage than a single-hide manor and so on. The pattern of core fields comprised well-drained lands with lighter soils lying on ridges or slopes, and there was a succession of these along the valley of the Hindwell Brook, an area where good arable was limited. In more favoured environments such small arable kernels would, as population rose, have quickly been absorbed into more extensive and complex field systems. However, neither the Hindwell nor indeed the Lugg valleys ever fully developed the characteristics of champion landscapes in the Central Province.

The case of Tidenham, south Gloucestershire, outside the area just discussed, is worth considering in this context. An ancient royal estate belonging to the kings of Wessex, it was set on the English side of Offa's Dyke and in 956 was granted by charter to the Abbot of Bath (Seebohm 1883, 148–59; Faith 1994, 39–51). A multiple estate, it amounted to 30 hides of land, 9 of demesne and 21 set with tenants. In addition to Tidenham it contained the hamlets of Stroat ('Street' – significantly on a Roman road), *Cingestune* (now Sedbury), *Bishopstune* (now Old Bishton Farm), an enigmatic *Middeltun*, and *Landcawet* (now Llancaut), a Welsh hamlet set amid woodlands as the name implies. The arable of Street, Middleton and Sedbury was assessed in terms of *gyrda gafollandes* 'rent paying yardlands', possibly open townfields; in the woodland portion of the estate, at Bishton and Llancaut, these elements are absent from the land assessments. The estate, with access to the Severn estuary and the river Wye, was rich in fishweirs, but it is two details of the labour services that are singularly revealing. In addition to weir building and the construction of wattled fish traps, the tenants were required to construct '15 yards of acre fencing, or ditch 15 yards' and 'ditch one yard of burh-hedge'. The measures involved must be land-yards, rods, poles or perches: we may speculate between 15 or 20 feet. The 'acre fences' (*Æcertyninge*) must be the vital fences around the arable lands, both demesne and tenant, protecting them from the depredations of wild and domesticated animals; though in an area with alluvial flatlands these may have been ditches rather than live or dead fences. The *burh-hedge* must be the delimiting feature around a *burh* or defensive site, surely that at Sedbury. Here is a late tenth-century estate with English and Welsh elements; set within the Northern and Western Province, but linked culturally and administratively to the Central Province, and which can be glimpsed in 956.

As in the north of England, the picture is one of field cores, perhaps not even subdivided at first – for it is perfectly possible to share crops rather than land. We may postulate that increasing population, subdivision by inheritance, and taking in new arable gradually generated more complex systems. Once these had appeared, restructuring and reorganisation of the holdings within them was feasible, as was the imposition of formalised rotations in two, and eventually three fields. In the small field kernels of the Hindwell valley can be seen the sort of arable cores that must have formed the nuclei of more complex systems, antecedents of arrangements such as those seen at Marden. Here, also, are smaller versions of the core arable areas discussed in Chapter 4.

We have explored here these 'outliers' of the Central Province in order to take up a line of research suggested by Harold Fox. He has proposed that the 'clues to the circumstances of the adoption of the Midland system are provided first by places which never accepted it *outside* the Midland zone and in places where it was taken up *outside* the limits of the period which saw its general adoption' (Fox 1981, 91). We will now return to the Central Province itself, attempting to provide some overall characterisation of its development. We begin with its north-eastern and south-western extremities.

The extremities of the Central Province

The North-east

This zone embraces much of Northumberland and Durham. As noted earlier the townfields were largely enclosed before 1700 (Fig 5.3), either by private agreement among freeholders or by the lord's decision. Traces of these changes, leading both to the consolidation of large farms from many small ones and to a dispersal of farmsteads, can be seen in the much shrunken or even wholly deserted villages. Nevertheless, as early maps attest, townfields were once present in this zone in some numbers. They generally covered less than 40% of the area of a township, but sometimes, in more favoured regions, townships are found with as much as 60% of their surface under townfield cultivation (Butlin 1973, fig 3.3), a level commensurate with what is found in Northamptonshire. The enclosure of Durham has been particularly well documented because of the relatively uniform landholding arrangements, with the two largest estates being ecclesiastical and inherently conservative. Hodgson has shown that the peak of activity was between 1625 and 1675, but late sixteenth-century cases are known, as are survivals well into the eighteenth (Hodgson 1989, fig 6.4). 'Enclosure by agreement' took place over a period of two or three days, when the open strip holdings were surrendered in the Bishop's Halmote court to a named individual, who then readmitted the tenants to their new compact farms. A key factor encouraging these changes was undoubtedly the presence of the most vigorously developing coalfield in Europe. It was a region whose trading links and ship construction allowed the import of Baltic grain, and whose prosperous populations were able to consume more dairy produce. By the seventeenth century there was an over-arching need for horses and fodder for the burgeoning industrial expansion along with food for the local population, stimuli enough for radical change. Nevertheless, too little is yet known about the admixtures of townfield land and enclosed land within the regional farming system, and the whole zone contained diverse terrains and diverse field systems. That some enclosed farms were of ancient foundation is not to be doubted: thus Edderacres is documented in 1185 (Austin 1982, 20-21; Greenwell 1857, 127). And there are others, ranging from specialist demesne enterprises to scatters of small hamlets and single farmsteads that emerged in zones of active land taking (Roberts 1981, 152–61).

What is known of the origins of these townfield landscapes? Documentation in the period between c 1550 and 1800 (Butlin 1973, 100–1) shows that three-field systems occurred throughout the region's valleys and plains, although intermixed with systems of one, two and four or more fields. At other locations it is not possible to document more than the presence of 'common fields' or 'townfields'. Butlin's conclusions on their medieval antecedents are relevant: 'it is possible ... to postulate the existence ... of an embryonic field system. This comprised a number of furlongs, loosely grouped for the purposes of crop rotation and in some cases more permanently grouped into larger common fields. In time, with the continued expansion of the arable area in regions of increasing population, the grouping of furlongs into two, three or more common fields became a more widespread occurrence' (Butlin 1973, 142). A critical stage in the appearance of the more elaborate field systems may be represented by the appearance of the region's regular planned villages, in the late eleventh and twelfth centuries. That this involved the regularisation of preceding agrarian structures cannot be doubted, and Göransson has mapped the areas subject to extremely organised systems of field layout by collecting references to *solskifte* (Fig 5.5).

Butlin's conclusions imply that village-based townfield systems were preceded by simpler systems based upon hamlets and linked farmstead clusters, but his carefully weighed words establish no chronology. By 1185 the Boldon Book, a survey of holdings on the Bishop of Durham's estates was describing vills in terms of bovates, and while these fiscal tenements extended far beyond the classic townfield arrangements (Fig 5.5), they clearly represent, in this context, holdings whose descent can be traced through the records to the townfield enclosures of the seventeenth century. There is a strong case for linking bovated townfields with village plantation at a time of conquest and devastation falling between the 1070s and the decades before 1185 (Roberts 1972). Given that the construction of the great cathedral at Durham was achieved by 1133, and given the considerable local resources that must have been consumed in the course of realising that project, there are grounds for compressing many developments in that particular county into the years between 1070 – the effective date of the Norman take over – and 1093, when construction commenced. This is a remarkably short period. In Durham the sustained needs of the great ecclesiastical corporations ensured, in general, stronger control over tenants and the greater formalisation and expansion of the townfield arrangements than occurred further north and west. These developments took place behind a screen of substantial castles extending between the Tweed and the Tyne and in an environment with greater agricultural potential than is found in Cumberland and Westmorland.

Nevertheless, amid the rising spurs of west Durham is a group of small villages possessing arable cores, in effect single arable fields, divided into long strips of the order of 200–250m in length (Roberts 1987, figs 9.3 and 9.5). In settlements known to have been developing during the twelfth century, these were a means of dividing a limited amount of arable between a few tenant farmers. Once again these are probably useful indicators of one of the antecedent forms of the larger, more fragmented and more complex systems of later centuries. They closely parallel cases in the Eden Valley although the strips are rather smaller.

To generalise about these northern areas: the plantation of regulated villages and the formalisation of the townfield systems, with standardised fiscal tenements and regular parcel allocation, are likely to represent a phase of reorganisation falling between the Conquest and devastations of the late eleventh to early thirteenth centuries. In spite of the possibly short time involved in Durham, these changes should not in general be envisaged as a single phase, but as a series of overlapping waves, transformations, intensifying as well as extending, as ideas spread from vill to vill, from estate to estate and from region to region. The adoption of new ideas may occur for the most pragmatic of reasons. For instance, the associated crop yields from a particular arrangement of the arable lands may be seen to be good: nothing will influence farmers more than better yields experienced on adjacent lands. On a broader scale, landowners, or their stewards, must have been powerful agents in the diffusion of new ideas for the physical arrangement of farmsteads and farmholdings as well as for agrarian practices, as manifest a century or so later in agricultural treatises (Oschinsky 1971). The end result of such developments was to draw these northern areas into the Central Province by the thirteenth century, although it was inevitable that the Eden Valley would remain, on the map, an outlier.

The South-west

The south-western portion of the Central Province (Fig 5.2), West Wessex, embraces much of Somerset and west Dorset. This area was already substantively enclosed by the seventeenth century (Gonner 1912, fig D). The extremely diverse terrains have always given varied economic potential, able to support villages and hamlets in great profusion. Published maps of pre-enclosure township layouts suggest that there were some places like Stoke sub Hamdon, in Somerset, where (in 1776) over 80% of the township was under townfield arable, with indications that much of the remainder had been enclosed from open strips (Dunning 1974, 236). In other pre-nineteenth-century townships, for example Crewkerne (c 1842), Martock (1824), Long Sutton (1814) and Somerton (1806), there were discontinuous blocks of open arable (Dunning 1974, 141, 156; Dunning 1978, 6, 80). Sometimes these formed a ring entirely round the nucleation, as at Crewkerne, – perhaps representing the survival of a few townfield holdings. Elsewhere they formed dispersed blocks lying in an asymmetrical relationship with the settlement focus and intermixed with earlier enclosed lands. The latter occur either as fragments complementary to the townfield land, or in substantial blocks, some of which may be enclosed townships or 'tithings'. In 1810 Charlton Mackerell possessed characteristic Somerset townfield remnants (Dunning 1974, 82), whereas Charlton Adam appears as wholly enclosed. The tiny hamlets of Cooks Cary, Lytes Cary and Cary Fitzpaine – the latter little more than a single farmstead – have no documented traces of townfields. While such small settlements can be identified as enclosed demesnes – their place-names suggest this – this attribution in no way explains their origin. They could represent either late reclamations, or ancient farmsteads or hamlets never assimilated into the nucleations with their associated townfields and tenancies. The fact they do not appear

in Domesday Book need not invalidate the latter argument, for each entry in the Inquest must conceal many settlement variations.

Surviving into the seventeenth and eighteenth centuries as functioning entities, these townfield systems had medieval roots, although piecemeal enclosures were underway by the late seventeenth century in places like Somerton (Dunning 1974, 140). Of the root structures, ie the layout of the furlongs in the townfields, it is possible to say little. At Stoke sub Hamdon there is a clear tendency for rather irregular blocky furlong structures to prevail near the settlements – there are two nuclei. Further away, furlongs based upon larger units appear, long rectangles divided ladderwise, in what are clearly very regular blocks broken from waste or marsh (Dunning 1974, 236). This provides a glimpse of what may be a fundamental model: four rings, comprising (a) the village tofts plus some enclosures (possibly including former demesne); (b) irregular blocky furlongs, perhaps created from antecedent rectangular fields; (c) more regular peripheral structures in a recurrent pattern. Finally (d) the common waste, forms an outer ring, but may also intercalate with rings (a) to (c). Two underlying issues permeate this discussion. The first is the balance at the township level between communal resources on the one hand (townfield arable and meadow, common waste and woodland), and, on the other, areas of enclosed land in severalty. The second issue is the deep structures discoverable within the morphology of the townfields that may have a bearing upon their origins.

Mick Aston has explored settlement nucleation and townfield development in Somerset in a series of both extensive and intensive studies. His county-wide investigations have broadly confirmed this part of the Central Province boundary, with nucleations in central and eastern Somerset, and smaller, more scattered settlements in the west (Aston 1983; Aston 1985, 81, fig 8.1). Even within the zone of nucleation, however, the incidence of large medieval village settlements and regular townfield systems seems to have been very patchy. Aston cites a number of nucleations, such as Cheddar, with two-field systems (only occasionally three), but even these seem not to have completely dominated the countryside as their equivalents did in the east Midlands. At Draycott, for example, there was a regular townfield system and a well-planned village, but elsewhere within the same parish there was an irregular pattern of farmsteads. In some cases, lands in two-field systems were shared not only by the farmers in the village but also by the inhabitants of neighbouring hamlets (Aston 1994, 226–8). At the other end of the Central Province, in Northumberland, the lowlands came to be dominated by townfield villages, whereas in Somerset there were still many hamlets: 'very mixed and varied field systems were in use in the Middle Ages, often with extensive areas of woodland and common pasture available to the local farmers' (Aston 1994, 233). No doubt the early demise of townfield systems was partly due to the existence of extensive non-townfield resources.

The chronology of nucleation and townfield creation also seems to have been very variable – a conclusion which cautions against assuming that the spread of regular townfield systems proceeded in a gradual and uniform fashion. Aston has used a number of indicators to study the change from hamlets to village, among them the names 'huish', 'worth' and 'wick'. In western Somerset (within the Northern and Western Province) these are still to be found attached to isolated farmsteads. Elsewhere, especially in the east, such names are attached to fields and furlongs, indicating settlement sites abandoned at the time of nucleation (Aston 1994, 220–21). At Shapwick, another two-field village, Aston has suggested the tenth century as the period of nucleation. It may have been associated with the monastic reforms of that time, and there may have been contemporary nucleation on other parts of the Glastonbury estate: 'it begins to look as if, on selected arable estates, a deliberate decision was made by some large monasteries to re-order both landscape and settlement on an impressive scale, probably to increase revenue' (Aston and Gerrard 1999, 29). Christopher Thornton's detailed analysis of Rimpton has led him to identify in that village a core settlement enclosure perhaps established by the tenth century, with later phases of village planning and townfield development being instigated by the estate owners between the mid-tenth and late eleventh centuries (Aston 1994, 227, 229). Not all nucleations originated in the pre-Conquest period. Some may be signified in tenurial changes between 1066 and 1086, as recorded by the Domesday survey. Stoke sub Hamdon is one such vill, where the three manors of 1086 had been created out of the lands of eight thanes in 1066. Others may have been reorganised in the mid-twelfth to thirteenth centuries (Aston 1985, 84, 91, 93; Aston 1989, 127).

Pre-Conquest origins of townfield systems

It should be emphasised at this point that when thinking about townfield origins we do not conceive of a single location from which diffusion took place. What is envisaged is an infinitely more complex process, as indicated in the Somerset studies, by which widespread tendencies already present within earlier agrarian systems were gradually strengthened. Sawyer has shown (1978, 41–8) how the origins of Wessex and Mercia lay in a number of sub-kingdoms, small and unstable cells, in varying degrees of subjugation to an overlord, such as Ine and Penda. These rulers had an opportunity to establish law-codes and impose, revitalise or formalise, rents, renders and dues within their imperium. In Wessex, Ine was able to do this by 678–726. This is not to say that there were no earlier codes, perhaps even unwritten ones, but it does suggest that codes and territorial control – rather than codes and people – were becoming linked. Conquest brought new land rights to the successful ruler (Sawyer 1978, 47-8, 52); grants of land and formal taxation eventually followed. The core of Ine's kingdom probably extended from the mixed lands of Somerset and much of Dorset, to the chalk lands of Wiltshire, with some fluctuating control over the Upper Thames valley. Whatever the historical sources tell of devastations in the wars of conquest against the Britons, or of conflicts between nascent Anglo-Saxon kingdoms, peasant farming continued. It was the source of taxes and it was therefore in the interests of any ruler to give it support and to develop it. We can postulate, but never prove, the sustained presence of a mixture of farming types, some in effect continuing Romano-British structures, others created or modified by incomers and incoming influences. In such conditions, variety must have prevailed, including many 'unspecialised arrangements' (Fig 3.4 E). New laws and new taxes may have created the impetus towards greater uniformity, which was gradually manifest in the field systems.

The laws of Ine contain clauses about the maintenance of a communal boundary around 'meadow or other land divided into shares ....' owned by ceorls. These are worth requoting here: 'A ceorl's homestead must be fenced both winter and summer. If it is not fenced, and his neighbour's cattle get in through his own gap, he has no right to anything from that cattle: he is to drive it out and suffer the damage' (Whitelock 1955, 368, clause 40). More significantly, 'If ceorls have a common meadow or other land divided into shares to fence, and some have fenced their portion and some have not, and [if cattle] eat up their common crops or grass, those who are responsible for the gap are to go and pay to the others, who have fenced their part, compensation for the damage that has been done there. They are to demand with regard to those cattle such reparation as is proper' (Whitelock 1955, 368–9, clause 42). Of course this need not, and probably does not, imply a fully fledged townfield system. Indeed, it is as likely to refer to shares within the ring-fenced ovals already examined in Chapter 4. The concepts expressed here can be compared with an eighteenth-century law from Jamtland in Sweden:

> anyone who has fenced in private estate, whether one or several [ie one person or a group], that is to say, anyone in the village itself or outside it has enclosed field or meadow, must keep a wattled fence valid in law around this or blame himself. If any damage is done on such enclosed estate no other person shall be fined or penalised. Those who have gathered about such an enclosure may leave their cattle to graze in autumn and spring.
> *(Erixon 1966, cited in Roberts 1981, 161)*

As Swedish maps from the seventeenth century show (Erixon 1961, figs 2, 4, 5 and 6) areas of meadow or arable need only be shared between a small number of farmers. The formality of the statement suggests that the problem was a prevalent one, implying perhaps that tenants as well as kinsmen were involved in the shares. A system of open townfields cultivated in common lay firmly on the tenancy side of the kinship/tenancy social divide. Another clause from Ine's laws, which states that a man need not accept labour services unless his lord gives him a house (Whitelock 1955, 371, clause 67), surely represents a powerful factor fostering nucleation. It may indicate that the two key ingredients of the classic townfield/nucleation arrangements were already present within parts of Wessex by the end of the seventh century.

There are no descriptions of the introduction of these systems into the heartlands of the Central Province. David Hall, in a very thorough analysis of Northamptonshire, argues that some at least of the open (town)fields originated in long broad strips, laid out over large blocks of landscape, later reduced to a 'checkerboard pattern' by cross divisions. A regular tenurial order of parcels was then created within this pattern, and Hall suggests an origin for 'subdivided fields at the end of the Middle Saxon period, say in the eighth century' (Hall 1995, 137). This chronology is based upon the observation that the furrows of the open fields overlie both Roman and Middle Saxon sites as revealed by pottery scatters. These same sites often preserve in their field names the element -cot, or names that appear to incorporate possible Saxon personal names, suggesting that those who laid out the strip fields knew that the Saxon settlements had existed (Hall 1995, 129–31; Fox 1981, 88–91). This is a compelling argument. Such an early date does not contradict our hypotheses about the broader patterns of adoption and assimilation. From Segenhoe, Bedfordshire, in a wooded section of the south-eastern angle of the Central Province, Fox describes a set of documents in which intermingled shares together with assart lands were, in about the 1160s, subjected to a procedure of 'surrender and admittance', with the lands being surrendered, presumably to the corporate body of the manorial court. Then, on the advice of six old men, they were 'by the measure of the perch divided, as if they were newly won land, assigning to each a reasonable share'. Although the material is rather opaque, Fox holds the view that this was the point at which a two-field system was being established in an area which retained its woodland in 1086 (Fox 1981, 96–7). During the middle decades of the twelfth century surviving woodlands were being assarted, and the documents, concerning a small property of Dunstable Priory, record the absorption of these assarts within a formal townfield structure of eight hides held in villeinage. This specific and detailed case is indicative of what must have happened elsewhere many times in the preceding centuries.

By the later eighth century, if Hall's chronology is correct, arrangements antecedent to townfields were appearing in the east Midlands, at least in Northamptonshire. This was at a time when, as Hall also shows, 'late Saxon' settlement was becoming linked with the development of settlement upon the sites of the present villages (Hall 1995, 130). Figure 5.4 suggests that by the tenth century incipient townfield systems were present throughout all of the central portions of what was to be the eventual geographical range of the townfield systems. Between two broad dates, 'later eighth century' and 'tenth century', lie events of national importance, namely the Scandinavian invasions and settlement. Northamptonshire lies at the southern limit of Scandinavian settlement as indicated by names in -by (Fig 5.6). While the south-west portion of the county was virgated, most was assessed in bovates (Fig 5.5; Jolliffe 1935–6, map). The Midlands saw warfare and devastation both during the later eighth century (Hill 1981, 40 and 42) and during the reconquest by the English in the first two decades of the tenth century. By this stage the Midlands area of the Central Province comprised cleared zones interspersed with some tracts of wooded countryside (Fig 1.12). Within this 'inner frontier zone', society and agriculture must at times have been under very great stress. Here are tenable contexts – geographical, economic, social and political – for increasing nucleation and communal cultivation. The rise of communality took place within the valuable grain producing, well-populated, cleared land in the Central Province (Fig 1.12). Of course, all of these elements existed as tendencies long before these developments. Nevertheless, the need to sustain basic grain production in a war zone may have encouraged the formalisation of regional economic systems towards this one goal, and its relative efficiency may thus have been demonstrated to local aristocrats, to their overlords and, above all, to the farmers themselves. A further significant factor may well have been the imposition of Danegeld: much of the outflow of this wealth must have represented the depletion of long-accumulated high value goods and bullion. English aristocrats became impoverished, and rents from tenants provided one source of replacement (Hunter-Blair 1960, 96–7; Jones 1968, 213n, 132, 356, 364–7, 399).

The boundary established between Guthrum and Alfred had wholly collapsed by 921. Athelstan, who ruled between 924 and 954, had sufficient resources to be able to extend the wider boundaries of the English state, but inevitably some localised and internal warfare and campaigns continued into the eleventh century (Hill 1981, 60, 68, 71). Stability was only restored upon the accession of Cnut, who on the death of Edmund finally became the ruler of the whole kingdom in 1016. As early as 939 the Danish settlers of the Midlands had shown that they preferred their 20 years under West Saxon rule to the domination of the heathen Norse under Eric Bloodaxe, ruler of York (Hill 1981, 61). By the later decades of the tenth century conditions were probably such that these settlers had long been subjected to the same pressures as English farmers, and were recognising the productive capacities of the formalised, communally organised townfield systems. Familiarity with such systems by Cnut's administrators and companions may be a crucial link in the transfer of the idea to Scandinavia, a possibility identified by Göransson (1961). In England, the focus of such ideas would have been the grain-producing capacity of the strong loams of the Midlands (Fig 2.1) for which the arrangements were ideally suited. In effect each township was converted into an extremely stable grain-production machine, with yields secured by the scale of the formal rotations and the integration of arable, meadow and pasture. Its success is evident in its persistence. The Norman take over in the years immediately after 1066 reinforced this tendency, while an increasing need for oats, to help sustain the horses of the knights, ensured both the maintenance and extension of the systems, as well as their transfer to other regions. There is, however, a further dimension to the discussion, for the economic impact of the Scandinavian invasion was by no means confined to the 'English' side of the Danelaw boundary.

The Danelaw

In the Danelaw south of the Humber, medieval Lincolnshire was dominated by townfields. As the excellent, detailed studies by the Russells have shown, a high percentage of each township was still under townfield arable in the late eighteenth and early nineteenth centuries (Russell and Russell 1983; 1985; 1987). Nettleton is typical, and the evidence from the award of 1791 (Russell and Russell 1987, 114–18) can be tabulated (Table 5.1). In villages where neither common waste nor old enclo-

Table 5.1 Nettleton parish, Lincolnshire

Town closes and other closes	168 acres	4.9%
Town fields – East	1080 acres	
Town fields – West	1082 acres	63%
Common wastes	690 acres	20%
(probably excluding a portion of about 100 acres)		3.0%
Common meadows (*ings*)	323 acres	9.3%
Total (excluding the 100 acres)	3343 acres	

Table 5.2 Saleby parish, Lincolnshire

Town closes and other closes unspecified (estimated)	9 acres	
Old enclosures	1057 acres	59%
Town fields	631 acres	35.3%
Common wastes (fens and carrs)	92 acres	5%
Roads etc	9 acres	0.7%
Total	1798 acres	

sures were present the townfield land reach 80% or more, while significant old enclosure adjusted this figure downwards, for instance in Saleby (Table 5.2; Russell and Russell 1987, 149–51). By the mid-eighteenth century, 'old enclosures' could occupy as much as 60% of a parish or township. Blocks of such lands were, however, comparatively rare, sometimes involving a whole small township (with a deserted hamlet or village, such as Corringham and Springthorpe: Russell and Russell 1983, 29–38), sometimes representing a former block of common land (Fulstow: Russell and Russell 1983, 6–16), or sometimes resulting from the enclosure of a demesne or grange holding.

Turning to the administrative units containing these field systems, parish boundaries in the county fall into two broad categories. On the Wolds and in South Kesteven irregular polygons prevail, while around the coasts, along Lincoln Heath, along the Wash coast and in measure along the valley of the Trent, classic strip parishes appear. These cut across the diverse terrains to give economic variety, with the nucleated settlements forming lines in the preferred settlement zones along the lower portions of the scarps. This is a rational division based upon topographic controls, with subdivision of some townships generally also being lengthways; indeed, even the

field systems of such strip parishes may be so divided (as at Searby: Russell and Russell 1987, 168–70). Along the North Sea coast, however, there are strong hints that they were broken in two crossways (as Ludboro-Fulstow-Marsh Chapel: Russell and Russell 1983, 60–3, 6–16, 72–4). Such divisions represent basic frames within which fully developed forms of the townfield system emerged. Because of the limitations of the sources, few of the Russells' reconstructions based on the Enclosure Awards show the details of strip structures. Nevertheless, it is clear from several examples that the strips and the parish/township boundaries are in accord (as in Corringham and Fulstow: Russell and Russell 1983, 6–16, 29–38). Specifically, small-scale angled irregularities in the lines of parish boundaries are normally found where these pass *between* adjacent villages. This suggests that in such cases the administrative boundary was defined only *after* the furlongs of adjacent field systems had interlocked, or at a time when a larger territorial unit was being divided up between two communities. The remaining portions of each parish/township, fen and carr, clayland and heathland pasture could be divided by straight lines or along watercourses. Furlongs continued to be added within these defined frameworks, but the new blocks of ploughing respected the established boundaries.

To what extent can we assemble chronologies for the creation of both the parish/township units and the nucleated settlements and field systems in this part of the Danelaw? Use of Roman roads as axes for some boundaries suggests either a Roman or a post-Roman date for the parishes (Owen 1981, 1–19). As far as the settlements within them are concerned, Paul Everson and his colleagues have concluded from their work in West Lindsey that 'planning and replanning of villages was a phenomenon of the 10th to the 12th centuries' (Everson *et al* 1991, 22). The two to three centuries implied by this phrase need not represent chronological imprecision, for as we have repeatedly emphasised, the process was protracted. Can we build upon the slight irregularities found in the strip-parish boundaries, and see a first stage when inner-core field systems were limited to the areas immediately surrounding the initial settlement, followed by second phase of expansion within the formal framework of the township/parish?

Certain historical events assist the formulation of a possible chronology. The kings of Lindsey had become permanent tributary kings under Offa and were finally absorbed into the Mercian nobility by 800 (Hill 1981, 78). By 879 the area was under Danish control (Hill 1981, 40); indeed Lindsey seems to have been part of the settlement of 877 (Hill 1981, 40; Fellows Jensen 1978, 297–8). In spite of dense Anglo-Saxon settlement (Fellows Jensen 1978, figs 1 and 2, with 3 and 4), the take over by warriors with their ship-base in the Humber must have been disruptive, devastation and dislocation affecting Anglo-Saxon lord and peasant alike. Whatever pre-Danish settlement was like, the extension of cultivation into the main bodies of the parishes and townships, beyond the limited areas implied by the lengths of irregular boundary, perhaps took place *after* the end of the ninth century. The development of the putative arable cores could be pre-Scandinavian, and we may postulate that a degree of aggregation of pre-Scandinavian hamlet settlements into village-sized nucleations took place both during and after the take over, with surviving tenants being valued for their productive capacities. An initial cultural separation is possible, with single farmsteads in the hands of Danish settlers (Fellows Jensen 1978, 10–12, 276–8, 369–70), and with English tenants concentrated in nucleations.

In his study of the twelfth-century Danelaw charters, Sir Frank Stenton indicated that he believed the Scandinavians had played a major role in the replanning of field systems. His analysis of those systems as recorded in the twelfth century emphasised a number of points. First, while the bovate was the normal unit of peasant tenure, there appear to have been great variations in its size and structure, with its form varying from a compact block, or a large long single strip, to scattered parcels. Secondly, Lincolnshire holdings in particular appear to have functioned within a two-field system; indeed, parcels of land not described in terms of bovates (ie non-assessed land), are often divided by charters between the two great arable fields. Demesne holdings normally 'lay dispersed, but in furlongs not in strips'. Thirdly, and here Stenton is quite precise, 'all this means we cannot expect to find any conclusive twelfth-century evidence of a distribution of strips according to a consistent sequence of holders. Traces of such a rota are at no time frequent in this region'. He continued:

> The forces which were making for the dissolution of tenements during the twelfth century were numerous and powerful, but they do not by themselves explain the irregularity with which shares were distributed over the open fields. From the time when the lands of this region were first plotted out by its Scandinavian invaders the distribution of shares must to some extent have reflected the wealth and station of those who held them. No doubt the fields of a village inhabited only by sokemen and their immediate dependants ... (some thirty examples are known from Domesday Book) ... may well at one time have been distributed in equal holdings, each possessed by one man, and each dispersed in strips, whose sequence was determined by a pre-arranged rota. It must be added that no direct evidence of this ideal symmetry has hitherto been observed. *(Stenton 1920, lvi)*

Göransson has, however, recorded a number of terminological usages that do in fact suggest regularity of strip allocation in this county (Fig 5.5). Yet he has also argued that the Danish warriors were unlikely to have brought the townfield system into England, because there is no evidence for its presence at that date in Denmark. This may be so, but once initial Scandinavian steadings began to expand and as tenants were accreted, then the mind-set which could produce the logical geometry of a site such as Trelleborg, Jutland, was capable of creating regular agrarian structures. This would occur even if an older structural framework were evident in the form of ring fences around arable, march fences between grazings and other, slighter field remains around depopulated settlements. The warrior settlers, at first lacking female kin and household dependants, were faced with more than creating farmsteads in the style of their homeland: they were faced with the problem of handling – and perhaps even gathering – peasant cultivators. Military conquest brought new problems and social aspirations. In other parts of the country lower densities of Scandinavian names and the presence of Grimston and Carlton hybrids suggest different circumstances. We believe that in this zone, where the Scandinavian impact can hardly be questioned, agrarian development was associated with settlement agglomeration linked to 'tenant collection'.

Next, we turn to the northern Danelaw, the great tract of diverse terrains north of the Humber. Understanding the character of the Vale of York is important. Physically it is a south-to-north corridor between enclosing hill masses, a bridge between many local cultures. Its villages, field systems and manorial arrangements were apparently substantially reorganised as a result of changes wrought by the Norman Conquest, even if the 'devastation' is in measure a record of estates not fully productive rather than true on-ground destruction (Bishop 1934; 1935–6; 1948; Kapelle 1979, 158). June Sheppard has suggested that four categories of village settlement can be identified: first, regular plans laid out in the late eleventh century on lands recolonised by rent-paying tenants; secondly, demesne vills which originated in the same period; thirdly, a small group of plans remodelled after 1150, and finally some plans which were of pre-Conquest origin (Sheppard 1966; 1974; 1976; 1979). Working on the settlement and field plans of East Yorkshire and Holderness, Mary Harvey believed that she could detect two phases of landscape reorganisation, one in the late eleventh century, following devastation (Harvey 1983, 103), and a second in the late ninth century, inevitably largely obscured by the first. In both cases, very long and rather broad strips were involved.

Systems possessing similar long broad strips have also been identified on the Wolds (Hall 1995, 131–2), and indeed such arrangements are still visible along the northern side of the Vale of Pickering, as far west as Middleton by Pickering, where traces appear even on modern maps (Ordnance Survey 1:25,000 map of North York Moors, eastern sheet). We are left with the question of the Viking contribution to the appearance of such distinctive arrangements. Göransson's conclusion, that the introduction of regular village plans and regulated field systems into Scandinavia postdates the Viking control of much of England suggests either that they were indigenous developments or that they resulted from concepts derived from further south in Europe.

Finally, we turn to the Scandinavian impact upon the assessment of land, rather than its physical layout. Cyril Hart has argued that:

> the primitive hide was a measure of assessment based upon the complete agricultural package requirement for the maintenance of a family. At an early stage, individual hides became split into a number of virgates or smallholdings owing rent and services to the landlord. Estates evolved, each comprising a number of hides, usually a factor or multiple of ten. Early in the tenth century a fresh cadastre was introduced throughout hidated England, and also in territories newly recovered from the Danes. This newly imposed pattern of assessment was the direct result of the enormous disruption caused by the Danish settlement, and the partial recovery of some of the Danish-held territory, which was brought under English rule. *(Hart 1992, 304–5)*

He continues 'during this upheaval, the regular issue of royal land–books had been suspended', concluding that in the Danelaw this occurred in the half century before 942, and in the rest of England 'during the last twenty years of the reign of Edward the Elder' (ie 905–925), thus providing a *terminus post quem* for developments in each zone (Hart 1992, 294–5). Further, he suggests that soon after the settlement of Scandinavian warriors on the land wapentakes were formed, each comprising a number of 'hundreds' of 12 ploughlands, equalling 96 oxgangs for the purposes of assessment. Each ploughland (or carucate) was based upon arable land, presumably the tillage by a team of eight oxen in one year, and an oxgang (bovate) was one-eighth of this (Maitland 1897, 458).

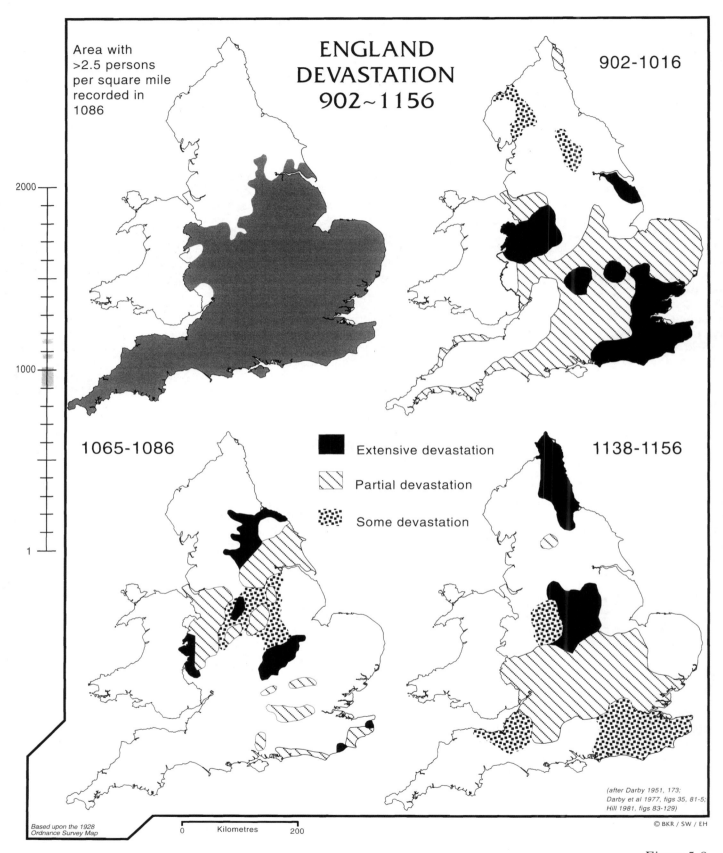

Area with >2.5 persons per square mile recorded in 1086

ENGLAND DEVASTATION 902~1156

902-1016

1065-1086

1138-1156

■ Extensive devastation

▨ Partial devastation

▨ Some devastation

2000

1000

1

0   Kilometres   200

Based upon the 1928 Ordnance Survey Map

(after Darby 1951, 173; Darby et al 1977, figs 35, 81-5; Hill 1981, figs 83-129)

© BKR / SW / EH

Figure 5.8

Hart notes that 'both words are Scandinavian loan borrowings, brought to England by the Danes to describe their units of arable land, ploughed by teams which ideally comprised eight oxen' (Hart 1992, 317). He concludes his thesis with the suggestion that when Edward the Elder established his new cadastre in Wessex and Mercia in about 920, he modelled each of the 'new' English hides on the ploughlands of the Danelaw' (Hart 1992, 317–19). In this is perhaps the root of the important idea that both the English hide and the Danish ploughland were regarded as consisting of 120 'geld' acres.

This raises, in turn, more important questions about the development of settlement and associated field systems. By the later tenth century, men of Viking descent in England, at least at the top level, had been assimilated into English society (John 1996, 140–42), so that the appearance of a unified system is conceivable, but one may question this by the 920s. The troubled question of what the 'Danes' did or not bring must remain an open one. The period is both complex and thinly and tantalisingly documented. Furthermore, more than a century separates the end of the reign of Alfred in 899 from the accession of Cnut in 1016, a time when rural life was constantly interrupted by devastation caused by the movement of armies. Figure 5.8 attempts a summary of nationally important devastation between 902 and 1156. As Darby pointed out 'although it was sporadic, local and relatively ephemeral ... repeated devastation was an ingredient of no mean importance in the life of England in the earlier Middle Ages' (Darby 1951, 173). These maps are necessarily very approximate, and for this reason they are produced at a small scale; nevertheless, they serve as a reminder of the importance of devastation in moulding the earlier medieval institutions and landscapes of all three provinces. By the end of the tenth century peace was obtained by paying for it, and in 994, 1002, 1007 and 1012 the English paid £250,000 at a time when the largest coin was a silver penny (John 1996, 145), a prodigious outpouring of bullion. Political troubles did not cease with the accession of Cnut; indeed, stability – we can now see – emerged only after the Norman Conquest (John 1996, 151–95). We may note, however, that whatever the misfortunes of the period 1065–86, the century between 902 and 1016 seems to have inflicted rather

less devastation on the northern Danelaw. Certainly, the prevalence throughout the north of the bovate, already part of the fiscal scene by 1086 and first documented in 963 at Sherburn in Elmet (Hart 1992, 317), suggests developments towards regular field systems before, if not well before, the later eleventh century. A charter issued at the same time and concerning North and South Newbald refers to '7 ilc oder acra be fastan hode', interpreted to mean that every other acre in Hotham Field (east of Hotham) is to be included within the estate (Hart 1975, 120–2, 185–6). Thus, bovation had arrived on both flanks of the Vale of York by the mid-tenth century.

Further layers of complexity were added by later eleventh-century political developments, strengthening lordship and creating new opportunities for restructuring and regularising older arrangements. So, too, did subsequent developments such as field expansion, the subdivision and amalgamation of holdings, reorganisations, changes of rotation from two fields to three fields and the processes of contraction and/or holding re-disposition. Figure 5.9 introduces a further element into the argument. It is a reminder of the simple fact that in terms of localities, royal demesne lands in 1086 were concentrated in the north, and these may well have been foci for innovation. Most of these lands had come into William's hand by right of conquest, and Elizabeth Hallam's map reveals distinctive concentrations of lands held by Edward the Confessor in the eastern portion of the Danelaw, notably in six areas (Hallam 1986, maps 3–13). From south to north these are: east of Leicester and south of Melton Mowbray, between Mansfield and Retford, around Bakewell in the Peak District, around Goole, at the head of the Humber, throughout much of West Yorkshire and south of Ripon. There are smaller concentrations in the Vale of Belvoir, south of Derby, and north of Nottingham. Of course, in terms of hides, Domesday evidence emphasises that the greatest royal wealth was concentrated in the heartlands of Wessex. Nevertheless, the presence of these royal holdings, as with the extensive demesne holdings of King William, is likely to be a reflection of the reimposition of control over areas formerly in Scandinavian hands, whose existing tenurial and administrative structures had largely been destroyed.

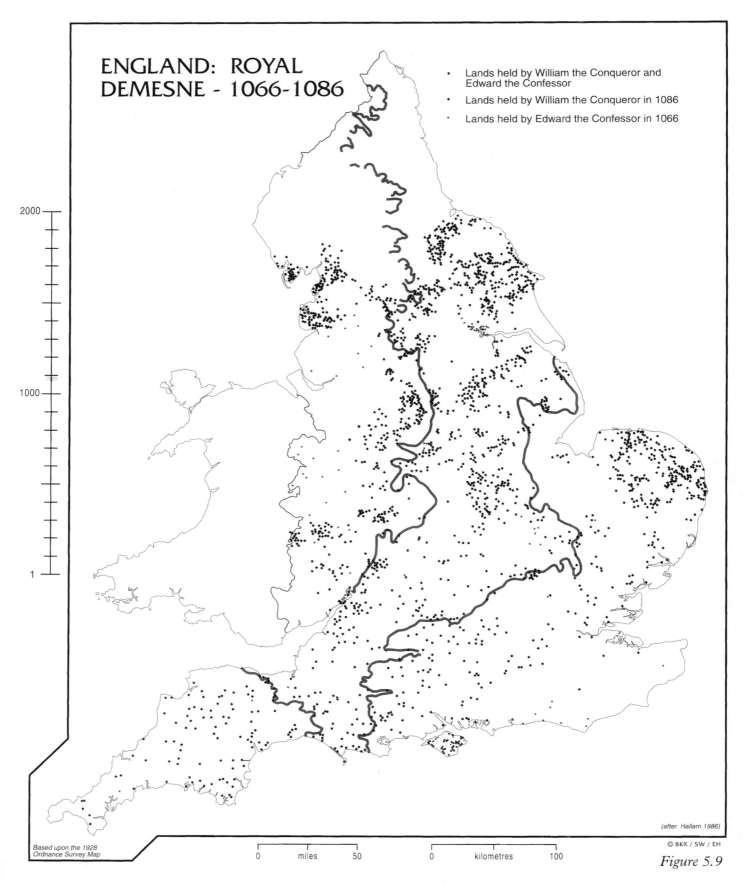

ENGLAND: ROYAL
DEMESNE - 1066-1086

- Lands held by William the Conqueror and
  Edward the Confessor
- Lands held by William the Conqueror in 1086
- Lands held by Edward the Confessor in 1066

2000

1000

1

(after Hallam 1986)

Based upon the 1928
Ordnance Survey Map

0   miles   50   0   kilometres   100

© BKR / SW / EH

Figure 5.9

Conclusions and questions

In spite of the difficulties of dating, the material available for this assessment of the chronology of townfield development in the Central Province presents a reasonably coherent picture. We envisage this process as being at least as complex as the later transformation known as the 'enclosure movement' (Fig 5.1), although it was different in character. Fifteenth-century village depopulations and enclosures by agreement suggest that the enclosure of townfields began as a series of specific local preferences, with individuals and/or particular communities taking decisions or having them forced upon them by local circumstances. These tendencies were widespread, and were eventually superseded and reinforced by powerful movements diffused by means of polemical literature and, finally, by nationally applicable Acts of Parliament. In fact, the enclosure of townfields was not a single movement but, mainly, a series of over-lapping waves, discontinuous in both space and time. In this picture of enclosure there are general lessons about both the possible time span during which the genesis of the townfield systems took place, and the spatial complexity of the forces at work.

Case E in Figure 3.4 is the least specialised of the field system types. We envisage that before and during the emergence of the Central Province similar shares in arable land were found all over England, and for that matter Scotland and Wales, in circumscribed patches of variable size. What happened throughout the Central Province was an exaggeration and magnification of tendencies already well-developed and long-established in the core of the province in the Cotswold Scarps and Vales (CCTSV), the Inner Midlands (CINMD), the East Midlands (CEMID) and the Trent Valley (CTRNT: all Fig 1.4) but also in adjacent localities. We believe that these areas were affected earliest and most strongly because they were anciently cleared land, already, by later prehistoric times, devoted to grain production (Fig 1.13). We stress that we do not see these cleared lands as homogeneous, but imagine local pockets of dense rural populations interspersed with areas of significantly lower density, where some open pasture, wood pastures and 'wold' lands survived.

From these shadowy beginnings, present in Wessex by the end of the seventh century, the advantages of a concentrated tenantry and a system of joint grain production was further stimulated by the inter-state frontier troubles of the eighth century, the Viking invasions of the ninth century and the demands of royal taxation. By the end of the tenth century elements of the system were prevalent throughout the later townfield areas of the Midlands, a region subject to constant warfare (Kerridge 1992, 22). Agricultural success on heavy clays, heavy loams and calcareous loams further encouraged its adoption. It is as a result of the intensification of population that we envisage the imposition of more formalised arrangements, particularly as the common grazing lands of local communities were given over to the plough, and the maintenance of general fertility by fallow grazing became necessary. Throughout the tenth, eleventh and twelfth centuries, amid the pressures of increasing manorialisation and lordship and the shocks of military activity, more developed 'systems' emerged. These drew together more and more of the morphological, functional and tenurial characteristics associated with the documented systems of the later centuries (Campbell 1981, 113–18). Eventually, often in association with planned villages and post-Conquest planned towns, these assemblages, in the form of the classic 'Midland system' described by H L Gray, were carried into the more peripheral regions of the Central Province and into the more productive parts of the outer provinces.

Figure 5.10 draws together in one map the distribution of townfields as recorded by Slater and those suggested by Orwin and Orwin. The latter, we are told, was prepared 'by shading all those parishes where Open Fields were proved or might be presumed ... the whole of the parish in which any evidence of open field has been found has been shaded, for it was impossible on a map of this scale to distinguish between inclosed and champion country within so small a unit, even were the data available. Thus, the map is a diagram of the geographical spread of the Open Fields, not a measure of their extent' (Orwin and Orwin 1938, 59–66). The map is unusual because it moves beyond the records of enclosure and backwards in time to a selection of medieval sources (Orwin and Orwin 1938, 60–61). This was a large-scale project, undervalued in the literature: the fact that it has not been used and reproduced suggests it has not been generally

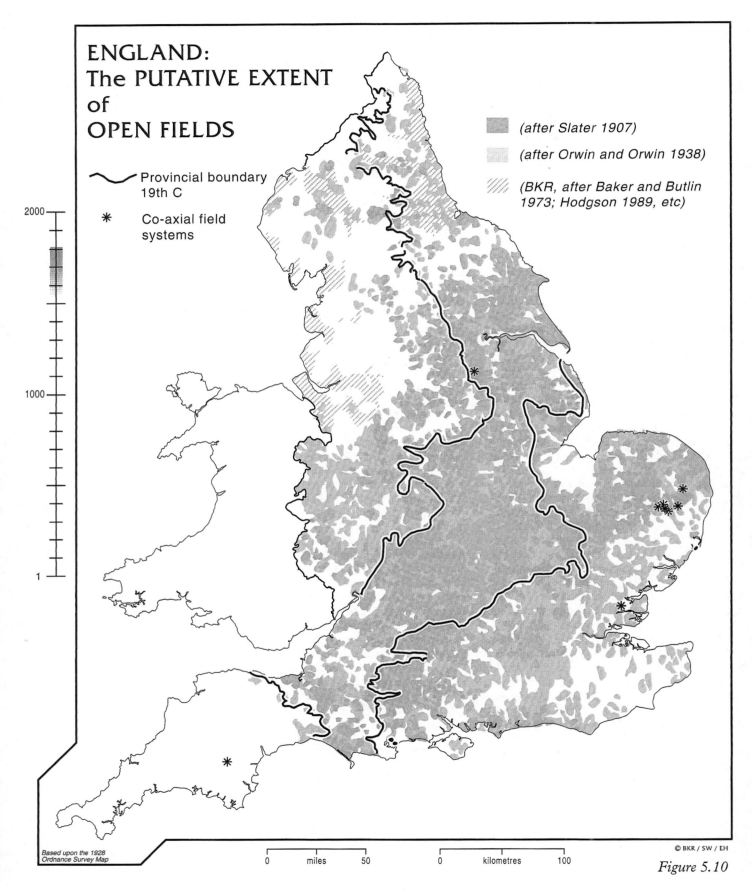

ENGLAND:
The PUTATIVE EXTENT
of
OPEN FIELDS

Provincial boundary
19th C

* Co-axial field systems

(after Slater 1907)

(after Orwin and Orwin 1938)

(BKR, after Baker and Butlin 1973; Hodgson 1989, etc)

Based upon the 1928
Ordnance Survey Map

© BKR / SW / EH

Figure 5.10

0 miles 50

0 kilometres 100

understood. To the Orwins' base have been added other indications of the presences of 'open fields' in the North and West. Nevertheless, what emerges is a crude surrogate of reality. A key point which should be understood is that the shading of the parishes exaggerates the presence of townfield lands in the outer provinces, where core shared lands would have occupied much smaller areas. We have at the moment no means of rectifying this distortion. At the point in time when these townfield systems were at their maximum, perhaps in the later thirteenth century if population levels are a guide, the contrast between the heartland areas of the Inner and East Midlands and the peripheral zones, with thinner scatters of townfields, each of restricted extent, must have been clear. While we cannot demonstrate it given the limited data available, we believe that this distribu-

tion would have more closely mirrored that of nucleations seen in Figure 1.1.

More challengingly, the arguments presented in the first paragraph of this section are modelled in Figure 5.11. In this, we picture field systems within the Central Province evolving under the influence of several factors. First, the population was, in general, rising: this statement by no means excludes national, regional or local reductions, particularly in the earlier stages of development, but the overall trend was upwards, and was associated with both local pressures on land and with colonisation. Secondly, there was an increase in both royal and seigniorial power, linked with a transition from social obligations based upon kinship to one with obligations linked to taxation, service and tenancy (see also Chapter 7). With this was associated a switch from taxation based upon territory, to taxa-

Figure 5.11

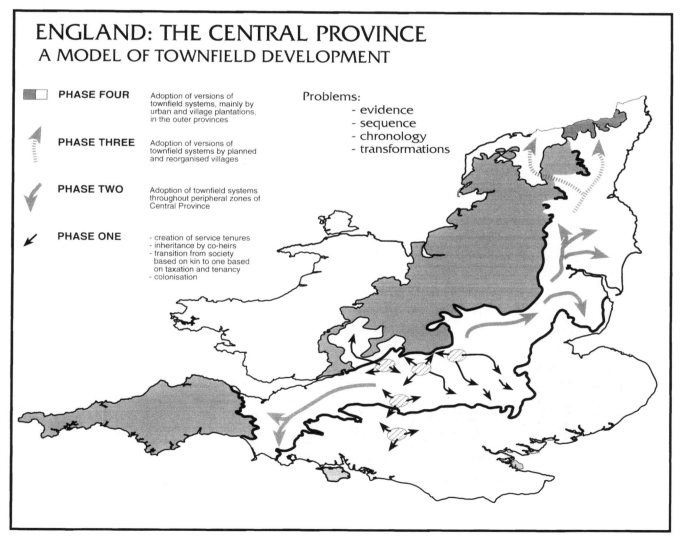

ENGLAND: THE CENTRAL PROVINCE
A MODEL OF TOWNFIELD DEVELOPMENT

PHASE FOUR   Adoption of versions of townfield systems, mainly by urban and village plantations, in the outer provinces

PHASE THREE   Adoption of versions of townfield systems by planned and reorganised villages

PHASE TWO   Adoption of townfield systems throughout peripheral zones of Central Province

PHASE ONE
- creation of service tenures
- inheritance by co-heirs
- transition from society based on kin to one based on taxation and tenancy
- colonisation

Problems:
  - evidence
  - sequence
  - chronology
  - transformations

tion based upon arable lands. The latter was more appropriate in a society in which clerks of the royal household were taking steps towards refining a bureaucracy. Finally, the expansion of arable tillage within the Central Province resulted in townfields that were the dominant form of land use. This picture is by no means complete. In individual local regions the sequencing of the varied elements of change will surely need adjustment while others will need adding. At the level of the individual township or manor, a measure of cyclical change may have been present. At first, the expansion of the fields under the influence of a rising population stimulated the emergence of a fresh local balance between tillage and pasture. Then, after a few generations, parcel fragmentation encouraged the revision of the system, both in the disposition of the holdings and in the rotations practised, while the fallow cycle of the new rotations helped to augment the pasture supply, allowing more reclamation. This eventually led to the emergence of new stable conditions.

Figure 5.11 may be seen to imply an inevitable and strident advance: this is in the nature of such images, but study of Figure 5.1 provides a valuable corrective. The adoption of the agrarian system based upon townfields took a long time, varied from estate to estate, from manor to manor and from terrain to terrain. This gave the 'frontier' a ragged quality, with developments in favoured but discrete locations, leaping ahead when circumstances were appropriate. There is an added complexity. The varied ingredients of field systems, the elements of field layout, the disposition of holdings, the rules affecting cropping and the grazing of the wastes and the fallows, and the manner in which these were all implemented, are all likely to possess individual and distinct chronologies. We cannot depict this complexity in Figure 5.11. Nevertheless, the result was the assimilation of large tracts of central England into an agrarian system in which communal townfields were the dominant agricultural form.

6
Landscapes of old enclosure: the outer provinces

Introduction

Just as the Central Province has been defined as a zone of nucleated settlements normally associated with extensive townfield systems of agriculture, so the dispersed zones of the outer provinces are normally associated with rather different agricultural systems. There is a general correlation between dispersed settlements and more 'enclosed' landscapes, though this does not mean that subdivided, open townfield systems were absent – or, indeed, even uncommon there. It is probable that most of the communities had some land – perhaps even land within enclosed fields – subdivided into small parcels, tenanted or owned by different members of the community. The community itself might be housed in several small clusters of dwellings – hamlets – which either shared subdivided lands or held them separately. Furthermore, most towns and market villages possessed townfields, and these were spread across the three provinces with relative uniformity (Fig 1.1; Unwin 1990, fig 5.2; Everitt 1967, fig 9). In the outer provinces, however, the nucleated settlements and their associated field systems by no means dominated the areas of land available to the individual communities. Unlike the Central Province, large reserves were available for other forms of land use, and it was these that generated the differences.

Some of the key issues addressed in this book concern the chronological relationships between the central and the outer provinces and the landscape elements of which they are constituted. These have already been discussed in Chapter 3. Figure 3.12(a) presents a cross section of England from north-west to south-east, from the Northern and Western Province, across the Central Province, to the South-eastern Province. It depicts the planned countrysides of the Central Province as superimpositions over a base layer of more ancient countrysides. In this reading, a great swathe of older landscape was substantially

destroyed by the imposition of regularly organised townfield systems and the subsequent centuries of cultivation that followed. The similarities between the outer provinces, in terms of their agrarian structures, have been drawn out in the case studies of Chapter 4. They are, perhaps, surprising when we note that the terrains of the north and west are fundamentally different from those of the south and east, differences reflecting latitude, relief, climate, soils and vegetation (Figs 2.1 and 2.3). Our discussion must now turn directly to the difficult questions arising from these 'ancient landscapes'. How can they be characterised and explained? What developmental stages have they passed through? In what way do the limited, often fragmented, areas of townfield and the tracts of woodland, heathland, marshland and upland fit in to a broader picture of provincial development? Finally, do the outer provinces provide vicariously a picture of the earlier landscapes of the Central Province, landscapes that have disappeared under the sustained pressure of population and the assault of the plough teams? Table 6.1 and Figure 6.1 provide an initial framework from which to approach these questions.

Table 6.1 could be extended and refined, but it draws upon published studies and accepted chronologies to create a pattern reflecting the types and periods of enclosure likely to be represented in nineteenth and twentieth-century landscapes. The higher up the tabulation, the more the phase represents an element visible in the present landscape. There is much that could be challenged, for instance should (B) really precede (C), but above all, the temporal phases (C), (D) and (E) pose the most questions. Identifying and dating these is difficult: they blend inextricably at both the purely local scale – the individual township – and at a county or a national scale. Nevertheless, a crucial issue is that the term 'ancient countrysides' as used by Rackham, is legitimate only if phases (A) to (C) contribute a significant amount to the structure of the countryside in the twentieth century. If enclosures created in time phases (D) to (I) predominate, then we must conclude that the landscapes of the outer provinces are broadly *of the same date* as those of the Central Province, and the term 'ancient' is a misnomer. On the other hand, phases (C) to (E) may conceivably contain substantial elements which are significantly earlier, perhaps even originating in phase (A). Phase A itself, of course, compresses into a single line more centuries than are represented by the succeeding nine phases.

In addition, this simple model assumes a succession of phases running in one direction. It takes no account of complexities introduced when, for example, enclosures recede and 'waste' expands again.

While some specific phases in this model can be dated, most have not been. We should, therefore, avoid the assumption that 'same form equals same date'; nothing could be further from the truth. There are examples of what may well be fossil Romano-British field systems, recovered by aerial photography, that in terms of scale and layout

Figure 6.1

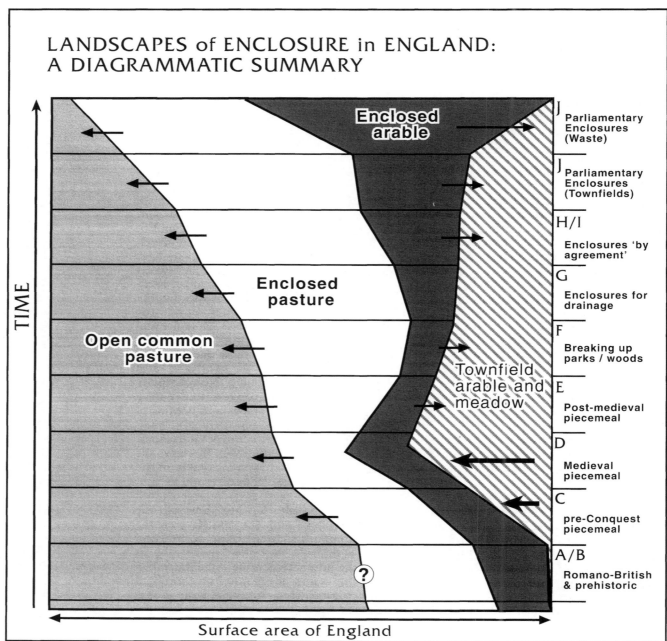

LANDSCAPES of ENCLOSURE in ENGLAND: A DIAGRAMMATIC SUMMARY

most closely resemble those of eighteenth-century enclosures. In our attempt to break away from the analysis of specific cases and reach towards the general picture, we are all too aware of the deficiencies in evidence. A further problem inherent in the table is expressed in Figure 6.1. In this the vertical scale shows time, and the horizontal represents the land surface of all England. This is divided up, subjectively but, we hope, intelligibly, into simple land use categories. The townfields that were the subject of Chapter 5 form the diagonally shaded portion to the right: they expanded and then contracted. On the left hand side lie the common pastures, including both wholly open land and some woodlands. These form the raw material from which enclosed fields, arable, pasture and meadow, have been fashioned. The precise proportion of each land category present in each period is of course, highly speculative. Nevertheless, the attempt to create this diagram was challenging, and we have no doubt that such an audit will remain a necessary step in evaluating the effect of human society on the environment.

In this chapter we are concerned with the intermediate categories in Figure 6.1, the enclosed arable and enclosed pasture. We begin with a discussion of the physical characteristics of enclosure boundaries, leading to a national map that classifies the landscapes of the two outer provinces in terms of the *mixtures* of enclosures likely to be present. This establishes a framework for a series of regional studies and comments. The arguments derived from this analysis are finally drawn together in Chapter 7, which considers the regional balances between townfield land, enclosed land, and the residue of common grazing.

The nature of enclosures

Enclosure is by no means easy to define. In general, the term is applied to the construction of distinct bounding features around pieces of land, parcels or plots of varied size, be these units of ownership, tenure, usage, working or management. Tillage, meadow and pasture or wood will be involved. When dealing with archaeological features, an 'enclosure' can be recognised by the physical remains of boundaries. Yet we normally have no idea of the extent to which what has been detected was further divided into more ephemeral parcels. These might be bounded by no more than dead hedges, fences of small stakes, lines of stones or unploughed baulks. What appears to us to be a single rectangular block-field may even have been cultivated and grazed in common, its produce being shared by several farmers. However, irrespective of ownership, tenancy or usage arrangements, it is the physical enclosure of individual land parcels that defines distinctive countrysides. The most sensible way of achieving an understanding of them is through their physical appearance, their chronological development and the varied tenurial and farming systems they represent. Chapter 4 dealt with a number of specific cases, but building up a general picture from such cases would require far more detailed studies than we have so far assembled. We are left with field form and the physical structure of enclosure boundaries, from the stone walls of the northern uplands to the hedges of the Midland bocages and the wet ditches of Essex. Even then we cannot yet assemble from these a securely based national distribution. Indeed the only map yet attempted is

Table 6.1 Enclosure: a subjective temporal classification

Parliamentary enclosures – townfield and waste ('by Act of Parliament')	(J)
Pre-parliamentary planned enclosures involving townfields ('by agreement')	(I)
Pre-parliamentary enclosures from waste ('intakes')	(H)
Pre-parliamentary planned enclosures from waste ('draining')	(G)
Parkland and woodland enclosures ('breaking up')	(F)
Piecemeal intakes from waste ('post-medieval')	(E)
Piecemeal intakes from waste ('post-Conquest, medieval')	(D)
Piecemeal intakes from waste ('pre-Conquest')	(C)
Planned intakes from waste ('co-axial systems' and 'ring-fenced enclosures')	(B)
Romano-British and prehistoric enclosures ('survivals')	(A)

based on Luftwaffe aerial photographs (Pollard *et al* 1974; Hartke 1951). To bypass these problems we must create models from such data as are available.

Figure 6.2 is a way of beginning an analysis of enclosed landscapes by defining various categories of enclosing materials. The three elements, land (both country rocks and drift materials), soil and vegetation provide raw materials from which enclosures can be formed. The brackets show varied associations of these elements, so that ditches, banks and hedges can all appear together, but all can – at least theoretically – appear independently. The letters differentiate landscape types. Reality is, of course, far more complex than the diagram implies. Take, for instance, Type N, landscapes of fences. These are now either combined with barbed wire to make relatively cheap stock-proof barriers or appear in contexts where they represent only a minute portion of the total capital investment – for instance, where horses are bred, reared or trained. However, to imply that there were no medieval or pre-medieval enclosures with stake-and-rail work, wattled fencing and the like, would be nonsense, for these forms of enclosure appear in medieval illustrations. Built of perishable materials they never survive as functional elements of modern landscapes; they are archaeologically detectable only with difficulty, for much evidence may have been lodged in the surface soil rather than in the subsoil. The permanence of stone walls, or the strings of stone resulting from dumping at clearance or from wall collapse, together with the near indelibility of ditches are apt to give the impression that these were the dominant enclosure forms. A journey through timber-rich Scandinavia quickly reveals the variety and impressive character of wooden fences. Many of them are set on the soil as much as in it, and occur in combination with various forms of stone walling.

Thus, Figure 6.2 subsumes many variations. A ditch can appear without a bank (Type J) provided that the initial waste and all subsequent scourings are spread over the adjacent fields rather than merely piled nearby. Banks can appear without ditches if they are built of turf and other land-clearance debris, the end result being wholly different from a true stone wall or revetted stone dyke. Parts of the South-west carry substantial enclosure banks which, when seen in section, rarely show many large stones. There may be a link here with the paring of turf from long

grass fallows, normal in western environments, because wooden ploughs shod with iron parts could not easily cope with a well-formed sod such as developed in the warmer and wetter west. This is not to deny that field stone clearance gradually added more material, but is a way of emphasising the profound linkages between enclosure and farming practices. Land taken into cultivation for the first time generates certain materials with which to demarcate and construct boundaries. At this stage the farmer must enclose, even if the land is intended as townfield land, to avoid the damage from animals pastured on the common wastes. Residual bushes, stones picked from the broken tilth and even stubbed up rootstocks or residual timber trees, particularly fruit trees and the like, were undoubtedly used to frame initial enclosures. Thus, clearance from the wild is intimately associated with the enclosure and protection of arable land, as Gonner identified (Gonner 1912, 82, n2).

In contrast, the materials needed in order to fence consolidated townfield strips and intakes from common grazings or open ground – quarry stone or hawthorn quicks – lend themselves to a formal, regular geometry of enclosure characteristic of more recent centuries. In Figure 6.2, Types A and K, they are associated with these late enclosures, either by agreement or under Parliamentary Act. Between these two extremes lies the case of long-tilled land, where inherited initial boundaries tend to be gradually eliminated, both as encumbrances to the run of the ploughs and as wasteful of productive land. Such boundary clearance signified that communal rights were superseding individual rights or the rights of co-parceners within an enclosed field. In intensively cultivated areas, live hedges, harbouring pests, as well as usable timber and brushwood, were gradually eliminated by excessive grazing and cutting, while within claylands, any field stone formed useful material for buildings and trackways. Dead-hedges and fences eventually rot, and earthen banks and ditches eventually fall to the plough. In short, open landscapes are the product of usage and time. The stimulus for change must be found in decisions taken by the farming community, and as we noted in Chapter 5, the demands of grain production are the most likely factor leading towards the relative homogenisation of champion countrysides through the assimilation of farming systems towards a culturally imposed norm.

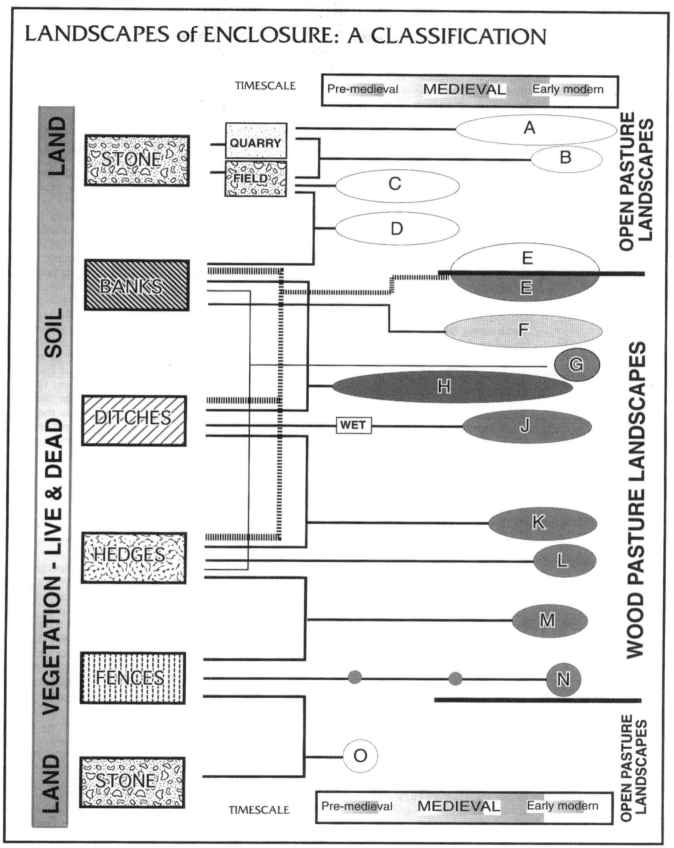

Figure 6.2

The varied types of enclosing boundary in Figure 6.2 are arranged in two broad groups: those associated with open pastures and those linked with wood pasture landscapes. We have also attempted to place the varied combinations within a crude chronological framework. Certain well-known categories can be recognised. Type A, of quarry stone, is characteristic of upland margin landscapes of Parliamentary enclosure of the eighteenth and nineteenth centuries: it is distinctive, the walls bound together by bands of through stones into a coherent yet highly flexible wall. There are fundamental contrasts between these and the older walls, constructed of field stones, to be seen in the South-west, and the older walling of the Pennines and the Lake District (Type C). Such ancient walls are normally patched with quarry stone and often – at least throughout the Pennines – closely associated with even older enclosures using banks (Type D) or large basal boulders. The former often possess ditches, and lead to the 'catch-all' category of Type E, enclosures based upon banks, ditches and hedges, found in diverse contexts. Cases occur with hedges set upon near negligible banks (Type L), sometimes with more substantial banks, and a marked ditch (Type K). The use of substantive banks without ditches but with hedges, Type F, is seen in south-west England. However, we must stress that this diagram is simply a reminder of both regional diversity and chronological variation found within the all-embracing term 'enclosed landscapes'. It is an attempt to break into a way of thinking that passes beyond the rather vague 'early' or 'late', and 'regular' or 'irregular'.

Figure 6.3 moves to land patterns and uses sets of simple models to suggest ways in which three types of enclosure patterns can be organised by using the morphological characteristics. Shown as a stylised landscape, varied types are identified by means of appended letters; these refer to the types shown in Figure 6.2.

Regular blocks. These are constructed of quarry stone, or earthen banks mixed with some field stones and hedgerows in the uplands, and low banks with or without small ditches set with hedges or fences in the lowlands. They are primarily associated with Parliamentary enclosure of both common grazings and townfields. Similar block fields, initially larger but then subjected to subdivision, are linked with pre-Parliamentary intakes of wasteland in the seventeenth and eighteenth centuries. Linked to improved accuracy in land survey these field patterns are geometrically regular impositions and appear in both wood pasture and open pasture landscapes. A sub-group is found in regular wetland enclosures using drainage ditches.

Irregular blocks. These comprise field stone walls with some quarry stone patching, and banks, ditches and hedges. They are landscape elements linked with the continuum of medieval and post-medieval enclosure in both wood and open pasture regions. It is often possible to identify several significant sub-groups. First, in upland countrysides, upward-curving lines result from the creation of a series of head dykes at increasing altitudes. Between adjacent upward loops a downward funnel focuses upon a farmstead, so that the two enclosing sides make a cattle track, to protect the arable and meadow grass of the enclosed inby. These arrangements may be associated with a succession of roughly parallel roads, bridleways and footpaths running along the valley sides; they are common features of the uplands. Secondly, in lowland countrysides, there is the subdivision of large intakes, often with 'geographically logical' boundaries, where a tract of land between two streams, extending from the edge of a flood plain up the slope towards the crest, has formed a coherent unit for clearance. This may be confirmed by the limits of landownership or tenancy. There is also a category involving the division of former parkland or other 'specialist' enclosures.

A second and particularly important sub-group can be seen in distinctive looped or curvilinear enclosures – 'ring-fenced enclosures' – which when they appear in groups, leave swathes of common lands between the protected improved lands. Given that they are normally the focus for important farmsteads, halls, and even township or parish foci, they may be of considerable antiquity, perhaps ranging in date from pre-medieval to medieval, however this be defined. In some situations the settlements lie peripheral to the enclosed ovals. Such arrangements have been identified in contexts as far apart as Suffolk, Lancashire and Devon (Chapter 4), and appear to represent a perfectly logical taking in of areas of 'better land' with the least effort. This wide geographical range leads to an interesting question about their origins. In the uplands

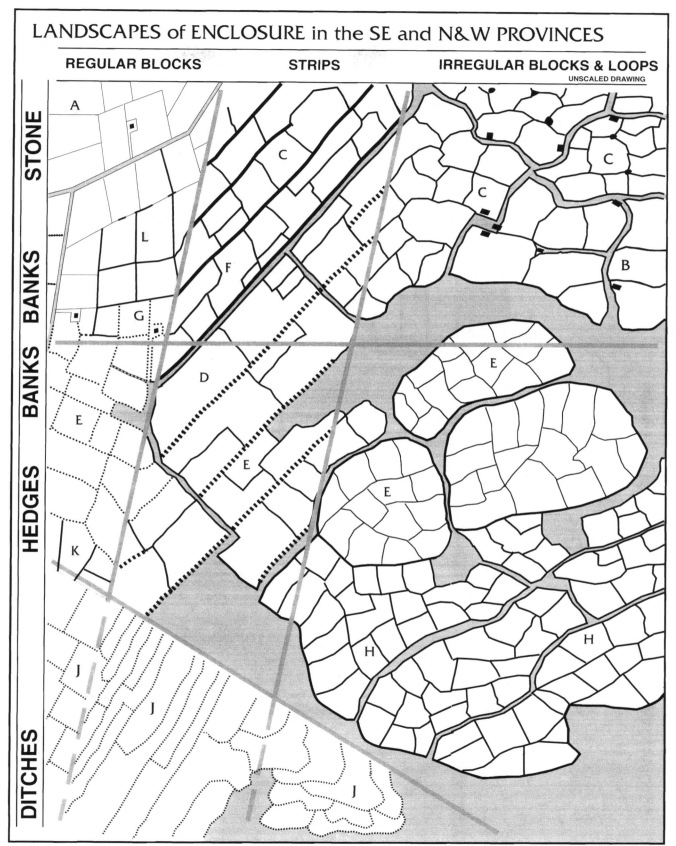

LANDSCAPES of ENCLOSURE in the SE and N&W PROVINCES

Figure 6.3

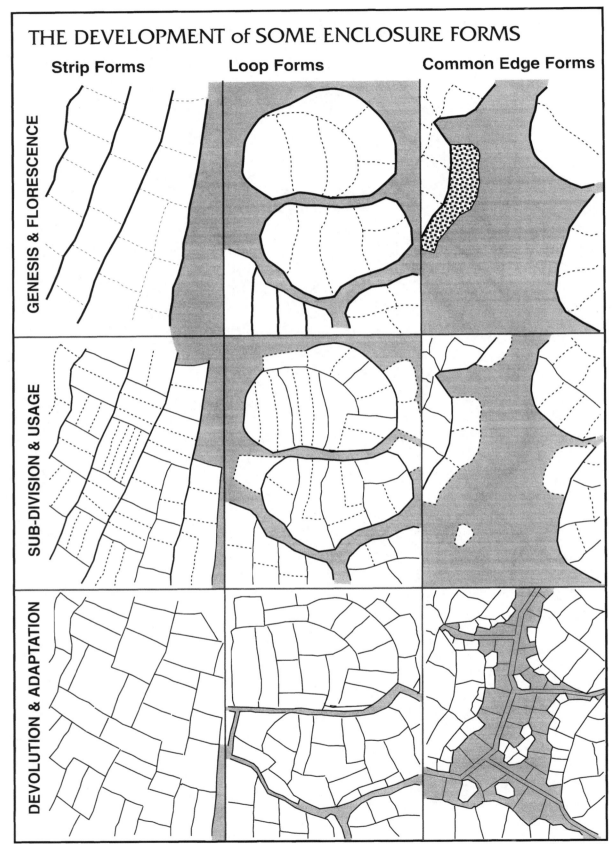

Figure 6.4

they may be pastoral, associated with stock production. It is possible that the ring-fenced enclosures of south-east England are also pastoral in origin, linked with turning wood pastures, suitable grazing for cattle, goats and pigs, into grass pastures more suitable for sheep. If pigs were initially fenced within such ovals they would, if the trees had been removed, speedily clear the land of its vegetation, so as to allow colonisation of the bare soil by herbaceous plants and, eventually, the plough.

The chronology of all these features presents fundamental difficulties, which can be illustrated at Steward Shield Meadow, a distinctive ovoid enclosure of inby land amid the heather and grass moors of upper Weardale, County Durham (Roberts *et al* 1973, 207–21).The element 'shield' in the name suggests an origin as a temporary settlement associated with summer grazing. Occupation became permanent during the thirteenth century, with desertion at some date between the second and eighth decades of the fourteenth century, and reoccupation in the seventeenth century: a brief episode of settlement history, simply told. Yet the pollen diagram shows a much longer history of clearance which, according to a radiocarbon date, culminated in the pre-Roman Iron Age about 100 BC. Some of the banks and ditches may, therefore, be prehistoric in origin, rather than medieval. This is an example of the problems of 'dating' such an upland site. At Roystone Grange in Derbyshire, an even greater complexity has been revealed (Hodges 1991).

Strips: In south-east England there appear areas of 'co-axial field systems', where the land surface is divided by a series of roughly parallel boundaries, of clearance stone or earthen banks. It is important to distinguish between these and the exceptionally long townfield strips found in some parts of the North. A normal townfield ploughstrip is characteristically 220 yards (200m) long and five, seven, eight or as much as eleven yards (4.6 to 10m) in width, to be seen in the landscape as ridge and furrow. A parcel, the unit of tenure or ownership, may comprise one, two, three or even more ploughed lands. In contrast, the great strips are 400m, 600m, or more rarely up to 1200m in length, and correspondingly wide, 30m, 40m or more. Nevertheless, they are part of a townfield system (Maitland 1897, 422–62). In contrast, the published diagrams of co-axial field systems show that the strips of which they are comprised can

be several kilometres – two, three, five and as many as eight – in length. Width is more difficult to state accurately because the features show as traces across substantial tracts of countryside. The system itself may be several kilometres wide (Warner 1996, figs 3.3, 3.4, 3.6). They may be compared with the prehistoric land divisions known as reaves, on Dartmoor (Fleming 1988), although many of the East Anglian strips possess lateral boundaries which are gently curved, perhaps reflecting an origin as plough-strips. Thus, the great strips and co-axial systems overlap at the extremes of their dimensions, but both differ markedly from the normal ploughstrip, and it is hard to conceive of a ploughstrip extending for several kilometres in length. This question may be resolved by detailed analysis in the field.

The first two columns of Figure 6.4 take two of the basic clearance 'frameworks', the strip and the loop – seeing the individual block as a simpler version of the former – and then suggest three developmental phases. The assumption is that these basic forms are shapes that are created during land clearance, be this from wildwood or from heath or moor. The diagram then depicts forms which develop through sustained usage and subdivision, to a point at which the original frameworks are almost wholly destroyed. This is a model, involving a constant interplay between continuity and change; nevertheless, this type of thinking, and the assumptions upon which it is founded, underlie much morphogenetic analysis (eg Fowler 1971, 176–9; Rippon 1991). Strips may be wholly regular, irregular, wedge-shaped or, more commonly, rather sinuous, reflecting topography. Cross divisions result in a more or less regular 'ladder' pattern. The final column generalises a distinctive pattern which may be equally important as an antecedent feature in enclosed landscapes: the 'negatives' which are created when an area of common waste survives as a residual feature, set amid surrounding enclosures. Encroachments of varied size can and do occur, but the final stage of a formal act of complete enclosure inserts a new geometry into the landscape. Not included in these generalisations are small strips, characteristically resulting from enclosures by agreement, which were created by fencing small blocks of townfield parcels (Fig 4.19). These often follow the former patterns sufficiently closely to reveal the character of the antecedent system.

Landscapes of enclosure: the national picture

Figure 6.5, a and b, a map that attempts to summarise enclosed landscapes at a national scale, uses an icon or ideogram to encapsulate the typical landscape elements of each region. The regional divisions seen on the map are, with a few exceptions, the divisions based upon the settlement sub-provinces already defined in Figure 1.4. This is a logical procedure, because the contrasts in real countrysides derive from the varied balances between townfield land, enclosed land and common pasture; and these are, in part at least, reflected also in settlement characteristics. The constituent elements of the landscapes of the two outer provinces are characterised by the icons in Figure 6.5b. Two things differentiate the regions: first, the varied proportions of each element present within a given landscape; and secondly, the appearance of some regionally specific elements, perhaps present elsewhere but only in insignificant quantities. The following discussion of cases and problems is divided according to the regions shown on the map, and each is preceded by a short summary of its general characteristics.

Eastern English enclosure landscapes

Eastern England can be divided into three distinct zones that broadly reflect land quality and farming potential. The first, the Fenland, forms a distinct *pays*, and the history of its colonisation and drainage, and hence 'enclosure' history, has been the subject of numerous analyses (Darby 1974; Hallam 1965; Ravensdale 1974; Hall and Coles 1994). Rimmed by somewhat higher lands, this former shallow bay, of which the Wash is a remnant, has been partially filled by silts, clays and peats. These deposits have varied according to delicate balances between the relative levels of the land and the sea. Between the clays of the coastal salt marshes and the silts and peats of the inner basin there runs a low silt ridge, the southern end of which breaks into smaller patches to form the 'islands' associated with Ely, Thorney and March. As Figure 1.1 emphasises, nucleations are concentrated on these slightly higher areas, although, since systematic post-medieval drainage, some small hamlets have appeared along the dykes and causeways of the drained peat fen. The fen edge, a classic preferred settlement zone, carries a dense chain of nucleations. The place-names of Domesday Book imply that this pattern of settlement nodes, perhaps hamlet clusters, often with parish churches, was already present by 1086. The surrounding lowlands formed common grazings, and patterns of linear parish boundaries, running from washlands to the dry land of the silt ridge and thence to the fen, emphasise this. The history of subsequent colonising activity can be generalised as the gradual extension of improved lands into the fen edges: 'fen dykes' were created around the islands and on the western, landward side of the ridge; and 'sea dykes' were established on the eastern or seaward sides of the settlement zones (Hallam 1965, end-pocket map; Hall and Coles 1994, fig 86).

There is little doubt that forms of arable townfields were present on the silt ridge, islands and fen edges (Hallam 1965, 137–61; Ravensdale 1974, 85–120, fig 1; Spufford 1974, 120; Hall and Coles 1994, 140). Other attractions for settlement lay in varied fen resources: in pasture and turbary, fisheries and salt pans, reeds, rushes and bird life. The battle with water was constant; it was, as Hallam's detailed analysis shows, at once a valuable resource and an ever-present hazard (Hallam 1965, 119–36). Modern maps of the region still allow earlier curvilinear patterns of intakes to be distinguished from the rigidly rectangular patterns resulting from systematic drainage and reclamation of the flat silt and peat fens in the seventeenth century. The region's exceptional physical circumstances have generated conditions which allow aerial photography also to reveal extensive traces of the antecedent patterns (Hallam 1970, A–L; Hall and Coles 1994). Thus, when the details of Romano-British landscapes of the Fenlands are projected onto a scale of 1:25,000, the resultant patterns of farm and field boundaries and settlement – both nucleated and dispersed – are at least as intricate as the detail of the modern Ordnance Survey map.

East of the Fens, the Good Sand and Brecklands of the western portion of East Anglia have in this study been identified as a distinctive sub-province. This is very variable land: at best it is some of the best general quality farmland in the country, but at worst, notably in the Brecklands, the poor sandy and gravely soils are suited only for lowland heaths. They were worked traditionally by balancing crop production. On the one hand there was a continuously cropped area manured with dung from the homesteads and folded sheep. On the other, there were intermittently cropped areas called 'brecks'; these were taken from the waste, used for a few years and then allowed to revert to sheep pasture until ploughed again (Stamp 1937–44, vii, fig 15, 128–9). The maps give the impression of open landscapes that are in general dominated by comparatively recent remodelling, as a by-product of agricultural improvement occasioned by the advent of the turnip as a field crop. This is not to say that traces of former landscapes are not recoverable, but to recognise a contrast similar to that between Westmorland and Northumberland. In the former, ancient landscapes are still both a part of the everyday functioning scene, and visible in field patterns and earthwork remains, while in Northumberland a substantive 'newness' has been superimposed by extensive townfield development and subsequent wholesale improvement.

The third zone comprises the sub-province of the clayland plateaux of the east and south of East Anglia. These plateaux extend from northern Norfolk, across High Suffolk, north-western Essex, and thence into eastern Hertfordshire and northern Middlesex, where they abut the Chilterns. Together they form one of the most continuous tracts of good quality general-purpose farmland in the country. Needless to say, there are within this zone many variations. In the north-eastern sector of Norfolk the clays are associated with glacial sands and gravels, giving more loamy soils. The sandier wedge, extending southwards from Lowestoft and broadening inland to spread along the northern flank of the Stour Valley, forms a countryside known as 'The Sandlings'. Much of this area has long been enclosed and all the indices of medieval wealth suggest that this was a zone of great and populous prosperity (Glasscock 1975, map 1). Its mixed farming system involved arable maintained by the folding of sheep, and the grazing of many commons and wood pastures by varied stock.

The characteristics of these countrysides bring into focus the question of clay soils. H Rider Haggard, writing in 1899, at a time when he was farming clay land near Bungay, north of the Waveney, in Norfolk, says: 'Heavy land … does not necessarily mean bad land … if I were given a choice I would … undertake a heavy-land farm in good order than one liable to 'scald', which refuses to produce a crop of hay or roots unless deluged day by day with rain … the heavy lands are corn-growing lands, and when it no longer pays to grow the corn they are supposed to be of no value …' (Haggard 1899, 8). When not kept in good heart and in good order, however, clay lands are expensive to bring back into production. Maps of the late eighteenth century show that Norfolk then contained substantial tracts of open common grazings and heathland, particularly extensive in the Breckland area north of Thetford. To these must be added large tracts of fen and marsh in the east and west of the county. Such commons are largely absent from the 'Good Sand' region to the north-west. Across the clay plateaux, although smaller, they are nevertheless present as a recurrent landscape feature, often with long roadside tongues reaching from one common towards the next (Barringer 1996; Denman et al 1967, map no 19). Around Haggard's farms very small commons were the rule, but the area carried significant small patches of woodland. In contrast, to the south, in Suffolk, the clays carried fewer and even smaller commons. For both the Essex and the East Hertfordshire boulder clay plateaux, Gonner's generalised figures suggest that the commons caught by the Enclosure Commissioners were generally less extensive than those of Norfolk (Gonner 1912, 285). In practical terms the picture must be envisaged as dynamic. By the later eighteenth century traditional practices had long felt the impact of the London market. There must have been circumstances in which, on the one hand, proximity to London helped preserve tracts of open grazing and woodland, particularly those in royal hands, while in other circumstances the location must have helped accelerate piecemeal enclosure.

In terms of settlement this sub-province is characterised by significantly lower densities of nucleations, hamlets, villages and market towns than the English Midlands. A figure of 55 nucleations per 25 by 25km square contrasts with the 70–80 usual for the Central Province. Towards the coast, amid the Sandlings and the Broads, there are even lower densities. Only in the Norfolk portion of the sub-province do significant numbers of deserted villages appear. There is a consistent presence of medium to very high densities of dispersed

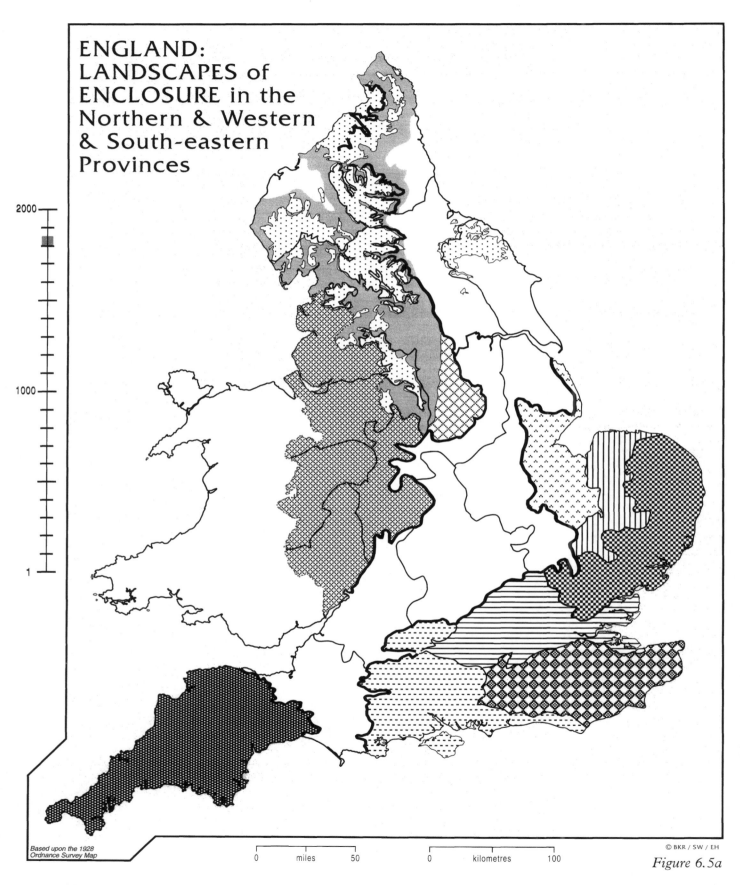

ENGLAND:
LANDSCAPES of
ENCLOSURE in the
Northern & Western
& South-eastern
Provinces

Based upon the 1928
Ordnance Survey Map

© BKR / SW / EH

Figure 6.5a

Northern Enclosures

Northern Uplands

— Open common pastures with intakes

— Post-medieval intakes and Parliamentary enclosures

— Medieval irregular closes

— Townfield lands

North & West Midlands Enclosures

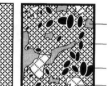

— Open common pastures with intakes

— Medieval irregular closes: some ring fences

— Townfield lands

— Post-medieval intakes and Parliamentary enclosures

Sherwood

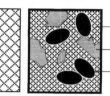

— Medieval irregular closes

— Open common pastures with intakes

— Townfield lands

Eastern England Enclosures

Fens

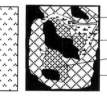

— Post-medieval intakes and Parliamentary enclosures

— Coastal marshes

— Medieval irregular intaking

— Townfield lands

Sands and Brecklands

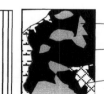

— Open common pastures with intakes

— Townfield lands

— Post-medieval intakes and Parliamentary enclosures

Clay Plateaux

— Townfield lands

— Open common pastures with intakes

— Medieval intaking: irregular blocks, strips and ring fences

LANDSCAPES OF ENCLOSURE ~ KEY

South-eastern Enclosures

Thames

— Open common pastures with intakes

— Woodland survivals

— Medieval irregular closes

— Townfield lands

Weald

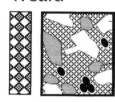

— Woodland survivals

— Townfield lands and 'yokes'

— Open common pastures with intakes

— Medieval / post medieval irregular closes

Chalk and Sands

— Townfield lands

— Earthwork survivals

— Post-medieval intakes and Parliamentary enclosures

— Medieval irregular closes

— Woodland survivals

— Open common pastures

South Western Enclosures
South West England

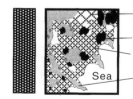

— Post-medieval intakes and Parliamentary enclosures

— Townfield lands

— Medieval irregular closes

Sea — Open common pastures

Figure 6.5b

settlement: isolated halls, large farmsteads and churches. These are scattered in landscapes with large numbers of wet-ditched moated sites, loosely structured hamlets bearing 'green' names, all formerly associated with long chains of roadside commons, linking together the scattered larger blocks of common land. Overall, the area is dominated by dispersed settlements, with some regions – notably in Essex, Suffolk and southern Norfolk – having very high densities. The essential patchiness of these eastern English landscapes is their characteristic feature, a lack of uniformity over large areas reflecting ancient roots. Faden's map of Norfolk in 1797 provides a powerful image, for even if parkland is excluded the woodland, common and heathland, fen, carr and marshland must account for 15–20% of the total surface area at that date. It is probable that this proportion was even higher in the medieval period, before the introduction of rotations which allowed the permanent integration of intakes into the system of tillage. These extensive pastures, ranging from dry sand and gravel areas, through wet bottoms to coastal marshes, supported the sheep flocks that brought prosperity to the area.

Work by Gray and Douglas attested that a form of open townfield was present in East Anglia. Areas were limited, and good heart was maintained by fold coursing, the folding of sheep flocks on the arable, so that their urine enriched the soil. Douglas showed that in medieval East Anglia there was a multiplicity of small manors, and furthermore that the geld was not assessed in carucates but distributed among the vills or townships, each contributing so many pence to every pound of geld (Douglas 1927, 3–4). He demonstrated in some detail that the basic fiscal tenement, the *tenementum*, comprised 12 acres of arable land, more or less, a unit which tended to retain its integrity through time, even when subdivided. The tenement, and the shared acres associated with it, were of ancient foundation (Douglas 1927, 17–67). Nevertheless, these open townfields never came to dominate the entire landscape. The presence of large open commons and wood pastures, plus the tradition of folding, helped sustain the system. Neither the demesne nor tenant land was divided into two or three cropping units of equal size. Warner has shown how the ring-fenced enclosures are a part, but only a part, of a system of land occupation present in and before 1086. Links between these structures

and the formal fiscal tenements have yet to be defined. An assessment of the dimensions of one of the examples he illustrates, Wenhaston Old Hall, suggests a size of the order of 350ha (over 850 acres: Warner 1987, 30, 33).

Our impression is that the three structural elements noted above underlie and frame landscapes in proportions that vary spatially. Ring-fenced enclosures and areas of townfield are more usual in Norfolk; Suffolk is characterised by ring-fenced enclosures and long 'co-axial' strips. Remodelled patterns were gradually inposed in both counties. Faden's map of Norfolk in 1797 and J Hodskinson's late eighteenth-century map of Suffolk suggest a line of contrast extending from Great Yarmouth, though Diss to Bury St Edmunds (Barringer 1996; Stamp, 1937–44, vii, 336). To the north and west of this, commons are larger and more numerous, while to the south and east (south-east Norfolk extending into the boulder clay region of central Suffolk), commons are fewer and smaller. It is to the south and east of this line that, in general, the densest areas of dispersed settlement appear by the nineteenth century (Fig 1.13).

Stephen Rippon's thought-provoking analysis of the early planned landscapes of south-east Essex represents a ground-breaking study of the complexities of multi-layered ancient countrysides in the South-eastern Province. His conclusion is worth citing:

> It would appear therefore that the following conclusions can be reached. Firstly, the regular landscape is not all one entity: there are numerous morphologically distinct landscapes in this area, with a generally similar orientation perhaps due to a framework of earlier trackways. Secondly, individual morphological zones were deliberately planned out. Thirdly, the landscape as it exists is a palimpsest, including both Roman and Saxon/medieval elements, though most of the regularity evident in the modern landscape probably dates to the middle or later Saxon period. *(Rippon 1991, 55)*

These developments, dating to the period between the eighth and the tenth centuries, are described as a 'major reorganisation of the landscape' (Rippon 1991, 57–8). There is some evidence that this reorganisation took place over antecedent agrarian structures of Roman date; but the key point is that, if Rippon is correct, these countrysides were taking their visible form *in the same period* as that in which the landscapes of the Central Province were also taking shape.

South-eastern enclosure landscapes

In Figure 6.5b three sub-provinces are used as a framework for dividing the zone into 'Chalk', 'Thames' and 'Weald'. Once again we emphasise the pragmatic nature of this step: we appreciate that each sub-province contains many local regions. The Weald basically comprises an oval arrangement of inward-facing escarpments and a sandstone central ridge, with upstanding chalk and sandstone beds separated by clay vales. The scatter of nucleations is light, and with a marked preferred settlement zone appearing in the north, the Vale of Holmsdale. Evidence from the Petworth estates suggests that the nucleated villages and larger hamlets may well have once had regular plans and that these suffered subsequent devolution (Leconfield 1954, maps). Everitt expresses the opinion that many of the Kentish villages may have originated as little market towns rather than purely agricultural communities; while others, if traced back, are seen to originate in small hamlets or single farmsteads. His cautious and qualified comments indicate the need for research focused upon settlement origins (Everitt 1986, 39–40). This is, in his words, 'an essentially different type of countryside' from that of the classic Midland plain, in which farmsteads of medieval age, associated severalties and common edge strings of small farmsteads and cottages, intermix with forge and hammer houses and specialist settlements such as 'denns' or 'denes'. Nucleations are a product of more recent centuries.

With the exceptions of the Canterbury-Thanet local region and Romney Marsh the intensity of dispersion is uniformly high. Hamlets, both close structured and loose structured, often around small areas of common waste, probably represent relatively ephemeral features of this landscape: farmstead clusters can be added to, cottage and farmstead strings can be infilled, or conversely, farmsteads and cottages can disappear. The presence of industrial elements within the economy, the working of minerals or the processing of woodland products, are pressures towards more speedy change than is perhaps normal under conditions dominated by agricultural production. The presence of open commons creates conditions in which common edge squatting occurs, generating distinctive strings. It is possible that buried within these landscapes, truly ancient elements may survive, perhaps preserved by and beneath a post-Roman phase of woodland regeneration.

'Thames' (the sub-province ETHAM: Fig 1.4) embraces the London Basin but includes within it the escarpment of the Chilterns. The southern boundary has been drawn along the foot of the dipslope of the Chalk, a delineation which reflects nineteenth-century settlement patterning. The heart of the sub-province lies in the floodplains and gravels of the Thames and its tributaries, with associated heathlands and clayland tracts. The Chilterns, to the northwest, give a distinctive local region where the Chalk carries surface layers of clay. Between the two is a complex gradation. To the south of the Thames both claylands and alluvium and gravels appear on rising slopes, while east of London, marshlands are characteristic. In a national context this sub-province is a pivotal, transitional countryside, where local regional variations are often of sharp importance, and where ancient characteristics have long been masked first by the influence of the capital, and eventually by the sprawl of urban and suburban landscapes. In the light of this, it is paradoxical that with the exception of a single local region the whole sub-province was, in the middle decades of the nineteenth century, characterised by low densities of nucleation. The exception is the mid-Thames terraces to the west of London. There, concentrations of villages were such that a 25 by 25km square sample recorded 92 nucleations, an exceptionally high figure. These do not appear to be directly associated with the diffusion of 'suburbanisation' from London itself, but represent an older layer of settlement: there are clear signs that the area was once dominated by townfields.

Gray, writing in 1915 about the field systems of the area, puts a precise finger on the problem: 'what is clear is that the plain on both sides of the Thames west of London constituted a region where the midland system and the Kentish system came into contact ... the outcome was a hybrid system difficult to follow in its origins, and indeed this difficulty prevails to the field arrangements which characterised the entire lower valley of the Thames. Scarcely any part of England is so dependent upon conjecture for the writing of this early history' (Gray 1915, 402). Roden (1973, 325–76) adopted an explanatory model which interrelated two factors: the varied conditions of soil and slope, and the broad sequences of colonisation. Early settled zones tend to possess townfields, while later – possibly post-twelfth century colonisation – generated fragmented communal systems and severalty.

Further west, the chalkland node and associated lowland basin, so distinctive in their settlement characteristics, could well be designated a separate small province. Equally, there are arguments for attaching the area to either the Central Province or the South-eastern Province. All three possibilities could be justified, but here it is described with the South-eastern Province because of the relatively low overall densities of nucleations. Its distinctive rolling swells seen in the chalk downs, with deep, smoothly contoured valleys with winter stream flows, contrast with the lower heathlands and woodlands of the Hampshire Basin proper. Throughout this sub-province the location of nucleated settlements is strongly affected by terrain: they often form into chains along the valleys where water supply was assured. There is also a greater concentration of villages and hamlets along the coastal plain, extending into Sussex. Because of topographic constraints, in neither of these contexts is a meaningful 25 by 25km square sample possible. The area is one with, in general, extremely low densities of dispersion. Only along the coast east of Southampton water and in the Isle of Wight do higher densities appear by the nineteenth century, reflecting the kindly climate, proximity to major harbours and relative proximity to London. Paradoxically, this area is both pivotal and peripheral. It is pivotal because of important harbours at Southampton, Portsmouth and Chichester with their access to the Channel. But with generally poorer soils on the chalk and the newer rocks of the Hampshire Basin (the basis of the New Forest), it is peripheral to the political focus of the London Basin, to the grain-producing sub-provinces of the Midlands, and to the rich and diverse lands to the west.

Christopher Taylor has argued for the kernel and periphery model of landscape development in Dorset, with ancient foci, perhaps no more than single farmsteads, accreting population, acquiring a form of townfields, and then developing into larger nucleations with more elaborate field systems. In the chalk valleys rational patterns of land division appeared, with strip parishes, townships and manors cutting across the valley at right-angles, so as to obtain shares of bottom land, valley slopes and chalkland grazings. Eventually chains of near continuous nucleation appeared along the lower valley slopes (Taylor 1970, 87). As long ago as 1966, Colin Bowen and Peter Fowler argued that the basic factor conditioning the survival of traces of Romano-British and earlier field systems was the limit of the medieval and post-medieval permanent arable (Bowen and Fowler 1966, 59, 62). In short, whatever the process of transition from the Romano-British or earlier systems to the medieval, the sustained cropping of the townfield systems essentially eliminated the traces of the earlier systems. No doubt more survivals will be discovered through both ground survey and aerial photography, but what Bowen and Fowler enunciated is probably a general rule, and must raise the question at a national scale of the degree to which pre-medieval fields occupied the same areas as the later townfields.

Throughout the whole of this south-eastern zone, common pastures were formerly present in considerable quantities, both as open pastures and as wood pastures. The survival of prehistoric and Romano-British field boundaries on the chalklands attested, until comparatively recent ploughing campaigns, the many centuries during which they existed as open, grazed downlands. The extensive wood pastures of the Weald, and the heaths, commons and marshlands of the middle and lower Thames are survivals of once more extensive tracts, the raw materials from which assarts and enclosures were structured. Our knowledge of the agrarian patterning in this zone would benefit considerably from studies focusing – like Rippon's in Essex – on the broader patterns of enclosed fields, roads and trackways.

Northern enclosed landscapes

Discussion now moves to the northern portion of the Northern and Western settlement province, to landscapes where great tracts of common pasture dominated – and to some extent still dominate – the region's landscapes (Fig 1.13). A survey of Gilsland, Cumberland, in 1603 calculated the estate to be some 74,000 acres in extent, of which no less than 50,000 acres, two-thirds, were commons, waste or forest land (Graham 1934, 162–4). The icon in Figure 6.5b models the balances between the characteristic elements of land use, although this was dynamic rather than static. Northern enclosure landscapes comprise areas of irregular closes, forming a blocky pattern of hedged or walled enclosures along the floors and sides of main and tributary valleys (Fig 6.5b). Many are likely to be medieval; some may be older. However, evidence from County Durham is a useful pointer. The assessed lands of the Boldon Book of 1183 – generally described in terms of bovates – appear in a similar guise in 1380, but at that date they are swamped, in the western dales, by great amounts of 'exchequer land'. These rendered only a cash rent to the Bishop's exchequer, and can only be interpreted as land reclaimed piecemeal between 1183 and 1380, or more likely by about 1300 (Austin 1982, 39–43; Greenwell 1857, 60–76). Named farms show that these intakes were located between the areas of townfield on the better lands of the valley floors and sides, and a head dyke set at or about the 300m contour. The gradual process of upslope encroachment has left successions of upward-looping head dykes, set at progressively higher levels, with funnel-shaped drifts, cattle tracks, leading down slope to the older and more important farmsteads (Fig 3.4 H). Above such enclosures, at higher levels up the valley slopes, post-medieval additions include some larger-scale intakes from the commons, often distinguishable because of their greater dimensions and use of quarry stone as a walling material (Fig 6.2B).

All of these enclosures were held in severalty and are associated with dispersed farmsteads and small hamlets. On the better quality soils of the valley floors and sides, however, are to be found traces of townfields enclosed early, by agreement. These are distinctive because of the presence of rather small rectangular fields whose hedged or walled boundaries show clear evidence of aratral curves. Normally, these indicators are adjacent to small market towns and villages, but they may also be linked with the most substantial hamlets. In Figure 6.5a these landscapes are modelled by identifying four principal constituent elements. Versions of ring-fenced enclosures with curvilinear, near-circular or oval enclosing boundaries, as discussed in Chapter 4, have been identified in several northern contexts. Small versions appear at the core of some townfield systems, perhaps being a first cleared foothold furlong. These grade imperceptibly into rather larger, rectangular, cores based upon long strips as at Cockfield, Iveston and Frosterley in County Durham (Roberts 1987, fig 3.11), and as at Cumwhitton, Cumberland (Roberts 1987, fig 3.12). Elsewhere are to be found enclosures for specialist enterprises, shielings, vaccaries, stud farms, parks and the like.

In all these countrysides, careful field study suggests that it is typical for a 'bank and ditch phase' to precede the addition of walling. The latter normally comprises quarry stones with an admixture of field stones. In Wharfedale, however, Raistrick identified at Linton a townfield core surrounded by walls consisting of massive field stone boulders, presumably the erratic blocks and other surface stone cleared by agricultural colonists and representing several phases of intakes (Hoskins 1967, 130–4). The primary kernel was just over 28ha (70 acres) in extent, and its boundary is c 1.5m (4 to 5 feet) wide at its base, and c 1.7m (5 to 6 feet) high. At Cockfield, County Durham, both primary and secondary kernels seem to have been of the order of 12ha (30 acres).

The study of Roystone Grange, Derbyshire (Fig 4.12), based upon wall typology, earthworks, and excavation, has permitted the identification of the many periods of use of an upland steading, set between 240m and 335m above sea level (Hodges 1991). The two looped enclosures which signify the Romano-British occupation, and which have been discussed in Chapter 4, were each about 30ha (74 acres) in extent, with double-orthostatic walls, the same order of magnitude as those at Linton. In an interesting section Hodges expresses some surprise at the huge effort put into making the original bounds of the enclosed landscape, into the twin looped enclosures which appear to have been designed for collective use by the community (Hodges 1991, 85-6). One Romano-British enclosure seems to have been for arable and the second, higher one, for stock. Of course, such enclosures could either protect arable crops from the animals grazing the surrounding pastures, or protect livestock from wild animals. Temporally, a transition from an initial pastoral enclosure to an arable field is inherently probable, for the manuring by stock eventually enhances the initial soil quality, allowing crops to be taken (Bodvall 1960).

What emerges from these admittedly limited examples is that the ring-fenced enclosures of the South-east are substantially larger than are those of northern England. In some northern contexts they are the frameworks within which a rudimentary strip division takes place, while in other cases they form the basis for farms in severalty. The scale differences between those of the South-east and those of the North must reflect environmental factors, the different problems of land clearance in the two areas and local population levels. The labour of making soils by moving stones in the one context must be set against the need to clear timber, underwood or rough grass in the other. Both the ring-fenced enclosures and the large co-axial strips could be very ancient, Roman or even pre-Roman, and they represent two distinct processes of land taking, one relatively informal, the other seemingly planned, organised and rationally structured. We are left with many areas of indeterminate enclosures.

Nevertheless, it is far too easy to concentrate upon such archaeologically interesting elements. Northern landscapes are effectively dominated by the ingredients defined in Figure 6.5b. Large areas of open, common upland pastures still survive; and if we add to these only the post-medieval intakes and the lands enclosed by Act of Parliament, we can reconstruct vast tracts of former open pasture. Enclosed landscapes with single farmsteads and small hamlets fill the valley and dale sides, and it is only around the nuclei – sometimes hamlets, sometimes market villages and market towns – that traces of communally cultivated systems appear, with former strips showing in the patterns of enclosure or as archaeological features.

North and west Midlands enclosure landscapes

The north and west Midlands zone (Fig 6.5a) embraces not only the conventional west Midlands, but extends westwards to the Welsh Border, and northwards, through Cheshire into Lancashire. The precise boundaries between this region and 'the north' proper in terms of types of enclosure

are open to question, but important transitions must occur where the Lancashire Plain merges with the Pennines. The same landscape elements are present as in the north, but the proportions of each element show considerable differences. While unenclosed common grazing land is present, it is characteristically diffused throughout the landscape as small patches, rarely exceeding a few hundred acres. Larger blocks appear where hill masses such as the Clee Hills or the Long Mynd intrude, or where soils are particularly poor, as on the slopes rising towards the Malvern Hills (Hoskins and Stamp 1963, 223, fig 38). Basically, however, in Cheshire, Shropshire and Herefordshire the accumulated totals of common land are minute compared with those of the Pennines or Wales (RCCL 1958, 27, map 1). Moving downslope from the head dyke, tracts of Parliamentary enclosure from the common wastes are limited in extent, in both Hereford and Shropshire accounting generally for less than 10% of the land (Gonner 1912, 273 and 275) and affecting generally less than 20% of townships. This contrast is often clearly seen in situations where old enclosures directly abut common pastures (Curtis *et al* 1976, fig 4.1). Indeed Williams, writing of Bringsty Common (285 acres) in Bromyard, concluded that after the fourteenth century its boundary became 'firmly fixed' and jealously guarded. Even then there appear to have been accumulations of small encroachments (Williams 1987, 177–201).

In general, all of these borderland hills and commons lie within an enveloping tide of small hedged closes, some rather regular but others highly irregular, the end product of many centuries of reclamation. The zone contains some royal forests, but these are generally small compared with those of the south-east and far north. Dean is the largest, in itself a distinctive *pays*, but there are also Hereford Hay, Feckenham, Kinver and Cannock, and a scatter of smaller entities in Shropshire. Further north are the Wirral, Delamere and Macclesfield in Cheshire, the High Peak in Derbyshire and a group in southern Lancashire – Simonswood, West Derby, Croxteth and Toxteth. All are pointers to specialist wood pasture landscapes. In Figure 6.5a Sherwood has been included as an outlier of this zone. As Glasscock notes, such forests were not only timber reserves and hunting grounds, but also important grazing areas for deer, cattle, pigs and horses. Intakes were created, but the existence of these zones 'outside' the common law of the realm was a significant factor retarding the spread of a uniform pattern of enclosure (Glasscock 1973, 164–7).

Nevertheless, a fundamental paradox exists in the fact that few of these areas contain the largest amounts of recorded woodland in 1086, although this may be merely because they contained fewer settlements possessing rights over woodlands, and were still intercommoned wood pastures. In contrast, the Forest of Arden in north Warwickshire, the Bromyard area in Herefordshire and the Forest of Mondrum on the south Cheshire upland were all markedly wooded. As Higham notes, citing Dodgson, the name element 'Lyme' (otherwise Lime or Lyne) is associated with the tract of country extending from the steep western edge of the southern Pennines, and the hills which continue that line. The name means 'elm', and the woodland involved may indicate the presence of a tenth-century boundary zone (Higham 1993, 95–6; Gelling 1992, 63–5). Like many 'forest' names of the west Midlands, applied to both the royal forests and to less determinate wooded tracts, 'Lyme' had been adopted by the Anglo-Saxons from the British name for this area (Gelling 1984, 189; 1992, 63–4). It is no accident that the woodland countrysides of the Midlands occur, in general, where upfaulted blocks of pre-Carboniferous, Carboniferous and sometimes Triassic age form low plateaux, often with rather acidic sandy soils less attractive to agriculture (Fig 2.1).

Townfields are known to have been present throughout the zone. They are seen in their most classic forms where small market towns and villages are set within local areas of potentially high production. Elsewhere, they often formed less regular systems or small cores (Sylvester 1969, fig 23; Rennell of Rodd 1958, 84–118). To understand the short distance variations, the characteristics of local terrain, geology and soils are crucial. As Figure 2.1 shows, the area is divided between those parts with extensive, often thick deposits of glacial drift, and those where the drift is discontinuous and thin. The soils of these drift landscapes vary greatly: the origin, lithology and age of the parent material is crucial, as is the degree to which the fluvio-glacial components have been sorted. Calcareous tills tend to occur in southern Warwickshire and Worcestershire, in the champion countrysides of that part of the Central Province.

In the northern and western Midlands as defined here, the soils have a tendency to be acidic, inherently containing less calcium carbonate. Today, they are domesticated, farmed: the end product of many centuries of tillage, drainage and, ultimately, land clearance. In their pristine, wildwood condition, before agricultural occupation, where the drift lay thickly, the drainage would have been significantly poorer than it now is. Where sand or gravel was the dominant parent material there was a strong tendency for post-clearance soils to acidify because of the leaching away of nutrients once the trees had been felled. Heathland vegetation with heather and thorns speedily appeared. Thus it was that clays, often ameliorated by admixtures of other materials, offered the best long-term tillage prospects; but these needed sustained husbanding to bring out their better qualities.

All discussion of soils is fraught with problems: there are enormous difficulties involved in the processes of field recognition, classification and mapping. In one authoritative text, the clay and marl lowlands of the midland portion of the Central Province are discussed wholly in terms of their drainage problems, noting that they are 'liable to waterlogging' because 'the fine particle size of the substrate often causes serious impedance of water movement'. It fails to mention that these same soils have been, at least until recent decades, almost universally covered with ridge and furrow indicative of their former use as grainlands! Even Primrose McConnell describes the Lias clays as 'too stiff to cultivate', although conceding that 'drainage sometimes converts these clays into good arable land' (McConnell 1922, 123). In the north and west Midlands the varied drifts and their depositional circumstances, together with the problems of local drainage amid varied and complex topographic situations, have long posed problems for the farmer. For sustained arable production, soils in which a clay base is ameliorated by some admixture of gravel or sand tends to be sought, preferably set on sloping land so that drainage can be encouraged by the direction of the ploughing. Those soils where sands and gravels predominate, or the wetter clays of the bottomland, will be avoided because one is 'hungry', while the other is better for grass production. The heterogeneous local conditions of this area generated great diversity, and this poses problems when attempting to summarise regional characteristics.

In Figure 6.6, Sylvester's individual maps of woodland clearance for Cheshire, Shropshire and Herefordshire have been synthesised to allow a wider perspective to be assembled. In effect this is a portion of Figure 1.13 mapped in a different way. Surviving woodland and that likely to have been present in 1086 are recorded using two different keys, while the areas in grey are where place-names in *-leah* (*-ley*), *-hyrst* (*-hurst*), *-wudu* (*-wood*) and *-graefe* (*-grove*) appear. What is left are distinctive swathes of lowland characterised by place names such as *-ingham*, *-ham*, *-bury*, *-ingaton* and *-tun*. Superimposing her map of field systems over this woodland base reveals the complexity of the spatial patterns. Overall, there is a broad correlation with land quality, the most developed systems appearing on the better lands, while the fragmented systems and kernels appear in less favoured contexts. Of course, this is not the whole story, because the area has been a marcher zone, a frontier, and the multitude of Norman castles and small planted towns must have been agents by which more organised field systems were diffused throughout the area (Merlen 1987).

The few detailed maps published by Sylvester suggest that most townships possessed some common grazings which, when pictured in the eighteenth and nineteenth centuries, were already in the process of dissolution, without need of Acts of Parliament. Richard Gough's account of Myddle, south-east of Wem, Shropshire, written between 1700 and 1706, contains a particularly revealing note. Concerning Bilmarsh Farm, part of the Earl of Bridgewater's land, he notes, 'it was formerly a common ... in that every man has land adjoining to it, does enclose from it, except a little piece of common called Bilmarsh Green, and from this Bilmarsh farm does make hayment, and therefore it may seem that this little green is part of Bilmarsh farm, and that it was left out when the rest was enclosed' (Razzell 1981, 70). The presumption must be that in the absence of a communally organised farming system those with access to such small residual commons could, with the agreement of the lord of the manor, undertake such enclosures. In his account of the Shropshire landscape Rowley describes the 'colonising of the woodland' in terms of clearings created by monastic houses and freeholders: these are substantively seen as post-Conquest, that is relating to phases D-F and H in Table 6.1 and Figure 6.1.

The nature of settlement in the Forest of Arden can be illustrated by the case of a single parish, albeit a large one. At Tanworth in Arden an arable townfield kernel formed only a small proportion of the area of the parish, the 200 acres or so representing about 2% (Fig 6.7; Roberts 1965, 530). Charters show that between 1200 and 1250 there was assarting on the edge of the townfield area, creating, for example, 'Rydding', a close that stayed in severalty to 1500 and beyond. Other crofts, Bancroft (which 'John son of Alard claimed'), Dunscroft, Longcroft, Hethcroft, Birchcroft and Shirwoldescroft, have names which imply intakes in severalty. Nevertheless, Whetedych – *Wheat-eddish* – 'the wheat field' (Seebohm 1883, 376-80) – appears to represent a core area of shared arable strips, while field names such as Oldbury (later Bury), Willeworth, Weserworth, Apelton, Bickerscote, and possibly Lullenham are pointers to more ancient clearance and settlement. All are Old English names and extend down the undulating valley below the hill upon which Tanworth sits. All contain name-elements that could imply the presence of a scatter of farmsteads or even fortifications before the emergence of the demesne – church-village pattern of the twelfth and thirteenth centuries. The demesne surely replaced and took its name from 'Bickerscote' – 'the beekeeper's cottage'. An enigmatic letter from Dugdale, reports the discovery of 'a multitude of men', in a trench, interpreted as the site of 'some battell', but associated with 'a speare head of iron' and 'divers potsherds ... about two inches thick'. These are said to lie on 'Mr. Archers land', and hint at an otherwise unrecorded Anglo-Saxon cemetery exposed in the seventeenth century (Burman 1930, 50).

From this nucleus of activity, the bulk of post-1200 colonisation thrust northwards into the heaths and woodlands of the plateau surface, creating hedged enclosures, many of which were carved from substantial block grants. Thus to Thurstan de Sileby:

> all that land and wood ... of my new assart at Benetford, in length from the heath of Benetford to the hedge of Roger Durvassal as far as Rodmor, and from Rodmor up the hedge to Betlesworth Heath as far as the hedge of Roger Durvassal extends. *(BM Cart Harl, 45.1.31)*

Nevertheless, the place-name 'Betlesworth' indicates that there were already older settlement foci set in this waste, and there

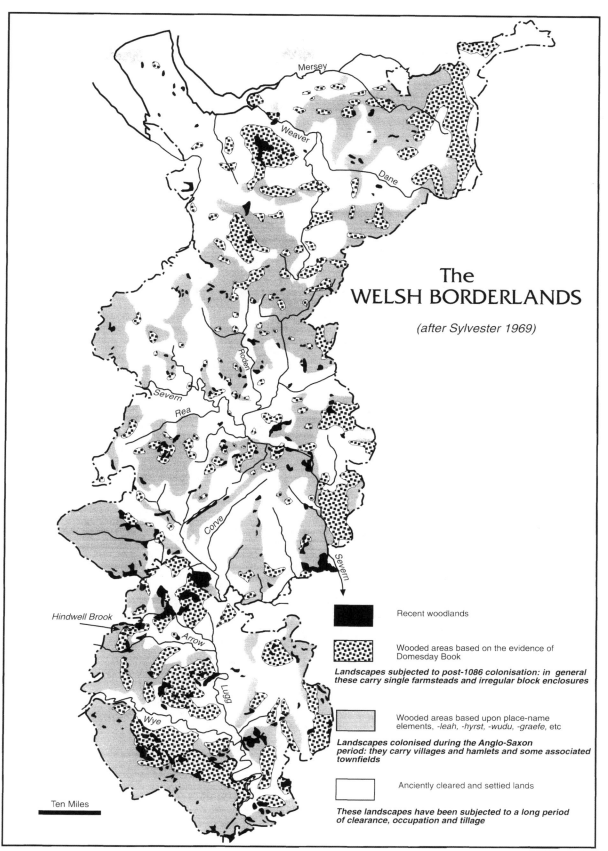

The
WELSH BORDERLANDS

(after Sylvester 1969)

Recent woodlands

Wooded areas based on the evidence of Domesday Book

Landscapes subjected to post-1086 colonisation: in general these carry single farmsteads and irregular block enclosures

Wooded areas based upon place-name elements, *-leah, -hyrst, -wudu, -graefe,* etc

Landscapes colonised during the Anglo-Saxon period: they carry villages and hamlets and some associated townfields

Anciently cleared and settled lands

These landscapes have been subjected to a long period of clearance, occupation and tillage

Ten Miles

Figure 6.6

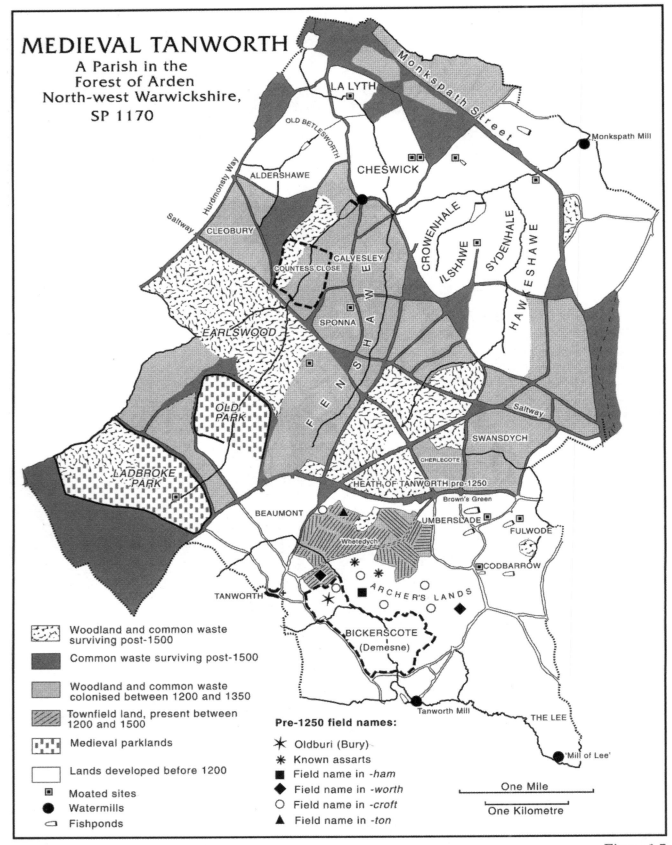

MEDIEVAL TANWORTH

A Parish in the
Forest of Arden
North-west Warwickshire,
SP 1170

Woodland and common waste
surviving post-1500

Common waste surviving post-1500

Woodland and common waste
colonised between 1200 and 1350

Townfield land, present between
1200 and 1500

Medieval parklands

Lands developed before 1200

▣ Moated sites

● Watermills

◠ Fishponds

Pre-1250 field names:

✳ Oldburi (Bury)

✴ Known assarts

■ Field name in -ham

◆ Field name in -worth

○ Field name in -croft

▲ Field name in -ton

One Mile

One Kilometre

Figure 6.7

are hints of ring-fenced enclosures (Fig 6.7). Area names such as Earlswood, Aldershawe, Ilshawe, Hawkeshawe, Fenshawe confirm the presence of stands of woodland; others, Calvesley, Cheswick, Crowenhale and Sydenhale are more ambiguous, and may imply pre-Conquest settled locations (Mawer and Stenton 1936, 292–6). Overall, the picture is one of early 'islands' of intakes amid a larger tract bearing a mixture of heathland, woodland and scattered groves, broken into blocks by trackways. There is little doubt from a wider study of the general pattern of colonising activity in Arden that seigniorial decisions radically affected the trajectory of an individual parish or township. For successive earls of Warwick, Tanworth was a locality where individual colonisation was encouraged. The action of a land market allowed certain tenants to consolidate small estates, quasi-manors, and the existence of these families accounts for the unusually large number of moated sites in the parish (Roberts 1968). In this case, the main manor is not listed in Domesday Book, but as Dugdale saw, it is represented in 1086 by the block of woodland attached to Brailes, south Warwickshire, of which Tanworth was a hamlet.

The Welsh Border counties in general, and Tanworth in particular, provide a fundamentally simple model. Long-established nuclei, bearing Old English settlement names, at some stage acquired townfields. The more favourable the environment, and the more extensive the townfields, the more closely they approximate, in both organisation and extent, to the classic systems of the Central Province. In peripheral regions, and Tanworth in Arden is such a case, systems appear which are smaller in extent, less formalised, and prone to piecemeal absorption into the general mass of enclosures in severalty. Around these kernels, accrete masses of piecemeal enclosures, sometimes involving assart land – woodland clearance – but more often involving the improvement of common grazings bearing underwood, heath, moorland and marsh. This activity appears to be largely post-Conquest in date, although we must allow for the persistence of some of the earlier steadings. A pre-Conquest picture, throughout the north and west and probably also in the south and east, is of settlement and cultivation nuclei, surrounded by extensive, at times enormous, tracts of uncultivated land, either intercommoned or manorial wastes, sometimes with wholly unappropriated tracts (RCCL 1958, 150–51, paras 5–11).

Here we reach a paradoxical conclusion: Rackham's 'ancient landscapes' are in fact *not* chronologically older than the landscapes of the Central Province, except for long-established nuclei and associated arable kernels. The bulk of the enclosures are later than the townfields that had developed in the core of the Central Province. It was the surviving blocks of ancient woodland, old hedgerows cut from woodlands, and tracts of commonable waste, elements present only in smaller amounts in the cleared lands of the Central Province, that preserved a more distinctive, richer, more ancient flora – in effect Rackham's 'ancient landscapes'. Refuges existed, from which communities of woodland plants could be sustained and reinforced, so that the hedgerows of such regions may still bear wild garlic and the bluebell. The enclosures themselves are associated with phases D, E, F and G of Table 6.1. This is not, we emphasise, to deny that there may be traces of extremely ancient enclosures concealed amid the post-townfield enclosures, and which have by their presence influenced the form and character of later developments.

South-western enclosure landscapes

A final large region, a single sub-province in Figure 1.4, has been defined on the basis of settlement characteristics, although it can easily be divided into no less than 24 local regions. Its eastern boundary is distinguished by a sharp break in the overall density of nucleations, while the sea not only forms the remaining boundary but has also had a powerful impact upon climate and lifestyles. Cornwall has been the subject of a detailed landscape survey. The historic component of this, by Nicholas Johnson and his team, achieves a level of detail far exceeding what is appropriate in a synoptic survey (Herring 1998, 15–51). This is a diverse terrain, ranging from the granite uplands, through rolling dissected plateaux, to clay lowlands further east. Basically the land is a powerfully rolling, undulating plateau surface. Above this rise the uplands and some sharper ridges, but an intricate drainage network has cut deep valleys. Towards the mouths of the rivers downcutting has been so great that a rising sea level has been able to invade, resulting in distinctive estuaries which penetrate the land. The settlement map reveals substantial variations at the level of the local region. The Devon lowlands and South Hams have sufficient numbers of nucleations to warrant inclusion within the Central Province. In other areas, notably the moorlands, clusters of any significant size are generally absent. With the exception of the largely empty granite moorlands the sub-province is characterised by densities of dispersion which lie above the 'medium' level. There are even some areas in which very high densities occur – reflecting the higher populations associated with extractive and mineral processing industries.

The presence of ancient hard formations and former deep weathering in an area never glaciated has long meant that land clearance has implied stone clearance as much as the removal of trees and other vegetation: much field stone remained in field boundaries. The Cornwall Archaeological Unit has found examples of what appear to be essentially prehistoric fields still determining existing farm boundaries (Herring 1998, fig 16). As Hatcher remarked in 1988, 'the sources for the study of south-western field systems and rotations in this period (1042–1350) are deficient in both quantity and content (Hatcher 1988, 383). He concluded that 'settlements with subdivided fields did not flourish throughout Devon and Cornwall', although they may well have been familiar on the fertile soils of the south Devon coastal regions, the north Devon valleys and the northern and southern coastal regions of central Cornwall (Hatcher 1988, 385).

One of the peculiarities of Devon and Cornwall is the relatively large number of borough foundations (Beresford 1967, table IX.10; Beresford and Finberg 1973). In general, these are very small (Beresford 1967, 417). None was engineered by the Crown; most represent foundations by lay lords in the late twelfth and thirteenth centuries. Size for size a plantation such as South Zeal was physically no larger than an average planted village such as can be found in northern England. The curves of its property boundaries show that it was laid out over a portion of the arable strips of South Tawton, the parent settlement. Some 800m to the west, Sticklepath, a wholly rural village, was laid out in the same manner (Roberts 1987, 10.2). In effect, these small towns represent the South-west's response to the factors leading to nucleation in the Central Province. They involved tenantry and arable as well as trade; and it is likely that all were provided with sufficiently extensive supporting arable townfields, as in the case of Kenton (Finberg 1969, fig 2). Braunton and Down Thomas (Finberg 1969, figs 1 and 3) are a reminder that substantive subdivided fields were not limited to 'urban' contexts.

Nevertheless, as the case of Rashleigh shows (Chapter 4, Fig 4.14) these larger systems contrast with older, less extensive, less complex shared arable plots in Devon, integrated within the ring-fenced enclosures and sub-rectangular field mosaics which dominate much of the countryside (Hatcher 1988, 383–7). Similar small cores of shared land also appeared in Cornwall, and, as Uhlig pointed out, these were a part of the cultural landscapes of many more peripheral or agriculturally more marginal areas of Europe (Uhlig 1961, 294). Throughout the whole of the South-west it is reasonable to postulate a fundamental dichotomy between indigenous sharelands, with small patches of subdivided fields shared among kin or tenants (resembling types B and E in Figure 3.4), and the planted nucleations, either villages or small towns, with larger, planned, communally worked arable fields (as in type C).

Townfield land and enclosed land: a general analysis

As will no doubt be evident to the reader, we have found it extremely difficult to provide any meaningful generalisations about the character and development of agrarian structures in the outer provinces. This is because we have located few studies at the required scale to enable us to avoid, on the one hand, a simple recital of detailed investigations, and, on the other, statements that are far too generalised to be of much use. Nevertheless, we can make a few preliminary suggestions. The first is that the enclosed landscapes we see in these provinces are likely in the main to *postdate* the development of townfield systems. In terms of acreage, the Northern and Western Province in particular is dominated by field patterns that originated in enclosure from waste during the twelfth, thirteenth and later centuries. There are undoubtedly earlier elements present, particularly, as noted above, in the South-west, but these are not in overall terms a dominant feature.

Figure 5.10 indicates, with asterisks, some of the main groups of remains that can be categorised broadly as 'co-axial' field systems, including Riley's 'brickwork' field systems of the north Midlands (Riley 1980) and Fleming's 'reaves' in the South-west (Fleming 1988). Currently, they seem to occur mainly on the margins of the principal areas of townfield development, though this pattern could be radically altered by further work – in the South-east, for example. Large-scale land division no doubt occurred at different times in different places, and for different reasons. As far as the East Anglian examples are concerned, however, scholarly opinion seems presently to be moving towards a common view. The systems may be based upon sinuous, roughly parallel tracks, droveways, created in prehistoric times, perhaps in the Iron Age; but the detail of the systems is probably coeval with, or later than, the development of townfields in the Midlands.

As far as the townfield cores in the outer provinces are concerned, it is likely that they represent lands cultivated long before Anglo-Saxon times. On good soils, carefully husbanded and fertilised, they represent a vital and long-lasting resource to successive generations of farmers. Continuity between prehistoric and Romano-British systems and medieval townfield cores has fundamental implications for understanding the occupation of land – and the consequent patterning of archaeological data – in this country. In general, then, townfield land represents anciently cultivated land. This is not to say that what became townfield cores was always worked in common: all the indications are that communal organisation was stimulated by increasing populations, increasing lordly control and the development of more elaborate systems of land division and crop rotation. This land was normally the arable of Domesday Book, plus new furlongs added to the core fields during the next two centuries or so. Regional variations had, at their root, the fundamental contrasts between cleared land and woodland, and between tilled lands and pastures, either open or wooded. Within these framing structures, communally organised field systems developed.

The lands dominated by irregular block enclosures in the two outer provinces (phases C, D and E of Table 6.1) represent accretions around these ancient townfield arable cores. No doubt some are ancient, even prehistoric, but in general we conclude they represent intakes from woodlands and open pastures, and the majority are likely to be post-Conquest. A corollary of this is that unenclosed pastures were formerly a very significant component of earlier landscapes, as modelled in Figure 6.1. We will attempt to quantify land use in the next chapter, but we envisage that both 'outer' provinces were once dominated by land usages drawing upon these extensive pastures. These involved grazing cattle, goats and pigs in unenclosed wood pastures, and maintaining areas of pollarded and coppiced woodland to provide supplies of building materials, fuel and other woodland products. The grazing of wood pastures led to their inevitable degradation, eventually allowing sheep to be grazed on the emergent open pastures. As Darby notes, 'roughly speaking there were, in Norfolk, fewest sheep where there was most wood' (Darby 1952, 144). Those counties for which listings of demesne stock survive indicate the importance of sheep, with swine and goats being most prevalent in the most wooded counties (Table 6.2). We emphasise here the single word *demesne*, for Domesday Book excludes the tenant stock and there is no basis for interpolating these numbers from the

Table 6.2 Demesne stock in 1086

counties	sheep	swine	goats	cattle	horses	animals
Norfolk	46,354	8,074	3,020	23	1036	2,107
Suffolk	37,522	9,843	4,343	9	654	3,083
Essex	46,095	13,171	3,576	237	917	3,768
Dorset	22,977	1,567	780	72	163	541
Somerset	46,981	6,847	4,505	117	834	4,289
Devon	49,999	3,682	7,263	23	477	7,357

Source: Darby *et al* 1952–77

demesne animals. In addition there would have been a multitude of other woodland products, not least honey from the bees (Crane 1983, 87–90) and timber and cord-wood: the uses of the wood were manifold (Glacken 1967, 320–2).

It is possible that the South-eastern Province does indeed retain elements of 'older' landscapes, in as much as the oldest arable foci, although subjected to varying degrees of reorganisation and expansion, have been assimilated into townfield or quasi-townfield areas. Nevertheless they normally retain asymmetries and irregularities which speak of less formal antecedents. Around these cores appear enclosed fields resulting from the gradual colonisation of the former wood pastures and open pastures in medieval and post-medieval times. It is worth recalling that as late as the last three decades of the eighteenth century as much as 20% of Norfolk was still common grazing land, on heath and in marsh. This theme, the overall balances between the varied categories of land use, will be pursued in our concluding chapter.

7
A synoptic view

The keys to this book are the two maps introduced in Chapter 1, one a record of mid-nineteenth-century settlement (Fig 1.14), the other a plot of Late Anglo-Saxon woodland (Fig 1.13). Chapter 1 included a discussion of the methods by which these datasets were constructed, summarising the more detailed account in *An Atlas of Rural Settlement in England*. It also included some warnings about their problems and deficiencies, in terms of both the data sources and the methods of representation. Nevertheless, despite – and, sometimes, because of – their limitations, they have provided an unavoidable opportunity to explore some fundamental issues of rural settlement history.

The concept of nucleation and dispersion

The first of these issues concerns the settlement map, Figure 1.14, and the opposition of 'dispersed' and 'nucleated' settlement. Readers should understand that this opposition is a construct, devised for the purposes of investigating the diverse structures of rural settlement. As we have argued elsewhere (Roberts and Wrathmell 1998, 111–13), it is one which can and should be discarded once it has served its purpose. Thirty years ago, Sylvia Hallam argued that:

> Archaeologists, and indeed geographers, have tended to envisage settlement patterns in over-simplified terms – either isolated farms or nucleated settlements. This has deflected them from their real task of describing the varied states between dispersal and grouping which actually existed. If by 'dispersed settlement' we mean a scatter of small groups such as we have described for the Wash area [in Romano-British times], mainly twos, threes and fours, but with some isolated farms and some clusters of up to a dozen or so farms, then a 'dispersed' pattern is the general background throughout North-west Europe for the later development, in restricted areas, of more concentrated varieties of settlement ...

we need Estyn Evans's reminder that 'dispersion ... does not necessarily mean single farms' ... [L]andscapes of isolated farms are only a very recent development.' *(Hallam 1970, 62)*

The results of this 'over-simplification' are evident in our difficulties over the categorisation of EWASH (E) and EWEXE. Western Norfolk, lying in the first of these sub-provinces, is classified as dispersed. As can be seen in our distribution maps, however, it appears to have many 'Central Province' characteristics: it has numerous records of deserted medieval villages and of open-field enclosures. EWEXE, a sub-province marked by distinctive terrain contrasts, is equally ambiguous. Its valleys contain strings of settlements ranging from single farmsteads, through 'irregular attenuated rows' and 'loosely clustered agglomerations' to nucleations (Lewis 1994, 174, fig 8.5). Added to these, a further sub-province, CPNSL, seems to change its attribution, belonging in the Middle Ages to the Northern and Western Province but forming part of the nucleated zone in the mid-nineteenth century.

These ambiguities highlight the point that the nucleation/dispersion contrast is not solely a matter of distance between farmsteads. There is a second, albeit unstated opposition: that between planned and regulated development on the one hand, and organic growth on the other. The thirteenth-century villages of EWASH (E) and the early nineteenth-century nucleations of CPNSL often resulted from large but essentially unplanned increases in the density of existing settlement, not from a conscious decision to replace dispersed with nucleated settlement. In these regions, and at these times, we would not expect to find that kind of planning and regulation, of townfields as well as of settlements, so characteristic of the Central Province. On this basis, our construct ought theoretically to encompass settlement morphology, since planning and regulation are detectable in settlement structures. The reason it does not do so is quite simply because morphological data revealing the contribution of planning to each local settlement region are not yet available on a national scale.

Without some kind of construct it is impossible to frame research questions. Furthermore, unless the research community sees that construct as relevant and usable, it will have no impact on the course of research. Our exploration of individual case studies, in Chapter 4, is an attempt to demonstrate the value of our broader framework to those involved principally in the study of detailed agrarian structures at a regional level. Whether or not the individual interpretations stand the test of time is less important than the new perspective that the national framework of provinces and local regions provides. We have demonstrated that there are remarkable similarities between the two outer provinces, similarities that override the obvious differences between, say, Lancashire and Suffolk, in terms of location, socio-economic circumstances and terrain. It suggests that, whatever the regional variations, there was at some stage an underlying uniformity in the approach to farm management. The aim of that approach was to provide a community with access to contrasting resources. Furthermore, the most efficient way to exploit such resources was to locate the community's farmsteads on the boundaries between those resources: hence the emphasis on settlement sites which were peripheral to the arable 'ovals'; hence the centrality of agrarian structures in any study of rural settlement. Farmsteads were ephemeral elements of countrysides that were framed and articulated by the boundaries demarcating the different resources, and by the routeways giving access from one to another. Glanville Jones's (1985) 'girdle' settlements are an expression of this approach, and Richard Hingley (1989) has used the same arrangement to model Romano-British settlement. As noted above, rising population densities could create settlements which might be termed 'villages', and the arable lands of the ovals might be subdivided among an increasing number of tenants, leading to forms of 'open field'.

Such trends are likely to have been generated by the custom of partible inheritance among kin groups, a topic discussed in more detail later in this chapter. They can be seen operating, at a late date and in exceptional circumstances, in parts of Cumberland and Northumberland during the fifteenth and sixteenth centuries. In North Tynedale for example, manorial control, visible in the records of bondage tenements during the thirteenth and early fourteenth centuries, broke down under the pressures of the Anglo-Scottish wars and cross-border raiding. Bondage tenure was replaced, not by customary husbandland tenure as elsewhere in Northumberland, but by tenant right which allowed the tenants to sell off or otherwise alienate all or part of their holdings. In contrast to neighbouring Redesdale, North Tynedale provides no reliable evidence of a custom of partible inheritance, but it is clear that tenants exercised their rights of disposal to provide holdings for more than one heir. In both dales there was a growth in the size of hamlet settlements, and a fragmentation of arable holdings. In both there was an emergence of kin groups, 'surnames', such as the Charltons who provided all three tenants in the hamlet of Dunterley in the early seventeenth century (Wrathmell 1975, 269–74). These late medieval developments may offer some indication of the nature of social and agrarian structures elsewhere at much earlier times.

Regional experience

The underlying similarities in the agrarian structures of the South-eastern and Northern and Western Provinces, and their possible origins in Roman or earlier times, might indicate that model 'a' in our 'stratigraphic section' (Fig 3.12) is the correct one: that the zone which became the Central Province had previously contained similar structures to those on either side. The Late Saxon woodland map (Fig 1.13), however, and its varying relationships to archaeological distributions of earlier times indicates a more complex picture. Whatever the recording errors in the location of individual blocks of woodland, the trend between the Late Saxon period and the nineteenth century is undoubtedly one of progressive woodland clearance in the Central Province. Clearance took place between, on the west, the Avon-Trent line, and, to the south and east, the line of the Icknield Way. Countrysides with relatively small arable cores and wood pastures were converted to extensive townfields served by village settlements. The transition is recorded in the survival of furlongs bearing the habitative names of former dispersed settlements; it can also be seen, we have argued, in the agrarian structures of townships in west Cambridgeshire. By the mid-nineteenth century, only a few small patches of dispersed settlement, notably in North Bedfordshire and Buckinghamshire, remained sufficiently distinctive to be visible still at a national scale.

The Avon-Trent line (along with some other areas of the Central and South-eastern Provinces) was substantively clear of woodland in the Late Saxon period. It was, we have argued elsewhere, a key corn-growing region in and before the Roman period, with the Fosse Way acting as the arterial route for grain transportation (Roberts and Wrathmell 2000b, 93–4). We have further argued that these lands remained extensively and continuously under tillage in post-Roman times, becoming closely associated with Early Anglo-Saxon burials. If so, the preponderance of arable over pasture, so evident in later centuries, may already have demanded idiosyncratic agrarian and social structures, different from those of the wood-pasture zones. Here, we are approaching not model 'a' in Figure 3.12, but model 'e'.

In other parts of the country, regions that appear to have been significantly wooded in Late Saxon times have produced large numbers of Roman villa sites. Villas will, of course, have had a major requirement for fuel, both for hypocaust systems and for the 'drying kilns' frequently represented among their outbuildings. They will have needed extensive resources of coppiced woodland, presumably sited on their estates; and the abandonment of the villa estates will have led to rapid woodland regeneration. Such may be the circumstances that have produced the coincidence of numerous villa sites and significant records of Late Saxon woodland in areas such as Hertfordshire and part of the Cotswolds. In contrast to our hypothesis of continuity along the Avon-Trent line, we suggest that these areas may mark regions of discontinuity in the early post-Roman period.

The question of 'continuity' during the fourth to sixth centuries brings us to another fundamental issue which has emerged from our research: the relationship between regional diversity and national synthesis. To ask whether Roman Britain's agrarian communities continued to function during the fifth and sixth centuries, without any substantive break, is a question

to which there is, in our view, no single answer. Others have come to a similar conclusion. As Helena Hamerow has written with regard to the 'migration' question: 'our perspective may become at once insufficiently regional and too insular ... we lack a model which is sensitive to regional variability with regard to the scale and impact of Germanic immigration' (Hamerow 1994, 174). Experience of continuity, like migration, varied from one region to another, some seeing fundamental changes if not abandonment, others continuing much as before, though perhaps under new management. Indeed, we would argue that many of the key questions about rural settlement as a whole have been obfuscated by the assumption that there is a single answer for the whole of England. The classic example of this has already been discussed in Chapter 4: did nucleation and the townfield revolution take place before the Norman Conquest or after? The answer is both. As Chapter 5 has shown, the growth of the townfield zone to its greatest extent probably took just as long as the process of enclosing those same townfields.

Another example of the necessity of a regional perspective, a more recent topic of debate, is the idea of 'closure' in the later Middle Ages (Johnson 1996). One recent contributor has written that 'enclosed fields were not a new feature of the later Middle Ages, but had always been a part of everybody's landscape, and open fields were to remain a part of many people's until the eighteenth century' (Hinton 1999, 180–1). We argue that the assumed commonalty of experience that underlies this statement is misplaced. People's experience of open fields and enclosed fields will have varied enormously throughout medieval times, depending upon which part of the country they inhabited. Such variation will have had a significant impact on their view of family and community and of social relations in general. Furthermore, in some ways such regional variations could be seen to transgress the traditional period divisions. In woodland settings, the character of archaeological remains and composition of archaeological assemblages may be seen to have basic similarities whether they are Romano-British, Anglo-Saxon or medieval, and to have greater contrasts with the material culture of open environments. Too great an emphasis on 'period' divisions will obscure the long-term persistence of such similarities and contrasts.

A final issue clarified in the course of our research is the relationship between these varied regions and the administrative and political structures that contained them. As indicated in Chapter 5, there is reason to expect manorial and state policy to have influenced the course of the townfield revolution, just as it did the course of townfield enclosure. There is, however, no sign that woodland regions were incorporated into different administrative areas from those encompassing open countrysides. Whether we take wapentakes, hundreds or shires (or, for that matter, 'Celtic' tribal regions or Anglo-Saxon polities), there is no 'fit' to the regions identified. There are, on the contrary, grounds for suggesting that many midland shires were structured so as to include both cleared land and woodlands. More importantly in terms of historical analysis, when historical data are assembled by the unit of wapentake, hundred or shire, any marked regional contrasts crossing these units will be smoothed. Equally, administrative boundaries will themselves show marked lines of contrast where none existed, as the distribution of partible inheritance indicates (Fig 7.1).

A social context for pre-Conquest settlement

The varying forms of agrarian structures are a reflection of the varying interests of individuals and communities, of families and kin groups, in the lands that supported them. Therefore we introduce at this point some ideas which have been supplied by social historians, to provide a context for the changes we have modelled, and the further hypotheses we wish to develop with regard to Anglo-Saxon settlement. The earliest English law codes (Whitelock 1955, 357), with their clear focus upon compensation payments to be made for the injury or death of kin, find their context in societies in which resources belonged to the kin group as a whole:

> family land belonged to the whole family; every member had a claim to support from it, from generation to generation. Responsibility for its management could lie with a generation-set, or with a single representative, but the position was one of stewardship, not of ownership. *(Howell 1976, 113–14)*

From the time of our earliest historical records, however, there was a gradual weakening of the hold of kin groups on their lands. It has been argued that this trend was promoted by the Church in order to increase the amount of land alienated permanently to ecclesiastical institutions, and to reduce the opportunities of the donor's kin to claim residual rights in a holding which had passed to the Church (Howell 1976, 121; Goody 1983, 123–5, 133–56). In the words of Jack Goody:

> by setting itself against certain 'strategies of heirship' that would assist a family line to continue – namely adoption, cousin marriage, plural marriage or concubinage, unions with affines, or the remarriage of divorced persons, the Church brought about the further alienation of family holdings. Its teaching emphasised the elementary family as all-important, thus eroding the rights of collaterals and of wider kin groups. *(Goody 1983, 123)*

One aspect of these broad social changes, one of particular importance to the story of rural settlement, was the move away from partible inheritance to unigeniture, a move which 'involved a reduction in the claims of kin' (Goody 1983, 120). To what extent are the diverse physical records of agrarian societies a reflection of these changes? Our hypothesis is that land subject to partible inheritance, with reversion to the kin group as a whole, will have resulted in the fluidity of settlement patterns. On the one hand, the operation of partible inheritance would lead to the fragmentation of holdings, and the multiplication of farmsteads. On the other hand, the residual rights of kin groups would lead to the re-absorption of holdings, either upon the failure of direct heirs, or through endogamy (see Faith 1966, 80). Cicely Howell has described how kin groups in early Irish society were limited to a specific number of generations:

> Membership of the kindred gave [an individual] a claim to a share in its land, both arable and pasture; this share varied in its exact position and extent, as the total membership of the kindred was redefined once every generation. *(Howell 1976, 115)*

Within the broad generational limit, presumably itself related to the extent of available resources, we see again the considerable potential for change. In marked contrast, societies that practised unigeniture, where tenements were passed, intact, down generations of elementary families, provide a context for unchanging land shares and permanent tenurial structures. This is not to deny the capacity of such structures to accommodate widows' shares, joint arrangements among siblings, sub-tenancies and the like. Nor is it to deny that such structures could be subject to complete or partial reorganisation from time to time. It is, however, to argue for a broad correlation between the practice of unigeniture and the townships of the Central Province, where agrarian structures were permanently written into the soil in the form of toft and croft earthworks and ridge and furrow, and where individual virgate holdings can be traced century after century. Equally, in the outer provinces, where the impact of the nucleation-town-field revolution was never sufficient to create wholesale transformations, the opera-tion of kin-group interests in general, and partible inheritance in particular, will have fostered continued fluidity in farmstead location and land shares. The result was the kind of mobility in settlement sites evident on the margins of greens and commons in Norfolk and Suffolk. It is a correlation that is supported by the recorded incidence of partible inheritance.

Over thirty years ago, Rosamond Faith reviewed the evidence for inheritance customs in medieval England. Her starting point was the geographical distinction drawn by Homans between, on the one hand, Kent and East Anglia, where the farming unit was in the hands of patrilineal kinsmen, and, on the other, Central England, where open-field holdings were farmed from compact villages by 'nuclear' families. Faith's purpose was to explore the origins of this contrast, which Homans had attributed to the varied customs of the different German tribes that participated in the Adventus. She concluded, on the contrary, that 'partible inheritance was very probably the general peasant practice throughout Anglo-Saxon England' (Faith 1966, 79). Medieval and later records of partible inheritance and the related custom of Borough English (Faith 1966, 83) 'show that we cannot relate differences in inheri-tance custom at all reliably to racial origins' (Faith 1966, 84).

Figure 7.1 displays the evidence for partible inheritance and Borough English as collected by Faith. It records, by shading, those areas where such customs were wide-spread (Essex, Furness, Hampshire, Kent, Middlesex, Norfolk, Rossendale, Shrop-shire, Suffolk, Surrey, Sussex; Faith 1966, 81–4); late medieval partibility in parts of Northumberland has been considered earlier in this chapter. The South-eastern Province is almost completely shaded, and it should be remembered that our sources, which refer to customs by county, have undoubtedly created a false edge on the administrative boundaries. There are also widespread records of such customs in the Northern and Western Province. The black dots on Figure 7.1 show records of partible inheritance and Borough English in partic-ular localities outside the counties which are wholly shaded (Faith 1966, 93–5), excluding, as we are concerned with rural settlement, those places which were boroughs (Beres-ford and Finberg 1973). A couple are located well within the Central Province: in the Soke of Rotheley, Leicestershire, and at Brigstock in Northants. The others seem very much to cluster along the provincial boundaries, a circumstance which may well signify the reason they were recorded: the customs of manors on the boundaries between partible and impartible regions were perhaps more likely to be challenged.

Pre-Conquest settlement tendencies

Having described what we see as the broad social context for changes between the end of Roman Britain and the Norman Conquest, we now offer a series of hypotheses on the social and economic changes which may have generated some of the landscape characteristics we have identi-fied. They are presented not as conclusions, but as a contribution to further debate.

Up to the Middle Saxon period, though particular areas of land were farmed from particular farmsteads, or local groups of farmsteads, the concept of a kin-group territory underpinned a farming system in which the group had strong residual rights to the farmlands if direct heirs failed. The ability of single members of a group to alienate property individually was thus circumscribed. Territories over which rights existed were more important than the char-acter of the places from which these territo-ries were exploited. In the archaeological record this state of affairs is manifest in farmsteads or even larger settlements that had a tendency to be archaeologically ephemeral, and not substantively defined in the ground: few substantial ditches are

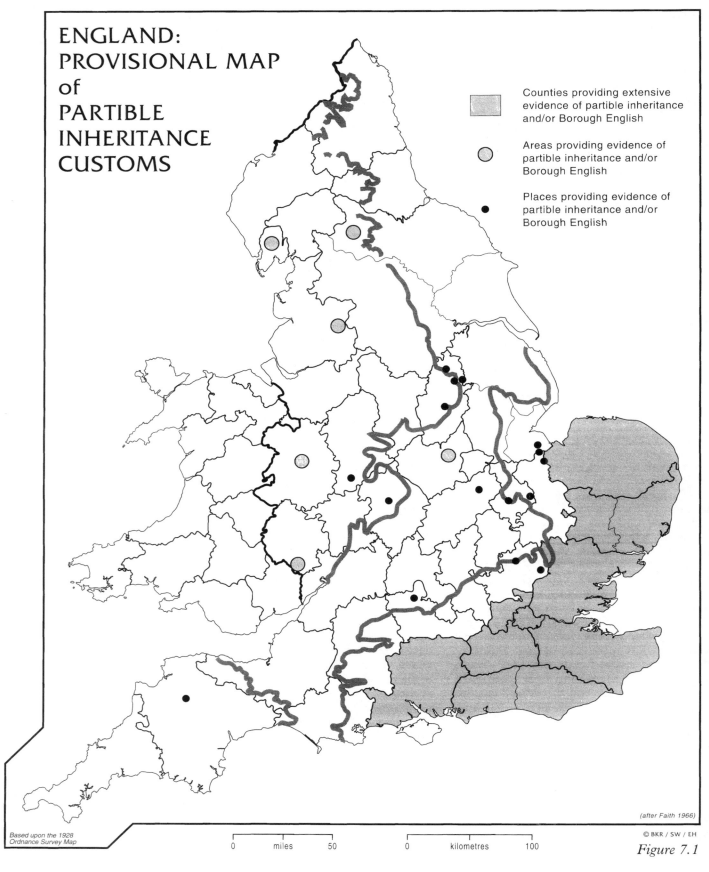

ENGLAND:
PROVISIONAL MAP
of
PARTIBLE
INHERITANCE
CUSTOMS

Counties providing extensive
evidence of partible inheritance
and/or Borough English

Areas providing evidence of
partible inheritance and/or
Borough English

Places providing evidence of
partible inheritance and/or
Borough English

(after Faith 1966)

Based upon the 1928
Ordnance Survey Map

0   miles   50

0   kilometres   100

© BKR / SW / EH

Figure 7.1

archaeologically detectable. Buildings were constructed wholly of organic materials, whose effective life was limited to little more than one or two human lifetimes, although their major timber elements could be transported to new sites with relative ease. This does not exclude the possibility of substantial fences of timber or thornbushes essentially set *on* the land, but it probably signifies that settlements shifted relatively easily, if not frequently. Furthermore, it is likely that the inevitable accumulation of dung and urine both on and around a settlement site made it attractive as farm-land or garden land after a few generations. Here we would point to the numbers of pre-Conquest settlement sites that have been discovered because they were drawn into the tillage, surviving merely as field and furlong names or pottery scatters. Broken by plough or spade, such manured sites would have been inherently productive areas, and indeed were conceivably the very portions of the farm-group tillage that were most readily subdivided into strips (Fig 3.4 e).

With scattered communities operating amid heterogeneous landscapes, a diversity of practice would be expected, not least because of interaction between Anglo-Saxon and Romano-British communities possessing differing traditions. For the first centuries of the Anglo-Saxon period small rural settlements were the norm. Most hamlets would have been inhabited by small groups of farmers linked by blood ties, together with their household slaves. In this pattern, larger congregations of farmers, including those with craft skills as well as the underprivileged – perhaps Romano-British – dependants of a powerful local or regional family would have a logical place. Emergent royal vills, drawing together an even greater diversity of communities and farming environments would characterise the next level in the hierarchy. The numerous Old English place-names expres-sive of estate geography, function or depen-dency signified these diverse layers. While name changes would have inevitably occurred as part of such a dynamic system (Sawyer 1976, 6–7; Roberts 1996a, 123), the arrival of written evidence of land holding helped to perpetuate them long after they ceased to be descriptive.

For the vast majority of the population this dynamic system would have been closely bonded to the arable land, both that farmed at an earlier stage and that added through intakes of open pastures and

assarts of woodland. At the level of the indi-vidual settlement, partibility and co-aration within the kin group led to the appearance of irregular patchworks of strips and block-fields. Strips perhaps appeared first upon the more favourable, more valuable, long-farmed and manured lands, worked from irregular hamlets and loose girdles of farm-steads that increased in size and number as population grew. That such arable cores were surrounded by a fence to protect the crops from the depredations of both wild animals and domestic stock cannot be doubted; as Ine's law of 690 implies (Whitelock 1955, clause 42), its mainte-nance was an important liability. Neverthe-less, flexibility and change were normal in such a system, with settlements shifting sites within their territories (Roberts 1996a, 120-7). More permanent settlement centres – Alan Everitt's 'seminal places, where things happen' – were provided by the chief centres and halls of magnates.

In the matter of agricultural clearance Sawyer concluded that 'the resources of many parts of England were already being fully exploited in the seventh century' (Sawyer 1976, 5), or more informally that 'the Anglo-Saxon period was not one long assart'. In support of his argument we can see no extensive evidence for Anglo-Saxon name-elements which are indisputably linked to the *process* of woodland clearance, as opposed to the *presence* of woodland. Although the varied forms of the root *ryd* and *rydding* imply 'clearance from wood-land' (Smith 1956, 89–91; Gelling 1984, 208), they are by no means common in place-name formation. Of course, we would not deny that clearances were taking place, but would question the scale involved. Increases in population in the Anglo-Saxon period, and an associated expansion of tillage led to closer definition of any unde-fined territories, and to the degeneration of wood pastures to open pastures. The dynamic qualities of the system were enhanced by political instability which brought warfare and episodic devastation (Hill 1981; Fig 5.8); but all developments, both local and 'national', were framed by the antecedent landscapes inherited from Roman Britain. In this, we picture local regions of relative stability set alongside, and within, areas of sustained and vigorous change, and the location and character of these would have varied spatially, tempo-rally and internally within the territories over which local magnates exercised control. Figure 5.1 is a powerful reminder of the spatial complexity likely to have been present at this stage. Some of these territories were undoubtedly ancient estates, perhaps the lineal descendants of Roman territorial units, while others were wholly new assemblages. The 'multiple estate' seems to represent a general model for what emerged (Figure 1.7), an arrangement in which the resources of a rather large territory were focused at a central place or places for the support and use of a king or aristocratic landholder (Jolliffe 1926, 161–99; Rees 1963, 148–68; Barrow 1973, 7–68).

New settlements, perhaps including those with place-names in -worth, appeared in these newly reclaimed areas. When plotted and viewed as an individual distribution (Fig 7.2) the element -worth, including also the related forms -worthy and -wardine, both of which have clear regional affinities, generates no clear-cut nationally significant distribution. Nevertheless, when this seemingly random scatter is superimposed upon the national distribution of woodlands seen in Figure 1.13, a pattern of associative peripherality is seen. There is no doubt in our mind that these names, in early use in the Anglo-Saxon period (Smith 1956, 273–7; Cox 1976), represent a category of individual farmsteads established within or on the edges of woodland tracts. The facts that many are linked with personal names and that there are very few compounds with -ingas- and -ham (Smith 1956, 273–7) supports the suggestion that these represent steadings resulting from land taking by individual colonists. Their diffusion throughout the three provinces, with concentrations occurring only in parts of the two outer ones, again suggests that the term had a general rather than a purely local meaning. How far woodland clearance was involved we cannot know, but the laws of Ine of Wessex (688–726) contain clauses which are designed to stop the erosion of timber resources by specifying a fine for cutting down a tree big enough to shelter 30 swine (Finberg 1972b, 404).

The socio-economic origins of the Central Province and the trend towards dependent tenancies in the hands of elementary families are possibly evident in one of Ine's laws, which states that:

> If a man takes a yard of land, or more, at a fixed rent, and ploughs it, and the lord requires service as well as rent, the tenant need not take the land if the lord does not

give him a dwelling: but in that case he must forfeit the crops. *(Finberg 1972b, 411; Whitelock 1955, Ine, clause 67)*

Finberg interprets its purpose as being to encourage new gains for the plough, and that the husbandman was not to be deterred from enlarging his ploughland by the fear that he would incur a heavier liability for service on his lord's demesne. Nevertheless, the fact that the king attaches the liability for labour services to the house, the messuage, rather than to the arable holding, has important implications for the plantation of nucleations. Lloyn notes that 'three general conclusions seem perfectly permissible: (1) that a lord may, if he so wishes, demand labour services (*weorc: opus*) in place of or as well as rent (*gafol: gablum*); (2) that if he has not provided the tenant with a house then the tenant may refuse weorc, though at a loss of tenure and of seed; (3) by implication that a tenant who has a house, a *botl*, committed to him can be held to labour services' (Lloyn 1962, 165). Furthermore, the doom implies that there was a distinction between those who possessed their own dwellings and those – tenants – who lived in dwellings provided by their lord. The latter are linked with arable land described as a 'yard', a unit later latinised into *pertica* (perch) and *virgata* (virgate or yardland), eventually the normal holding of a typical husbandman in a tenant village. The creation of communities made up of neighbours – tenants rather than kin – was associated with the planting of tofts and crofts and with permanence and stability in rural settlement.

This particular clause is associated with others concerning the migration of a nobleman (a *gesith-born* man), who could move elsewhere with his reeve, his smith and his children's nurse. Further, 'he who had twenty hides must show twelve hides *gesettes landes* when he departs, he who has ten hides must show six, and he who has three must show one and a half'. The term *gesette land* is normally considered to mean 'land settled by tenants', and whatever the shades of meaning present (Lloyn 1962, 163–4; Seebohm 1902, 421–2), the implication is that tenanted, cultivated land was seen as an important resource, worthy of royal attention. The tenth-century document known as the *Rectitudines Singularum Personarum* states that in some places it is the custom, when settling a *gebur* or farmer on the land, that there shall be given to him

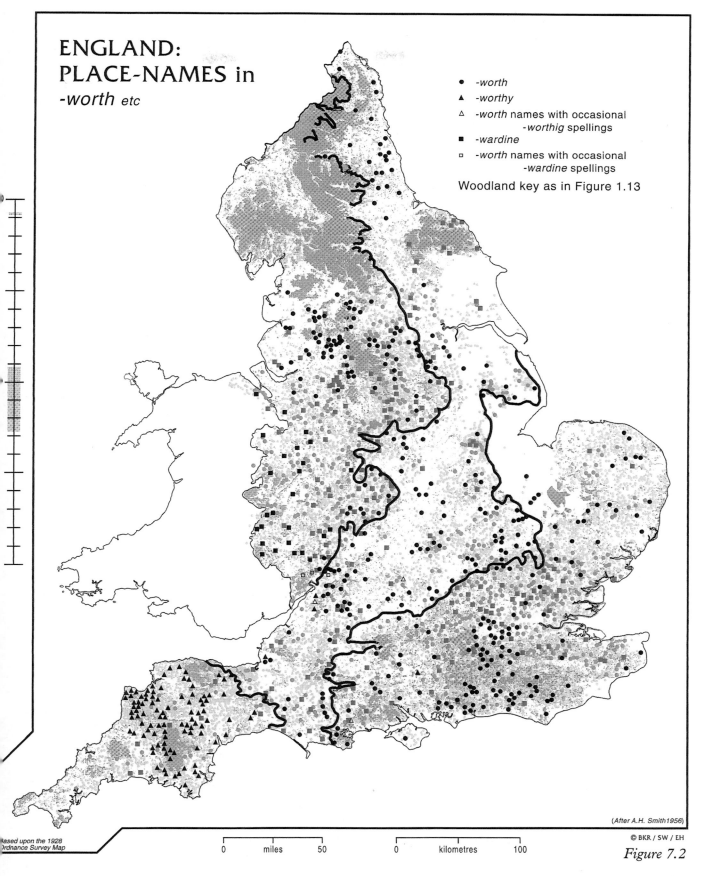

ENGLAND:
PLACE-NAMES in
-worth etc

- ● -worth
- ▲ -worthy
- △ -worth names with occasional -worthig spellings
- ■ -wardine
- □ -worth names with occasional -wardine spellings

Woodland key as in Figure 1.13

(After A.H. Smith 1956)

Based upon the 1928 Ordnance Survey Map

0   miles   50

0   kilometres   100

© BKR / SW / EH

Figure 7.2

'to land setene' (ie an outfit), namely two oxen, one cow, six sheep and seven acres sown on his yardland or virgate (Seebohm 1883, 129–59). It is generally the case that four yardlands together made a hide of land, the eight oxen for the four tenants combining to make a full ploughteam. Such provision was essential for a new tenant, and we see in this group of clauses necessary conditions for the appearance of new nucleated, planted hamlets and villages. The variations emphasised by the author of the *Rectitudines* – 'the geburs services are various, in some places heavy, in others moderate' – would reflect the varied circumstances of land settlement. It is clear that the new tenant was excused rent for a year, for the account continues: 'Wherefore after that year he must perform all services which pertain to him'. The fact that 'he must have given to him tools for his work, and utensils for his house. Then when he dies his lord takes back what he leaves' emphasises the complete dependency of the new arrival, a dependency we interpret as real rather than a legal fiction. The crop from the seven sown acres would be enough to feed at least two people for a year, with sufficient surplus, even were yields low, for seed grain for the next year (van Bath 1963a, fig 6, 21). The 'seven acres sown' needs to be explained in the context of 20 or 30 acres which traditionally constitute the yardland or virgate. In the case of a 20 acre virgate – no doubt varying in size according to the customary lengths of rods and poles in particular regions – a two-course rotation would imply ten acres of cropland each year. The seven acres of the document probably represent this, less one-tenth tithe, while the remaining two-tenths represent the 24 *sesters* of barley and the seed grain for three acres the *gebur* owed as part of the rent. In this account a clear link with woodland regions is evident in the statement that the outfit is provided 'on that land' where 'two and two (ie two tenants) feed one hound' (for hunting purposes of course), and 'each *gebur* gives vj loaves to the swineherd when he drives his herd to the mast'.

As nucleated tenanted settlements evolved, and when lord and peasant so agreed, the toft in the hamlet or village could become 'the mother of the acre', ie part of the paradigm for organising the distribution of arable strips amid fields which were subjected to intensive and sustained arable cultivation. When field systems grew larger, and as rotations became formalised, a regular disposition of strips became desirable. Ultimately this regularity was manifest in *solskifte* (Vinogradoff 1911, 175–9, n33; Homans 1960, 83–106; Göransson 1961, 80–104). Such developments were part of the practices of landscape and tenemental formalisation in a society in which at first the physical structures of toft and croft, ridges and furlongs and the 'mind of man' constituted the primary record, rather than the written survey or the map. The reformation of agricultural practices in the ninth to twelfth centuries was only one step along the way to the expression of full social 'individualisation' through farming practices. Such trends were reinforced and reiterated by the trauma of extensive devastation after the Viking wars and the Conquest of 1066. Of course, this is in no way to underrate the significance of other produce, particularly forest produce, the meat of pigs and cattle, honey, fruits and nuts, cheeses and ale, vegetables, as well as the meats of birds and fish. Nevertheless, grain was the staff of life, a storable commodity, for conversion into bread or drink. The roots of the fiscal tenements are to be found in the arable landscapes of the seventh and eighth centuries (Finberg 1972b, 411–16; Jolliffe 1935–6) and it is to the basis of fiscal tenements – the assessed land – that we must now turn.

Assessed and non-assessed land

The regular fiscal tenement emerged during the centuries before the Norman Conquest bonding together royal taxation, social obligations and service and the physical structures of field systems and settlements. How did the concept spread? Radding and Clark (1992, 3) writing of medieval architecture in its cultural context summarise the key problem of spatial connection in the following way:

> in contrast to a mere parallelism, the connection ... is a genuine cause-and-effect relation; but in contrast to an individual influence, this cause-and-effect relation comes about by diffusion rather than by direct impact. It comes about by the spreading of what may be called, for want of a better term, a mental habit.

The similarities and parallels seen in the characteristics of settlement, field systems, social arrangements, farming practices and fiscal systems are all part of an aggregation of habits of mind of proven worth within the context of a particular 'village firm' (Dahlman 1980, 204–10). The regional and local diversity we detect in medieval and post-medieval sources shows clearly that the adoption of these habits was never uniform and never universal: there were false starts, inertia and failures. There is no doubt that a diffusion of 'habits of mind' took place, but we are rarely, if ever, dealing with any single uniformly imposed system, even in the case of royal taxation. A given idea, a given practice, was invariably thought through differently and applied differently in varied regional and local contexts. Some elements were imposed externally, while others, the need to share, arose from within the community of the vill. The result has created diversity not unity, yet paradoxically the unity within the diversity – the generality rather than the detail – is what we seek to observe and describe in order to create tools for thinking, analysis and explanation. Figure 7.3, a generalisation cast in the form of a cartogram reflecting the shape of England, brings together several components: assessment systems, land use and the quantity of assessed land within the territories of individual communities. The importance of this to our general theme is direct. This assessed land was generally – for there are always exceptions – land long-cultivated, land that was cleared: effectively open townfield land.

Beginning in the Central Province, holdings assessed in virgates and bovates and at root hides and carucates, dominate the assessment system. This land is shown as a shaded symbol within the area of each hexagon, while peripheral notes comment upon the characteristics of the assessments. The hexagons symbolise the individual townships and parishes making up each province, and the inset map provides a reminder of the varied size of parishes on a national scale, and of the manner in which townships – *tithings* in the South-west – are variously combined to make parishes. The remaining portions of each hexagon, shown grey in the Central Province and white in the two outer provinces, comprise some enclosed land held in severalty, some woodland and any residual areas given over to open common pastures. By 1086, some parts of the champion zone, especially the central portions of the Central Province, had already been long cleared. Their populous settlements, villages and large hamlets, and highly organised field and farming

systems, with their operating rules and assessments based upon fiscal tenements using virgates and bovates, resulted from political, social and agrarian pressures. Moving outwards from the central Midlands, the proportion that the assessed lands represented of the total township area – and concurrently the proportion they represented of the total land surface – decreased, with concomitant increases in other forms of land usage. In the two outer provinces, assessed land, usually a form of townfield land, represents in most cases only a small proportion of each township. While we cannot be certain that the *tenementa*, the fiscal tenements of East Anglia, and the *sulungs*, *leynes*, and *virgates* of the South-east were wholly incumbent upon anciently cleared lands, there must be a strong presumption that they were. These lands were, *in large*, the areas which are eventually documented as townfields (Fig 5.10).

The inset to Figure 7.3, ultimately drawing upon the maps created by the Genealogical Society (Humphery-Smith 1984) attempts a simple synoptic view of variations in parish sizes and their shape characteristics. This is an imperfect map, because it is based upon ecclesiastical parishes: townships are noted only where coterminous with chapelries, so the lines, which have been drawn so as to define the essential spatial contrasts observable within the texture within the map, cannot be wholly accurate. Nevertheless, the tract of the Trent Valley, between the rising ridges of Sherwood and the Fenland edge is the site of an important transition. Throughout the Midland portion of the Central Province parishes tend to be small and irregular, and contain three or fewer townships, while to the north they are notably larger, even very large, and normally contain between two and seven townships (Sylvester 1969, 166–71). The transition is marked throughout the scarplands and fenlands of Lincolnshire and south Yorkshire by the appearance of tracts of countryside divided into remarkably regular patterns of linear, strip-like parishes and townships, arranged so as to cut at right-angles across the grain of the land in a region where linear terrain contrasts closely reflect the underlying geology. Similar patterns appear along some areas of the scarp and vale in south-eastern England.

The main model in Figure 7.3 emphasises the varied amounts of assessed land present, both in the three provinces and in

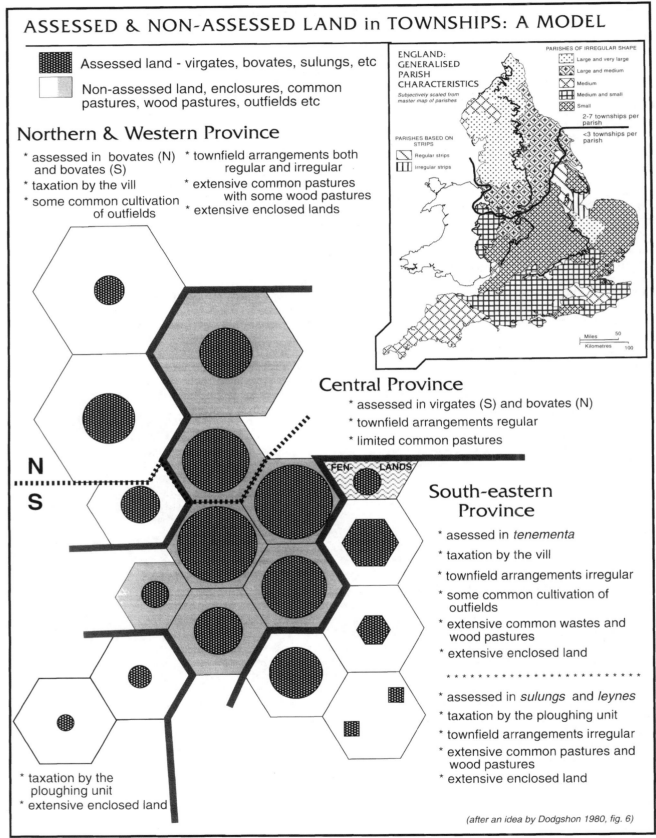

ASSESSED & NON-ASSESSED LAND in TOWNSHIPS: A MODEL

Assessed land - virgates, bovates, sulungs, etc

Non-assessed land, enclosures, common pastures, wood pastures, outfields etc

ENGLAND: GENERALISED PARISH CHARACTERISTICS
Subjectively scaled from master map of parishes

PARISHES OF IRREGULAR SHAPE
- Large and very large
- Large and medium
- Medium
- Medium and small
- Small

2-7 townships per parish
<3 townships per parish

PARISHES BASED ON STRIPS
- Regular strips
- Irregular strips

Northern & Western Province

* assessed in bovates (N) and bovates (S)
* taxation by the vill
* some common cultivation of outfields
* townfield arrangements both regular and irregular
* extensive common pastures with some wood pastures
* extensive enclosed lands

Central Province

* assessed in virgates (S) and bovates (N)
* townfield arrangements regular
* limited common pastures

FEN-LANDS

South-eastern Province

* asessed in *tenementa*
* taxation by the vill
* townfield arrangements irregular
* some common cultivation of outfields
* extensive common wastes and wood pastures
* extensive enclosed land

* *

* assessed in *sulungs* and *leynes*
* taxation by the ploughing unit
* townfield arrangements irregular
* extensive common pastures and wood pastures
* extensive enclosed land

* taxation by the ploughing unit
* extensive enclosed land

(after an idea by Dodgshon 1980, fig. 6)

Figure 7.3

sub-provinces within them. Given the fact that we have not been able to discover great tracts of countryside in which traces of extremely ancient, pre-Anglo-Saxon enclosures are clearly present – the co-axial systems of the Waveney valley and the enclosed systems of Essex may represent important exceptions – then the areas of townfield land present, say, at the time of Domesday Book must have been set amid great tracts of open pasture and wood pasture. If this is true of the South-east, then this must to an even greater degree have been the situation in the West and the North. There are possible exceptions in some portions of the far South-west, where stone-dyked enclosures preserve ancient patterns (eg Herring 1998, fig 17). Nevertheless, for both outer provinces a picture emerges of vast areas of unploughed land. Some of these were grass pastures, sometimes wet, sometimes dry, but these graded into pastures with stands of trees and galleries of surviving woodland. Enclosed woods established some areas of protected timber, and these graded into a few zones, often eventually Royal Forest, where extensive woodlands persisted around only limited areas of assessed land. No doubt some parts of this 'waste' had once been cultivated land, areas where it had proved impossible to sustain soil fertility given the limitations of the farming practice available, or where devastation by war, plague or policy had reduced the local population. Nevertheless, we have a picture of an English countryside in which there were extensive tracts of land for which the term 'temperate savanna' may not be inappropriate.

A glimpse of landscape conditions in the Anglo-Saxon and Anglo-Scandinavian periods comes from a surprising source: royal law codes treating travelling, trading and livestock. The earliest of these, the laws of the Kentish kings, largely deal with infringements of the peace, personal contact and injury, manslaying and oath-taking (Whitelock 1955, 357–61) but a doom of Whitred (695, clause 28: Whitelock 1955, 364) provides a succinct image:

> If a man from a distance or a foreigner [ie someone unknown to the local community] goes off the track, and he neither shouts nor blows a horn, he is to be assumed to be a thief, to be either killed or redeemed.

'Goes off the track' carries the implication that if travellers on honest business stuck to recognised routes, then there were no problems. Only those of dishonest intent were to be expected away from the tracks, moving covertly, amid the open pastures and wood pastures. This doom appears, almost word for word, in clause 20 of the code of Ine of Wessex (690: Whitelock 1955, 364–72) which also provides important evidence about local landscapes. The famous 'If ceorls' clause (41) treats the need to fence communally organised meadow or arable, and the fact that marauding stock could be killed by those suffering such depredations (clause 42) indicates the seriousness of such trespass. Like humans, cattle can acquire bad habits. Of course, landowners had the duty to fence and could expect no compensation for trespass by a neighbour's stock if this were not done (clause 40). Future problems are seen in two further clauses. The first allows unsound beasts to be returned to a seller within 30 days, unless the latter swears there was no fault in the sale, a defence against theft, while another concerns a wife's liability when a husband steals cattle (clause 57). Finally, there are clauses (48–49.1, 49.2 and 49.3) touching the stealing of mast pasture by putting swine on it, while a further set concerning trees 'in a wood' notes that 'fire is a thief' while the axe, a noisy tool, is an informer. The imposition of fines shows that as early as 690 it was necessary to have a royal doom upon standing timber, particularly substantial timber, for a tree 'under which 30 swine could stand' can hardly have been small. Its mast-bearing quality made it particularly valuable.

Over 150 years later, the laws of Alfred (871–99: Whitelock 1955, 372–80) show the theft of stock to be a matter of a compensation fine (clause 16). However, a sign of change is found in a clause which states that if anyone entrusts property to a friend and loss follows: 'If it ... were livestock, and he [the friend] says that the army took it, he need not pay for it' (clause Int 28: Whitelock 1955, 372). Athelstan's code, issued at Grateley, Hampshire (Whitelock 1955, 381–6) in 924–39, is much more specific. One clause (9) concerning the 'attaching' of livestock – placing stock under the control of a court – suggests that neighbours were called upon to witness legal possession, while in the case of exchange (clause 24) the witness of a reeve, priest or the lord of an estate was necessary. Proof of action was crucial, to the degree that if a purchase were in any way challenged (clause 24) then the seller had to take the beast back. Establishing the legality of a sale, in a society where the word of witnesses represented proof of ownership raised fundamental problems. A further clause qualified the statement that 'one is not to buy outside a town' except with the witness of the town reeve or another reliable man or of other reeves in a public meeting, unless the goods were under 20 pence in value. This reiterates the problem of establishing the legitimacy of transactions. A further doom, issued by Athelstan at Exeter (Whitelock 1955, 386–70) contains a dramatic image (clause 2):

> And he who tracks cattle into the land of another – he who owns the land is to follow the trail out [of his land] if he can: if he cannot, the trail is to serve instead of the preliminary oath [ie the formal oath that a crime had been committed] if he [who lost the cattle] accuses anyone on that estate.

There is an assumption here that stolen cattle could be tracked. This task would have been difficult but not wholly impossible along established routeways, but far easier amid extensive open pastures and wood pastures. The theme is developed further in an ordinance associated with the bishops and reeves of the London district (Whitelock 1955, 387–91), a set of rules formulated by a 'peace guild', whose activities, in addition to feasting, included quests after stolen cattle. In these, formal statements about tracking were included. It is evident that something approaching a 'posse' was to be assembled for pursuit (clause 4) and this pursuit could result in the death, by hanging, of the thief (clauses 7 and 12). Sometimes the need to track cattle could arise because 'many heedless men do not care how their cattle wander out of over-confidence in the peace' (clause 8.7), while tracking could flow from one shire to another (clause 8.4). Edgar's code issued at 'Whitbordesstan' in 962–3 (Whitelock 1955, 397–401) demands that beasts purchased 'unexpectedly' by a man on a journey were to be brought to the common pasture with the witness of his village (clause 8). If however, the stock remains on the common pasture for five days unannounced, then the cattle are forfeit and the herdsmen are to be flogged – presumably because such action must have been taken with their complicity (clause 9). Underlying all of these dooms is the problem of theft,

and Athelstan states 'that it is my will that villagers and their herdmen may hold the same investigation among my livestock and among those of my thegns as they hold amongst their own' (clause 13). This was to apply to both men of English and Danish blood, for the code was 'to be common to all of us who inhabit these islands' (clause 14.2).

We can speculate about why the post-Alfredian codes laid such emphasis upon theft and the witness of actions designed to inhibit theft. During the troubled times of the Viking wars there was more disruption than that caused by the armies under the control of ealdormen and jarls: casual brigandage and rieving, the stealing of movable, consumable wealth, must have become all too common. In the context of peripheral brigandage an earlier doom of Ine (clause 13.1) makes sense: 'We call up to seven men 'thieves'; from seven to thirty-five a 'band'; above that it is an 'army''. Athelstan's codes represent a reassertion of royal authority following strife and actual warfare (Hill 1981, 60–1), representing a law and order campaign (John 1996, 111) and must be linked with such other public acts as his circumnavigation of the realm. Eric John appears to be the only scholar who has commented on some of the clauses examined above, and he too uses terms such as 'rustling' and 'posse', images which are inescapable. 'Cattle and horses', he notes, 'were very big business in that world', and had the particular advantage that they could be walked away (John 1996, 110). The enactments make sense in the context of the 'temperate savannas' defined earlier, some of which were true common pastures closely attached to local communities while others, the more extensive, were substantive wildernesses into which stock could disappear leaving no more than their spoor. The proportions of waste and enclosed ground are crucial to the history of land settlement and land use.

Auditing land characteristics

If we are to explore the land use history of even a single parish or township we need to know, for varied periods of time, the extent of the arable and meadow of the townfields, the extent of rough, common grazing lands, the quantity of surviving woodland, and the extent of land enclosed and worked in severalty. Of course, these are crude divisions. The term 'grazing lands' for example, might encompass lands freely intercommoned and lands appropriated to a manor, commonable wood pastures and enclosed woodlands, enclosed and stinted or unstinted pastures, marsh and fen, parkland and chase, forest and warren. The proportions of each category of land can be assembled at the level of the township or parish, but can we assemble figures that relate to larger scales of analysis? To do this we are again forced to return to the straightjacket of the administrative county, the level at which data are available.

We begin with Northamptonshire, a county in the Central Province. It is largely dominated by townfields, although including areas of woodland in Rockingham and Whittlewood. Its total area is of the order of 585,000 acres (Philip 1928, 18; Darby and Terrett 1954, fig 146). In their work on Domesday Book, Darby and Terrett (1954, 379–416) recorded 2253 ploughteams in the county. If each worked 100 acres (a conservative estimate) they account for in excess of 225,300 acres, suggesting that 38.5% of the county was then tilled. Warwickshire, on the other hand, was divided between townfield landscapes and woody landscapes approximately in the proportion 3:2 (Darby and Terrett 1954, fig 105). It may have had only 32.5% of its area tilled (an area of 624,000 acres, set against 2030 ploughteams). In Berkshire tillage by the 1885 ploughteams probably accounted for 40.6% of the area, and in Norfolk the 5006 teams again accounted for 38.5% of the land surface. Shropshire provides contrast, where 20.3% of the 862,000 acres were cultivated by the 1750 teams. Herefordshire is an interesting anomaly: 2417 teams were working the 539,000 acres, and may account for as much as 44.7%. For clarity, the full comparative figures are shown in Table 7.1.

If our earlier suppositions are correct, then most of the remainder of each county in 1086 was 'waste', with varied mixtures of woodland and heathland, subjected to varied types of management which normally involved rights of common. The proportion of uncultivated lands in 1086 ranged between about 60 and 80%. These 'wastes' were 'temperate savannas', mixtures of woodland, scrubland and heath and grass pasture, the raw materials from which new townfields and landscapes of enclosure were created. In their study of the estates of Rievaulx abbey, Yorkshire, at the end of the twelfth century, Fergusson and Harrison (1999, 42) estimate that 'about half of the land included within the granges and totalling about 600 acres (243ha) was meadow and common pasture; about twenty per cent was arable and the same proportion was waste land or marshland or scrub'. Thus, in all, about 70% was meadow and common pasture, and waste, marshland or scrub. While the North York Moors were in some respects unusual we should not forget that the western end of the Tabular Hills, where Rievaulx is located, was in many respects well-settled by 1086, and the scatter of granges represents a fair sample of the terrains of eastern Yorkshire (ibid figs 3–6).

On a national scale large areas of the common pastures were finally subjected to enclosure under Parliamentary Act. The tracts of common land still found in present landscapes, prolific in the northern counties but more restricted elsewhere, represent the last residuals of this vast reserve. Our problem, modelled in Figure 6.1, is to obtain a concrete measure of the proportion of waste present at crucial time thresholds: let us say at the end of the thirteenth century, the end of the fourteenth century and at the end of the sixteenth century.

Table 7.1 Land area, Domesday ploughteams and proportion tilled in 1086 in six sample counties (area in thousands of acres)

county	area (A)	1086 ploughteams x 100 (B)	(B) as % of (A)
Berkshire	464	188.5	40.6
Northamptonshire	585	225.3	38.5
Warwickshire	624	203	32.5
Norfolk	1300	500.6	38.5
Shropshire	862	175	20.3
Herefordshire	539	241.7	44.7

Table 7.2 Land area and late enclosed waste in six sample counties (all in thousands of acres)

county	area	estimate of late enclosed common pasture	% of area
Berkshire	464	6.4	1.4
Northamptonshire	585	13.7	2.3
Warwickshire	624	11.3	1.8
Norfolk	1300	79.6	6.1
Shropshire	862	336.2	39.0
Herefordshire	539	5.9	1.1

This cannot yet be done. An estimate of the extent enclosed by Act of Parliament can, however, be obtained from Tate's data (Turner 1978) and this is summarised as Table 7.2.

Only in Shropshire does late enclosed waste form more than a small percentage of the county area. The difference between the two percentage figures for each county in Tables 7.1 and 7.2 represents land reclaimed between 1086 and the later eighteenth century. There is no secure way of differentiating between that which was added to the townfield land of 1086 and that which was enclosed directly from the waste. If, however, we take figures from the Land Use Survey of the 1930s (Stamp 1962, 196–200), Table 7.3 can be created. Its final column contains a figure that must represent the combined acreage of both the townfield areas and those enclosures accreted in medieval and post-medieval centuries before 'late enclosure', ie enclosure by Act of Parliament. If we could take from these the acreages representing the areas of the townfield lands, the result would indicate (and no more) the likely quantities of land involved in medieval and post-medieval enclosing activity (again before enclosure by Act of Parliament).

The estimates of townfield areas in Table 7.4 have been derived from Tate's enclosure data, but these figures exclude any enclosures by agreement as well as enclosures resulting from village depopulations and emparking. The estimates of the maximum extent also take into account the calculations based upon Domesday Book.

The final figure, 'B minus A' is an estimate of the amount of old enclosure present in each county. That for Berkshire represents nearly 30% of the total land surface, that for Northamptonshire just over 30%, that for Warwickshire 38.4%, while that for Norfolk is 32.5%. It is a surprisingly consistent proportion. Shropshire represents 25.3% and Herefordshire 29.4%, but these estimates are less reliable because of the uncertain histories of townfields in these counties. As gross figures none of these is in conflict with Gonner's calculations (1912, fig D). Reviewing work by Lennard and

Table 7.3 A summary of land use in six sample counties (all in thousands of acres)

county	area	estimate of late enclosed common pasture (after Turner 1978)	rough pasture+ woodland in 1930s	arable+grass (in 1930s) all enclosed	arable+grass (in 1930s) minus late enclosed common pasture
Berkshire	464	6.4	62.7	365.1	358.7
Northamptonshire (including Peterborough)	585	13.7	30.1	514.0	500.3
Warwickshire	624	11.3	30.7	500.8	489.5
Norfolk	1300	79.6	190.4	1002.9	922.4
Shropshire	862	336.2	96.2	729.7	393.5
Herefordshire	539	5.9	82.6	414.3	408.4

Table 7.4 Estimate of amount of land enclosed piecemeal (all in thousands of acres)

county	area*	townfields* (after Turner 1980)	estimate of max. area of townfield A	enclosed arable +grass (in 1930s) minus late enclosed common pasture B	B minus A
Berkshire	464	140	(220)	358.7	138.7
Northamptonshire	585	263.8	(316)	500.3	184.3
Warwickshire	624	162.8	(250)	489.5	239.5
Norfolk	1300	310.7	(500)	922.4	422.7
Shropshire	862	4.3	(175?)	393.5	218.5
Herefordshire	539	16.7	(250?)	408.4	158.4

Maitland, Darby concluded that the arable area of 1086 was conservatively some 7.2 million acres, possibly as much as 8.6 million. This figure may be compared with 7.7 million acres in the Agricultural Returns of 1914 (Darby 1977, 129–33) and 8.3 million present in the later 1930s (Stamp 1962, 196). This latter figure is reduced to 6.33 million if we exclude the four northern counties that do not appear in Domesday Book. For the 28 counties recorded in Domesday Book, Lennard calculated 8.6 million acres of arable at 120 acres to the team or 7.2 million acres at 100 acres. Of course, the distribution of arable in 1086 differed greatly from that of 1914, and there were many sharp local variations. The area of England is some 32 million acres, although the counties with the more usable Domesday returns account for only some 22.5 million acres. If approximately one-third of this latter were arable – the Domesday arable figure of about 8 million is inevitably weighted towards these same counties – then we arrive at a generalised figure of about 35.5% tilled. This is well in accord with the county totals presented above, where the average of the tillage areas for the six counties is nearly 36%.

It is a pity, as Darby concludes, that the Domesday references to pastures are 'limited and unsystematic'. Nevertheless, they reveal the extent to which even the coastal marshes such as Canvey Island carried large amounts of stock. In the fens this marshland grazing was anciently divided among inland parishes (Darby 1977, 157–9). The terminology of 'pasture for sheep' in Essex, linked to those manors that had access to coastal marshes, indicates that the extensive wood pastures which dominated elsewhere in the county were pastures for cattle. In the South-west there are inexplicable variations in the 1086 data: for example, the very large amounts of pasture associated with the chalklands of Dorset as compared with those of Wiltshire. The deficiencies of the record are emphasised by the curious absence of large amounts of recorded pasture associated with the manors surrounding Dartmoor. That very large amounts of pasture land could be involved is illustrated by the cases of Melksham in Wiltshire and Frome in Somerset, the former returning 7 leagues by 7 leagues of pasture, the latter 17 furlongs by 17 furlongs (ie 1.4 leagues by 1.4 leagues: Darby 1977, 154–5). A Domesday league is generally considered to be 1? modern miles.

Developments after 1086 involved the colonisation of both open pastures and wood pastures. There were three aspects to this: first, the addition of new furlongs to existing arable townfields; secondly, the creation of new townfields where old foci were being expanded or new settlements planted; thirdly, the addition of new enclosed fields, peripheral to the old cores, either for new specialist enterprises or to create new farms in severalty. These are not, of course, wholly discrete categories. The fundamental question is why the expansion of townfields, either through direct assarting or through the absorption of assarts made in severalty, came generally to an end (Bishop 1935–6; Roberts 1973, 228–9). The context, like that of townfield development in earlier centuries, is both legal and fiscal. Three factors are likely to have been of importance. First, a shift in royal taxation: from the geld, to levies upon the movable wealth of individuals. Danegeld, a form of taxation structured around the existence of land-based fiscal tenements was taken for the last time in 1162 (Poole 1955, 418). In origin the assessment of a shire was fixed first, and each shire was held to contain a number of taxable units, hides, carucates or *sulungs*. Shires were further subdivided into hundreds, wapentakes, rapes, leets and individual townships, and each appears to have been allocated an appropriate share of the tax. Although the geld is commonly associated with taxation by Aethelred (979–1016) to buy off Danish armies, the roots may be very much older, originating in ancient levies of tribute. By the end of the twelfth century, however, taxes on movables were appearing, and were used, for example, to raise the ransom of Richard I. This transition was never clean-cut: a form of geld was brought in as an emergency measure in 1194 (Poole 1955, 418); but once the land tax declined in importance then geldable land, assessed in terms of carucates and hides and their subdivisions, was no longer relevant in the taxation system. New land was not gelded.

Second, new types of real action, legal procedures concerned with land, were introduced during the reign of Henry II. The action of *novel disseisin* took the form of the litigant alleging before the Royal courts that a recent (novel) dispossession (disseisin) had taken place. The matter was put before twelve jurors, and if the answer was that it had, then the status quo ante was restored (Simpson 1961, 27–31). It is probable that the king was more concerned with preventing disseisins than protecting seisin, or legal possession, but the effect was that the king took freeholders under his wing. These freeholders formed a social group intimately associated with intakes of new enclosures from the common pastures, lands granted by charter which passed into severalty. Although it could be used in either direction, to protect encroachments or protect the pasture, on balance this action represented a protection of the rights of the freeholder and not the rights of the community. In this lies its importance: the new action was a corollary of social change. The greatest opportunities for reclamation by individuals were present within the two outer provinces.

Finally, by 1235 the *Statute of Merton* (the Commons Act 1236) permitted lords of the manor to enclose common pasture provided that sufficient common was left for the free tenants (RCCL 1958, 154).

More formally, this allowed a lord to fence, enclose or 'approve' any of the waste, against his freehold tenants' rights of pasture appendant or appurtenant, provided that sufficient pasture was left for their beasts levant and couchant (Gonner 1912, 8–11, 49–51; Denman 1958, 130–1). The very existence of this legislation provides confirmation of an ongoing process. Although we cannot be certain, there is a strong presumption that the intakes envisaged by the Act were held in severalty, and were fenced, embanked, walled or hedged. They were not extensions of townfield arable, over which rights of common pasture – at the fallow time – were, of course, preserved even after their absorption into the townfields. This is a key point. The passing of the Act, the first of its kind, is a broad indication of the pressures building up, and by the thirteenth century the by-laws noted in manor court rolls record limitations upon the number of beasts which could be carried on the commons. By the mid-thirteenth century in Leicestershire, definite stints of the common pasture appear. These specify the number of stock allowed per yardland or arable land (RCCL 1958, paragraph 21). Thus, in the two outer provinces the great reserves of common pasture provided contexts in which increasing agricultural populations could be accommodated without any vast expansion of townfield arable.

Lennard concluded that in the England of 1086, Anglo-Saxon farmers were 'not nibbling at the edges of an unsubdued wilderness', and that 'villages, hamlets and farmsteads were to be found throughout the length and breadth of the country' (Lennard 1959, 3–5). Commenting on the absence in 1086 of 'fine fields of permanent grass' he noted that 'the pastures consisted mostly of very rough grazing lands'. We do not question his view that 'village fields were in many cases severed from neighbouring [ones] by a thin belt of land that remained in a wild state'. We emphasise, however, that this was true only of well-settled zones of our Central Province. In the outer provinces the cumulative amounts of rough grass pasture and wood pasture were very extensive indeed.

Conclusion

This study began with a national map of settlement (Fig 1.1). Figure 7.4 is an attempt to picture what lies beneath that distribution by using a visual cross section of

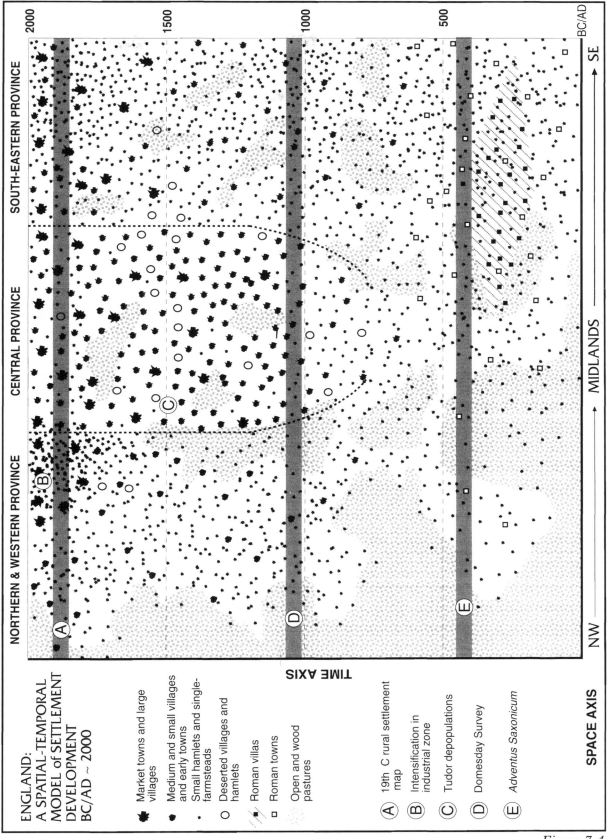

ENGLISH:
A SPATIAL-TEMPORAL
MODEL of SETTLEMENT
DEVELOPMENT
BC/AD ~ 2000

Market towns and large villages

Medium and small villages and early towns

Small hamlets and single-farmsteads

Deserted villages and hamlets

Roman villas

Roman towns

Open and wood pastures

(A) 19th C rural settlement map

(B) Intensification in industrial zone

(C) Tudor depopulations

(D) Domesday Survey

(E) Adventus Saxonicum

Figure 7.4

191

time and space, following ideas discussed in the cross section models of Figure 3.11. This takes a long-term view of settlement evolution, and while it is necessarily built around nucleations, towns, villages and hamlets, the background shading of wood pastures and open pastures hints at the locale of dispersion. At worst this diagram merely reveals the complexity underlying the simple distribution map. At best, it suggests the way in which subtle temporal shifts in local settlement geography gradually led towards the appearance of strongly differentiated local regions, and the emergence of the three provinces. By depicting time as a stratigraphic succession instead of a series of discrete phases, this diagram emphasises the artificiality of all such divisions. Life and work were a continuum; changes, at first limited to certain regions, were disseminated to adjacent and more distant regions. It is difficult to ascertain the nature of the actual linkages, the vehicles of transmission, but we have attempted to define the circumstances and contexts of transmission.

As the reader will by now have come to realise, this book is not a conventional work of synthesis. It does not pull together a multiplicity of case studies and attempt to identify *on the basis of those studies* a series of generally applicable themes and trends. There have, indeed, been a number of valuable 'bottom-up' syntheses of this kind, but even in these the authors measure (even if silently) the individual case studies, singly or collectively, against their own generalised perceptions of what is, or is not, important in the period or topic under consideration. In the end, syntheses of this sort are not that much different from our own approach, even if the perceptual framework is not openly articulated and is perhaps even unacknowledged.

Rarely are true 'bottom-up' syntheses attempted; few are the occasions on which general meaning has really been created from an archaeological or historical dataset of particular cases. The reason is that such datasets are usually wholly inadequate to the purpose. For example, a courageous attempt, over a decade ago, to establish regional variation in medieval settlements was based on 35 excavated sites which had provided detail of 162 buildings (Astill 1988, 41). Yet we estimate that England contained in the order of 15,000 township communities in the early fourteenth century, housed in nucleated settlements, hamlets or fully dispersed farmsteads. Omitting towns and boroughs, they will still have occupied well over half a million farmsteads and cottages. It is difficult to imagine that such a small excavated sample, 'to some extent arbitrarily determined by where archaeologists have chosen to excavate' (Astill 1988, 41), can realistically provide a basis for regional differentiation.

We hope that researchers will, instead, reference their local studies to our national frameworks. This is not because they will invariably find national and local perspectives in accord: there will often be discord. Nevertheless, it is this interaction of detailed investigations and general hypotheses that drives research forward. All too often archaeological investigations proceed without such interaction, with the result that we know something once existed somewhere, but little more than that. Settlement remains should, instead, be referenced to a hierarchy of contexts, local, regional and national. Their perceived characteristics will either conform to or diverge from what is known and understood, however limited, of the contextual hierarchy.

When the decision was made to prepare a series of case studies for this volume, it soon became evident that the published studies that focused exclusively on individual groups of habitation sites were of little value. The best were those which extended, in cartographic as well as written form, across the whole of a community's resource base, expressed physically as the township area. As we have emphasised in earlier chapters, farmsteads were positioned in the landscape with reference to the layout of those resources, and to the trackways which gave access between them. Indeed, it is the trackways not the farmsteads which often seem to represent constants in the landscape, especially in areas of dispersed settlement. We believe that many more township scale studies are essential for exploring and giving depth to the broader frameworks outlined in this book.

Bibliography

Aberg, A (ed), 1978 *Medieval Moated Sites*, CBA Res Rep, **17**, London

Adams, I D (ed), 1976 *Agrarian Landscape Terms: a Glossary for Historical Geography*, London

Alcock, N W, 1981 *Cruck Construction. An Introduction and Catalogue*, CBA Res Rep, **42**, London

Armstrong, A M, Mawer, A, Stenton, F M, and Dickens, B, 1950–2 *The Place-Names of Cumberland*, Cambridge

Astill, G, 1988 Rural settlement: the toft and the croft, in *The Countryside of Medieval England* (eds G Astill and A Grant), Oxford, 36–61

Aston, M A, 1983 Deserted farmsteads on Exmoor and the Lay Subsidy of 1327 in West Somerset, *Somerset Archaeol Nat Hist*, **127**, 71–104

_____ , 1985 Rural settlement in Somerset: some preliminary thoughts, in Hooke 1985c, 81–100

_____ , 1989 A regional study of deserted settlements in the West of England, in Aston *et al* 1989, 105–28

_____ , 1994 Medieval settlement studies in Somerset, in Aston and Lewis 1994, 219–37

Aston, M A, and Costen, M D (eds), 1994 *The Shapwick Project, fifth report*, Bristol University Department of Continuing Education, Bristol

Aston, M A, and Gerrard, C, 1999 'Unique, traditional and charming': The Shapwick project, Somerset, *Antiq J*, **79**, 1–58

Aston, M A, and Lewis, C, 1994 *The Medieval Landscape of Wessex*, Oxford

Aston, M A, Austin, D, and Dyer, C (eds) 1989 *The Rural Settlements of Medieval England*, Oxford

Aston, T H, 1958 The origins of the manor in Britain, *Trans Royal Hist Soc*, **8**, 59–83

Atkin, M A, 1985 Some settlement patterns in Lancashire, in Hooke 1985c, 171–85

Atkin, M, and Tompkins, K, 1986 *Revealing Lost Villages: Wharram Percy*, London

Austin, D (ed), 1982 *Boldon Book. Northumberland and Durham*, Chichester

Baker, A R H, 1968 A note on the retrogressive and retrospective approaches in historical geography, *Erdkunde* **22**, 244–5

_____ , (ed), 1972 *Progress in Historical Geography*, Newton Abbot

_____ , 1973 Changes in the later Middle Ages, in Darby 1973, 186–247

Baker, A R H, and Butlin, R A (eds), 1973 *Studies of Field Systems in the British Isles*, Cambridge

Barringer, J C, 1996 *Faden's Map of Norfolk in 1797*, Dereham

Barrow, G W S, 1973 *The Kingdom of the Scots*, London

Bell, M, and Boardman, J (eds), 1992 *Past and Present Soil Erosion*, Oxbow Monogr, **22**, Oxford

Bennett, S, and Bennett, N, (eds), 1993 *An Historical Atlas of Lincolnshire*, Hull

Beresford, M W, 1950 The deserted villages of Warwickshire, *Trans Birmingham Archaeol Soc*, **66**, 49–106

_____ , 1967 *The New Towns of the Middle Ages*, London

Beresford, M W, and Finberg, H P R, 1973 *English Medieval Boroughs. A Handlist*, Newton Abbot

Beresford, M W, and Hurst, J G (eds), 1971 *Deserted Medieval Villages*, London

_____ , 1990 *Wharram Percy Deserted Medieval Village*, London

Best, G, 1979 *Mid-Victorian Britain 1851–75*, London

Best, R H, and Rogers, A W, 1973 *The Urban Countryside*, London

Bishop, T A M, 1934 The distribution of manorial demesne in the Vale of York, *Engl Hist Rev*, **49**, 386–407

_____ , 1935–6 Assarting and the growth of open fields, *Econ Hist Rev*, **6**, 13–29

_____ , 1948 The Norman settlement of Yorkshire, in *Studies in Medieval History Presented to Maurice Powicke* (eds R W Hunt, W A Pantin and R W Southern), 1–14, Oxford

Bodvall, G, 1960 Expansion of the permanently settled area in Northern Hälsingland, *Geografiska Annaler*, **42**, 244–9

Bowen, H C, and Fowler, P J, 1966 Romano-British rural settlements in Dorset and Wiltshire, in *Rural Settlement in Roman Britain* (ed C Thomas), CBA Res Rep, **7**, 43–167, London

Brown, A E, and Taylor, C C, 1989 The origins of dispersed settlement; some results from fieldwork in Bedfordshire, *Landscape Hist*, **11**, 61–81

_____ , 1999 Chellington field survey, *Bedfordshire Archaeol*, **23**, 98–110

Brown, W (ed), 1906 *Yorkshire Inquisitions*, **4**, Yorkshire Archaeol Soc Rec Ser **37**

Brunskill, R W, 1978 *Illustrated handbook of Vernacular Architecture* (London)

Burman, J, 1930 *The Story of Tanworth in Arden, Warwickshire*, Birmingham

Butlin, R A, 1964 Northumberland field systems, *Agricultural Hist Rev*, **12**, 99–124

_____ , 1973 Field systems of Northumberland and Durham, in Baker and Butlin 1973, 93–144

Campbell, B M S, 1981 Commonfield origins – the regional dimension, in Rowley 1981, 112–29

_____ , 1990 People and land in the Middle Ages, in Dodgshon and Butlin 1990, 69–121

Catt, J A, 1978 The contribution of Loess to soils in lowland Britain, in Limbrey and Evans 1978, 12–20

Clay, C T (ed), 1947 *Early Yorkshire Charters 7*, Yorkshire Archaeol Soc Rec Ser, Extra Ser 5

Conzen, M R G, 1949 Modern settlement, in *Scientific Survey of North-Eastern England* (eds P C G Isaac and R E A Allan), Newcastle upon Tyne, 75–83

Corner, J, and MacLean, A S, 1997 *Taking Measures across the American Landscape*, Newhaven and London

Cox, B, 1976 The place-names of the earliest English records, *J Engl Place-name Soc*, **8**, 12–66

Crane, E, 1983 *The Archaeology of Beekeeping*, London

Croom, J, 1988 The fragmentation of the Minster *parochiae* of south-east Shropshire, in *Minsters and Parish Churches: the local church in transition* (ed J Blair), OUCA Monogr, **17**, 67–81, Oxford

Crump, W B, 1925 Clifton and its common fields, *Trans Halifax Antiq Soc 1925*, 105–35

Curtis, L F, Courtney, F M, and Trudgill, S T, 1976 *Soils in the British Isles*, London

Dahlman, C J, 1980 *The Open Field System and Beyond*, Cambridge

Darby, H C, 1951 *An Historical Geography of England before 1800*, Cambridge

_____ , 1952 *The Domesday Geography of Eastern England*, Cambridge

_____ (ed), 1973 *A New Historical Geography of England*, Cambridge

_____ , 1974 *The Medieval Fenland*, Newton Abbot

_____ , 1977 *Domesday England*, Cambridge

Darby, H C, and Campbell, E M J, 1962 *The Domesday Geography of South-East England*, Cambridge

Darby, H C, and Maxwell, I S, 1962 *The Domesday Geography of Northern England*, Cambridge

Darby, H C, and Terrett, I B, 1954 *The Domesday Geography of Midland England*, Cambridge

Darby, H C, and Versey, G R, 1975 *Domesday Gazetter*, Cambridge

Darby, H C, and Welldon Finn, R, 1967 *The Domesday Geography of South-West England*, Cambridge

Dark, K, and Dark, P, 1997 *The Landscape of Roman Britain*, Stroud

Darling, F Frazer (ed), 1956 *West Highland Survey: an Essay in Human Ecology* (rev edn), Oxford

Davison, A, 1988 *Six Deserted Villages in Norfolk*, East Anglian Archaeol, **44**, Dereham

_____ , 1990 *The Evolution of Settlement in Three Parishes in South-East Norfolk*, East Anglian Archaeol, **49**, Dereham

_____ , 1996 *Deserted Villages in Norfolk*, North Walsham

Denman, D R, 1958 *Origins of Ownership*, London

Denman, D R, Roberts, R A, and Smith, H J F, 1967 *Commons and Village Greens*, London

Dodgshon, R A 1980, *The Origin of British Field Systems: an Interpretation*, London

Dodgshon, R A, and Butlin, R A (eds), 1990 *An Historical Geography of England and Wales* (2nd edn), London

Dodgson, J McN, 1966 The significance of the distribution of English place-names in *-ingas*, *-inga-* in south-east England, *Medieval Archaeol*, **10**, 1–29

Douglas, D C, 1927 *The Social Structure of Medieval East Anglia*, Oxford Stud Social and Legal Hist, **9**, Oxford

Dunning, R W (ed), 1974 *The Victoria History of the County of Somerset, 3*, Oxford

_____ , 1978 *The Victoria History of the County of Somerset, 4*, Oxford

Dyer, C, 1982 Deserted medieval villages in the West Midlands, *Econ Hist Rev*, **35**, 19–34

Edwards, R, 1995 Hampshire village survey, *Medieval Settlement Res Group Annual Rep*, **10**, 11–12

Elliott, G, 1973 Field systems of Northwest England, in Baker and Butlin 1973, 42–92

Erixon, S, 1961 Swedish villages without systematic regulation, in Helmfrid 1961, 57–74

Evans, E Estyn, 1956 The ecology of peasant life in Europe, in *Man's Role in Changing the Face of the Earth* (ed W L Thomas), 217–39, Chicago

Everitt, A, 1985 *Landscape and Community in England*, London

_____ , 1986 *Continuity and Colonisation: The Evolution of Kentish Settlement*, Leicester

Everson, P, and Williamson, T (eds), 1998 *The Archaeology of Landscape*, Manchester

Everson, P, and Wilson-North, R, 1993 Fieldwork and finds at Egerton, Wheathill, *Shropshire Hist Archaeol*, **68**, 65–71

Everson, P, Taylor, C C, and Dunn, C J, 1991 *Change and Continuity: Rural Settlement in North-West Lincolnshire*, RCHME, London

Faith, R, 1966 Peasant Families and inheritance customs in medieval England, *Agric Hist Rev*, **14**, 77–95

_____ , 1994 Tidenham, Gloucestershire, and the origins of the manor in England, *Landscape Hist.* **16**, 39–51

_____ , 1997 *The English Peasantry and the Growth of Lordship*, Leicester

Farrer, W (ed), 1916 *Early Yorkshire Charters, 3*, privately publ

Faull, M L, and Moorhouse, S A (eds), 1981 *West Yorkshire: an Archaeological Survey to AD 1500*, Wakefield

Faull, M L, and Stinson, M (eds), 1986 *Domesday Book: Yorkshire*, Chichester

Fellows-Jensen, G, 1978 *Scandinavian Settlement Names in the East Midlands*, Copenhagen

Fergusson, P, and Harrison, S, 1999 *Rievaulx Abbey*, Newhaven

Field, J, 1993 *A History of English Field-Names*, London

Finberg, H P R, 1969 *West-Country Historical Studies*, Newton Abbot

_____ , 1972a *The Early Charters of the West Midlands*, Leicester

_____ , (ed), 1972b *The Agrarian History of England and Wales, 1* Cambridge

Fleming, A, 1988 *The Dartmoor Reaves*, London

_____ , 1998 Prehistoric landscapes and the quest for territorial pattern, in Everson and Williamson 1998, 42–66

Ford, W J, 1976 Some settlement patterns in the central region of the Warwickshire Avon, in Sawyer 1976, 274–94

Fowler, P, 1978, Lowland landscapes: culture, time and personality, in *The Effect of Man on the Landscape: the Lowland Zone* (eds S Limbrey and J G Evans), CBA Res Rep, **21**, London, 1-12

Fowler, P J, 1971 Early prehistoric agriculture in western Europe: some archaeological evidence, in *Economy and Settlement in Neolithic and Early Bronze Age Britain and Europe* (ed D D A Simpson), 153–84, Leicester

_____ , 1983 *The Farming of Prehistoric Britain*, Cambridge

Fox, C, 1952 *The Personality of Britain*, Cardiff

Fox, H S A, 1989 The people of the Wolds in English settlement history, in Aston *et al* 1989, 77–101

Fraser, C M, 1968 *The Northumberland Lay Subsidy Roll of 1296*, Newcastle upon Tyne

Frere, S, 1987 *Britannia: a History of Roman Britain* (3rd edn), London

Fulford, M, and Nichols, E, 1992 *Developing Landscapes of Lowland Britain: The Archaeology of the British Gravels – a Review*, Soc Antiq London Occas Pap, **14**

Gay, E F, 1902–3 Inclosures in England in the sixteenth century, *Q J Econ*, 2nd ser, **17**, 576–97

Geertz, C, 1973 *The Interpretation of Cultures*, New York and London

Gelling, M, 1978 *Signposts to the Past: Place-names and the History of England*, London

_____ , 1984 *Place-names in the Landscape*, London

_____ , 1992 *The West Midlands in the Early Middle Ages*, Leicester

Glacken, C, 1967 *Traces on the Rhodian Shore*, Berkeley

Glass, D V, and Eversley, D E C, 1965 *Population in History*, London

Glasscock, R E, 1973 England *circa* 1334, in Darby 1973, 136-85

_____ , 1975 *The Lay Subsidy of 1334*, Br Acad Rec Soc Econ Hist, new ser, **11**, London

Gonner, E C K, 1912 *Common Land and Inclosure*, London

Goody, J, 1983 *The Development of the Family and Marriage in Europe*, Cambridge

Göransson, S, 1961 Regular open-field pattern in England and Scandinavian *solskifte*, in Helmfrid 1961, 80–104

Gover, J E B, Mawer, A, and Stenton, F M (eds), 1931–2 *The Place-names of Devon*, Engl Place-name Soc, **8** and **9**, Cambridge

_____ , (eds) 1936 *The Place-names of Warwickshire*, Engl Place-name Soc, **13**, Cambridge

Graham, T H B, 1934 *The Barony of Gilsland: Lord William Howard's survey taken in 1603*, Cumberland Westmorland Antiq Archaeol Soc, extra ser, **16**, Kendal

Gray, H L, 1915 *English Field Systems*, Cambridge, Mass

Greenway, D E, 1972 *Charters of the Honour of Mowbray, 1107-1191*, Br Acad Rec Soc Econ Hist, new ser, **1**, London

Greenwell, W, 1857 *Bishop Hatfield's Survey*, Surtees Soc, **32**

Grenzbach, K, 1984 *Siedlungsgeographie-Westafrika, Afrika Kartenwerk*, Beiheft W9, Berlin and Stuttgart

Gulley, J L M, 1961 The retrospective approach in historical geography, *Erdkunde* **15**, 306–9

Gurney, N K M, and Clay, C (eds), 1971 *Fasti Parochiales, 4*, Yorkshire Archaeol Soc Rec Ser, **133**

Hadley, D M, 2000 *The Northern Danelaw: Its Social Structure, c.800–1100*, Leicester

Haggard, H Rider, 1899 *A Farmer's Year*, London

Hall, D, 1989 Field systems and township structure, in Aston *et al* 1989, 191–205

_____ , 1995 *The Open Fields of Northamptonshire*, Northamptonshire Rec Soc, **38**, Northampton

Hall, D, and Coles, J (eds), 1994 *Fenland Survey: an Essay in Landscape and Persistence*, London

Hallam, E M, 1986 *Domesday Book Through Nine Centuries*, London

Hallam, H E, 1965 *Settlement and Society: a Study of the Early Agrarian History of South Lincolnshire*, Cambridge

_____ , (ed), 1988 *The Agrarian History of England and Wales 1042–1350, II*, Cambridge

Hallam, S J, 1970 Settlement round the Wash, in Phillips 1970, 22–88

Hamerow, H, 1994 Migration theory and the Migration period, in Vyner 1994, 164–77

Harmer, F E, 1952 *Anglo-Saxon Writs*, Manchester

Hart, C, 1975 *The Early Charters of Northern England and the North Midlands*, Leicester

_____ , 1992 *The Danelaw*, London

Hartke, W, 1951 Die Heckenlandschaft: der geographische Charakter eines Landeskulturproblems, *Erdkunde* **5**, 132–52

Harvey, M, 1982 Regular open-field systems on the Yorkshire Wolds, *Landscape Hist*, **4**, 29–39

Harvey, M, 1983 Planned field systems in eastern Yorkshire: some thoughts on their origin, *Agric Hist Rev*, **31**, 91–103

Harvey, P D A, 1965 *A Medieval Oxfordshire Village*, Oxford

Hatcher, J, 1988 Farming techniques in south-western England, in Hallam 1988, 383–98

Havinden, M A, 1966 *Estate Villages*, London

Hayfield, C, 1987 *An Archaeological Survey of the Parish of Wharram Percy, East Yorkshire, 1: The Evolution of the Roman Landscape*, BAR, Brit Ser, **172**, Oxford

Helmfrid, S (ed), 1961 Morphogenesis of the agrarian cultural landscape, *Geografiska Annaler*, **43**, nos 1–2

Herring, P, 1998 *Cornwall's Historic Landscape*, Truro

Higham, N J, 1986 *The Northern Counties to AD 1100*, London

_____ , 1993 *The Origins of Cheshire*, Manchester

Higham, N J, and Jones, B, 1985 *The Carvetii*, Stroud

Hill, D, 1981 *An Atlas of Anglo-Saxon England*, Oxford

Hingley, R, 1989 *Rural Settlement in Roman Britain*, London

Hinton, D A, 1999 'Closing' and the Later Middle Ages, *Medieval Archaeol*, **43**, 172–82

Hodges, R, 1991 *Wall-to-Wall History: The Story of Roystone Grange*, London

Hodgson, R I, 1989 Coalmining, population and enclosures in the sea-sale colliery districts of Durham (Northern Durham) 1551–1810: a study in historical geography, unpubl PhD thesis, Univ Durham

Hodson, Y, 1991 *'An Inch to the Mile' – The Ordnance Survey Map 1805–1974*, London

Hollinshead, J E, 1981 Halewood township: a community in the early 18th century, *Trans Hist Soc Lancashire Cheshire*, **130**, 15–36

Homans, G C, 1960 *English Villagers of the Thirteenth Century*, New York

Hooke, D, 1985a *The Anglo-Saxon Landscape: the Kingdom of the Hwicce*, Manchester

_____ , 1985b Village development in the West Midlands, in Hooke 1985c, 125–54

_____ , 1985c *Medieval Villages: A Review of Current Work*, OUCA Monogr, **5**, Oxford

_____ , 1998 *The Landscape of Anglo-Saxon England*, London

Hoskins, W G, 1963 *Provincial England: Essays in Social and Economic History*, London

_____ , 1967 *Fieldwork in Local History*, London

Hoskins, W G, and Stamp, L Dudley, 1963 *The Common Lands of England and Wales*, London

Houston, J M, 1963 *A Social Geography of Europe*, London

Howell, C, 1976 Peasant inheritance customs in the Midlands, 1280–1700, in *Family and Inheritance* (eds J Goody, J Thirsk, and E P Thompson), 112–55, Cambridge

_____ , 1983 *Land, Family and Inheritance in Transition: Kibworth Harcourt 1280–1700*, Cambridge

Huggett, J W, 1988 Imported grave goods and the early Anglo-Saxon economy, *Medieval Archaeol*, **32**, 63–96

Humphery-Smith, C R (ed), 1984 *The Phillimore Atlas and Index of Parish Registers*, Chichester

Hunter-Blair, P, 1960 *An Introduction to Anglo-Saxon England*, Cambridge

John, E, 1996 *Reassessing Anglo-Saxon England*, Manchester

Johnson, M H, 1996 *An Archaeology of Capitalism*, Oxford

Johnson, S, 1980 *Later Roman Britain*, London

Jolas, T, and Zonabend, F, 1977 Tillers of the field and woodspeople, in *Rural Society in France – Selections from the Annales Economies, Sociétés, Civilisations* (eds R Forster and O Ranum), 126–51, Baltimore and London

Jolliffe, J E A, 1926 Northumbrian institutions, *Engl Hist Rev*, **41**, 1–42

_____ , 1935–6 A survey of fiscal tenements, *Econ Hist Rev*, **6**, 157–71

Jones, G , 1968 *A History of the Vikings*, Oxford

Jones, G R J, 1953 Some medieval rural settlements in North Wales, *Trans Pap Inst Br Geog*, **19**, 51–72

_____ , 1971 The multiple estate as a model framework for tracing early stages in the evolution of rural settlement, in *L'Habitat et les Paysages Ruraux d'Europe* (ed F Dussart), 251–67, Liege

_____ , 1985 Forms and patterns of medieval settlements in Welsh Wales, in Hooke 1985c, 155–69

Jones, G R J, 1990 Celts, Saxons and Scandinavians, in R A Dodgshon and Butlin, R A, *An Historical Geography of England and Wales*, 2nd edition, London, 45-68

Kapelle, W E, 1979 *The Norman Conquest of the North*, London

Kerridge, E, 1969 *Agrarian Problems in the Sixteenth Century*, London

_____ , 1992 *The Common Fields of England*, Manchester

Kershaw, I (ed), 1970 *Bolton Priory Rentals and Ministers' Accounts, 1473–1539*, Yorkshire Archaeol Soc Rec Ser, **132**

Kosminsky, E A, 1956 *Studies in the Agrarian History of England in the Thirteenth Century*, Oxford

Lamb, H H, 1966 *The Changing Climate*, London

_____ , 1982 *Climate History and the Modern World*, London

_____ , 1984 *Climatic History and the Future*, Princeton

Lawton, R, 1964 Historical geography: the Industrial Revolution, in Watson *et al* 1964, 221–44

_____ , 1986 Population, in *Atlas of Industrializing Britain* (J Langton and R J Morris), London

_____ , 1992 Demographic change from the 1830s to the 1890s, in Lawton and Pooley 1992, 117–38

Lawton, R, and Pooley, C G, 1992 *Britain 1740–1950*, London

Lebon, J H G, 1952 *The Evolution of Our Countryside*, London

Leconfield, Lord, 1954 *Petworth Manor in the Seventeenth Century*, Oxford

Leighton, R, 1995 Rural settlement and population in England between 1676 and 1851, unpubl MA Dissertation, Univ Durham

Lennard, R, 1959 *Rural England 1086–1135*, Oxford

Le Patourel, H E J, 1973 *The Moated Sites of Yorkshire*, Soc Medieval Archaeol Monogr Ser, **5**

Lewis, C, 1994 Patterns and process in the medieval settlement of Wiltshire, in Aston and Lewis 1994, 171–93

Limbrey, S, and Evans, J G (eds), 1978 *The Effect of Man on the Landscape: the Lowland Zone*, CBA Res Rep, **21**, London

Lloyn, H R, 1962 *Anglo-Saxon England and the Norman Conquest*, London

Mackinder, H J, 1915 *Britain and the British Seas*, Oxford

Maitland, F W, 1897 *Domesday Book and Beyond*, Cambridge

Margary, H (ed), 1975-81 *The Old Series Ordnance Survey Maps of England and Wales*, 8 vols, Lympne

Mayhew, A, 1973 *Rural Settlement and Farming in Germany*, London

McConnell, P, 1922 *The Agricultural Notebook*, London

Mercer, R (ed), 1981 *Farming Practice in British Prehistory*, Edinburgh

Merlen, R H A, 1987 *The Motte and Bailey Castles of the Welsh Border*, Ludlow

Morgan V, 1979 The cartographic image of 'The Country' in early modern England, *Trans R Hist Soc*, **29**, 129–54

Millett, M, 1990 *The Romanization of Britain*, Cambridge

Mills, D R, 1980 *Lord and Peasant in Nineteenth Century Britain*, London

Muir, R, 1998 The villages of Nidderdale, *Landscape Hist*, **20**, 65–82

Oosthuizen, S, 1997 Prehistoric fields into medieval furlongs? Evidence from Caxton, Cambridgeshire, *Proc Cambridge Antiq Soc*, **86**, 145–52

_____ , 1998 The origins of Cambridgeshire, *Antiq J*, **78**, 85–109

Orwin, C S, and Orwin, C S, 1938 *The Open Fields*, Oxford

Oschinsky, D, 1971 *Walter of Henley and Other Treatises on Estate Management and Accounting*, Oxford

Owen, D M, 1981 *Church and Society in Medieval Lincolnshire*, Hist of Lincolnshire, **5**, Lincoln

Parry, M L, 1978 *Climatic Change, Agriculture and Settlement*, Folkestone

Passmore, J B, 1930 *The English Plough*, London

Perring, F H, and Walters, S M (eds), 1962 *Atlas of British Flora*, London

Pevsner, N, 1967 *The Buildings of England: Yorkshire West Riding* (2nd edn), London

Philip, G (ed), 1928 *Administrative Atlas of England and Wales*, London

Phillips, C W (ed), 1970 *The Fenland in Roman Times*, London

Bibliography

Phythian-Adams, C, 1977 Rutland reconsidered, in *Mercian Studies* (ed A Dornier), 63–84, Leicester

Pollard, E, Hooper, M D, and Moore, N W, 1974 *Hedges*, London

Poole, A L, 1955 *From Domesday Book to Magna Carta 1087–1216* (2nd edn), Oxford

Postan, M M, 1972 *The Medieval Economy and Society*, London

Rackham, O, 1986 *The History of the Countryside*, London

Radding, C M, and Clark, W W, 1992 *Medieval Architecture, Medieval Learning: Builders and Masters in the Age of Romanesque and Gothic*, Newhaven and London

Raftis, J A, 1964 *Tenure and Mobility*, Pontifical Inst Medieval Stud, Stud Texts, **8**, Toronto

Ravenhill, W, 1992 *Christopher Saxton's 16th-century Maps*, Chatsworth

Ravensdale, J R, 1974 *Liable to Floods: Village Landscape on the Edge of the Fens, A D, 450–1850*, Cambridge

Razzell, P (ed), 1981 *The History of Myddle*, London

RCCL, 1958 *Royal Commission on Common Land 1955–1958, Report*, London

RCHME, 1960 *A Matter of Time*, Royal Commission on Historic Monuments (England), London

RCHME, 1968 *West Cambridgeshire*, Royal Commission on Historic Monuments (England), London

RCHME, 1970 *Dorset, vol 3 Central, part 1*, Royal Commission on Historic Monuments (England), London

Rees, W, 1963 Survivals of ancient celtic custom in medieval England, in *Angles and Britons* (ed H Lewis), 148–68, Cardiff

Rennell of Rodd, Lord, 1958 *Valley on the March*, Oxford

Reynolds, P, 1981 Deadstock and livestock, in Mercer 1981, 97–122

Riley, D N, 1980 *Early Landscapes from the Air*, Sheffield

Rippon, S, 1991 Early planned landscapes in south-east Essex, *Essex Archaeol Hist*, **22**, 46–60

_____ , 1997 *The Severn Estuary: Landscape Evolution and Wetland Reclamation*, Leicester

_____ , 1998 Medieval settlement on the North Somerset Levels: the third season of survey and excavation at Puxton, 1998, *Archaeol in the Severn Estuary*, **9**, 69–78

Rivet, A L F, 1969 *The Roman Villa in Britain*, London

Roberts, B K, 1965 The Forest of Arden 1086–1350, unpubl PhD thesis, Univ Birmingham

_____ , 1968 A study of medieval colonisation in the Forest of Arden, Warwickshire, *Agric Hist Rev*, **16**, 110–16

_____ , 1972 Village plans in County Durham: a preliminary statement, *Medieval Archaeol*, **16**, 33–56

_____ , 1973 Field systems of the West Midlands, in Baker and Butlin 1973, 188–231

_____ , 1981 Townfield origins: the case of Cockfield, County Durham, in Rowley 1981, 145–61

_____ , 1982 Village forms in Warwickshire: a preliminary discussion, in *Field and Forest – An Historical Geography of Warwickshire and Worcestershire* (eds T Slater and P J Jarvis), 125–46, Norwich

_____ , 1987 *The Making of the English Village*, London

_____ , 1989 Nucleation and dispersion: distribution maps as a research tool, in Aston *et al* 1989, 59–75

_____ , 1993 Some relict landscapes in Westmorland: a reconsideration, *Archaeol J*, **150**, 433–55

_____ , 1996a *Landscapes of Settlement: Prehistory to the Present*, London

_____ , 1996b The great plough: a hypothesis concerning village genesis and land reclamation in Cumberland, *Landscape Hist*, **18**, 17–30

Roberts, B K, and Wrathmell, S, 1998 Dispersed settlement in England: a national view, in Everson and Williamson 1998, 95–116

_____ , 2000a *An Atlas of Rural Settlement in England*, London

_____ , 2000b Peoples of wood and plain: an exploration of national and local regional contrasts, in *Landscape, the Richest Historical Record* (ed D Hooke), Soc Landscape Stud, 85–95

Roberts, B K, Turner, J, and Ward, P F, 1973 Recent forest history and land use in Weardale, northern England, in *Quaternary Plant Ecology* (eds H B J Birks and R G West), 207–21, Oxford

Roden, D, 1973 Field systems of the Chiltern Hills and their environs, in Baker and Butlin 1973, 325–76

Rostow, W W, 1971 *The Stages of Economic Growth* (2nd edn), Cambridge

Rowley, T (ed), 1981 *The Origins of Open Field Agriculture*, London

Rowley, T, and Wood, J, 1982 *Deserted Villages*, Princes Risborough

Russell, R C, and Russell, E, 1983 *Making New Landscapes in Lincolnshire: the Enclosures of Thirty-Four Parishes*, Lincolnshire Hist, Ser 5, Lincoln

_____ , 1985 *Old and New Landscapes in the Horncastle Area*, Lincolnshire Hist, Ser 7, Lincoln

_____ , 1987 *Parliamentary Enclosure and New Lincolnshire Landscapes*, Lincolnshire Hist, Ser 10, Lincoln

Salter, M de Carle S, 1921 *Rainfall of the British Isles*, London

Salzman, L F, 1952 *Building in England down to 1540*, Oxford

Sawyer, P H, 1968 *Anglo-Saxon Charters: an Annotated List and Bibliography*, London

_____ , (ed), 1976 *Medieval Settlement: Continuity and Change*, London

_____ , 1978 *From Roman Britain to Norman England*, London

Scargill, C, and Lee, J R, 1986 *Spen Valley: a Landscape of Hamlets*, Leeds

Scott, E, 1993 *A Gazetteer of Roman Villas in Britain*, Leicester Archaeol Monogr, 1, Leicester

Scull, C, 1992 Before Sutton Hoo: structures of power and society in early East Anglia, in *The Age of Sutton Hoo* (ed M O H Carver), 3–22, Woodbridge

Seebohm, F, 1883 *The English Village Community*, London

_____ , 1902 *Tribal Custom and Anglo-Saxon Law*, London

Sheppard, J A, 1966 Pre-enclosure field and settlement patterns in an English township, *Geografiska Annaler*, **48**, ser B, 59–77

_____ , 1974 Metrological analysis of regular village plans in Yorkshire, *Agric Hist Rev*, **22**, 118–35

_____ , 1976 Medieval village planning in northern England: some evidence from Yorkshire, *J Hist Geogr*, **2**, 1, 3–20

_____ , 1979 *The Origins and Evolution of Field and Settlement Patterns in the Herefordshire manor of Marden*, Univ London Occas Pap, **15**

Shotton, F W, 1978 Archaeological inferences from the study of alluvium in the Lower Severn-Avon valleys, in Limbrey and Evans 1978, 27–32

Simpson, A W B, 1961 *An Introduction to the History of the Land Law*, Oxford

Slater, G, 1907 *The English Peasantry and the Enclosure of Common Fields*, London

Smith, A H, 1956 *English Place-name Elements*, Engl Place-name Soc, 25–6, Cambridge

_____ , 1961a *The Place-names of the West Riding of Yorkshire, part 2: The Wapentakes of Osgoldcross and Agbrigg*, Engl Place-name Soc, **31**, Cambridge

_____ , 1961b *The Place-names of the West Riding of Yorkshire, part 6: The Wakentakes of East and West Staincliffe and Ewcross*, Engl Place-name Soc, **35**, Cambridge

_____ , 1967 *The Place-names of Westmorland*, Engl Place-name Soc, **43**, Cambridge

Smith, J T, 1965 Timber framed building in England: its development and regional differences, *Archaeol J*, **122**, 133–58

Spufford, M, 1974 *Contrasting Communities: English Villagers in the Sixteenth and Seventeenth Centuries*, Cambridge

Stamp, L D (ed), 1937–44 *The Land of Britain*, County Fascicules, R Geogr Soc, London

_____ , 1962 *The Land of Britain: its Use and Misuse*, London

Stenton, F M, 1920 *Documents Illustrative of the Social and Economic History of the Danelaw*, Oxford

Stoertz, C, 1997 *Ancient Landscapes of the Yorkshire Wolds*, RCHME, Swindon

Sylvester, D, 1949 Rural settlement in Cheshire. Some problems of origin and classification, *Trans Hist Soc Lancashire Cheshire*, **101**, 1–37

_____ , 1956 The open fields of Cheshire, *Trans Hist Soc Lancashire Cheshire*, **108**, 1–33

_____ , 1969 *The Rural Landscape of the Welsh Borderland*, London

Tansley, A G, 1939 *The British Isles and Their Vegetation*, Cambridge

Tate, W E, 1967 *The English Village Community and the Enclosure Movements*, London

Taylor, C C, 1970 *The Making of the English Landscape: Dorset*, London
_____ , 1989 Whittlesford: the study of a river-edge village, in Aston *et al* 1989, 207–27
_____ , 1992 Medieval rural settlement: changing perceptions, *Landscape Hist*, **14**, 5–17
Thirsk, J (ed), 1967 *The Agrarian History of England and Wales 1500–1640, vol 4*, Cambridge
_____ , (ed), 1984–5 *The Agrarian History of England and Wales 1640-1750, vol 5*, Cambridge
_____ , 1987 *England's Agricultural Regions and Agrarian History, 1500–1750*, London
Tubbs, C, 1968 *The New Forest – An Ecological History*, Newton Abbot
Turner, M E, 1978 *A Domesday of English Enclosure Acts and Awards*, Reading

Uhlig, H, 1961 Old hamlets with infield and outfield systems in western and central Europe, in Helmfrid 1961, 285–312
_____ , 1971 Fields and field systems, in *Man and His Habitat* (eds R H Buchannan, E Jones and D McCourt), 93–125, London
_____ , (ed), 1972 *Rural Settlements*, Giessen
Unwin, P H T, 1990 Towns and trade 1066–1500, in Dodgshon and Butlin 1990, 123–49

van Bath, B H Slicher, 1963a *The Agrarian History of Western Europe AD 500–1850*, London
_____ , 1963b Yield ratios, 810–1820, *Adfedling Agrarische Geschiedenis Bijragen*, **10**, 12–264, Wageningen
Vinogradoff, P, 1908 *English Society in the Eleventh Century*, Oxford
_____ , 1911 *The Growth of the Manor*, London
Vyner, B E (ed), 1994 *Building on the Past*, R Archaeol Inst, London

Wade-Martins, P, 1980 *Village Sites in Launditch Hundred*, East Anglian Archaeol **10**, Dereham
Warne, H M, 1985 The place names and early topography of Burgess Hill, *Sussex Archaeol Collect*, **123**, 127–43

Warner, P, 1987 *Greens, Commons and Clayland Colonisation*, Dep Engl Local Hist Occas Pap, 4th ser, **2**, Leicester
_____ , 1996 *The Origins of Suffolk*, Manchester
Watson, J Wreford, and Sissons, J B, 1964 *The British Isles: A Systematic Geography*, Edinburgh
Watts, V, 1976 Comments on 'The evidence of place-names' by Margaret Gelling, in Sawyer 1976, 200–2
Whitelock, D (ed), 1955 *English Historical Documents, c.500–1042*, London
Wildgoose, M, 1991 The drystone walls of Royston Grange, *Archaeol J*, **148**, 205–40
Williams, P, 1987 *Bromyard: Minster, Manor and Town*, Leominster
Williamson, T, 1998 The 'Scole-Dickleburgh field system' revisited, *Landscape Hist*. **20**, 19–28
Winchester, A, 1987 *Landscape and Society in Medieval Cumbria*, Edinburgh
_____ , 1990 *Discovering Parish Boundaries*, Princes Risborough
_____ , 1993 Field, wood and forest, landscapes of medieval Lancashire, in *Lancashire Local Studies* (ed A G Crosby), 7–27, Preston
Withington, L (ed), 1876 *Elizabethan England, with Introduction by F J Furnivall*, London
Wrathmell, S, 1975 Deserted and shrunken villages in southern Northumberland from the 12th to the 20th centuries, unpubl PhD thesis, Univ Wales
_____ , 1989a Peasant houses, farmsteads and villages in north-east England, in Aston *et al* 1989, 247–67
_____ , 1989b *Wharram. A Study of Settlement on the Yorkshire Wolds, VI: Medieval Peasant Farmsteads*, Univ York Archaeol Publ 8, York
_____ , 1992 Excavation and survey at The Old Hutt, Halewood, in 1960, *J Merseyside Archaeol Soc*, **8**, 1–46
_____ , 1994 Rural settlements in medieval England: perspectives and perceptions, in Vyner 1994, 178–94

Yelling, J, 1977 *Common Field and Enclosure in England 1450–1850*, London

Index

Index

Index